Dun & Bradstreet's Guide to

$YOUR INVESTMENTS$™ 1984

Twenty-Ninth Edition

C. COLBURN HARDY

1817

HARPER & ROW, PUBLISHERS • **NEW YORK**

CAMBRIDGE, PHILADELPHIA, SAN FRANCISCO, LONDON
MEXICO CITY, SÃO PAULO, SYDNEY

The title *$Your Investment$* is a registered trademark of
Harper & Row, Publishers, Inc.

DUN & BRADSTREET'S GUIDE TO $YOUR INVESTMENTS$: 1984. Copyright © 1984, 1983, 1982, 1981, 1980, 1979, 1978, 1977, 1976, 1975, 1974, 1973 by Harper & Row, Publishers, Inc. All rights reserved. Printed in the United States of America. No part of this book may be used or reproduced in any manner whatsoever without written permission except in the case of brief quotations embodied in critical articles and reviews. For information address Harper & Row, Publishers, Inc., 10 East 53rd Street, New York, N.Y. 10022. Published simultaneously in Canada by Fitzhenry & Whiteside Limited, Toronto.

Designer: Helene Berinsky

ISBN 0-06-015255-9

ISBN 0-06-091097-6 (pbk.)

LIBRARY OF CONGRESS CATALOG CARD NUMBER 73-18050

Contents

EDITOR:

C. Colburn Hardy

SENIOR EDITORS:

Jonas Blake
Hart Munn

EDITORIAL ASSOCIATES:

Ruth E. Hardy
Clark Hunt

FOUNDING AUTHOR:

Leo D. Barnes, Ph.D.

About the Editor:

C. Colburn Hardy has edited *Your Investments* since 1974, when he started early retirement after many years as a public relations executive. In this second career as an author, he has written over 1,500 articles on investments, money management, estate/financial planning and retirement. He has written/revised/ghosted or collaborated on 20 books including *ABCs of Investing Your Retirement Funds, Your Money & Your Life, Investor's Guide to Technical Analysis, Your Guide to a Financially Secure Retirement,* and *How to Make the Most of Your Personal Pension Plans.*

He is financial editor of both *Physician's Management* and *Dental Management,* has been a featured speaker at financial seminars, has taught at colleges and is a frequent guest on local and national radio and TV shows.

A Phi Beta Kappa graduate of Yale, Mr. Hardy continues to be active in community, state and national affairs, primarily in areas concerned with aging/retirement . . . "which," he says, "has been possible only because of the extra income generated from following the advice in books such as *Your Investments.*"

With Professional Assistance from:

Alph C. Beane, Sr., *Dean Witter Reynolds*
Alph C. Beane, Jr., *Dean Witter Reynolds*
Robert J. Bernstein, *RBA Group NA*
Richard Blackman, *Richard Blackman & Co.*

Garrett Cole, *Penntower Corp.*
Leroy Gross, *Dean Witter Reynolds*
Craig Hall, *Real Estate Consultant*
John B. Halper, *Real Estate Consultant*
Hans Jacobsen, *Herzog, Heine & Geduld*
Jack Maurer, *Indicator Digest* ˙
Thomas C. Noddings, *Noddings, Calamos & Associates*
Bob Rollins, *First Financial Planners*
Robert W. Ross, *Shearson-American Express*
Gary Sellari, *Blalock, Martin & Sellari*
Robert W. Stovall, *Dean Witter Reynolds*
Howard J. Wiener, *Palm Beach Tax Attorney*
James Wolpert, *L. S. Rothschild, Towbin, Unterberg*
John Winthrop Wright, *Wright Investors' Service*

American Municipal Bond Association
Barron's
Boardroom Reports
Bottom Line
Business Week
Canadian Business Service
Chicago Board of Options
Chicago Board of Trade
Comex Exchange
Commodities
Dental Management
Financial World
Forbes
Fortune
International Monetary Exchange
Investment Company Institute
Medical Economics
Merrill Lynch
Money
Moody's Investors Service
Municipal Bond Insurance Association
New York Times
Physician's Management
Post-Times
Prudential-Bache
Research Institute of America
Securities Research Company
Standard & Poor's
T. Rowe Price & Associates
United Business Service
Vanguard Group
Wall Street Journal
Wright Investors' Service

And special thanks for information from:
American Stock Exchange
National Association of Securities Dealer
New York Stock Exchange
No-Load Mutual Fund Association
Securities and Exchange Commission

DUN & BRADSTREET'S GUIDE TO $YOUR INVESTMENTS$®: 1984

1

Introduction

Now's the time to raise your sights to look for investment returns that can double your money in the next four to five years. There are no tricks, no real risks. All you need is consistent savings, quality securities, prompt reinvestment of income, common sense and the discipline to adhere to proven profitable rules as outlined in the pages that follow. Specifically, investment targets for 1984 should be:

• *For the conservative:* 14% total returns: with *utility stocks:* 8% to 9% dividends plus 5% to 6% annual appreciation; with *discount bonds:* 11% to 12% interest plus 2% to 3% rise in value toward maturity or through lower interest rates.

• *For the aggressive:* 20%—4% to 5% dividends plus 15% to 16% average annual capital gains.

These are close to the goals that have been achieved by sample portfolios in previous editions of *Your Investments.* This year, the big difference is TIME: everything will happen more quickly in the bull market that appears to be ahead. These total returns will, often, come in less than one year compared to the 24 to 36 month time frame set before.

These targets are not headlines written for promotion or publicity. They are based on the results attained by suggested buying and selling securities as outlined in this guide since 1973 when I became editor of this handbook.

You should do better because you can continue to manage your holdings. My selections are made in May and cannot be changed except by formula. Still, the total returns . . . income plus appreciation minus losses . . . have averaged well over 20% a year!

The reader, who, in 1973:

1. Set up a $10,000 trust fund, invested in quality stocks listed in *Your Investments* and managed the portfolio—selling at target prices for gains of 35% to 50% or more and for losses of no more than 15%—would now have over $74,300.

2. Contributed $5,000 a year to a Keogh plan ($55,000) would have a nest egg of $165,000.

The securities themselves are not as important as the methods used in selection and management. Their superior performance emphasizes the basic concept of this book: *that if you buy quality stocks when they are undervalued and corporate prospects improving, you will always make money in the long term of an investment program.*

In successful investing, the key factor is the *corporation,* not the stock. As long as the company retains its quality status, its shares will be worth more . . . in time. The action of the stock, as shown by its market price, is temporary; the value of the quality corporation will continue to grow.

Booming Stock Market BUT . . .

In the euphoria of a bull market, it's easy to denigrate the past and overoptimize the future. At this time, the stock market is roaring up to new peaks. Many investors (and even more speculators) made more money (usually on paper) in the first half of 1983 than they ever did in any previous two years!

But study the figures of the Dow Jones Industrial Average (DJIA). Note that the prior high, of 1020, was reached way back in 1972. Then came the sharp decline to 616 in less than two years, a fast bounce-back to 1005 in 1976, meandering for the next five years and, finally, the upsurge only in the last 12 months.

Most analysts expect the rise to continue because:

• Corporate earnings will improve in 1983 and 1984: for the DJIA: from $103 to $134.50 per share.

• The price/earnings ratio will rise, from 8.1 in 1981 to 11 by 1984.

• The prime interest rate will decline from about 10% today to 8% by 1985.

• The inflation rate will stay close to 4% . . . easily offset by rising sales.

There are, of course, many fears, that:

• The money supply has expanded so fast and the deficits are still uncontrolled so that the Federal Reserve Board will be forced to raise the cost of money and retrigger inflation.

• Banks will be hard hit by defaults in loans of foreign countries.

• Too many debt-heavy corporations will be unable to float equity to ease fixed obligations.

Still, most fears never come to pass and when they do, are less severe than anticipated.

To the optimists (and, over the years, they have been right far more often than the pessimists), there have been significant improvements in well-managed corporations:

• The break-even points (where sales equal costs) have been lowered so profitability should bounce back quickly.

• Are doing more with less: fewer plants, fewer employees, and the elimination of unprofitable products/services.

• Reporting greater cash flow through liberalized depreciation, liquidation of inventory and cutbacks in overhead.

DOW JONES INDUSTRIAL AVERAGE

YEARLY PERFORMANCE AND RATES OF RETURN

Year	Closing Price	% Change in Year	% Divi- dend*	Total Change
1950	235.41	+17.6%	8.1%	+25.7%
1951	269.23	+14.4	6.9	+21.3
1952	291.90	+ 8.4	5.7	+14.1
1953	280.90	− 3.8	5.5	+ 1.7
1954	404.39	+44.0	6.2	+50.2
1955	488.44	+20.8	5.3	+26.1
1956	499.47	+ 2.3	4.7	+ 7.0
1957	435.69	−12.8	4.3	− 8.5
1958	583.65	+34.0	4.6	+38.6
1959	679.36	+16.4	3.6	+20.0
1960	615.89	− 9.3	3.1	− 6.2
1961	731.14	+18.7	3.7	+22.4
1962	652.10	−10.8	3.2	− 7.6
1963	762.95	+17.0	3.6	+20.6
1964	874.13	+14.6	4.1	+18.7
1965	969.26	+10.9	3.3	+14.2
1966	785.69	−18.9	3.3	−15.6
1967	905.11	+15.2	3.8	+19.0
1968	943.75	+ 4.3	3.5	+ 7.8
1969	800.36	−15.2	3.6	−11.6
1970	838.92	+ 4.8	3.9	+ 8.7
1971	890.20	+ 6.1	3.7	+ 9.8
1972	1020.02	+14.6	3.6	+18.2
1973	850.86	−16.6	3.5	−12.7
1974	616.24	−28.0	5.4	−22.6
1975	852.41	+38.0	5.1	+43.1
1976	1005.00	+18.0	4.4	+22.4
1977	831.00	−17.0	5.1	−11.9
1978	805.00	− 3.0	6.1	+ 3.1
1979	838.74	+ 4.2	6.3	+10.5
1980	965.99	+14.9	5.7	+20.6
1981	875.00	− 9.0	6.4	− 2.8
1982	1046.54	+20.0	5.2	+25.2

* On year-end price

PROJECTED	High	Low
1984	1450	1150
1985	1585	1285
1986	1750	1400
1987	1900	1500

SOURCE: Wright Investors' Service

More than ever before, it pays to concentrate on *quality* stocks. These are shares of companies whose managements have proven their ability to make more and more money. Stocks of some of these companies are already overvalued but there are still hundreds of quality stocks that have excellent prospects of providing total returns of 50% over the near future.

In the year ahead, the single biggest investment danger will be *greed:* trying to make a fast killing with shares of new, small, high-technology firms that have little more than a specialized product/service, backing by a venture capital group that will sell out to the gullible public and an aggressive underwriter whose registered representatives paint glowing pictures of huge profits from new "concepts."

The harsh reality, of course, is that the small investor is too often sold on exciting concepts and exciting concepts are how he will lose money. As adviser John Train puts it, "The small investor is typically moved by ignorance and passion and hypnotized by the movement of a stock without knowing whether his shares are worth $10 or 50¢."

Yet, the wise investor can make as much money with almost complete safety with quality stocks. Look at what happened to a few of the leaders in the last 12 months:

Company	May 1982	May 1983
IBM	60	120
Ralston Purina	13	23
Scott & Fetzer	28	45
Sonat, Inc.	22	34
Tandy Corp.	26	65

As is stressed throughout this book, there are always profitable investments for those who are willing to do their homework, insist on strict standards, buy when shares are undervalued and sell when they become fully priced or, when a mistake is made, quickly at a small loss.

Quality, value, and timing will be explained in detail later, but when you invest in shares of *quality* corporations (generally, companies that are financially strong, are leaders in their fields and have fairly consistent records of high, profitable growth), you will *always* make money over a period of time.

Here's why:

If a company earned 15% on stockholders' equity (the money invested by shareholders), it ends the year with 15¢ per dollar more. Generally, the dividend payout is about 5¢ per share. That leaves 10¢ to be reinvested for future growth. Thus the underlying value of the corporation doubles in about 7.5 years. The same 15¢ rate of return will produce double earnings and, often, double the dividends. Eventually these extra values will be reflected in the price of the common stock. That's why the best investments are shares of companies that keep on making a lot of money.

With *value* (the ratio of tomorrow's price to today's market quotation), the profits will come by buying when the stock is underpriced and selling when it becomes fully valued. Even if you buy too soon, you will profit as long as the company prospers.

Timing purchases and sales enhances profits and reduces losses. As is explained by many examples, the key points of timing can be determined by technical analysis—primarily charts, but often by other indices.

But, always, there must be common sense!

Keep in mind that when an *investor* buys any stock, he is acquiring a share in a business enterprise because he feels it is worth holding regardless of any short- or intermediate-term action. When a *speculator* buys a security, he assumes that someone else will pay more; the sooner, the better.

Successful investing takes time and patience. Dramatic moves, up or down, are exciting, but they seldom last and they are usually followed by equally sharp reactions. The slow, steady advance is best because it builds a strong base and, when the upmove continues, protects capital and provides opportunities for big profits. The long view is hard to find in the financial press, but you can rely on your own research and common sense in making investments. You will be right 80% of the time, which is a much better record than that of most so-called professional money managers. The sample portfolios prove this. *To repeat:* Anyone with common sense can make money with investments in securities. This Guide will help you to do this.

The Magic of Compounding

One thing that most people neglect is the Magic of Compounding: earning income on income by prompt reinvestment of all interest, dividends and realized capital gains. As shown by the tables, even with modest rates of return, savings can mount at an astonishing rate . . . in time. For a quick calculation of how long it takes to double your money at various rates of return, use the rule of 72: divide 72 by the yield. Thus, at 8%, it would take nine years; at 10%, seven years; at 12%, six years.

Some specific examples are worth repeating:

• **A $10,000 trust fund** set up at the birth of a child, with the money invested at 12% and the income reinvested annually, will grow to $96,463 when the youngster is 20 years old (not counting commissions, fees and taxes).

• **Annual contributions of $2,000** to an Individual Retirement Account, starting at age 40, with a modest 10% yield, will swell to $196,700 in 25 years and to $328,980 when retirement starts at age 70. That later sum will assure almost $50,000 a year income for as long as most people can expect to live!

Over the long span of a true investment program, everyone can accumulate sufficient assets to assure a financially comfortable retirement. Don't be greedy. Just be sensible.

No Quick Formula for Success

This logical approach is far different from the "sure-fire" formulas "revealed" by some financial wizards and the gloomy warnings of future disaster predicted by some self-styled "experts" or "authorities." They make more money from their books, lectures and letters than they do from following their own counsel.

These modern medicine men denigrate American business and government. They sell verbal snake oil as the cure for all financial ills and as the magic ingredient in building wealth. And, sad to say, they attract a large following.

But the record shows that their "advice" has been, and still is, detrimental to the financial health of the investor. For a short period their elixir may work wonders, but over the long term it can be devastating.

What's Ahead

As most investors have already learned from experience, the stock market can do anything . . . and usually does. Over the short term, it is seldom logical. It can suddenly slow down after sharp gains; it can break wide open with no news to justify such optimism; and it can plummet because of a rumor or headline that can be more startling than true.

As will be explained later, there are certain patterns that tend to repeat themselves over the years. Here are two that have proven reasonably accurate:

• The two years *before* a presidential election are bullish with modest to strong upswings; the two years *after* the election (1984 and 1985) are mediocre to poor. But quality stocks will almost always perform better than the overall market: *up* more in good times; *down* less in bear periods.

• After recessions, the market gains are strong. The key here is when a recession ends. Right now, most pundits believe that the real recession is over but there are those who are not so sure.

They tell you to buy gold at $800 an ounce, yet its price falls below $300. They tout "stocks of the future" at $2 and $3 per share and headline their wisdom when they soar to $30 or higher in a few years. But they seldom mention the majority of selections that fail to fulfill their promise, and won't even answer questions when the price of last year's favorite plummets below its initial "value."

And with real estate, they let you in on the secret of making millions with other people's money: $100 down and the balance financed with a big, long-term mortgage. That approach may have had some merit when the interest rate was 10% and the annual appreciation 15%, but it won't work when you have to pay 15% and appreciation slows to 5% or less. And be sensible: if a person lets you acquire property with no money down, the odds are that there's something wrong. People are not as stupid as these shills would have you believe.

Everyone genuinely interested in becoming a successful investor should heed these comments by two of the deans of the investment world:

THE POWER OF COMPOUND INTEREST

A regular investment of $100 per year, invested at:	* Will, compounded annually, at the end of each year, grow to this sum after this number of years.							
	5	10	15	20	25	30	35	40
6%	$564	$1,318	$2,328	$3,679	$5,486	$7,906	$11,143	$15,476
8	587	1,449	2,715	4,576	7,311	11,328	17,232	25,906
10	611	1,594	3,177	5,727	9,835	16,449	27,102	44,259
12	635	1,755	3,728	7,205	13,333	24,133	43,166	76,709
14	661	1,934	4,384	9,102	18,187	35,679	69,357	134,202
16	688	2,132	5,166	11,538	24,921	53,031	112,071	236,076

To get the corresponding total for any other annually invested amount (A), multiply the dollar total given above for the yield and the number of years by $\frac{A}{100}$. Example: You plan to invest $75 per month, $900 a year. What capital sum will that provide after 35 years, at 12% compounded annually? Check where the lines cross for 12% and 35 years: $43,166 $\times \frac{900}{100}$ = $388,494. N.B. The totals will be greater if: (1) the deposits are made at the beginning of the year; (2) compounding is more frequent.

SOURCE: David Thorndike, ed., THE THORNDIKE ENCYCLOPEDIA OF BANKING & FINANCIAL TABLES (Boston: Warren, Gorham & Lamont, 1980)

• Benjamin Graham, whose books have become standard texts: "Investment must be based on thorough analysis and must promise safety of principal and a satisfactory return. Lacking one of these, it is a speculation."

• T. Rowe Price, who built one of the major money management firms: "I do not have the ability to guess the ups and downs of the stock market averages or the trends in individual stocks. Most fortunes are built on ownership of successful business enterprises over a long period of time."

STOCK MARKET AFTER RECESSIONS

RECESSION	MARKET LOW S&P 500	MARKET HIGH Date	MARKET HIGH S&P 500	GAIN: S&P 500 Low to End	GAIN: S&P 500 End to High
12/48-12/49	13.55	1/53	26.66	18.5%	66.0%
7/53-5/54	22.71	8/56	49.74	24.4	76.0
8/57-4/58	38.98	8/59	60.71	8.0	44.2
4/60-2/61	52.30	12/61	72.64	18.1	17.6
12/69-11/70	69.29	1/73	120.24	20.1	44.4
11/73-3/75	62.28	9/76	107.83	31.0	32.2
1/80-7/80	98.22	11/80	140.52	16.3	23.0
7/81-1/83	102.42			37.3	....

SOURCE: Standard & Poor's OUTLOOK

Inflation

No book on investments can ignore inflation. But now that the official Consumer Price Index is down to about 4%, inflation is no longer as awesome nor as destructive as in the past. Inflation does erode purchasing power so that you will need more money to buy the same goods and services. With a current base of $10,000 you will have to have $12,200 in five years and $14,800 in 10 years.

But remember that inflation works both ways. It also increases the yields on investments, especially those with fixed income. Even with a modest 10% rate of return, that $10,000 will grow to $16,100 in five years and to $25,900 in a decade (with compounding). These days, with low inflation, almost every worthwhile investment can keep you ahead of inflation even when you deduct the taxes!

To get the best returns, you must be flexible: moving out of stocks into money market funds and bonds when yields

HOW TO CALCULATE THE EFFECT OF INFLATION

Years From Now	4%	5%	6%	7%	8%
5	1.22	1.28	1.34	1.40	1.47
10	1.48	1.63	1.79	1.97	2.16
15	1.80	2.08	2.40	2.76	3.17
20	2.19	2.65	3.21	3.87	4.66
25	2.67	3.39	4.29	5.43	6.85
30	3.24	4.32	5.74	7.61	10.06

SOURCE: David Thorndike, ed., THE THORNDIKE ENCYCLOPEDIA OF BANKING AND FINANCIAL TABLES (Boston: Warren, Gorham & Lamont, 1980)

rise above 12%; back to stocks, when they fall below 11% or so. In investing, look for the best returns within your objectives. If you opt for income, you will have to accept lower returns when inflation—and interest rates—are low. If you are wise and shoot for total returns, you will always stay ahead of inflation, be able to pay taxes and still build your assets.

About This Edition

In this 1984 edition of *Your Investments,* there are many important revisions. Some reflect the vast changes that have taken place in the financial world: interest rates of 10% compared to 16.5% last year; new types of securities: zero coupon bonds for taxable and tax-exempt bonds; units of limited partnerships for everything from oil/gas deals to real estate packages of home mortgages; new types of financial futures and, most speculative of all, options on a score of futures contracts ranging from debt issues to stock indexes. Wall Street has become the biggest, most imaginative packager of all!

There are also major revisions in the chapter on pension plans as the result of new legislation: higher contributions to Keogh plans and lower contributions for corporate plans; less discrimination against employees and better terms for eligibility and vesting. As a result, the investment of these fiduciary funds is more important than ever before.

Many of the changes involve details that, too often, are overlooked but, if not heeded, can eliminate benefits and boost taxes. Some tax-avoidance schemes are no longer permitted and the benefits of others have been restricted. In a real sense, investing in 1984 will be a brand new ball game!

In the original revision, I included a chapter on high-technology stocks (more don'ts than dos) but, on second thought, this was eliminated. These "hot" stocks are almost all speculations and, it seems to me, not suitable for an *investment* guide that seeks to explain how to preserve capital, to earn income and to achieve long-term profitable growth of assets.

Throughout *Your Investments,* all material is designed and presented to help the individual investor with his or her personal savings—directly or through personal pension plan portfolios. The securities mentioned are suggestions, not recommendations. They are the types of holdings to consider when they can help you meet your investment goals. But take nothing for granted and always check the latest data before committing any money. Investigate *before* you invest; *while* you invest; and, to improve your skill, *after* you have made the sale.

None of the counsel or techniques are applicable to all stocks at all times. They should be used only when common sense tells you that they are likely to be effective.

If you have any doubts, do not spend your money. It's just as important to sleep well as to make money.

The goals of *Your Investments* are the same as they have been since the first edition: to provide information to help thoughtful investors understand securities and commodities, the operation of their markets and the standards and methods that have proven successful. In investing, there is

STOCK MARKET TRENDS 1964 — 1983

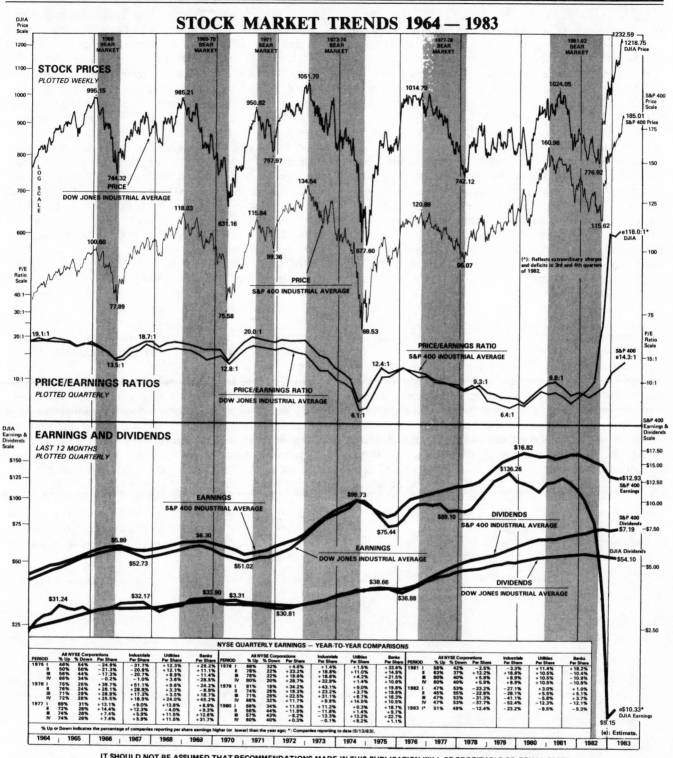

PERIOD	All NYSE Corporations % Up	% Down	Per Share	Industrials Per Share	Utilities Per Share	Banks Per Share	PERIOD	All NYSE Corporations % Up	% Down	Per Share	Industrials Per Share	Utilities Per Share	Banks Per Share	PERIOD	All NYSE Corporations % Up	% Down	Per Share	Industrials Per Share	Utilities Per Share	Banks Per Share
1975 I	46%	54%	-24.9%	-31.7%	+12.3%	+25.2%	1978 I	68%	32%	+4.6%	+1.4%	+1.5%	+33.6%	1981 I	58%	42%	-2.5%	-3.3%	+11.4%	+18.2%
II	50%	50%	-21.3%	-20.8%	+12.1%	+11.1%	II	78%	22%	+23.2%	+18.6%	+11.0%	+14.9%	II	63%	37%	+12.2%	+16.9%	+10.5%	-10.4%
III	56%	44%	-17.3%	-20.7%	+8.9%	-11.4%	III	78%	22%	+19.6%	+18.6%	+4.2%	+21.5%	III	60%	40%	+5.9%	+8.9%	+10.5%	-10.9%
IV	66%	34%	-0.2%	-1.0%	+3.6%	-28.5%	IV	80%	20%	+28.7%	+32.9%	+1.4%	+10.8%	IV	60%	40%	+5.9%	+8.9%	+10.5%	-10.9%
1976 I	75%	25%	+39.7%	+51.1%	+9.6%	-24.2%	1979 I	81%	19%	+34.2%	+43.1%	+9.0%	+19.8%	1982 I	47%	53%	-23.2%	-27.1%	+3.0%	+1.0%
II	76%	24%	+26.1%	+28.9%	+3.3%	-8.9%	II	74%	26%	+19.3%	+23.2%	+3.7%	+19.6%	II	45%	55%	-22.8%	-28.1%	+5.5%	+5.1%
III	71%	29%	+28.9%	+17.3%	+3.5%	+18.7%	III	71%	29%	+22.5%	+31.1%	+6.7%	+18.3%	III	47%	53%	-31.3%	-41.1%	-5.8%	+3.7%
IV	72%	28%	+25.5%	+18.3%	+24.0%	+45.2%	IV	68%	32%	+11.7%	+9.9%	+14.5%	+10.5%	IV	47%	53%	-37.7%	-52.4%	-12.3%	-12.1%
1977 I	69%	31%	+13.1%	+9.0%	+13.8%	+6.9%	1980 I	66%	34%	+11.5%	+11.2%	+0.3%	+18.7%	1983 I*	51%	49%	-12.4%	-23.2%	-8.5%	-5.3%
II	72%	28%	+14.4%	+12.3%	-4.0%	+9.3%	II	56%	44%	-11.9%	-11.8%	+1.4%	+9.7%							
III	74%	26%	+7.4%	+5.9%	+11.5%	+12.6%	III	57%	43%	-8.2%	-13.3%	+13.2%	+22.7%							
IV	74%	26%	+7.4%	+5.9%	+11.5%	+31.7%	IV	60%	40%	+0.3%	-0.1%	-8.2%	+1.1%							

% Up or Down indicates the percentage of companies reporting per share earnings higher (or lower) than the year ago; *: Companies reporting to date (5/13/83).

NYSE QUARTERLY EARNINGS — YEAR-TO-YEAR COMPARISONS

IT SHOULD NOT BE ASSUMED THAT RECOMMENDATIONS MADE IN THIS PUBLICATION WILL BE PROFITABLE OR EQUAL PAST PERFORMANCE. THE COMPLETE *WRIGHT INVESTMENT RECORD* IS AVAILABLE ON REQUEST WITHOUT COST OR OBLIGATION.

SOURCE: Wright Investors' Service

no substitute for knowledge, which, in turn, depends on information. Add a little luck and you can make your savings grow rapidly.

Your Investments is not an advisory service and has no products or services to sell. It is designed as a guide to the intelligent use of savings; through tables, charts and words, it shows you how to make more money with the money you have made or inherited.

Forget about fancy formulas, ratios, curves, square roots, the length of a dress hem, sunspots and such client-impressing terms as *alpha and beta*. All anyone has to do to accumulate wealth is to view the stock market as an investment device, not as a game or a gamble.

Your Investments is edited for the concerned investor, whether new or sophisticated. The information is as accurate as its source, and whenever possible it has been double-checked by authorities.

The techniques and recommendations are not gospel. They should be used only when common sense tells you that they will enhance your profits or reduce your losses. *They have three goals: to preserve your capital, to build your assets and to boost your income.*

As you will learn from reading this book, the stock market is not as mysterious nor as complex as many people would have you believe. Wall Street is often puzzling, usually frustrating and frequently foolish . . . for a short while. This is understandable because the stock market is the end result of the fears, hopes, prejudices and pride of millions of people and billions of dollars. Their actions and reactions are influenced by rumors and headlines; too few are the result of facts and common sense. Yet, over the long term, the stock market is logical, and facts and fundamentals will always prove rewarding.

In the stock market, there are profit-making opportunities regardless of the trend. There are certain industry groups or types of stocks which perform better than the averages. In this book you will find rules, concepts, facts and techniques to help you select those securities when they are undervalued and sell them when they become fully priced. Or, in erratic markets, to use leverage, sell short, use options or warrants, or cash in with bonds and convertibles. That's what money management is all about.

Unlike most books on the stock market, *Your Investments* seeks to show you how to avoid and minimize losses. *In successful investing, it is just as important NOT to lose money as to make a profit.*

Throughout the book, there are many warnings. They are important because, as Charles H. Dow wrote at the turn of the century, "The man who is prudent and careful in carrying on a store, factory or real estate business seems to think that totally different methods should be employed in dealing with stocks. Nothing is further from the truth."

The two most important elements in successful investing are *accurate information* and *common sense*. By stressing dangers and pitfalls, *Your Investments* hopes to persuade you to use your intelligence and business or professional experience to make wise decisions.

Before moving into details of successful investing, study this chart of Stock Market Trends: 1964–1983: 20 years that involve both bull and bear markets. Notice how the stock market averages have moved up and down over these two decades: from a 1966 high of 995.15 to a 1974 low of 577.60, back to 1014.79, down again (but not so far) to 764.12, up to 1024.05 in 1981, down to 776.92 and then skyrocketing to new highs in 1983.

Now check the bottom chart of earnings and dividends to get an idea of what really happened. Until 1983, with modest fluctuations, earnings continued to rise: on a per share basis for the S&P 400, from $5.89 to $16.82 and then down to $12.93 recently. *American corporations made more money.* In part, these reflected inflation but the long-term trend was *up* and, in 1984, can be expected to rise again.

Finally, note how dividends rose: for the DJIA, from $31.24 to $54.10 per share. This is significant because only rarely do major corporations reduce the dollars of their payouts. These higher dividends set a solid base for the future: for both income and total returns.

American business is stronger than ever. Major corporations have weathered some difficult years and are now moving ahead again. How far their stocks will go is anyone's guess but Wright Investors' Service projects that the DJIA will be between 1500 and 1800 by 1987. This may be optimistic for the overall market but such gains can be achieved with quality stocks bought and sold under the rules outlined in this guide.

porary swings in the price of stocks but they are *never* a sound reason for *investment* decisions. Find out the truth and then act if the stock you hold carries a quality rating. But if it's a marginal firm and you can still sell at a profit, get out. You'll keep peace in the family.

Specific Guidelines

Here are some valuable points as set by John Winthrop Wright, a leading fundamentalist:

Buy a stock when it is selling well below the average price/earnings ratio of the past decade and there are good prospects for rising earnings in a strong market.

Example: In 1982, Tandy Corp. stock was at 20 with a price/earnings ratio of 12, about the average multiple for the last decade. With excellent prospects, this was a bargain. By the spring of 1983, the stock price soared to over 60, a multiple of about 20 times estimated profits. This was the time to sell.

Review a stock when its P/E ratio goes to, or above, its average annual high ratio for the last five years.

Example: In early 1983, IBM stock broke above 120. This was 16 times the last 12-month earnings. In the 1978–82 period, the high end of the P/E range was 14. It was time to consider selling (especially as the stock had been purchased at about 60 the year before).

Sell a stock when it becomes fully priced in relation to past performance, future prospects and its historical P/E ratio. When any stock which, over the years, has sold at 8 to 10 times profits gets to a multiple of 12, watch carefully. At a P/E of 14, get ready to sell unless there are strong reasons to anticipate unusually fast and sustained growth or some temporary activity such as a possible takeover. Very few stocks continue to trade at ratios far above those of their industry or their past averages.

Concludes Wright: "It is always better to make Baron Rothschild's famous mistake of making a little less by selling too soon than to take the greater risk of overstaying the market in an overpriced stock."

To these can be added two other checkpoints used by analysts for stock review in determining sell points:

• When the price of the stock rises to a price that is considerably more than double the shareholders' equity at corporate book value per common share. When buyers are willing to pay more than twice the tangible value of a company, they are adding a hefty premium for future growth. Be sure this extra is justified. (N.B. This applies mainly to manufacturing firms with substantial equipment, buildings, etc. . . . not to drug/service/financial companies whose tangible assets are usually small in relation to total revenues.)

Example: At the start of 1982, V. F. Corp. had a book value of $29.80 per share and the stock was trading at 20. This was the time to buy. A year later, when the book value rose slightly to $30.86 per share, the stock was over 80: time to sell. Within a few weeks, V. F. stock started to drop.

• When the dividend yield falls below 3%. If the company is utilizing its cash for research, development and expansion, that's good. But growth has to be substantial to justify accepting a low current return for the use of your money.

Manage Your Portfolio

Selecting your investments is only the first step to financial success. It is important to review and revise your holding as conditions change: your own and those of the marketplace. Never forget that a stock does not care who owns it and that price/volume action is the result of forces far stronger and wealthier than you are and ever will be.

1. Follow the market trends. Do not try to buck the tide. If it's a bear market, be cautious and/or sell short. If it's a fluctuating period, think trade. If it's a bull market, take greater risks.

2. Limit your purchase until your forecast is confirmed. When you feel you have latched on to a "hot one," cut your original order in half even if it means buying less than a round lot. When the chart's trendline shows you are right, buy more. You may lose a few points of profit by waiting but you will minimize your losses.

A variation of this counsel is to average up when you pick a winner . . . buy more shares as the price of the stock rises. Be sure there's a solid basis for future optimism. Hopes of a stock split will push a stock up, but if the split does not occur, the shares will drop sharply.

3. Use leverage. When prospects are bright and interest rates not onerous, take advantage of margin. With stocks, this can give you two dollars of benefits for every dollar invested. But remember that in a down market, leverage can increase losses.

4. Watch the 12-month date. When you buy any stock, mark next year's calendar 12 months after: *(a)* the date on which the stock rise started (when investors with profits will start selling); and *(b)* your purchase date, so that your gains can qualify for the lower tax levy. Such a timetable can also be useful with losses, as you may be able to wait a few days to shift them from short to long term. This can be risky with a volatile holding.

5. Be skeptical. This is a repeat of that all-important *investigate before you invest* rule. As they used to say in the Old West, "I trust you, honey, but cut the cards."

Common Stocks for the Best Total Returns

Over the long term of true investments, the best total returns—income plus appreciation—are achieved by owning common stocks of growing, profitable corporations. You gain by: (1) constantly higher underlying values; (2) ever-increasing dividends; and (3) rising prices for corporate shares. In bull markets, such as appears likely to continue for some time, these benefits will come more rapidly.

There are, of course, times when temporarily greater rewards can be attained with fixed income securities: in periods of high interest rates, with CDs, money market funds, high coupon bonds for income and low coupon bonds bought at discounts. But the core of every investment portfolio, whether personal or pension fund, should be shares of financially strong corporations whose managements have proven records of profitable growth. As is repeated throughout this guide, the arithmetic is clear and compelling:

If a company earns 15% on the money invested by shareholders and pays out 5% as dividends, management reinvests 10% in new plants, products, services, markets, etc. In seven years, with the same rate of return, everything will double: the earnings, dividends, underlying worth of each share of stock and, at some point, the market value of the stock.

You will have to pay taxes on the dividends but the reinvestments will accumulate tax-free until you sell the shares.

Such progress will not happen every year with every stock. You must be ready to make changes when justified. There are a handful of stocks that you may never (well, hardly ever) want to sell, but, on the average, ample profits will come from securities held from three to five years after purchase. With stocks bought for income, such as those of utilities and banks, the time frame may be somewhat longer but, as noted in the previous chapter, only three of 27 utilities maintained a quality rating for 10 years!

Except in the Great Depression and the 1970s, common stocks, as measured by standard averages, have provided higher returns than bonds or Treasury bills in every decade in the twentieth century. And, in those 83+ years, stocks, as a group, have provided returns more than double those of bonds (9.1% vs. 4.2%) and almost triple those of T-bills (3.7%). With wise selections, investors did far better!

Advantages of Common Stocks

1. Growing values. Stocks are *live* investments. The good ones *grow*. Bonds and savings are *dead* investments.

Their basic values remain static. (*Note:* This doesn't mean you should always be fully invested in common stocks, no matter how rewarding. For maximum investment returns, it's important to be flexible.)

The market value of a common stock grows as the corporation prospers. This growth keeps pace and, hopefully, exceeds the erosion of inflation. The face value of bonds remains the same so that over the years, their real value, in terms of purchasing power, decreases.

Under normal conditions, investors, mindful of the debilitation of inflation, buy more common stocks. This tends to drive their prices up and their yields down. But these purchases are based on optimism which, usually, develops many months after the facts are available.

By contrast, the prices of bonds are almost completely controlled by interest rates and take effect immediately. When the cost of money rises, bond values drop to maintain competitive returns. Vice versa when interest rates decline. Bonds are traded by yields; stocks by what investors believe to be future corporate prospects.

Certainly, the stock market fluctuates, but the long-term trend has *always* been up and there has been a better than 3-1 edge for the years of gains versus those of decline. Right now, most analysts look for the greatest gains in history because, by traditional standards, most common stocks are undervalued.

With patience, experience and compounding, every investor should shoot for average annual rates of return of 20% with common stocks: 5% dividends, 15% annual appreciation. You won't score that well every time and, for balance, you will probably have some income holdings with lower yields, but, if you follow the rules of this book, use common sense and rub a rabbit's foot, you will end up with 16% which will double your money every 4½ years. Later, of course, there will be years with smaller rewards but, by then, you may be experienced enough to utilize money-adding techniques such as writing options. And, at all times, these welcome total returns can be achieved by *investing*, not speculating.

2. Bigger gains with real winners. The greatest gains come from a few stocks, typically, two of every 10 holdings. If you can score modest returns with the others, your average can be high . . . rarely possible with any other type of investments.

Examples: Automatic Data Processing: In 1975, 100 shares could be bought for 40: $4,000 investment. There were two stock splits, both 2-1: in 1976 and in 1981, so

COMPARATIVE INVESTMENT RETURNS

PERIOD	STOCKS	BONDS	90-DAY T-BILLS
1900-09	+ 9.4%	+ 4.2%	+ 5.7%
1910-19	+10.3	+ 2.6	+ 4.7
1920-29	+14.3	+ 6.4	+ 3.3
1930-39	0	+ 3.1	+ 0.4
1940-49	+ 8.5	+ 3.8	+ 0.5
1950-59	+18.9	+ 1.1	+ 1.9
1960-69	+ 5.3	+ 2.8	+ 3.7
1970-79	+ 5.2	+ 7.5	+ 5.7
1980-83 (mid)	+15.9	+11.8	+11.6
1900-83	+ 9.1	+ 4.2	+ 3.7

SOURCE: Wright Investors' Service

SOME MAJOR COMPANIES THAT HAVE BOOSTED DIVIDENDS IN EACH OF PAST 10 YEARS

COMPANY	% INCREASE 1973-82		% INCREASE 1973-82
Abbott Laboratories	546%	Lilly (Eli)	261%
Albertson's, Inc.	525	Malone & Hyde	484
Alco Standard	558	Masco Corp.	1000
American Brands	207	Melville Corp.	397
Am. Express/Shearson	410	MMM	233
Am. Home Products	279	Nicor, Inc.	65
Ametek, Inc.	233	Northwest Bancorp	150
AMP, Inc.	536	ONEOK, Inc.	192
Beatrice Foods	158	Penney (J.C.)	92
Bristol-Myers	250	Pfizer, Inc.	246
Carnation Co.	376	Philip Morris	674
Central & S.W.	61	Pillsbury Co.	239
Chesebrough-Pond's	218	Procter & Gamble	213
Coca Cola	202	Public Service Indiana	89
Colgate-Palmolive	150	Quaker Oats	189
CPC International	147	Ralston Purina	239
De Luxe Check	522	Raytheon Co.	833
Donnelley (R.R.)	215	Reynolds, (R.J.)	141
Dover Corp.	677	Rochester Telephone	222
Dun & Bradstreet	245	Rubbermaid, Inc.	357
Eckerd, Jack	966	Schering-Plough	265
Emerson Electric	250	Sonat, Inc	261
ENSERCH Corp.	166	Southwestern P.S.	113
Florida P&L	205	Sperry Corp.	220
Fort Howard Paper	823	Squibb Corp.	78
Foxboro Co.	511	Standard Oil (Calif.)	233
General Mills	275	Standard Oil (Ind.)	374
Genuine Parts	348	TECO Energy	126
Grainger (W.W.)	364	Texas Commerce Bank	276
Halliburton Co.	841	Thomas & Betts	292
Harland (John H.)	1450	Times Mirror	669
Harris Corp.	252	Tucson Electric	159
Heinz (H.J.)	370	U.S. Tobacco	365
Houston Industries	140	United Telecom	79
Interco, Inc.	132	Upjohn Co.	178
Johnson & Johnson	614	VF Corp.	492
Kellogg Co.	207	Vulcan Materials	369
K-Mart	488	Warner Lambert	108
Knight-Ridder News	607	Winn-Dixie Stores	172

SOURCE: Standard & Poor's OUTLOOK

that, in mid 1983, the investor owned 400 shares with a market value of $16,000. The dividends added $615.

Barry Wright: In 1978, 100 shares cost $1,200. In 1979 and 1980, there was 2–1 stock splits, so, by 1983, the 400 shares were worth $10,000 plus small dividends over the years.

Florida Power & Light: In 1978, 100 shares cost $2,400. In the next five years, per share dividends rose from $2.00 to $3.42, so the total income (through 1983) was $1,462. Add the 12-point price rise ($1,200 capital gain) and the total return of $2,662 was more than the original cost . . . an average annual rate of return of over 20%!

With stocks like these, you can reach your target if you can keep losses low and score moderate gains with the other winners. Note that I did not include such sky-rocketers as Schlumberger, Ltd. whose stock was split six times between 1972 and 1981 and, on an adjusted basis, shot up from 5 to 85. Or U.S. Shoe, whose shares zoomed from 23 in 1981 to 70 in early 1983.

3. Maximum safety. Quality stocks are just as safe as bonds. As long as the corporation meets quality standards—financial strength, growth and profitability—your money is safe. The company will continue to pay dividends, usually with periodic increases and, with higher earnings, the value of its shares will increase. If a well-known corporation pays dividends for more than 40 years, what risk is there in its stock as compared to its debt issues?

4. Effective tax shelter. The earnings that are *not* paid out to shareholders in dividends represent taxdeferred income. These profits are reinvested to make the company grow and prosper. As long as you own stock in a profitable company, your money is growing. You will pay no taxes on these "gains" until you sell and, then, if you hold the shares for 12 months, at the low capital gains rate: on only 40% of the realized appreciation.

5. Liquidity. Common stocks traded on major stock exchanges can be quickly bought or sold at clearly stated prices whose ranges are quoted in the financial press. You can instruct your broker to buy or sell at a specific price or at "market" which will be the best price attainable at that time. The complete transaction will take five working days but, immediately after the transaction, you can get exact data from your broker.

6. Growing dividends. This is important for investors who want ever-higher income. Almost all quality companies keep boosting their payouts because of higher earnings. Percentagewise, as shown by the table, these can be impressive: for Harland (John H.) 1,450% in 10 years: from 5¢ to 62¢ per share: for Rochester Telephone, in the same period, 222%: from 68¢ to $2.09 per share.

With fixed income investments (CDs, bonds, etc.), the original yield may be a bit higher but it will rarely be increased and then only with special types of securities that have limited marketability.

Caution: Dividend increases can be welcome but, to be really worthwhile, they must reflect improved earnings, not a higher percentage of flat profits. Over a decade, 19 major corporations—including Avon Products, Colgate-Palmolive, and Warner-Lambert—boosted their dividends at an annual rate of 10% compounded but the prices of their shares fell. *Reason:* Profits were down so that the percentage of earnings paid in dividends rose: for Colgate, to 51% from 46%. Directors cannot buy investor support with income alone. There must be profitable growth if the values of shares are to continue to rise.

Disadvantages of Common Stocks

Just to be sure that everyone understands that there are risks with ownership of common stocks, there are two disadvantages. The first does not apply to quality stocks and both can be controlled, if not overcome, by setting strict rules and using common sense.

1. The risk of permanent loss of capital. You may lose all your profits and some of your capital if you speculate in "poor" stocks (and, occasionally, if you do so with quality stocks). The problem is *you.* When you speculate in high-flying stocks which are temporarily popular, the odds are against success. Only a few strong-minded people have the courage to sell such stocks when they become overpriced. When such equities start down, too many people hang on in hopes of a comeback. This seldom happens.

Speculations in stocks should be limited to money half or all of which you can afford to lose.

2. Continual market-price fluctuations. Short-term swings in the prices of common stocks are unavoidable. That's the penalty you pay for the liquidity of your investment. If you bought the stock for steady income or long-term capital growth, forget about the weekly or monthly dips and squiggles. If the company's management has a proven record of financial success, the values of its shares will be recognized . . . in time.

These interim dips can be tough to take but if you buy the company rather than the stock, things will prove profitable. The difficult times come when a good—or pretty good—stock drops 2 or 3 points in one day solely because of some erroneous report or unconfirmed rumor. What happens is that, in an uncertain market, one big institution decides to sell. The large block of stock forces the price down to a stop-loss point set by another money manager on his computer. This signals another big sale and down it goes. By late afternoon, there's likely to be an upmove as wiser investors spot the bargain.

The alert investor can turn these price fluctuations to substantial advantage: buying quality stocks when they drop a couple of points, and, as their prices rise, adding to holdings on the temporary dips which almost always characterize a strong upswing.

Continuity/Stability

For investors who place safety first, the best common stocks are those of companies that have paid dividends for 40 years or more. There are many familiar names: Anheuser-Busch, Bristol-Myers, Chesebrough-Pond's, Heinz (H. J.), Johnson & Johnson, Melville Corp., Philip Morris and Woolworth.

But continuity is not necessarily a mark of quality. Some of the real old timers, such as utilities, are monopolies. Their continuing profits may be the result of their market position rather than managerial ability. And despite their famous names, neither Philip Morris nor Woolworth are quality corporations.

It's OK to start with companies listed here but *always* check their records to see if: (1) the dividends have been increased fairly consistently as the result of higher earn-

ings; (2) the company has been able to move ahead in recent years and appears likely to do even better in the near future. It's great to do business with an old store but only if the merchandise is up-to-date and fairly priced!

The corporation's past record is important but it is not a guarantee of its future. Managements change, markets shift, products become outmoded, governments regulate and consumer tastes are fickle. Well-run firms keep improving their goods and services, developing new areas, modernizing their plants and equipment and, overall, maintaining industry leadership. If you select any heirloom stock, be sure to check its recent record of profitability and growth. The name may be famous but the investment can be marginal. For example, PPG Industries (formerly Pittsburgh Plate Glass) has paid a dividend since 1896 but in the last four years, its per share profits have declined: from $6.41 to $6.23 to $6.12 to $4.21. But its dividends have risen from $1.88 to $2.36 per share. PPG stock has yo-yoed but, recently, with an eye on the comeback of the housing industry, has moved to a new high. Still, such a dismal record is *not* a sound reason for buying this stock . . . not yet, anyway.

Professional preference. These are stocks chosen by the "experts": managers of mutual funds, pension plans, insurance portfolios, endowments, etc. With rare exceptions, these are shares of major corporations listed on the New York Stock Exchange.

Institutional ownership is no guarantee of quality but it does indicate that some professionals have reviewed the financial prospects and, for some reason (not always clear) have recommended purchase or retention. Without such interest, no stock can move up!

In most cases, the companies must meet strict standards of financial strength, investment acceptance, profitability, growth and, to some extent, income. But too many institutions still buy name and fame and either move in after the rush has started or hold on after the selling has started. Use this list as a checkpoint for companies that appear attractive. If the stock is owned by more than 50 institutions, you'll be in good (but not always the most profitable) company. Information is available in Standard & Poor's *Stock Guide,* Moody's *Handbook of Common Stocks, The Value Line* and analyses available from brokerage firms and some investment advisory services.

And if you want to track portfolio changes, watch for reports on actions of investment companies in *Barron's Monthly Stock Digest* and the quarterly summaries published by *Lipper Analytical Services, Vickers Associates,* and *Wiesenberger Services.*

But be cautious. The public information comes months after decisions have been made. By the time you get the word, prices may have risen so much that your benefits will be comparatively small. Or you may be buying just before the Big Boys, realizing their mistakes, start selling.

It's also wise to check the type of fund. If it's designed for long-term holdings, following its action can be worthwhile if you are patient.

Following the leaders can also be profitable when you speculate. By watching institutional portfolios keyed to growth, you can find the names of AMEX and OTC stocks that have passed some sort of review. Usually these are companies that are "emerging" or "turnarounds" where

CONSISTENT DIVIDEND PAYERS FOR 50 YEARS OR MORE

These are industrial/service corporations that have paid at least one cash dividend annually for at least half a century. Most of them are listed on the New York Stock Exchange. Banks and investment/holding companies are not included. With such long records of profitable operation, these companies can be expected to keep on rewarding shareholders but take nothing for granted. One of the great claims of the Pennsylvania Railroad was its more-than-a-century record of dividend payments — before it went bankrupt — as Penn Central.

COMPANY	Dividends Paid Since	COMPANY	Dividends Paid Since	COMPANY	Dividends Paid Since
Abbott Laboratories	1926	Chesebrough-Pond's	1883	GATX Corp.	1919
AFA Protective	1889	Chicago Rivet	1932	General Electric	1899
Affiliated Publications	1882	Chubb Corp.	1902	General Foods	1922
Albany International	1922	Church & Dwight	1901	General Mills	1898
Alexander & Alexander	1922	CIGNA Corp.	1867	General Motors	1915
Alexander & Baldwin	1902	C-I-L, Inc.	1912	Georgia-Pacific	1927
Allied Corp.	1887	Cincinnati G&E	1853	Gibson-Homans	1922
Amerada Hess	1922	Cincinnati Milacron	1923	Gillette Co.	1906
American Bakeries	1928	Clark (J.L.) Mfg.	1921	Great Lakes International	1910
American Bell	1881	Cleveland Electric	1901	Great North. Nekoosa	1913
American Brands	1905	Cluett, Peabody	1923	Greit Bros.	1926
American Can	1923	Coca-Cola	1893	Guardsman Chemical	1918
American Dist. Telegraph	1903	Colgate-Palmoilve	1895	Gulf United	1932
American Electric Power	1909	Combustion Engineering	1911		
American Express/Shearson	1870	Cominco, Ltd.	1924	Hackensack Water	1886
American General Insurance	1929	Commonwealth Edison	1890	Handy & Harman	1906
American Home Products	1919	Cone Mills	1914	Hanover Insurance	1853
American Maize Products	1929	Connecticut Energy	1850	Harcourt Brace Jovanovich	1922
American National Insurance	1923	Conn. Natural Gas	1851	Harland (John H.)	1932
American Natural Resources	1904	Consolidated Edison	1885	Hartford Steam Boiler	1871
American Sterilizer	1914	Consumers Power	1913	Hawaiian Electric	1901
AMF, Inc.	1927	Continental Corp.	1854	Heinz (H.J.)	1911
Amfac, Inc.	1898	Continental Group	1923	Heller International	1921
Anchor-Hocking	1914	Conwood Corp.	1903	Hercules, Inc.	1913
Anheuser-Busch	1932	Corning Glass	1881	Hershey Foods	1930
Archer-Daniels-Midland	1927	Courier Corp.	1919	Holmes (D.H.)	1906
Arizona Public Service	1920	Courtlands, Ltd. ADR	1913	Home Beneficial	1906
Aro Corp.	1931	CPC International	1920	Honeywell, Inc.	1928
Arvin Industries	1925	CrownAmerica	1888	Hormel (Geo. A.)	1928
Atlantic City Electric	1919	CSX Corp.	1922	Houghton Mifflin	1908
Atlantic-Richfield	1927	CTS Corp.	1930	Household International	1917
Avondale Mills	1904			Houston Industries	1922
Avon Products	1919	Dart & Ktaft, Inc.	1924	Hydraulic Co.	1890
		Dayton P&L	1919		
Baker International	1929	Delmarva P&L	1921	Idaho Power	1917
Baltimore G&E	1910	DeLuxe Check Printing	1921	Ideal Basic Industries	1911
Bangor Hydro Electric	1925	Dentsply International	1900	Imasco, Ltd.	1912
Banta (George)	1927	Detroit Edison	1909	Imperial Chemical ADR	1927
Bay State Gas	1853	Diamond International	1882	Imperial Group ADR	1928
Becton Dickinson	1926	Dibrell Bros.	1925	Indianapolis Water	1926
Bekins Co.	1923	Discount Corp. of N.Y.	1920	Ingersoll-Rand	1910
Belknap, Inc.	1880	Dr. Pepper	1930	Ingredient Technology	1927
Bell & Howell	1915	Dome Mines, Ltd.	1920	INTERCO, Inc.	1913
Bell Telephone of Canada	1881	Donnelley (R.R.) & Sons	1911	IBM	1916
Bemis Co.	1922	Dow Chemical	1911	International Multifoods	1923
Beneficial Corp.	1929	Dow Jones & Co.	1906	Iowa Resources	1909
Berkshire Gas	1858	Duckwall-Alco Stores	1917		
Bird & Son	1924	Duke Power	1926	Jefferson-Pilot	1913
Blue Bell	1923	Dunlop Holding	1932	Jewel Companies	1928
Borden, Inc.	1899	DuPont (E.I.)	1904	Johnson Controls	1901
Borg-Warner	1928	Duquesne Light	1913	Johnson & Johnson	1905
Boston Edison	1890	Durham Corp.	1918	Joslyn Mfg.	1936
Briggs & Stratton	1929			Joy Manufacturing	1929
Bristol-Myers	1900	Eastern Utilities	1928	JWT Corp	1917
British Petroleum	1917	Eastman Kodak	1902		
Brown Group	1923	Eaton Corp.	1923	Kahler Corp.	1917
Burlington Industries	1931	El Paso Electric	1928	Kansas City Life	1907
Burroughs Corp.	1895	Emhart Corp.	1902	Kansas City P&L	1921
Business Men's Assurance	1924	ENSERCH Corp.	1926	Kansas G&E	1922
		Equifax, Inc.	1913	Kansas P&L	1924
Cabot Corp.	1931	Equitable of Iowa	1889	Kellogg Co.	1923
Calif. Portland Cement	1909	Exxon Corp.	1882	K-Mart, Inc.	1913
Calif. Water Service	1931			Kroger Co.	1902
Campbell Soup	1902	Farmers Group	1931		
Carpenter Technology	1907	Federal Co.	1924	Lane Co	1922
Carter-Wallace	1883	Federated Dept. Stores	1931	Lilly (Eli) & Co.	1885
Castle & Cook	1896	Firestone Tire	1934	Louisville G&E	1913
Caterpillar Tractor	1914	Fitchburg G&E	1859		
CBI Industries	1913	Fleming Cos.	1927	Macy (R.H.)	1927
CBS, Inc.	1931	Flickinger (S.M.)	1920	Madison G&E	1909
Ceco Corp.	1921	Fort Howard Paper	1922	Manhattan Life	1851
Central Hudson G&E	1903	Foxboro Co.	1916	Marsh & McLennan	1923
Central Illinois Light	1921	Freeport-McMoran	1927	May's Department Stores	1911
Champion Spark Plug	1919			McCormick & Co.	1929
Chattem, Inc.	1922	Gannett Co.	1929	Media General	1923

COMPANY	Dividends Paid Since	COMPANY	Dividends Paid Since	COMPANY	Dividends Paid Since
Melville Corp.	1916	Pillsbury Co.	1927	Sterling Drug	1902
Meredith Corp.	1930	Post Corp.	1921	Sun Chemical	1929
Middlesex Water	1912	Potomac Electric	1904	Sun Co.	1904
Mine Safety Appliance	1918	PPG Industries	1896		
MMM	1916	Pratt & Lambert	1905	Tasty Baking	1915
Mirro Corp.	1902	Procter & Gamble	1891	TECO Energy	1900
Mobil Corp.	1902	Protective Corp.	1926	Texaco, Inc.	1903
Monarch Capital	1867	Providence Energy	1849	Texas Utilities	1917
Monarch Machine Tool	1913	Provident Life & Accident	1925	Time, Inc.	1930
Monsanto Co.	1925	Public Service (Colo.)	1907	Times Mirror	1892
Morton Thiokol	1923	Public Service E&G	1907	Timken Co.	1921
Multimedia, Inc.	1921			Tokheim Corp.	1920
Murphy (G.C.)	1913	Quaker Oats, Inc.	1906	Toledo Edison	1922
		Quaker State Oil	1931	Towle Mfg.	1917
Nabisco Brands	1899			Travelers Corp.	1864
Nalco Chemical	1928	Raymark Corp.	1895	Trico Products	1928
Nashua Corp	1926	Redpath Industries	1930	Tucson Electric	1918
National Fuel Gas	1903	Reece Corp.	1882		
National-Standard	1916	Rexnord, Inc.	1894	UGI Corp.	1885
National Steel	1907	Reynolds (R.J.) Industries	1900	Union Carbide	1918
National Utilities	1923	Richardson-Vicks	1922	Union Electric	1906
New Process	1931	Robertshaw Controls	1941	Union Oil (Calif.)	1916
New York State E&G	1910	Rochester Telephone	1926	Union Pacific	1900
NL Industries	1906	Rockaway Corp.	1928	United Illuminating	1900
NLT Corp.	1920	Rohm & Haas	1927	U.S. Gypsum	1919
Noranda Mines	1930	Rose's Stores	1928	U.S. Shoe	1932
Norfolk Southern	1901			U.S. Tobacco	1912
Northeast Utilities	1927	Safeway Stores	1927	Universal Leaf Tobacco	1927
Northern States Power	1910	St. Paul Companies	1872	Upjohn Co.	1909
Norton Co.	1922	San Diego G&E	1909		
Noxell Corp.	1925	Savannah Foods	1924	Virginia Electric	1925
		SCOA Industries	1929		
Ohio Art	1930	Scott Paper	1915	Walco National	1890
Ohio Casualty	1923	Scovill Mfg.	1856	Walker Resources	1848
Ohio Edison	1930	Seibel Bruce	1916	Warner-Lambert	1926
Oklahoma G&E	1908	SFN Companies	1922	Washington Gas Light	1852
Olin Corp	1926	Shell Transport	1898	Washington National	1923
Orange/Rockland Utilities	1908	Sierra Pacific Power	1916	Washington Water Power	1899
Outlet Co.	1926	Singer Co.	1863	Waverly Press	1925
Owens-Illinois	1907	SmithKline Beckman	1923	Weston (George)	1930
		Sonoco Products	1925	West Point-Pepperell	1888
Pacific G&E	1919	Southern Calif. Edison	1909	Westvaco Corp.	1892
Pacific Lighting	1909	Southern Calif. Water	1931	Whirlpool Corp.	1929
Pacific Resources	1912	So. N.E. Telephone	1891	Wiley (John) & Sons	1904
Pacific Telephone	1925	Southland Royalty	1926	Woodward & Lathrop	1932
Penn-Virginia	1916	Springs Industries	1898	Woolworth (F.W.)	1912
Penney (J.C.)	1922	Squibb Corp.	1902	Wrigly (Wm.), Jr.	1913
Pennwalt Corp.	1863	SRI Corp.	1930	Wyman-Gordon	1916
Pennzoil Co.	1925	Stanadyne, Inc.	1905		
Peoples Drug Stores	1927	Standard Oil (Calif.)	1912	Xerox Corp.	1930
Petrolite Corp	1931	Standard Oil (Ind.)	1894		
Pfizer, Inc.	1901	Standard Register	1927	Zale Corp.	1925
Philadelphia Electric	1902	Stanley Works	1877		
Philip Morris	1928	Stauffer Chemical	1915		

SOURCE: Standard & Poor's STOCK GUIDE

---

there's hope of quick gains. Still, before you commit your savings, get a copy of the company's annual report, check advisory services for comments and wait until other major investors start buying. Such caution may cost a few points of profit but it will save a lot more in losses. And always remember that these are speculations, not investments.

Most Profitable Companies

The single more important standard of safety is high, consistent profitability. As explained later, this can be determined by calculating the rate of return on shareholders' equity, a minimum annual average of 11%. By sticking to these real winners, you will always make a lot of money . . . in time.

Wright Investors' Service proved this with the stocks of the 30 companies that make up the DJIA. It made a theoretical investment of $1,000 in each company and, 15 years later, sold out. With dividends reinvested, the shares of the 10 most profitable companies gained 208%; those of the least profitable, only 64%. Wright's conclusion: "Profitable companies listed on the NYSE will make more money with less risk than almost any other type of investment. If the investor takes time to shift to the ten top money makers of the DJIA each year, he will be rich while he is still young enough to enjoy his money."

INSTITUTIONAL FAVORITES

OWNED BY MORE THAN 500 INSTITUTIONS

American Home Products	MMM
Atlantic-Richfield	Mobil Corp.
Bristol-Myers	Monsanto Co.
Caterpillar Tractor	Pfizer, Inc.
Citicorp	Philip Morris
Coca Cola	Phillips Petroleum
Digital Equipment	Procter & Gamble
Dow Chemical	Raytheon Co.
DuPont (E.I.)	Reynolds (R.J.)
Eastman Kodak	Schlumberger, Ltd.
Exxon Corp.	Sears Roebuck
General Electric	Standard Oil (Calif.)
General Motors	Standard Oil (Ind.)
GTE Corp.	Tenneco, Inc.
Gulf Oil	Texaco, Inc.
Halliburton Co.	Union Carbide
IBM	Union Oil (Calif.)
Johnson & Johnson	Union Pacific
Merck & Co.	Xerox Corp.

BY 400-500 MAJOR INVESTORS

Abbott Laboratories	Lilly (Eli) & Co.
Aetna Life & Casualty	McDonald's Corp.
Avon Products	Morgan (J.P.)
Baxter Travenol	Penney (J.C.)
Dart & Kraft	PepsiCo, Inc.
Dresser Industries	SmithKline Beckman
Emerson Electric	Standard Oil (Ohio)
Hewlett-Packard	Texas Utilities
I. T. & T.	United Technologies
K- Mart	

BY OVER 250 INVESTMENT, INSURANCE COMPANIES

Alcan Aluminum	Hughes Tool
Aluminum Co. Of America	Illinois Power
Allied Corp.	Inco, Inc.
Amerada-Hess	Intel Corp.
American Brands	International Paper
American Cyanamid	InterNorth, Inc.
American Electric Power	Kerr-McGee
American Hospital Supply	Middle South Utilities
AMP, Inc.	Monsanto Co.
Anheuser-Busch	Nabisco Brands
Baker International	NCR Corp.
BankAmerica	NL Industries
Beatrice Foods	Norfolk & Southern
Boeing Co.	Pacific G&E
Burlington-Northern	Pennzoil Co.
Burroughs, Inc.	Perkin-Elmer
Central & Southwest	Public Service of Indiana
Champion International	RCA Corp.
Chase Manhattan	Revlon, Inc.
CIGNA Corp.	Royal Dutch Petroleum
Cities Service	Santa Fe Industries
Colgate-Palmolive	Schering-Plough
Commonwealth Edison	Shell Oil
Continental Corp.	Southern Calif. Edison
Cooper Industries	Sperry Corp.
CPC International	Squibb Corp.
CSX Corp.	Sterling Drug
Deere & Co.	Sun Co.
Delta Air Lines	Superior Oil
Disney (Walt)	Tandy Corp.
Duke Power	Texas Instruments
Dun & Bradstreet	Texas Oil & Gas
Federated Dept. Stores	Travelers Corp.
Florida P&L	TRW, Inc.
Ford Motor Co.	Union Camp
Gannett Co.	U.S. Steel
General Foods	United Telecommunications
General Mills	Upjohn Co.
Georgia-Pacific	Virginia Electric
Getty Oil	Warner Communications
Goodyear Tire	Warner-Lambert
Honeywell, Inc.	Westinghouse Electric
Hospital Corp. of America	Weyerhaeuser Co.
Houston Industries	

SOURCE: Standard & Poor's STOCK GUIDE

HIGH MULTIPLE STOCKS OUTPERFORM AVERAGE

GROUP	1973-82	1978-82	1980-82	1981-82
Top 50	+40.7%	+123.0%	+16.4%	+35.9%
S&P 500	+19.1	+ 47.9	+ 3.6	+14.8

Assumes investor: (1) invested in "median" top 50 stocks at end of 1972; (2) sold some or all stocks month later; (3) reinvested proceeds under same criteria at end of each successive month: January 1973, February 1973, etc. No deductions for commissions/fees which would be partially covered by dividends

SOURCE: Kidder Peabody

A corollary of this is the performance of high multiple stocks. According to a study made by Kidder Peabody over the 1978–82 period, the stocks with high price/earnings ratios outperformed the S&P 500 in four of the five years (exception: 1981). Their values rose +36% vs. +15% for the S&P.

The research assumed that the investor bought the 50 stocks with the highest P/Es and, each month thereafter, sold these shares and used the proceeds to purchase new shares under the same criterion. Of the original 50, the only survivors were: AMP, Automatic Data, Baxter Travenol, Electronic Data Systems, Hewlett-Packard and Wil-Mart stores. On the average, the expected growth rate averaged 21% which, in turn, justified a P/E of 21: double to triple that of the market average.

Common Stocks for Income

If you are looking for income only, common stocks may not always be the best investment. In periods of high interest rates, bonds and savings certificates will provide higher returns. But unless those fixed-income securities are bought at a discount, they will seldom appreciate in value so that your total returns will be limited.

The right kind of common stocks can provide income plus capital gains and, with lower taxes, can net more money. Under present laws, all income is taxed at the highest rate but only 40% of long-term profits (when the securities have been held 12 months) is subject to the federal income tax. Thus, the investor in the 50% tax bracket pays Uncle Sam 50¢ of every dollar in interest and dividends but only 20¢ of every dollar of long-term capital gains. In the 40% tax bracket, the investor keeps 60¢ of

$10,000 CAPITAL GAIN:
SHORT-TERM vs. LONG-TERM

REGULAR TAX RATE	SHORT-TERM Left After Tax	LONG-TERM Tax Rate	LONG-TERM Left After Tax	ADDED INCOME
28%	$7,200	11.2%	$8,880	$1,680
33	6,700	13.2	8.680	1,980
42	5,800	16.8	8,320	2,520
45	5,500	18.0	8,200	2,700
50	5,000	20.0	8,000	3,000

each income dollar and 84¢ of his capital-gains dollar.

The higher your total income, the greater the benefit of investments in common stocks.

Those tax advantages may not always be as real as they first appear. Lower-and middle-income investors (who pay taxes at a modest rate) may find that the higher net returns of capital gains, when compared to those of straight income, do not justify the risks.

It is always important to project capital gains on an annual basis. If you pay federal income taxes at a rate of 38% or less, 10% annual appreciation (not certain) may not be as rewarding as a sure 8% in dividends or interest. In a higher tax bracket (federal and state/local), however, there will be a significant difference.

Monthly Income from Dividends

Investors who rely on dividend income should select stocks according to their dividend payment dates, usually quarterly as reported in Standard & Poor's Stock Guide. Most payments are made about the middle of the month so retirees count on them to pick up the slack when Social Security has been expended. Ask your broker to help you set up a schedule like this:

January–April–July–October: Manufacturers Hanover
February–May–August–November: Rochester Telephone
March–June–September–December: Exxon Corp.

Or buy shares in a mutual fund and arrange for monthly checks. In some months, this may require the sale of some shares, but a well-managed fund should be able to increase the net asset value of shares so that your principal remains about the same. And once you've passed age 70, do not be afraid to invade capital (as you must do with pension plan payouts anyway). With a 15% annual rate of withdrawal, savings yielding 10% will last for 11 years.

And you can get monthly checks from Winn-Dixie, the profitable supermarket chain that has doubled its payout about every six years.

Calculating Rates of Return

To reach your target goals, you should monitor your rate of return on each investment hopefully a profit, but, occasionally, a loss. To make this calculation, divide the total end value by the starting value, subtract 1 and multiply by 100:

R = Rate of return
EV = Value at end of period
BV = Value at beginning of period

$$R = \frac{EV}{BV} - 1 \times 100$$

In early January, Sol Smith buys 100 shares of OPH stock at a cost of $3,315 (price plus commissions and fees). During the year, OPH pays dividends of $3 per share. In December, the stock is at 45. For that year, the rate of return is 44%.

$$R = \frac{4500 + 300}{3315} = \frac{4800}{3315} = 1.44 - 1 \times 100 = 44\%$$

If Sol had held the stock for two years and the dividends rose in the second year to $3.50 per share, but the stock price stayed at 45, the rate of return would be 32%.

$$\frac{4500 + 300 + 350}{3315} = 1.64 - 1 \times 100 = 64\%$$

But since this was over two years, the annual rate would be half that 64%, or 32%.

To make similar calculations with a time-weighted rate of return (where the rates of return vary and there are additional investments over a period of time), use the same general formula but calculate each time frame separately.

Sam Smith starts the year with a portfolio worth $10,000. He reinvests all income. At the end of March, it's worth $10,900; on June 30, it's up a bit to $11,100. On July 1, Sam adds $1,000. At the end of the third quarter, the value is $13,500 and, at year-end, savings total $15,000. Here's how he determined the rate of return:

March 30: $\frac{\$10,900}{10,000} = 1.09$ or 9%

June 30: $\frac{11,100}{10,900} = 1.01$ or 1%

September 30: $\frac{13,500}{12,100} = 1.12$ or 12%

December 31: $\frac{15,000}{13,500} = 1.11$ or 11%

Now use the quarterly figures according to the formula:

$$1.09 \times 1.01 \times 1.12 \times 1.11 = 1.37 - 1 = 37\%$$

Thus, 37% is the time-weighted rate of return but the average rate of return is much lower.

Stock Rights

One of the most rewarding ways to acquire more shares of common stock is through rights. These are a special form of option that permits current shareholders to buy corporate securities, usually common stock, ahead of the public and at a more favorable price, typically at a discount of 5% to 10% with no transaction fee.

Rights are issued by corporations seeking additional equity capital, especially utilities anxious to issue more common shares to balance their heavy debt obligations. Their discount reflects the fact that the new shares will dilute the value of the outstanding stock (total assets and earnings of the company are now divided among a larger number of shares). There are no commissions and if the shareholder does not want to exercise any or all of his rights, he can sell them in the open market.

To the issuing corporation, rights:
• *Lower costs of raising capital.* Existing stockholders are already favorably disposed toward the company so are likely to be anxious to subscribe, especially if they feel that the added capital will create greater profits.
• *Build shareholder good will* as the result of being able to acquire new stock at discount prices.
• *Broaden stock ownership at small cost.* With more shares, there are likely to be more shareholders. And because some people will not exercise their rights, from lack

CALCULATING GROWTH RATES

ANNUAL RATE OF EARNINGS INCREASE PER SHARE	JUSTIFIED P/E RATIOS			
	5 YEARS	7 YEARS	10 YEARS	15 YEARS
2%	15	15	13	12
4	17	17	16	16
5	18	18	18	18
6	19	19	20	21
8	21	22	24	28
10	23	25	28	35
12	25	28	33	48

Note that there should be only a small premium when a low growth rate remains static over the years. A 5% annual gain in EPS justifies the same P/E no matter how many years it has been attained. But when a company can maintain a high rate of earnings growth, 10% or more, the value of the stock is enhanced substantially.

SOURCE: Graham and Dodd, SECURITY ANALYSIS

ible securities, your equity is being constantly diminished. *True corporate growth must pay off to the stockholder on a per share basis.*

New SEC rules require that a corporation show per share earnings on both a regular and a fully converted basis (what the profits would be if all debentures or preferred stock were converted into common and all outstanding warrants or options were exercised).

With free-wheeling, leverage-minded outfits, dilution can be substantial and can reduce profits by 30% or more.

There's no harm in a small dilution, especially if there are prospects that the growth in earnings will continue. But beware of any company where there are heavy future obligations. It may take extraordinary growth to maintain the value of its stock.

2. Overdiscounted price. In bull markets, a few stocks sell at high multiples of over 30 times earnings. This is a steep price to pay. Such optimistic evaluations are rare today but will come again as they always have. This is the time to be cautious and take your profits. When any stock sells at a P/E that is double that of the overall market, be cautious. When the multiple triples the average, sell unless it's a roaring up-market. Huge price rises are almost always followed by equally huge declines.

From 1975 to 1978, stock of Dataproducts Corporation was a real winner: soaring from an adjusted price of about 1 to 12. Then, it fell almost straight down to 5½, bounced back to 22 in 1981, plummeted again, this time to 8 and, in 1982, started a steady climb to 25. Maybe DPC was overdiscounted half of the time but in other periods, it was overpriced. The only ones who made money were speculators who bought low, sold short at highs, covered at lows, etc. . . . that's a tough role for amateurs!

Advice from the Old Master

Benjamin Graham, in his book, *Security Analysis,* looks for bargains in stocks, which he defines as the time when they trade at:

• a multiple of no more than twice that of the prevailing interest rate: i.e., a P/E ratio of 16 vs. an interest rate of 8%.

• a discount of 20% or more from book value.

Example: In 1974, Dana Corporation stock was at an adjusted price of 8. This was a multiple of about four times earnings. The interest rate was 7¼%, and the book value was $12.34 per share.

Dr. Graham's formula worked. By early 1976, DCN stock was split 2 for 1 and could (and should) have been sold at over 30: a 364% gain.

Another opportunity came in early 1980 when Dana, with a book value of $27.37 per share, was trading around 18. With interest rates at record highs, Dr. Graham's criteria were no longer applicable. Still, by other standards the stock was a bargain, and soon it was up to 34 before easing down to 25 with the dismal automotive market.

If you think that because such calculations are simple they are not effective, hear this comment from Dr. Graham: "In 44 years of Wall Street experience, I have never seen dependable calculations made about common stock values or related investment policies that went beyond simple arithmetic or the most elementary algebra. *With complex calculations, you could take it that the operator was trying to substitute theory for experience and give to speculation the deceptive guise of investment."*

Relating Current Prices to Future Profits

In making projections of future prices of stocks, the most important bases are anticipated corporate earnings but most analysts also check past performance and mix in hope. To a degree, most professionals develop formulas which, they have found, are more or less reliable.

The most conservative approach is to project profits for the next three to five years. With this type of measurement, stocks of fast-growing, profitable companies that are selling at very high multiples of current earnings often appear to be more reasonably valued. But this approach is too often based on hopes rather than facts. Only rarely will a company that has grown at 25% a year maintain that pace for the the next five years.

But without some element of "reasonableness," there will not be a plausible explanation of why you should buy . . . and provide the broker with commissions.

WHAT ARE EARNINGS WORTH?

Annual Growth Rate	What $1.00 Earnings Will Become in 3 Years At Given Growth Rate	The P/E Ratio You Can Pay Today to Make 10% Annual Capital Gain & Expect P/E Ratio in 3 Years To Be	
		15X	30X
4%	$1.12	12.6	25.3
5	1.16	13.1	26.2
6	1.19	13.4	26.8
7	1.23	13.9	27.7
8	1.26	14.2	28.4
9	1.30	14.7	29.3
10	1.33	15.0	30.0
12	1.40	15.8	31.6
15	1.52	17.1	34.3
20	1.73	19.5	39.0
25	1.95	22.0	44.0

SOURCE: SHAKING THE MONEY TREE

QUALITY STOCKS LISTED ON THE NEW YORK STOCK EXCHANGE

APPAREL
Blue Bell, Inc.
INTERCO, Inc.
U.S. Shoe
V. F. Corp.

BEVERAGES
Coca-Cola Co.

CHEMICALS
American Cyanamid
Bandag, Inc.
Big Three Industries
Carlisle Corp.
Clorox Company
Colgate-Palmolive
Dexter Corp.
Ethyl Corp.
International Flavors
Loctite Corp.
Lubrizol Corp.
NCH Corp.
Nalco Chemical
Procter & Gamble
Rubbermaid, Inc.
Stauffer Chemical
Witco Chemical

CONSTRUCTION
CBI Industries
Masco Corp.
Pacific Lumber
Stone & Webster
Vulcan Materials

DIVERSIFIED
American Standard
Ametek, Inc.
Cabot Corp.
Emhart Corp.
FMC Corp.
MMM
Morton-Thiokol
National Service Industries
PepsiCo, Inc.
Rockwell International
Scott & Fetzer
TRW, Inc.
United Technologies

**.GS, COSMETICS &
. TH CARE**
Abbott ..   tories
American F.   ducts
American Hosp..
Avon Products
Bard (C.R.)
Baxter Travenol
Becton Dickinson
Bristol-Myers
Chesebrough-Pond's
Johnson & Johnson
Lilly (Eli)
Mary Kay Cosmetics
Medtronic, Inc.
Merck & Co.
Pfizer, Inc.
Revlon, Inc.
Richardson-Vicks
Rorer Group
Schering-Plough
Smithkline Beckman
Squibb Corp.
Sterling Drug
Upjohn Co.

ELECTRICAL
Emerson Electric

General Electric
Maytag Co.
Square D Co.
Thomas & Betts

ELECTRONICS
AMP, Inc.
Avnet, Inc.
Burndy Corp.
Computervision
Digital Equipment Co.
E. G. & G., Inc.
Foxboro Co.
General Instrument
General Signal
Harris Corp.
Hewlett Packard
IBM
Kollmorgen Corp.
Loral Corp.
M/A-Com, Inc.
Motorola, Inc.
Perkin-Elmer
Plantronics, Inc.
Raytheon Co.
Tektronix
Texas Instruments
Tracor, Inc.
Unitrode Corp.

FINANCIAL
Bank of New York
First City Texas
Interfirst Corp.
Manufacturers Hanover
Mercantile Texas
Morgan (J.P.)
NBD Bancorp
Northwestern Bancorp
Republic/Texas
Texas Commerce

FOODS
Archer-Daniels-Midland
Beatrice Foods
Borden, Inc.
CPC International
Campbell Soup
Campbell Taggart
Carnation Corp.
Consolidated Foods
Dart & Kraft
General Foods
General Mills
Gerber Products
Heinz (H.J.)
   .ey Foods
.   .
Nabisc.
Quaker Oa..
Ralston Purina

MACHINERY & EQUIPM.
Barry Wright
Briggs & Stratton
Colt Industries
Combustion Engineering
Cooper Industries
Daniel Industries
Diebold, Inc.
Dover Co.
Dresser Industries
Ex-Cell-O Corp.
Foster-Wheeler
Joy Manufacturing
Parker-Hannifin
Pitney Bowes

Snap-On Tools
Sundstrand Corp.
Xerox Corp.

METAL PRODUCERS
Brush-Wellman
Carpenter Technology
Nucor Corp.

**METAL PRODUCTS
MANUFACTURERS**
Crown Cork
Engelhard Corp.
Harsco Corp.
Hoover-Universal
Illinois Tool
Kennametal, Inc.
Keystone International
Stanley Works

**OIL, GAS, COAL &
RELATED SERVICES**
Atlantic Richfield
Baker International
Belco Petroleum
Exxon Corp.
Halliburton Corp.
Helmerich Payne
Hughes Tool Co.
Kerr-McGee
Louisiana Land
Mobil Corp.
Petrolane, Inc.
Phillips Petroleum
Schlumberger, Ltd.
Smith International
Standard Oil (Calif.)
Standard Oil (Ind.)
Union Oil, Calif.
Union Pacific Corp.

PAPER
Dennison Manufacturing
Fort Howard Paper
Great Northern-Nekoosa
Kimberly-Clark
Union Camp

PRINTING & PUBLISHING
De Luxe Check Printing
Donnelley (R.R.) & Sons
Dow Jones
Dun & Bradstreet
Gannett Company
Harland (John)
Knight-Ridder
McGraw-Hill
SFN Companies
Time, Inc.

RECREATION
American Broadcasting
Capital Cities
CBS, Inc.
Church Fried Chicken
Disney Productions
Eastman Kodak
MCA, Inc.
Milton Bradley
Warner Communications

RETAILERS
Dayton Hudson
Eckerd (Jack)
Edison Brothers
Federated Dept. Stores
K-Mart Corp.

Long's Drug Stores
Lowe's Companies
Lucky Stores
Macy (R.H.)
Melville Corp.
Mercantile Stores
Revco (D.S.)
Rite Aid Corp.
Standard Brands Paints
Tandy Corp.
Walgreen Co.
Winn-Dixie Stores

TEXTILES
Cone Mills

TOBACCO
American Brands
Reynolds (R.J.) Industries
U.S. Tobacco
Universal Leaf Tobacco

TRANSPORTATION
Consolidated Freight
Overnite Transportation
Transway International

UTILITIES
A. T. & T.
Arkla, Inc.
Centel Corp.
Central & Southwest
Columbia Gas
ENSERCH Corp.
Equitable Gas
Florida Power & Light
Florida Progress
Houston Industries
Houston Natural Gas
Internorth, Inc.
Midcon Corp.
NICOR, Inc.
ONEOK, Inc.
Panhandle Eastern Pipeline
Peoples Energy
Pioneer Corp.
Public Service Indiana
Rochester Telephone
Sonat, Inc.
Southern Union
Southwest Public Service
TECO Energy
Texas Eastern Corp.
Texas Gas Transmission
Texas Oil & Gas
Texas Utilities
Tucson Electric
United Telecommunications

MISCELLANEOUS
Alco Standard
Automatic Data
Bausch & Lomb
Flightsafety Inter.
Genuine Parts
Grainger (W.W.)
Hilton Hotels
Jostens, Inc.
Lenox, Inc.
Malone & Hyde
National Medical Care
Norton Co.
Philbro-Salomon
Rollins, Inc.
Super Valu Stores
Waste Management

Theoretically, the formulation of a future earnings figure is the exact number of years of estimated earnings included in the current price of the stock: "the payout time."

The standard price/earnings ratio represents the number of years of current profits in the prices of the stock. That is, if a stock sells at 20 times its last 12 months' earnings, it will take 20 years for these same earnings to add up to the price you now have to pay for the stock. The hope is that growth will reduce that time span. The lower this future P/E multiple, the shorter the payout period, and, other factors being equal, the better the value of the stock.

One way to make projections is to assure that earnings will continue to grow at pretty much the same rate as during the past decade. This may often be true of a few large, established corporations with long histories of steady growth, but it is a rash assumption for most smaller companies. The bigger you get, the tougher it is to maintain the same rate of growth. It is a lot easier to add 10% annually to $1 million in profits than to add $10 million to $100 million in earnings!

A reasonable frame of projection reference is five years. Many firms now prepare five-year advance budgets, and with a true growth company, this is a period long enough to balance out temporary dips and yet short enough to be reasonably accurate. If you read of such a long-range forecast in an annual report, clip the notes for your research file.

This Growth Stock Price Evaluator can be used for both projections. It is most useful when studying fast-growing companies with above-average growth rates and cash flow.

Example: The stock of a small high-technology corporation is selling at 30 times net current, per share profits. That sets a time span of 30 years. You estimate that, over the next five years, earnings will grow at an average annual compound rate of 20%. The table shows that, if this projection is correct, the stock will be selling at 12.1 times its anticipated five-years-hence profits.

This evaluation technique can be reversed. Today, the stock is selling at a multiple of 30 but you are not so sure about its future profits. From experience, you are willing to pay no more than 12 times future five-year earnings for any growth stock. Checking the table, you find that the average annual growth rate must be 20% compounded annually to meet your investment standards. This stock just meets your criteria.

The Growth Stock Price Evaluator does *not* show the *future* price-to-earnings multiple or cash flow. They might be lower than, the same as, or greater than they are today.

There is a built-in offset: when the earnings (or cash flow) growth of a company is uninterrupted, the price of its stock tends to rise faster than earnings. This is almost always the case when the stock's P/E ratio is still below the stratosphere. *Wall Street LOVES consistency and continuity.*

The greatest risk in buying and holding growth stocks lies in overestimating their probable future rate of growth in earnings. Too many investors project recent earnings growth automatically. That's OK if you have access to complete data and can make frequent revisions, but when such forecasts go awry, the price of such glamour issues can collapse. That's why it can be so costly to hold an overpriced equity.

ALWAYS be conservative in projecting future earnings and cash-flow growth rates. A sustained annual growth rate of 10% is good; 15% is excellent; only a handful of unusual corporations can maintain a 20% growth rate for many years. American business is too competitive; expansion into new products and new markets is too expensive; and unforeseen events are too frequent to permit even the best new companies to maintain supergrowth rates—30% or more—for longer than two or three years. In successful investing, be realistic. It is just as important NOT to lost money as to make profits!

A GROWTH STOCK PRICE EVALUATOR

HOW TO WEIGH PRICES OF GROWTH STOCKS IN TERMS OF THEIR FUTURE GAINS IN EARNINGS OR CASH FLOW

IF— a stock now sells at this many times its current earnings or cash flow:	—AND you believe its average annual growth in earnings or cash flow per share (compounded) will be:						
	10%	15%	20%	25%	30%	40%	50%
	THEN—here is how many times its projected earnings or cash flow per share five years hence the stock is currently selling at:						
12	7.5	6.0	4.8	3.9	3.2	2.2	1.6
14	8.7	7.0	5.6	4.6	3.8	2.6	1.8
16	9.9	8.0	6.5	5.2	4.3	3.0	2.1
18	11.2	9.0	7.3	5.9	4.9	3.3	2.4
20	12.4	10.0	8.1	6.6	5.4	3.7	2.6
22	13.7	10.9	8.9	7.2	5.9	4.1	2.9
24	14.9	11.9	9.7	7.9	6.5	4.5	3.2
26	16.1	12.9	10.5	8.5	7.0	4.8	3.4
28	17.4	13.9	11.3	9.2	7.5	5.2	3.7
30	18.6	14.9	12.1	9.8	8.1	5.6	3.9
32	19.9	15.9	12.9	10.5	8.6	5.9	4.2
34	21.1	16.9	13.7	11.1	9.2	6.3	4.5
36	22.4	17.9	14.5	11.8	9.7	6.7	4.7
38	23.6	18.9	15.3	12.5	10.2	7.1	5.0
40	24.8	19.9	16.1	13.1	10.8	7.4	5.3
42	26.1	20.9	16.9	13.8	11.3	7.8	5.5
44	27.3	21.9	17.7	14.4	11.9	8.2	5.8
46	28.6	22.9	18.5	15.1	12.4	8.6	6.1
48	29.8	23.9	19.4	15.7	12.9	8.9	6.3
50	31.1	24.9	20.2	16.4	13.5	9.3	6.6

How to Determine a Prudent P/E Ratio

Usually, analysts justify their recommendations by adjusting the multiple of the price of the stock by estimated rate of future growth or by cash flow per share rather than by reported earnings. In both cases, these are attempts to justify a predetermined decision to buy. These projections appear plausible especially when accompanied by tables and charts and computer printouts. But, in most cases, they are useful only as background and not for making decisions on the proper level to buy or, later, to sell. These calculations depend a good deal on market conditions and your own style but here's one approach for those "super-growth" stocks that will be suggested by your friends or broker.

Example: According to your "financial adviser," the stock of a "future" company now selling at 40 times its recent earnings will be trading at "only 16 times its projected earnings five years hence IF the company's average earnings growth is 20% a year." (See Evaluator Table.)

If you are speculating with this type of "hot" stock, you should compare it with other "opportunities" and, on

QUALITY STOCKS WITH BRIGHT PROSPECTS:
1983-88 AVERAGE COMPOUND RATE OF RETURN

COMPANY	GROWTH Dividends	GROWTH Earnings	DIVIDENDS REINVESTED	CHANGE P/E	TOTAL RETURN	RECENT PRICE	TARGET RANGE 1988
CHEMICALS							
Big Three	+12.0%	+17.7%	+2.7%	+ 6.74%	+27.1%	21	79- 55
DRUGS							
SmithKline Beckman	+16.6	+20.5	+3.1	+ 6.2	+29.8	71	277-185
FINANCIAL							
First Banc Texas	+12.2	+16.9	+5.4	+10.5	+32.8	23	93- 55
Interfirst Corp.	+10.2	+10.7	+5.9	+14.0	+30.6	21	77- 53
Texas Commerce	+17.5	+14.0	+3.8	+ 9.6	+27.4	38	129- 87
FOOD							
Kellogg	+11.8	+10.5	+6.1	+ 5.4	+22.0	27	67- 49
Nabisco Brands	+10.7	+ 9.5	+6.3	+ 7.7	+23.5	37	90- 70
MACHINERY/EQUIPMENT							
Cooper Industries	+ 9.6	+21.2	+3.8	+ 3.5	+28.5	32	113- 67
Daniel Industries	+17.6	+17.3	+1.7	+12.4	+31.4	10	50- 30
Xerox Corp.	+ 9.0	+19.3	+5.4	− 1.7	+23.0	45	111- 71
OIL/GAS							
Atlantic Richfield	+12.6	+15.4	+5.2	+ 6.4	+27.0	45	144- 92
Baker International	+10.0	+15.0	+4.0	+17.3	+36.3	19	100- 58
Helmerich & Payne	+10.5	+17.3	+1.6	+11.8	+30.7	20	88- 50
Schlumberger, Ltd.	+20.4	+20.3	+2.2	+11.3	+33.8	45	225-135
RECREATION							
Church's Fr. Chicken	+14.7	+21.5	+2.0	− 1.2	+22.3	28	83- 54
UTILITIES							
Enserch Corp.	+ 9.2	+14.8	+7.4	+ 6.3	+28.5	20	64- 40
Houston Nat. Gas	+13.4	+17.4	+4.3	+10.4	+32.1	37	159- 95
Pioneer Corp.	+18.4	+23.5	+4.9	+ 6.4	+34.8	23	95- 37
Sonat, Inc.	+14.8	+13.0	+5.4	+12.5	+30.0	38	101- 65

SOURCE: Wright Investors' Service

some basis, decide how reasonable this projection really is.

A handy formula is **PRU PER = G R Q M T.**

PRU = Prudent.

PER = P/E Ratio.

G = Growth. This is the company's projected growth in earnings per share over the next five years. The basic compound interest formula is $(1+G)^5$ where G is the projected growth rate, as shown in the Growth Stock Price Evaluator and Prudent P/E Multiples Table. This omits dividend yields because they are usually small in relation to the potential capital appreciation.

R = Reliability & Risk. Not all projected growth rates are equally reliable or probable. A lower projected growth rate is likely to be more reliable than a very high projected one (30% to 50% a year).

Logically, you can assign a higher reliability rating to a noncyclical company (utility, food processor, retailer) than to a corporation in a cyclical industry (steel, machinery, tools).

Another factor is the assumed length of the projected growth period. If you can realistically anticipate that the company will continue its rate of growth for the next 10 years, a 10% rate for its stock is more reliable than a 15% rate for a company whose growth visibility is only three to five years.

If you are uncertain about the corporation's consistency, you should consider the greater risk.

Q = Quality. As you know, this is the single most important *investment* consideration.

M = Multiple of price to earnings. This is a comparative measurement. The first step is to determine the P/E for an average-quality nongrowth stock. This is done by relating the current yield on guaranteed, fixed-income investments (savings accounts, corporate bonds) to the P/E multiple that will produce the same yield on the nongrowth stock.

$$PE + \frac{D}{IR}$$

PE = Price/Earnings ratio

D = Dividend as percentage payout of earnings

IR = Interest Rate

Thus, a stock yielding 8% on a 70% payout of profits must, over a five-year period, be bought and sold at 7 times earnings to break even on capital and to make as much income as could be obtained, over the same period, via the ownership of a fixed-income investment continually yielding 10%:

$$PE = \frac{7}{10} = 7$$

Note: This is NOT a valid comparison in terms of investment alone. Since the nongrowth stock carries a certain amount of risk in comparison to the certainty of a bond or money market fund, the stock should sell at a lower multiple, probably 5 to 6 times earnings.

PRUDENT PRICE-EARNINGS MULTIPLES FOR GROWTH STOCKS

If you project earnings per share (after taxes) to grow in next 5 years at average compounded annual rate of:	With these quality ratings*				
	B	B+	A−	A	A+
	these are approximate prudent multiples which represent the MAXIMUM current price to pay:				
5%	12.0	12.9	13.7	15.0	16.7
6%	12.5	13.4	14.3	15.8	17.4
7%	13.0	14.0	14.9	16.5	18.2
8%	13.6	14.5	15.6	17.1	18.9
9%	14.1	15.1	16.2	17.8	19.7
10%	14.6	15.7	16.8	18.5	20.4
15%	17.4	18.7	20.1	22.0	24.5
20%	20.2	21.8	23.4	25.7	28.6
25%	23.0	24.7	26.6	29.3	32.7
30%	25.2	27.3	29.4	32.5	36.2
35%	28.5	31.0	33.5	37.1	41.5
40%	31.9	34.8	37.7	41.7	46.7

*S&P designations. If not rated, use B; if new, untested firm, use a conservative rating based on comparison with similar companies, preferably in the same industry.

Checkpoints for Bargains

Norman Weinger of Oppenheimer & Co., ever on the lookout for bargains, developed special checkpoints for undervalued situations. His criteria:
- Current yield 33.3% above S&P 400 yield of 4.2%
- Current P/E is 33.3% below S&P 400 P/E ratio of 13.1
- Current price to book value is 33.3% below S&P 400's of 139%

He uses these as a starting point for discovering companies that have the potential for better-than-average upswings. His full list contained 82 stocks but the quality of some of these left something to be desired. Still, the concept has merit if you are willing to do your homework.

QUALITY STOCKS AT DEEP DISCOUNTS

COMPANY	Stock Price	Book Value	Yield	Price/ Earnings	Return on Equity
Bank of New York	54 1/4	69.19	6.27%	5.25	14.94%
1st City Bank Texas	20 1/2	25.86	6.34	5.26	15.08
Joy Manufacturing	23	26.68	6.09	6.93	12.44
Manuf. Hanover	43 1/4	59.34	7.05	5.51	13.18
Mobil Corp.	28 7/8	35.96	6.93	8.72	9.20
NBD Bancorp	35 1/4	61.93	5.90	5.56	16.16
Phillips Petroleum	34 3/8	37.70	6.40	8.13	11.22

SOURCE: Oppenheimer & Co., May 1983

Most Profitable Companies

In making their investments, conservatives should start with a quality list such as that of Wright Investors' Service. But always check recent reports and make certain that the corporation still ranks high.

The "best" corporations stay on the Approved Lists but to give you an idea of how quickly changes occur: just 10 years ago, the Automotive List included Champion Spark Plug, Clark Equipment, Dana Corp., Ford Motor, General Motors, Monroe Auto Equipment and Purolator and among the chemical stalwarts were DuPont, Firestone and Goodyear!

An aggressive investor might check statistical data in financial publications and start his search from a Corporate Scoreboard of the most profitable companies of the previous year. Note how many of these winners are also shown on the Wright Approved List. QUALITY COUNTS AND PAYS OFF!

COMPANIES WITH HIGH PROJECTED TOTAL RETURNS SOON

COMPANY	TOTAL RETURNS BY 1986	CURRENT PRICE	TARGET PRICE
CBI Industries	+28.3%	34	58
Central & Southwest	+25.5	18	27
Combustion Engineering	+25.1	34	55
CPC International	+24.8	38	55
Dresser Industries	+36.6	19	35
Foster Wheeler	+25.8	14	23
General Signal	+26.1	41	70
Houston Industries	+24.7	22	34
Hughes Tool	+31.3	19	33
Joy Manufacturing	+26.3	25	39
Lubrizol	+27.9	21	32
Midcon Corp.	+34.0	23	44
ONEOK, Inc.	+34.6	24	45
Panhandle Eastern	+34.8	27	48
Public Service - Indiana	+30.1	26	47
Republicbank Corp.	+29.9	33	58
Revlon, Inc.	+24.1	33	51
Richardson-Vicks	+25.0	27	40
Rollins, Inc.	+27.0	14	22
Rowan Cos.	+31.8	11	20
Smith International	+34.2	24	40
Southern Union	+38.1	18	34
Square D Co.	+23.9	35	51
Texas Eastern	+33.0	54	92
Texas Gas Corp.	+31.3	30	47

SOURCE: Wright Investors' Service

CORPORATE SCOREBOARD: MOST PROFITABLE COMPANIES: 1982

INDUSTRY/COMPANY	Return on Equity	Change from 1982
AEROSPACE		
Lockheed	58.1%	34
Grumman	27.5	22
Composite	12.9	−16
AIRLINES		
Southwest Airlines	14.7	0
PSA	9.1	−32
Composite	−8.9	NM
APPLIANCES		
Maytag	18.8	−1
Whirlpool	15.6	1
Composite	7.9	−23
AUTOMOTIVE		
Standard Products	14.1	19
Sealed Power	11.9	7
Composite	−4.0	NM
BANKS/HOLDING COMPANIES		
Allied Bancshares	23.5	26
Interfirst	20.0	15
Composite	12.7	3
BEVERAGES		
General Cinema	28.4	9
Heileman (G.) Brewing	24.8	13
Composite	17.2	8
BUILDING MATERIALS		
Valspar	17.0	5
Masco	16.9	4
Composite	2.8	−55
CHEMICALS		
Betz Laboratories	21.4	6
Petrolite	20.6	6
Composite	8.3	−32
CONGLOMERATES		
Northwest Industries	24.3	−27
Fuqua Industries	22.7	NM
Composite	10.8	−29
CONTAINERS		
Dorsey	17.1	−7
Ball	15.2	18
Composite	7.7	−33
DRUGS		
American Home Products	31.5	13
SmithKline Beckman	25.8	12
Composite	19.2	17
ELECTRIC/ELECTRONICS		
TIE/Communications	28.0	42
Tandy	26.1	23
Composite	15.1	5
FOOD PROCESSING		
Montfort/Colorado	33.3	87
Kellogg	26.2	11
Swift Independent	26.1	NA
Composite	13.5	−3
FOOD & LODGING		
McDonald's	20.5	14
Church's Fried Chicken	19.5	−7
Composite	15.5	2

NM = Not Meaningful

SOURCE: Business Week

INDUSTRY/COMPANY	Return on Equity	Change from 1982
GENERAL MACHINERY		
Pall	23.5	0
Bairnco	18.6	38
Composite	3.8	−72
INSTRUMENTS		
Pope, Evans & Robbins	25.6	53
Simmonds Precision	19.4	17
Composite	10.3	−14
LEISURE TIME		
Coleco Industries	58.3	482
Mattel	25.3	NM
Composite	14.1	2
METALS & MINING		
Engelhard	16.2	−9
Brush Wellman	13.7	−3
Composite	−5.8	NM
MISCELLANEOUS MANUFACTURING		
Williams Electronics	40.5	−24
Todd Shipyards	26.4	12
AFG Industries	24.4	19
Composite	10.2	−30
NATURAL RESOURCES		
Tosco	37.0	436
Standard Oil (Ohio)	27.2	−3
Texas Oil & Gas	26.5	27
Composite	13.1	−23
NONBANK FINANCIAL		
Nutri/System	46.9	76
Paine Webber	35.3	345
Composite	12.3	−3
OFFICE EQUIPMENT/COMPUTERS		
Safeguard Business	29.6	5
Telex	24.6	81
Apple Computer	24.6	56
Composite	15.9	8
OIL SERVICE/SUPPLY		
SEDCO	64.0	70
Schlumberger	26.9	6
Ocean Drilling	26.3	10
Composite	18.0	−16
PAPER/FOREST PRODUCTS		
James River	16.5	29
Kimberly-Clark	14.0	−4
Composite	3.9	−60
PERSONAL CARE		
Mary Kay Cosmetics	40.9	46
Chemed	34.5	−33
Composite	16.7	0
PUBLISHING/RADIO/TV		
Metromedia	108.9	127
Commerce Clearing House	41.5	10
Composite	16.6	7
RAILROADS		
Kansas City Southern	13.4	−14
Norfolk Southern	11.9	−18
Composite	8.7	−23

INDUSTRY/COMPANY	Return on Equity	Change from 1982
REAL ESTATE/HOUSING		
Pulte Home	26.9	144
Southmark	11.5	15
Composite	6.3	−3
RETAILING/FOOD		
Giant Food	24.1	145
American Stores	22.8	63
Composite	12.9	−2
RETAILING/NON-FOOD		
Limited Stores	25.5	42
Wal-Mart Stores	23.6	46
Composite	10.4	−6
SAVINGS & LOAN		
Financial Federation	0.5	NM
Great Western	−11.5	NM
Composite	−14.2	NM
SERVICE INDUSTRIES		
Stone & Webster	26.4	38
DeLuxe Check	26.3	21
Humana	25.0	30
Composite	13.0	−1
SPECIAL MACHINERY		
Dover	20.7	− 7
Joy Mfg.	11.7	−35
Composite	0	−98
STEEL		
Nucor	9.9	−36
Nortek	9.4	−34
Composite	−19.0	NM
TEXTILES/APPAREL		
VF	31.8	76
Farah Mfg.	23.3	67
Composite	9.2	−14
TIRE/RUBBER		
Bandag	22.5	1
Cooper Tire	20.3	10
Composite	5.3	−43
TOBACCO		
U.S. Tobacco	26.6	21
Philip Morris	22.0	19
Composite	20.2	12
TRUCKING		
Carolina Freight	17.7	20
Roadway Services	17.6	6
Composite	10.7	−27
UTILITIES		
MCI Communications	47.7	155
Entex	24.4	53
CELERON	20.3	−25
Composite	12.7	10

5

Value: The #2 Consideration in Profitable Investing

Value is the #2 factor in successful investing. It spotlights the range in which a stock should be bought or sold and, thus, provides a basis for investment profits. *The surest way to make money in the stock market is to buy Quality securities when they are undervalued and to sell them when they become fully priced.*

Value is relative. It can be measured by the ratio of the future price to the current price. That future price can be projected as the price at which a common stock can be expected to sell in relation to current and prospective earnings, dividends and corporate equity capital per common share: the company's ability to grow. Value indicates whether or not, and to what extent, a stock is likely to advance or decline from its present price.

Value is based on financial facts and relies heavily on the analyses of the corporation's past performance, present strength and future progress. When you select stocks on the basis of value (or undervaluation), you will almost always make money, usually quickly with speculative situations; often slowly with quality holdings.

Value is the approach used by fundamentalists. They prefer to pay one dollar for each two dollars of concrete assets and are seldom willing to "invest" 20 or 30 dollars for each dollar of prospective and possibly uncertain earnings some time in the future. These calculations should be based on the financial reports of the corporations whose shares you plan to acquire.

How to Analyze Financial Reports

Financial analysis is not easy for the uninitiated, but once you get the swing of things, you can pick the few quality stocks from the thousands of publicly owned securities, and if you are speculation-minded, you can find bargains with securities of mediocre or even poor corporations.

Basic figures and ratios show the company's current and prospective financial condition, past and prospective earning power and growth and, thus, investment desirability.

Publicly owned corporations issue their financial reports on an annual, semiannual or quarterly basis. Most of the important-to-the-investor information can be found in: *(a)* the balance sheet; *(b)* the profit and loss, or income, statement; *(c)* the change in financial position or the "flow of funds" data.

In each of these you can find or derive:
• The key quantities: net tangible assets, changes in working capital, sales costs, profits, taxes, dividends, etc.
• The significant rates and ratios: price/earnings multiples, profit rates, growth in net worth, earnings, dividends, etc.
• The relations between the criteria of one corporation with a standard: comparison of corporate performance with that of its industry, the stock market, the economy or some other broader base.

Here's how to find value (and other important information) for an industrial/service company. With variations, the same yardsticks can be applied to utilities, railroads, finance firms and insurance companies. The data and explanations are digested from *Understanding Financial Statements,* prepared by the New York Stock Exchange. Ask your broker to get you a copy for your review and files.

Balance Sheet Items

Here's an explanation of the items listed in the typical corporate balance sheet. The headings may vary according to the type of industry but the basic information will be similar . . . and just as important.

CURRENT ASSETS: items that can be converted into cash within one year. The total is $48.4 million this year, $4.2 million more than last year.

Cash: mostly bank deposits, including compensating balances held under terms of a loan—like keeping a savings account to get free checking.

Marketable securities: corporate and government securities that can be sold quickly. In the current year, these were eliminated.

Receivables: amounts due from customers for goods and services. This is a net amount after set-aside for items that may not be collected.

Inventories: cost of raw materials, work in process and finished goods. Statements and footnotes describe the basis, generally cost of current market price, whichever is lower. To handle the additional business, these were up over those of the previous year.

PROPERTY, PLANT & EQUIPMENT: the land, structures, machinery and equipment, tools, motor vehicles, etc. Except for land, these assets have a limited useful life and a deduction is taken from cost as depreciation. With a new plant, the total outlays were $11.6 million more with depreciation of $2.6 million.

OTHER ASSETS: Identifiable property is valued at cost. Intangibles such as patents, copyrights, franchises, trademarks or goodwill cannot be assessed accurately, so they are omitted form the computation of tangible net worth or book value.

If an increase in sales does not follow an increased investment, management may have misjudged the ability to produce and/or sell more goods or the industry may have reached overcapacity. If a company's plant and equipment show little change for several years during a period of expanding business, the shareholder should be cautious about the company's progressiveness. In this example, both fixed and total assets grew steadily.

LIABILITIES & STOCKHOLDERS' EQUITY: divided into two classes: current or payable within a year and long-term debt or other obligations that come due after one year from the balance sheet date.

Accounts payable: money owed for raw materials, other supplies, and services.

BALANCE SHEET

"Your Company"

Millions ASSETS	Dec. 31 Current Year	Dec. 31 Prior Year
Current Assets		
Cash	$ 9.0	$ 6.2
Marketable securities	—	2.0
Accounts and notes receivable	12.4	11.4
Inventories	27.0	24.6
Total Current Assets	$ 48.4	$ 44.2
Property, Plant and Equipment		
Buildings, machinery and equipment, at cost.	104.3	92.7
Less accumulated Depreciation	27.6	25.0
	$ 76.7	$ 67.7
Land, at cost	.9	.7
Total Property, Plant and Equipment	$ 77.6	$ 68.4
Other Assets		
Receivables due after one year	4.7	3.9
Surrender value of insurance	.2	.2
Other	.6	.5
Total Other Assets	$ 5.5	$ 4.6
Total Assets	$131.5	$117.2
LIABILITIES & STOCKHOLDERS' EQUITY		
Current Liabilities		
Accounts payable	$ 6.1	$ 5.0
Accrued liabilities	3.6	3.3
Current maturity of long-term debt	1.0	.8
Federal income and other taxes	9.6	8.4
Dividends payable	1.3	1.1
Total Current Liabilities	$ 21.6	$ 18.6
Other Liabilities	3.6	2.5
Long-Term Debt		
5% Sinking-Fund Debentures, due July 31, 1987	26.0	20.0
Stockholders' Equity		
5% Cum. Preferred Stock ($100 par: authorized and outstanding-60,000)	6.0	6.0
Common Stock ($10 par: authorized-2,000,000; outstanding-1,830,000)	18.3	18.3
Additional Paid-In Capital	9.6	9.6
Retained Earnings	46.4	42.2
Total Stockholders' Equity	$ 80.3	$ 76.1
Total Liabilities, and Stockholders' Equity	$131.5	$117.2

Accrued liabilities: unpaid wages, salaries and commissions, interest, etc.

Current long-term debt: amount due in next year. Usually, this requires annual repayments over a period of years.

Income taxes: accrued federal, state and local taxes.

Dividends payable: preferred or common dividends (or both) declared but not yet paid. Once declared, dividends become a corporate obligation.

Total current liabilities: an increase of $3 million needed to finance expansion of business.

Long-term debt: what's due for payment in the future less the amount due in the next year. Although the total was reduced to $20 million, an additional $7 million of debentures were issued.

STOCKHOLDERS' EQUITY (or CAPITAL): all funds invested in the business by lenders and stockholders as well as reinvested earnings.

Preferred stock: holders are usually entitled to dividends before common stockholders and to priority in the event of dissolution or liquidation. Dividends are fixed. If cumulative, no dividends can be paid on common stock until the preferred dividends are up to date.

Earnings before income taxes: the operating profit minus interest charges. When companies have complicated reports, this can be a confusing area.

Provision for taxes on income: the allocation of money for Uncle Sam . . . a widely variable figure because of exemptions, special credits, etc. . . . from about 5% for some banks to 45% for industrial corporations.

Net income for the year: *the bottom line.* This was 4.2% better than the year before—about the same as recorded in the previous period. This was no record breaker and works out better on a per share basis: $5.24 vs. $5.03.

One year's change is interesting but the true test of management's ability comes over five to 10 years.

Use this figure to make other comparisons: against sales: 8.5% vs. 8.6% the year before and then, relate this to returns of other companies in the same industry. The average manufacturing corporation earns about 5 cents per dollar of sales but supermarkets are lucky to end up with 1¢ . . . against shareowners' equity: the Profit Rate (PR) explained in the chapter on Quality. Here, the PR was a modest 13%.

To find the earnings per share, divide the net income (less preferred dividend requirements) by the average number of shares outstanding during the year. This is the key figure for most analysts. It is also used to determine the Price/Earnings (P/E) ratio: divide the market price of the stock by the per share profits. If the stock was selling at 30, the P/E would be 10—slightly above the average of most publicly owned shares.

Retained earnings: the dollars reinvested for future growth . . . always an important indication of future prospects. If the company continues to boost this figure, its basic value will increase. At the same PR, earnings will increase and, eventually, the value of the common stock.

Common stock: shown on the books at "par value," an arbitrary amount, having no relation to the market value or to what would be received in liquidation.

Additional paid-in capital: the amount of money received from the sale of stock in excess of the par value.

Retained earnings: money reinvested in the business.

Total stockholders' equity: the sum of the common par value, additional paid-in capital and retained earnings less any premium attributable to the preferred stock: what the stockholders own. The increase of $4.1 million is a rise of about 5%—not bad but not as much as should be the mark of a true growth company.

Income and Earned Surplus

Here's where you find out how the corporation fared for the past year in comparison to the two previous annual reporting periods: how much money the company took in, how much was spent for expenses and taxes and the size of the resulting profits (if any) that were available for distribution to shareholders or for reinvestment in the business. They are the basis for comparison within this company and firms in the same or similar business.

SALES: how much business the company does in a year. With public utilities, insurance firms and service organizations, the term "revenues" is often used. In the last year, corporate sales were up $5.8 million, a gain of 5.3%, not quite as good as the 5.5% rise the year before. Net income per share (middle) was also just slightly better: $.4 million (to $9.9 from $9.5), +4.2%. Check these figures against those of the industry and major competitors. They may be better than they appear.

STATEMENT OF INCOME AND RETAINED EARNINGS

"Your Company"

Millions	Current Year	Previous Year	2 Years Ago
SALES	$115.8	$110.0	$104.5
Less:			
Costs and Expenses:			
Cost of goods sold	$ 76.4	$ 73.2	$ 70.2
Selling, general and administrative expenses	14.2	13.0	12.1
Depreciation	2.6	3.5	2.3
	$ 93.2	$ 89.7	$ 84.6
OPERATING PROFIT	$ 22.6	$ 20.3	$ 19.9
Interest Charges	1.3	1.0	1.3
Earnings before Income Taxes	$ 21.3	$ 19.3	$ 18.6
Provision for Taxes on Income	11.4	9.8	9.5
Net income (per common share for year: Current-$5.24; Last-$5.03; 2 Years Ago-$4.97)*	$ 9.9	$ 9.5	$ 9.1
Retained Earnings, Beginning of Year	42.2	37.6	33.1
	$ 52.1	$ 47.1	$ 42.2
Less Dividends Paid on:			
Preferred Stock ($5 per share)	(.3)	(.3)	—
Common Stock (per share: This Year-$3.00; Last Year-$2.50; 2 Years Ago-$2.50)	(5.4)	(4.6)	(4.6)
Retained Earnings, End of Year	$ 46.4	$ 42.2	37.6

*After preferred share dividend requirements

Cost of goods sold: the dollars spent to keep the business operating. The $3.2 million more was less than the $5.8 million increase in sales.

Selling, general and administrative expenses: the costs of getting products/services to customers and getting paid. These will vary with the kind of business: high for consumer goods manufacturers and distributors because of advertising; lower for companies selling primarily to industry or governments.

Depreciation: a bookkeeping item to provide for wear/tear/obsolesence of machinery and equipment, presumably to set aside reserves for replacement. The maximum calculations are set by tax laws. Typically, a straight-line method might charge the same amount each year for a specified number of years. Or, with accelerated methods, the deductions would be higher in the early years.

With companies in the natural resource business, the reduction in value is depletion, again calculated over a period of years.

By changing the type of depreciation, a company can increase or decrease earnings, so always be wary when this happens.

OPERATING PROFIT: the dollars generated from the company's usual operations without regard to income from other sources or financing. As a percentage of sales, it tells the profit margin: a rising 19.5% in the last year compared to 18.5% the year before.

Interest charges: the interest paid to bondholders. It is deductible before taxes. The available earnings should be many times the mandated interest charges: in this case, a welcome 17 times before provision for income taxes.

Changes in Financial Position

This presents a different view of the financing and investing activities and clarifies the disposition of the funds produced by operations. It includes both cash and other elements of working capital—the excess of current assets over current liabilities.

The balance sheet shows that the working capital has increased by $1.2 million (current assets of $48.4 million exceeded current liabilities of $21.6 million by $26.8 million at the end of the year vs. $25.6 million the year before).

Sales and net income were up; the contribution to working capital from operations decreased to $13.6 million vs. $15 million the year before. This was narrowed to $.4 million by the proceeds of the $7 million in long-term debt, $1 million more than the proceeds from the sale of preferred stock the year before.

The difference between the funds used last year and the year before was $1.1 million, reflecting a heavier investment in productive capacity against a larger repayment of long-term debt the year before.

With increased capacity, the company should be able to handle higher sales. The additional cash may be a good sign but when too much cash accumulates, it may indicate that management is not making the best use of its assets. Still, in financially tense times, cash is always welcome.

STATEMENT OF CHANGES IN FINANCIAL POSITION

"Your Company"

MILLIONS	Dec. 31 Current Year	Dec. 31 Last Year	Dec. 31 2 Years Ago
FUNDS PROVIDED			
Net Income	$ 9.9	$ 9.5	$ 9.1
Changes not requiring working capital:			
Depreciation	2.6	3.5	2.3
Increase in other liabilities	1.1	2.0	1.4
Funds provided by operations	$13.6	$15.0	$12.8
Proceeds from long-term debt	7.0	—	—
Proceeds from sale of 5% Cum. Preferred Stock	—	6.0	—
Total funds provided	$20.6	$21.0	$12.8
FUNDS USED			
Additions to fixed assets	$11.8	$ .5	$ 6.2
Dividends paid on preferred stock	.3	.3	
Dividends paid on common stock	5.4	4.6	4.6
Payments on long-term debt	1.0	15.0	—
Increase in non-current receivables	.8	.1	.3
Increase in other assets	.1	—	.2
Total funds used	$19.4	$20.5	$11.3
Increase in working capital	$ 1.2	$ .5	$ 1.5
CHANGES IN COMPONENTS OF WORKING CAPITAL			
Increase (decrease) in current assets:			
Cash	$ 2.8	$ 1.0	$ 1.1
Marketable securities	(2.0)	.5	.4
Accounts receivable	1.0	.5	.8
Inventories	2.4	1.0	1.3
Increase in current assets	$ 4.2	$ 3.0	$ 3.6
Increase in current liabilities:			
Accounts payable	$ 1.1	$ .9	$ .6
Accrued liabilities	.3	.5	.2
Current maturity of long-term debt	.2	.1	.5
Federal income and other taxes	1.2	1.0	.8
Dividends payable	.2	—	—
Increase in current liabilities	$ 3.0	$ 2.5	$ 2.1
Increase in working capital	$ 1.2	$ .5	$ 1.5

Seven Keys to Value

	Current Year	Prior Year
1. Operating profit margin	19.5%	18.5%
2. Current ratio	2.24	2.38
3. Liquidity ratio	41.7%	44.1%
4. Capitalization ratios:		
Long-term debt	24.4%	20.8%
Preferred stock	5.7	6.3
Common stock and surplus	69.9	72.9
5. Sales to fixed assets	1.1	1.2
6. Sales to inventories	4.3	4.5
7. Net income to net worth	12.3%	12.5%

1. Operating profit margin (PM). This is the ratio of profit (before interest and taxes) to sales. The operating profit ($22.6) divided by sales ($115.8) equals 19.5%. This compares with 18.5% for the previous year. (Some analysts prefer to compute this margin without including depreciation and depletion as part of the cost because these have nothing to do with the efficiency of the operation.)

When a company increases sales substantially, the PM should be widened because certain costs (rent, interest, real property taxes, etc.) are fixed and do not rise in proportion to volume.

2. Current ratio. This is the ratio of current assets to current liabilities: $48.4 divided by $21.6 equals $2.24. For most industrial corporations, this should be about two to one. It varies with the type of business. Utilities and retail stores, for example, have rapid cash inflows and high turnovers, so they can operate effectively with lower ratios.

In your analysis, check the past record and watch for any major shift in this ratio.

When the ratio is high (5:1), it may mean that a company is not making the best use of its liquid assets. It may have too much money invested in securities. They provide high yields for a while but they do not expand the business.

3. Liquidity ratio. This is the ratio of cash and its equivalent to total current liabilities ($9 divided by $21.6 equals 41.7%). It is important as a supplement to the current ratio because the immediate ability of a company to meet current obligations or pay larger dividends may be impaired despite a high current ratio. This 41.7% liquidity ratio (down from 44.1% the year before) probably indicates a period of expansion, rising prices, heavier capital expenditures and larger accounts payable. *If the decline persists, the company might have to raise additional capital.*

4. Capitalization ratios. These show the percentages of each type of investment as part of the total investment in the corporation. Though often used to describe only the outstanding securities, capitalization is the sum of the face value of bonds and other debts *plus* the par value of all preferred and common stock issues *plus* the balance sheet totals for capital surplus and retained earnings.

Bond, preferred-stock and common-stock ratios are useful indicators of the relative risk and leverage involved for the owners of the three types of securities. For most industrial corporations, the debt ratio should be no more than 66⅔% of equity or 40% of total capital.

In this instance, the long-term debt plus preferred stock is 43.1% of the equity represented by the common stock and surplus, and 30.1% of total capital.

Higher ratios are appropriate for utilities and transportation corporations

5. Sales to fixed assets. This ratio is computed by dividing the annual sales ($115.8) by the year-end value of plant, equipment and land before depreciation and amortization ($104.3 plus $.9 equals $105.2). The ratio is therefore 1.1 to 1. This is down from 1.2 to 1 the year before.

This ratio helps to show whether funds used to enlarge productive facilities are being wisely spent. A sizable expansion in facilities should lead to larger sales volume. If it does not, there's something wrong. In this case, there were delays in getting production on stream at the new plant.

6. Sales to inventories. This ratio is computed by dividing the annual sales by year-end inventories: $115.8 divided by $27 equals a 4.3:1 ratio. The year before, the ratio was 4.5 to 1.

This shows inventory turnover: the number of times the equivalent of the year-end inventory has been bought and sold during the year.

It is more important in analyzing retail corporations

than manufacturers. A high ratio denotes a good quality of merchandise and correct pricing policies. A declining ratio may be a warning signal.

7. Net income to net worth (return on equity). This is one of the most significant of all financial ratios. It is derived by dividing the net income ($9.9) by the total of the preferred stock, common stock and surplus accounts ($80.3). The result is 12.3%: the percentage of return that corporate management earned on the dollars entrusted by shareholders at the beginning of each year. Basically, it's that all-important PR (profit rate).

This 12.3% is a slight decrease from the 12.5% of the prior year. It's a fair return: not as good as that achieved by a top-quality corporation but better than that of the average publicly held company. *The higher the ratio, the more profitable the operation.* Any company which can consistently improve such a ratio is a true growth company. *But be sure that this gain is due to operating skill, not to accounting legerdemain or extraordinary items.*

Ratios and Trends

Detailed financial analysis involves careful evaluation of income, costs and earnings. But it is also important to study various ratios and trends, both within the specific corporation and in comparison with those of other companies in the same industry. Usually, analysts prefer to use five- or 10-year averages. These can reveal significant changes and, on occasion, spot special values in either concealed or inconspicuous assets.

Example: When there is a wide difference between the book value of assets as carried on the balance sheet and their current market value, there may be important resources such as company holdings of valuable real estate, oil, gas or uranium.

Operating ratio. This is the ratio of operating costs to sales. It is the complement of *profit margin* (100% minus the PM percentage). Thus, if a company's PM is 10%, its operating ratio is 90%. It's handy for comparing similar companies but not significant otherwise.

PMs vary according to the type of business. They are low for companies with heavy plant investments (Borg-Warner) and for retailers for fast turnover (K-Mart) and high for marketing firms such as those providing information (Dun & Bradstreet), operating radio/TV stations (American Broadcasting) and for those manufacturing consumer products (Gillette).

For railroads and transportation corporations, a similar widely used test of operating efficiency is the *transportation ratio*—the percentage of revenues absorbed by the cost of handling traffic. *The lower the ratio, the greater the operating efficiency.* But because so many railroads have become holding companies that have diversified into non-transportation areas, this ratio is no longer overly useful.

Interest coverage. The number of times interest charges or requirements have been earned. Divide the operating profit (or balance available for such payments before income taxes and interest charges) by the annual interest charges.

Here, the interest (fixed charges) is covered 17.4 times in the past year and 20.3 times in the previous year. This is a

high, safe coverage. If earnings declined to only 6% of the past year's results, interest would still be covered. As a rule, a manufacturing company should cover interest five times; utilities, three times.

Keep in mind that when a company (except utilities or transportation firms) has a high debt, it means that investors shy away from buying its common stock. To provide the plants, equipment, etc., which the company needs, management must issue bonds or preferred shares (straight or convertible to attract investors). There are some tax advantages in such a course, but when the debt becomes too high, there can be trouble during times of recession. All, or almost all, of the gross profits will have to be used to pay interest and there will be nothing, or little, left over for the common stockholders.

On the other hand, speculators like high-debt situations when business is good. This means that when profits soar, all of the excess, after interest payments, will come down to the common stock. Typically, railroads, which have tremendous assets (almost all financed by debt obligations), are popular in boom times. An extra 10% gain in traffic can boost profits far more—percentagewise.

When corporations like utilities have small year-to-year fluctuations in earnings, a large amount of senior securities is no problem.

Payout ratio. This is the ratio of the cash dividends to per share profits after taxes. It reflects management's policy. Fast-growing corporations pay small dividends—less than 30% of each earned dollar; stable, profitable companies pay out about 50%; and utilities, which have almost assured earnings, pay 70% on the average.

It is pleasant to receive an ample dividend check, but for growth, look for companies that pay small dividends. The retained earnings will be used to improve the financial strength and operating future of the company; *and retained earnings are tax-free.*

Price to book value ratio. This is the market price of the stock divided by its book value per share. Since book value trends are, usually, more stable than earnings trends, conservative analysts use this ratio as a price comparison. They check the historical over- or undervaluation of the stock, which in turn depends primarily on the company's profitable growth (or lack of it).

Because of inflation, understatement of assets on balance sheets—and, in boom times, the enthusiasm of investors—often pushes this ratio rather high. On the average, only stocks of the most profitable companies sell at much more than twice book value. Investors believe that these corporations will continue to achieve ever-high earnings. But if the stock prices rise to too high levels, their declines, in a bear market, can be fast and far.

Price/earnings (P/E) ratio. This is calculated by dividing the price of the stock by the reported earnings per share for the past 12 months. Thus, the stock of Brandy-Dandy (B-D), with per share profits of $2.00 for the past year and selling at 24, has a P/E ratio of 12. This information is printed in stock tables in many financial publications.

This multiple of 12 was: *high* in comparison with that of the DJIA which at the time was 7; *low* when related to the company's historic range (over the past 10 years, a high of 17 and a low of 5.8).

B-D was a quality company, rated A by S&P. It was

financially strong; had an outstanding record of higher revenues and profits; reported a 10-year average profit rate of 17.4% and earned growth rate of 10.2%; and earnings were up at an annual rate of over 10%—from $1.21 to $2.80 per share.

B-D had ample capital, modest debt and able management. There were no visible reasons to indicate that the future would not be as favorable, especially when the number of institutional investors was rising steadily.

By fundamental standards, the stock of B-D was undervalued. In 30 months or so, the investor can *hope* for gains from 46% to 92% plus dividends of over 3% annually, to achieve total returns of from 53% to almost 100%. These projections are optimistic because: *(a)* the overall stock market may not move up; *(b)* the company may become unpopular with professional money managers who may not be enthusiastic about new policies or acquisitions; *(c)* there may be unfavorable governmental or legal problems affecting one or more of the industries in which B-D is involved; *(d)* the company may falter.

Two caveats: (1) Such projections can be made ONLY with stocks of quality corporations with long, fairly consistent records of profitable growth. They will not work with shares of companies that are cyclical, erratic or untested. (2) There can be no guarantee that these goals will be attained as soon as anticipated. Wall Street is often slow to recognize value and always takes time to come to intelligent decisions.

Cash flow. This yardstick is increasingly popular in investment analysis. Reported net earnings, after taxes, do not reflect the actual cash income available to the company. Cash flow shows the earnings after taxes *plus* charges against income that do not directly involve cash outlays (sums allocated to depreciation, depletion, amortization and other special items).

A company might show a net profit of $250,000 plus depreciation of $1 million. Cash flow is $1,250,000. Deduct provisions for preferred dividends, then divide the balance by the number of shares of common stock to get the cash flow per share.

According to some analysts, cash flow isn't what it used to be. In an effort to keep earnings high in inflationary times, accountants exercise "judgments" that tend to *overvalue* some assets and *understate* depreciation expenses. As a result, some companies are paying dividends with money they do not have or must borrow and, in effect, are cannibalizing the corporate structure to keep the stock price up.

This is a complicated area that reflects management's interpretation of established accounting policies.
Examples:

• When Company A owns over 20% of Company B, Company A can book B's earnings even though there's no transfer of funds.

• A retailer reports, as revenues, millions of dollars of receivables that have not been collected (and, in some cases, may never be).

• A corporation continues to show depreciation of $10 million a year on a facility, yet, because of inflation, the real replacement cost is $15 million.

To get more accurate figures, says *Forbes* magazine, analysts have developed two new figures:

Distributable cash flow: the amount of money the company has on hand to pay dividends and/or invest in real growth. If this is negative, there are problems. If it's positive, fine, *unless* the company pays out more than this figure in dividends and, thus, is liquidating the firm.

Discretionary cash flow: distributable cash flow minus dividends: how much money is left after allocations for maintenance and dividends, to grow with. Companies do not really set aside such funds, but, ultimately they have to have the money in some form—cash savings or borrowing.

Formulas for Value

With that background, let's see how some professionals use formulas to determine value and when to buy or sell a stock.

EARNINGS GROWTH: the rate at which profits have increased over the last several (preferably five or more) years. You can calculate this from summaries in annual reports or get the information from your broker. If you're a speculator, use the same rate for the future; if you're an investor, cut the percentage by 10% to 20%.

• **Index.** This involves an index based on the S&P 500 stocks. In good years, the average earnings growth has been +16% and the average P/E ratio 8, so the index is 2.

HIWHIZ has had a rapid earnings rise of +40% a year. Its P/E is 20, so its index is 2: not a bargain.

WHIZTECH's earnings have grown at a +70% annual rate. Its P/E is 30 so the index is 2.33: comparatively, cheap.

• **Percentage buying value.** This is a variation of the above formula developed by John B. Neff of Windsor Fund. It uses the current yield plus the rate of earnings growth dividend by the current P/E ratio. If the result is 2 or more, the stock is worth buying:

$$\frac{CY + EG}{PE} = PBV$$

CY = Current Yield
EG = Earnings Growth
PE = Price/Earnings ratio
PBV = Percentage Buying Value

Here's a comparison for judging growth (not income) potential between nondividend-paying, highly profitable Tandy Corp. and slow, steady Florida Power & Light:

TANDY $\dfrac{0 + 17}{22} = 7.7\%$ BUY

FLA. P&L. $\dfrac{8.9 + 5}{8} = 1.69$ SELL or DO NOT BUY

RETURN ON EQUITY AND P/E. Here, you divide the Return on Equity (ROE) by the multiple to get a ranking to indicate whether the stock price is too high or too low based on profitability.

Stock A has a ROE of 21% and a P/E of 7, so the quotient ranking is #3.

Stock B has a ROE of 14 and a P/E of 7, so its ranking is #2.

Comparatively, A is undervalued because both stocks have the same multiple but A has a record of higher profitability.

A further step could be to establish an average ranking for stocks: divide the median ROE by the median P/E, say

16 by 8, to get a #2 ranking. Now compare specific stocks with this base. Those with a ranking of between 1.7 and 2.4 are more or less fairly valued; one with a #3 ranking would be undervalued; one with a #1.5 would be overvalued.

Corporate cash position. This was developed by Dr. Benjamin Graham, granddaddy of fundamentalists. To use:

• Subtract current liabilities, long-term debt and preferred stock (at market value) from current assets of the corporation.

• Divide the result by the number of shares of common stock outstanding.

If the asset value per share is higher than the price per share, Graham would place the stock on his Review List.

Example: Puff Publishing has $100 million current assets, $20 million bonds, $10 million preferred stock and current liabilities of $25 million: a net of $45 million. With 1 million shares, this works out to $45 per share asset value. When the stock is at 35, PP meets Graham's requirements for an undervalued situation.

Checkpoints for Undervalued Stocks

1. A price that is well below book value, asset value and working capital per share.
2. Ample cash or liquid assets for both normal business and expansion.
3. A current dividend of 4.5% or more.
4. Cash dividends paid for at least five, and preferably 10, years without decrease in dollar payout.
5. Total debt less than 35% of total capitalization.
6. Minimum of $25 million net working capital . . . for liquidity.
7. Current dividend protection ratio of at least 1.4: $1.40 earnings for each $1.00 dividends.
8. A P/E ratio lower than that of prior years and, preferably, below 10 times projected 12-month earnings.
9. Earnings now depressed but, based on the historical record, with a strong probability of higher profits in the near future.
10. Assets with heavy depreciation and thus large cash flow. A company that earns $1 per share and that can write off $3 per share actually generates $4 in cash that can be used for future growth.
11. Realistically valued inventories. This is difficult to ascertain but can be checked by reviewing annual reports for the past several years.
12. Gain-to-loss ratio of a minimum of 2:1, i.e., based on past market action and future prospects, the probable gain should be twice as great as the possible loss: a potential gain of 10 points vs. a 5-point decline.

Low P/Es Pay Off

Most brokers get excited about stocks with high P/Es. They figure that these are so popular that their prices will keep on rising. But the facts prove otherwise: stocks with low P/Es (seemingly those with the worst prospects) outperform those with high multiples.

According to a 21-year study by analyst David Dreman,

80% of low P/E stocks scored better than average gains. He concludes that when investors become disappointed with high multiple stocks, they tend to overreact and dump their shares so their prices plummet. With low P/E groups, he found, the action is reversed. At the first sure sign of better earnings, their prices move up sharply.

Dreman, a Wall Street veteran, warns that it's essential to maintain a hard-headed approach, discounting hot tips and avoiding alluring concept stocks. "He must tell himself," he says, "that he is figuratively betting on a roulette wheel with more black numbers than red."

Here are his rules:

• *Buy large and medium-size established companies* whose stocks pay high dividends and have low P/E ratios. Such companies usually suffer less from accounting legerdemain than smaller companies do and have more staying power.

• *Select companies that are financially strong* and able to sail smoothly through the rough weather the low P/E firms can encounter.

• *Look for:* (1) current ratio (current assets divided by current liabilities) of 2:1 or higher; (2) total debt no more than 40% of capital (bonds, preferred stocks and common stock).

• *Diversify,* preferably 15 stocks in a dozen or more industries.

• *Be patient.* Success takes time, usually at least one year.

Ray Dirks, analyst-turned-author, seconds this approach. He insists that the lower the multiple, the more likely the rise in the price of the stock. He found that, over a decade, stocks with the lowest multiples gain $5 for every $1 while those with the highest P/Es returned only 84¢ on every invested $1. *His rule:* when the stock doubles its multiple, say from 3 to 6, it's time to sell. But, he adds, "You must be willing to accept some losses. In most cases, there will be a logical reason why the stock is so unpopular. So diversify and watch the portfolio."

Companies Repurchasing Their Stock

When corporations set up a program to buy back their shares, it's a bullish sign. Over a 12-month period, one survey showed, 64% of such stock outpaced the market.

Repurchase of a substantial number of shares automatically benefits all shareholders: profits are spread over a smaller total; there's more money for dividends and reinvestments; and there's temporary market support.

During periods of recession, many corporations feel that their stocks are at bargain levels and represent a wise and fruitful use of corporate funds. With shares at 50% of book value, the purchase acquires two dollars in assets for every one dollar spent. The savings on dividends could be applied against the interest on loans made for the stock purchase.

On the other hand, a steady stock purchase is a partial liquidation of the corporation, and the critics say, why not pay out more of the surplus cash and let the shareholders decide if the stock is worth buying?

Here's what happens: A company with 1,000,000 shares earns $2 million, for profits of $2.00 per share. If 50,000 shares are acquired and the company nets the same amount the next year, the earnings will be $2.10 per share. *Note:* That's a good reason to check the number of outstanding shares to be sure that the earnings growth is genuine.

Repurchased stock can be used for stock options, employee purchase plans, exercise of warrants, acquisitions, etc. The stock must be held for two years before it can be used in a pooling-of-interest merger. When it's paid out sooner, the deal becomes a straight purchase with more costly tax liabilities.

A corporation is required to make a public announcement of its intention to repurchase. When it's a listed stock, all transactions are handled by one broker for one day with a limit of 15% of the daily average volume for the preceding four weeks. To make it convenient for large shareholders, such as estates or foundations, to act without unduly disturbing the market, block purchases of $250,000 or more can be handled without restrictions.

Another point to watch: a suddenly announced repurchase at year-end. This could be window-dressing to boost the per share profits.

Companies with High Claims on Earnings

Income-seeking investors should look for companies that have only common stock outstanding or those with little or no debt. Since there are no interest payments for bonds, all profits come down to shareholders and, often, bring liberal payouts.

Since these corporations have no leverage in their capitalization, the prices of their shares tend to be more stable than competitors and, while they may move up or down slowly, they rarely swing erratically.

Comments

Value is "in here," not "put there" . . . as shown by corporate strength, growth and profitability. Value is not always what it should be or appears to be. A stock selling at 100 drops to 50 because some institutions lose confidence. Yet the company itself may stay much the same. The different values reflect what investors think of future prospects. And no one can ever predict such optimism or pessimism except over the long term.

Another factor is earnings. Even accountants are not sure. Often, profits are massaged or inflated with special adjustments. What it comes down to, says Heinz Beil, a Wall Street veteran, is "There are only two items on the balance sheet that are 'for real': *cash* which can be counted and *liabilities* that won't go away. Everything else—receivables, inventories, fixed assets and investments are *subject to* interpretation and may be over or understated." And, he might have added, "Most estimates of future earnings are wrong . . . except for those of established, quality companies."

6

Timing for Extra Profits, Lower Losses

Some analysts insist that Timing is the sole key to stock market profits. This may be true with speculations but, with investments, timing is only a tool to enhance profits and reduce losses.

A *speculator* may do well by buying a poor security before its price rises but profits will be more a matter of luck than skill. An *investor* always make money by buying a quality security if he's patient. Those gains will come faster when timing reflects corporate and market prospects. And with selling, the same conditions apply: with smart timing, there will be greater profits in buying and smaller losses . . . and greater profits . . . when selling. Timing is the third word in that money-making trio: quality, value and timing.

There are two types of timing: market and corporate. The first is related to the overall stock market. It is based on an investment policy that seeks to buy near cyclical lows and to accelerate profit-taking near cyclical highs. It determines whether or not it is a good time to invest in common stock. Action is taken against a background of fundamental factors—economic, monetary and political—that influences stock prices: earnings, dividends, financial strength, ratios, yields, interest rates, and, of course, future prospects for the economy, the industry and the company.

The fundamental investor acts with confidence that the stock market, over a period of time, will adjust to price levels reflecting these rational factors. His decisions are made on the basis of continuing business and economic forecasts. He pays little heed to the many psychological and short-run market forces that affect week-to-week, month-to-month and, often, year-to-year fluctuations in stock-market prices. With market timing, the fundamental investor works in general areas: low or *buy* ranges and high or *sell* areas.

This basic timing recognizes that most of the time the prices of common stocks move together and that there are four broad kinds of movements:

1. Major bull and bear markets. These seldom last less than two years. They include many short reversing fluctuations. It's not too difficult to spot long-term trends but is difficult to catch interim movements.

Typically, bear markets move downward much faster than bull markets move up. BUT NOT ALWAYS—as was demonstrated by the soaring phenomenon of 1981–83 when the Dow Jones Industrial Average rocketed up from below 800 to over 1200! In the stock market, past is usually prologue but there is nothing more predictable in general terms and more unpredictable in specifics. Once in a great while, some professionals may be right for a year or two but very few have called the shots accurately as to exact timing.

2. Intermediate market movements within a major bull or bear market. These usually run several months. These are ever-present, ever-changing. They are most rewarding (or most irritating) with groups of stocks.

3. Seasonal market movements of a month or so. These can be superimposed on intermediate swings. They tend to follow established patterns and often concern only a few stock groups significantly but generally apply to all securities.

4. Immediate short-term fluctuations of weeks or days. These are of importance only to traders although, on occasion, upsetting to investors.

There are hundreds of investment timing techniques which attempt to spot and pinpoint all four of these market movements. The conservative investor wants to catch the turn of major bull or bear markets; the less conservative watches for immediate movements; the speculator relishes the seasonal swings, but only the professional plays for the short, day-to-day fluctuations. *All serious investors should understand the broad trends and movements of the stock market in order to sharpen their own timing.*

Corporate timing involves industry groups and specific companies. Basically, this is keyed to individual stock transactions and involves buying after a long downtrend or a reversal and selling just before or after a price peak. Success requires self-discipline and adherence to logically determined conclusions, not hunches or rumors/tips. It is just as important to avoid losers as to pick winners.

As background, corporate timing must watch what's happening with specific industry groups as shown in the table on Stock Market Action. This is more important with trading than investing but can assure an extra point or two of greater profits and lower losses. Only rarely does any stock move out of line with its industry group.

The table shows how dramatically the stock market can change. After plus years in 1975 and 1976, it fell in 1977, bounced up a fraction in 1978 and handsomely in 1979 but then fell for two years and, in 1982, started its upsurge.

Note the significant differences in special stock groups: the Most Actives were winners all along; Traders' Favorites yo-yoed and, in recent years, were hardly worth the risks; and consumer goods and transportation did well over the eight years.

Before you make any major commitment, always check the long-term performance and concentrate on those groups that have bettered the averages. Chances are that they will continue to be winners.

Timing Errors

Before getting into the How To's, let's review the most frequent, and gravest, timing errors made by both amateurs and professionals:

STOCK MARKET ACTION

INVESTMENT GROUP

BOND MARKET	1982	1981	1980	1979	1978	1977	1976	1975
Corporate	+24	−10	−13	−13	− 7	− 2	+13	+ 1
Municipals	+36	−26	−29	− 4	−10	− 8	+19	+ 1
U.S. Long-Term	+26	5	−15	− 9	− 9	− 7	+10	− 3
STOCK MARKET								
NYSE Composite	+14	− 9	− 9	+15	+ 2	− 9	+21	+32
Dow Jones Industrials	+20	− 9	− 9	+ 4	− 3	−17	+18	+38
S&P 500 Stock Index	+15	−10	−10	+12	+ 1	−12	+19	+32
Value Line Unweighted	+15	− 4	− 4	+24	+ 4	0	+32	+44
SPECIAL STOCK GROUPS								
Most Active Stocks	+75	+136	+136	+405	+231	+46	+151	+262
Low Priced Stocks	+10	0	0	+24	+10	+10	+43	+84
Traders' Favorites	+16	−18	−18	+18	+20	−12	+40	+48
Institutional Favorites	+20	−13	−13	+ 8	+ 2	−14	+18	+34
MAJOR STOCK GROUPS								
Financial	+30	− 1	+ 3	+53	+ 6	0	+49	+19
Consumer	+44	+ 7	+16	+12	+ 6	+ 6	+31	+54
Defensive	+26	+ 8	+15	+17	− 1	− 1	+23	+37
Cyclical	+ 9	− 4	+23	+21	+ 3	+ 3	+39	+53
Utilities	+ 6	+10	+ 9	+ 5	− 9	− 9	+25	+37
Transportation	+24	+ 3	+28	+17	+ 4	+ 4	+39	+58

SOURCE: Wright Investors' Service

1. To refuse to sell after the price trend of the stock has reversed from up to down. If the stock is held at a loss and your portfolio can be strengthened by switching, the tendency is to take no action. As a result, you soon get locked in with your worst-performing stocks!

2. To refuse to sell when the stock you own soars to an unusually high level far beyond its normal range and its logical maximum value. This is the situation when stocks become popular. By definition, *this is the time to think about selling*—because the danger of a price drop is far greater than the probability of a further meaningful gain. *Best bet:* Set actual or mental stop orders at 10% to 15% below current market prices in a stable market.

3. To refuse to buy when the price of the stock is at a low ebb and when prospects for profitable growth by the company and the industry are good. This is the point at which stocks are unpopular and bargains can be found.

It is a sad truism that when stock prices are really low, most people are unwilling to buy and that when stock prices are really high, most people forget the logical prospects and buy avidly.

The basic rules for the successful timing of investments are to buy stocks when they are undervalued and unpopular and to sell when they become fully priced and are very popular.

Techniques of Timing

Market timing is always difficult. Technicians rely on charts and indicators. Fundamentalists look for bargains or overpricing. They both recognize that there are patterns that can be used successfully. For example, they know that, on the average, the price of a stock will swing 20% to 25% a year:

AMP, Inc.: 1978: 24 to 40; 1980: 34 to 56; 1982: 46 to 70.

Florida Progress (adjusted): 1980: 11 to 15; 1982: 12½ to 16½ (utilities, with their high dividends, move less erratically).

IBM: 1980: 50 to 71; 1981: 71 to 49; 1982: 53 to 100.

To take cognizance of such price movements, analysts have developed *relativity ratios.* These measure the rate of change in the price of a stock (or group of stocks) against a stock market index and thus indicate volatility.

The best known is "beta," based on the S&P 500 Stock Index. A stock with a beta of 1.25 has 25% more volatility (and thus, to a degree, risk) than the overall market. This means that it is likely to rise or fall 25% more than the general level of stock prices.

In terms of investing, the conservative should choose low-beta stocks: those rated under 1.00. In a down market, their decline will be less than average; in an up market, their gain will be smaller. The aggressive investor, and speculator, should concentrate on high-beta stocks.

Wright Investors' reverses the ratings and concentrates on stability. A stock rated 100% will move with the market; one rated 60% will be much more volatile. *Examples:* IBM: 91%; Computervision Corp.: 63%.

Both criteria are best for professionals because of the complex calculations but the wise amateur should check them to be sure that the stock fits his plan and sleep-well level.

YIELDS: STOCKS vs. BONDS

YEAR	S&P CLOSE	STOCK YIELDS	BOND YIELDS	DIFFERENCES vs. STOCKS
1962	66	3.4	4.1	−0.7
1963	79	3.3	4.2	−0.9
1964	90	3.0	4.4	−1.4
1965	98	3.1	4.6	−1.5
1966	85	3.3	5.4	−2.1
1967	105	3.2	5.8	−2.6
1968	113	3.0	6.5	−3.5
1969	101	3.1	7.5	−4.4
1970	101	3.6	7.8	−4.2
1971	113	3.0	6.9	−3.9
1972	132	2.6	6.7	−4.1
1973	109	2.9	7.5	−4.6
1974	76	4.1	9.2	−5.1
1975	101	4.1	9.0	−4.9
1976	119	3.8	8.5	−4.7
1977	105	4.5	8.2	−3.7
1978	107	5.0	8.6	−3.6
1979	121	5.2	9.4	−4.2
1980	154	4.9	12.0	−7.1
1981	137	5.2	14.0	−8.8
1982	158	4.6	12.0	−7.4

SOURCE: Wright Investors' Service

Another valuable broad timing aid is the spread between yields of stocks and bonds. This can be useful in determining when to move from bonds to stocks or back again. It was not effective in years of high yields but is becoming more valuable as interest rates decline.

The basic premise is sound: that there is always competition for capital between stocks and bonds. The total returns of common stocks—dividends plus capital appreciation—is weighted against the interest of bonds.

Note how the relationship has changed over the years, especially since interest rates began to rise. Back in the early 1960s, the difference was small, less than 1%. Most people preferred equity to debt.

In the bull-market years of the early 1970s, when stock prices were high and thus dividend yields low, the bond advantage widened so that some investors moved into bonds, especially with the stock-market downturn in 1974.

A timing signal was flashed in 1979 when the spread widened to over 4%—indicating that, for income, bonds were a better investment. This trend was confirmed in 1980 when the difference was a whopping 7.1% and again in 1982 when it rose to 8.8%. But in 1982, when the cost of money eased, the spread was moving down again—to 7.4%—and slightly less in early 1983.

Another professional timing tool is *value* as indicated by the price/earnings ratios: of the market, of the industry or of the stock. They *buy* when the multiple is below the long-term average; *sell* when it rises well above the historic range. This is better in theory than in practice but can be a useful confirmation check.

The problem is that value timing does tell you when a stock may be under- or overvalued but it cannot indicate when a favorable price movement will occur. Wall Street is slow to change its prejudices. The price changes that you believe should take place will come eventually but seldom as soon as you anticipate. They reflect psychology rather than logic.

Thus, if you buy a stock that you are convinced is undervalued, you may have to wait: hopefully a few months but, possibly, as long as one year. You may be right but, meantime, you tie up your money and miss potential profits that could be made by buying a fairly valued stock at the right time.

During 1972 and 1973, the prices of glamour-growth equities zoomed up and up. They soared far beyond traditional values and the fundamentalists cried in horror and dismay. *But they still kept moving up under the pressure of institutional buying.*

According to fundamental standards, even an aggressive investor should have sold Avon Products at around 100 in 1972–73 when the P/E ratio soared above 40. But AVP roared to a high of 140 with a multiple of 65 times earnings!

As usual, the fundamentalists were right but their timing was wrong. By late 1974, AVP had fallen way, way down to 19—along with almost all glamour-growth equities.

Keep in mind, too, that value, like growth, can be in the eye of the beholder. National Medical Care was touted as a super company and its stock, on an adjusted basis, rose from 7 in 1980 to 26 in 1981. But when earnings dropped, the stock plummeted to 5½!

In timing selections, the value approach, when combined with technical analysis, can spark excellent gains with minimal risk. But you must keep checking the financial facts to be sure that the value is growing. When any high-rider falters, the speculators will get out fast and most investors will have to take heavy losses.

When to Buy Stocks by Timing

There are so many tips/guidelines/rules for buying stocks throughout *Your Investments* that it is not necessary to go into details here. They all boil down to this: *when investing,* buy only quality stocks when they are undervalued, have good prospects and are becoming popular. Set your target at 35 to 50% gains in the next 24 to 30 months. This will assure average annual total returns—with dividends—of at least 16% in normal markets and more in bull markets. At times, you will have to be patient but, in a strong market, the appreciation can come almost too fast—before the 12 months needed to qualify for the low capital gains tax rate.

Whether you are trading or investing, the objective should be *to buy low and sell high.* But in an ebullient market, that aphorism can be expanded *to buy high and sell higher.*

When speculating, you can be more flexible in quality, but timing must be more precise: buying *up* stocks in an *up* industry in an *up* market. Or when you are selling short (where the buying comes later), the reverse. Your target goal should come faster, usually in six months or less.

This quick action is especially important in a bull market because, statistically, two-thirds of the gains come in the first six months before a reaction. That means it's smart to buy early and sell when there's a confirmed downtrend.

One way to use timing is to watch the number of new highs. With a chart, set up a Moving Average of these new peaks and once the line falls, and stays, below this guideline, sell unless there are specific reasons for optimism for any one holding. Only rarely does any stock move against the overall trend.

It's always pleasant to get a bargain but, experience shows, the best time to buy any stock is when its price is rising (unless you are willing to wait). The key, says technician Joseph E. Granville, is "Volume. This always comes before price."

He argues that unless a substantial number of people are interested in the stock, its price will move within a narrow range. Only where there is additional activity will the stock price change significantly: *up* when corporate news/prospects are bright; *down* when they are gloomy. In other words, he says, "Do not be afraid to buy a favored stock at a point or two above its current quotation. If the rise came with higher volume, the odds are that this uptrend will continue."

The reasoning back of this concept is that when sales increase, people know, or think they know, more than the rest of us. When the stock move is up, they are sufficiently confident to put up their money to back their opinion. Vice versa on the downside.

Despite his showmanship and iconoclastic approach, Granville continues to rely on volume indicators. But with the huge trading of recent months, the significance of volume alone appears to be less than in the past. Or at least more useful for speculating than for investing. A great many people who followed Granville's famous *sell* signal in early 1981 lost a great deal of money fast. The market did tumble but it quickly recovered to new highs. Timing is a double-edged sword: it cuts profits as well as losses unless one is nimble.

A more conservative approach is to watch those quarterly profits. If the company reports two consecutive quarters of better earnings, it is probably moving back to its traditional profitability and growth. But be cautious unless it's a strong market. Check to see whether that second quarter gain is against a very poor year-ago period or represents genuine progress. And be wary of recommendations by brokers or advisory services. They tend to be optimistic (to generate commissions for their representatives), and while their puffs may boost the stock price temporarily, market increases will depend on continually higher profits.

When to Sell Stocks by Timing

Selling stocks is more difficult and, for successful timing, demands strict adherence to strict rules. It is never easy to sell any stock when it is high-priced, popular and profitable. Such action is contrary to human nature and fails to accomplish two important objectives: to make your spouse happy and yourself boastful.

Yet it is the most logical approach. *How can you make real profits if you do not buy low and sell high?*

Sure, you can always operate on the "greater fool" theory that, regardless of how high the price of a stock becomes, a "greater fool" will come along and buy it from you. But what happens when the bubble bursts and there are no more devil-may-care buyers? *You can lose a lot of money FAST.*

Here are some guidelines for timing selling:

1. Take your profits when you have a worthwhile profit. In 1981, Dr. X bought American Home Products (AHP) at 28 and in a little more than 12 months (long enough to benefit from the lower capital gains tax), the stock was at 42. This was a 50% gain plus dividends that more than offset the commissions. Now, Dr. X had to decide whether to hold on for a few more points or to take his profit and put the proceeds in a more rewarding situation. AHP was a quality company, but based on research of past performance, Dr. X concluded that it would take a couple of years for AHP to rise another 50%: to 63. He sold and put the proceeds in Scott & Fetzer (SFZ) at 28, again shooting for a 50% gain.

As it turned out, this was a bit hasty because, in the strong 1982–83 market, AHP kept going to 50. But Dr. X was still OK because SFZ ran up to 44!

Taking profits makes more sense when corporate prospects dim. In late 1979, Dr. Y bought Schlumberger Ltd. (SLB) at 45 (later adjusted to 30 after a 3–2 stock split). The stock soared into the 80s for a whopping $50+ per share gain. This was a good time to sell under any conditions but became especially worthwhile when the financial reports showed that the company's profit rate was slipping as a result of the acquisition of Fairchild Camera: to 38.9% from 41.4% the year before. The timing was right: by early 1982, SLB stock was in the low 30s and a candidate for purchase again.

2. Sell when the original reasons for purchase no longer hold. There are three basic reasons to buy any stock:

• Your study shows that this is a sound company with good prospects for profitable growth.

• You believe that something good is going to happen: the stock may be split, the company is getting a big new contract, a new, profitable product, acquisition, etc.

• Reports and/or charts show that smart money is moving into the stock.

The last two are usually reasons for a quick rise in the price of the equity. There should be quick action. If there is not, *sell.* You were wrong.

3. Use stop orders. These can protect your profits or minimize your losses. There are two handy ways to do this:

Enter a good-until-canceled stop order. This will vary with the price range and the volatility of the stock, but as a rule, 10% to 15% below the purchase price or, if higher, the current value. With a stock at 50, set the stop at 45¼ or 42½. Use fractions because in a fast-falling market your round-number stop may not be executed. If the stock goes up to 55, move the stop up.

Use a mental stop order. This requires determination and constant surveillance of the stock market. It is valuable only for the disciplined investor. He should set a price below which he does not want to own the stock. Each night he checks the closing price and then decides his next day's action. If the price trend is down and the volume is up for several days, he should act promptly.

The difficulty with this approach is that it is too easy to delay, to get busy or to change your mind. Most people wait for a rally. By the time they do act, they have lost a couple of points more than anticipated.

4. Sell when the industry becomes unpopular. In late 1980, the chart showed that oil stocks, after hitting record peaks, were falling: Exxon from about 90 to 80 (before the split); Phillips Petroleum from 60 to 50, etc. For weeks, the oils were among the Most Active stocks with ever-lower prices. Clearly, these companies were out of favor with major investors and should be sold. *Never argue with Wall Street* unless you are willing, and able, to hang on with hope: in this case, for about 18 months!

5. Sell when the media is full of bad economic news: higher inflation, lower productivity, greater unemployment, bigger deficits, and dismal corporate reports. This is the time to switch from growth to income: to fixed income holdings that will assure steady interest/dividends and full or relatively stable values. This pessimism will be dramatically shown on the charts, as explained in Chapter 7. Use these primarily for confirmation of those upsetting headlines.

Conversely, when the news is optimistic, it's time to start buying—but the wise investor should have anticipated this and already be loading up with quality stocks at bargain prices.

6. Act when the stock's volume reaches a six-month high. With major corporations, this will show up first on the Most Active List. With smaller firms, check the charts to see the vertical lines at the bottom. When they grow taller, with lower prices, it's an almost sure sign of trouble ahead. The Big Boys are unloading.

When that volume comes with higher prices, investors are enthusiastic and will be willing to pay even more. *VOLUME PRECEDES PRICE.*

And now let's add some advice from Richard Blackman, a New Jersey discount broker and author of *Follow the Leaders.* He's a tough-minded professional trader who sticks to rules like these. He checks fundamentals but relies heavily on charts "because they report what is actually happening in the market-place. In successful trading, there's no room for emotional involvement. A stock does not care who owns it." All of these comments apply to selling:

7. After a big hit. If you have just sold at a substantial profit, take your time before reinvesting. Do not let your broker try to persuade you to sell and buy another stock. He's trained to "get the other side of every trade." Stop. Clear your head. Let the market go for a week. Then make sure that the next stock you buy has a potential gain of at least 25%. Otherwise sit on the sidelines.

8. After three straight losses. Blackman says, "When this sad situation occurs, sell everything. If you struck out three times in a row, it's not you if you have been playing by the rules. You're in a bad market and should recognize it."

9. After 12 months if you are fully invested. At this point, the market and up-moving stocks are likely to pause under the pressure of sales by profit-taking investors. They take control and, for a while, virtually stop the market from going up.

"When you judge this time span, do so from the week the uptrend started, not the date you bought the stock. Check the chart and make believe you bought at the bottom. Then mark your investment calendar one year ahead.

"This is a tough rule for most investors to accept. It should be used flexibly but it's backed by common sense and proven-profitable results."

10. When stocks break out of a consolidation pattern. This is a variation of Blackman's break in the uptrend-line. Stock seldom rise to a peak and then fall off. They usually form a consolidation area where the price moves up and down within a relatively narrow range. Charts show this quickly.

As long as the stock stays within this channel pattern, *hold.* But the minute there's a breakthrough on the downside, get ready. If the penetration is confirmed in the next day or so, *sell.*

And here are some final comments based on personal experience:

11. Sell when you have a short-term profit if there's a good chance that you might lose 20% before the 12-month capital gains period is over. You will have to pay full taxes on your profits but you may cut your losses.

The mathematics work out this way. For every $100 short-term profit, you will net $80 after taxes (assuming a modest tax bracket). If you can hang on for a year, the net will be increased to $84. But if your $100 profit is cut 22% to $78, your after-tax net will be only $50 even with the lower capital-gains tax.

This is a handy rule for volatile stocks. Suppose you bought 100 shares of Blowhard, Inc. at 36 in November. It jumps to 46 in March, so you have a $1,000 profit. Under this rule, you can afford to lose only $200 of the $1,000 profit. That's a two-point drop. Any stock that rises 10 points in five months can fall two points in seven months more. *It is better to sell and be happy.* (Blowhard did go to 50⅞, but at the end of six months, it was down to 30.)

12. When the dividend income falls short of your needs. People who need maximum income on their money should not hesitate to sell and take their capital gains if the return on their current investment is considerably lower than could be obtained elsewhere.

Example: You own 1,000 shares of Earache, Ltd., bought at 10 and paying 50¢ a share for a $500 annual income. Within the year, the stock becomes popular and jumps to 26. The profits are not up enough to justify much of a dividend increase, so your yield is now 2% with a possibility of a slight raise. You sell the shares, pay taxes and commissions and have some $20,000 to invest in 1,000 shares of a utility yielding over 9%. The income is almost $2,000 a year with the probability of future raises and a higher price for the stock.

13. Be cautious when the company announces plans to issue convertible debentures or preferred stock. Eventually, these will dilute the value of the common stock unless the corporation can use the money to boost profits. Most important, CVs are usually offered when the market is booming and the securities can command a high price because of investor optimism.

According to one study, of 141 NYSE companies that floated CVs in the up market of the late 1960s, the common stock of 70% of these firms fell 25% or more within the next nine months. Later, about half of these recovered but, with few exceptions, CVs are better for the issuer than the investor. *Best bet:* buy CVs when they are selling at discount prices.

14. Sell promptly when your stock runs up on news that it may be taken over because: *(a)* proposals do not always end in marriage; *(b)* there's no guarantee that the merger

will be successful; *(c)* it's difficult to accurately project future profits; and *(d)* such enthusiasm is temporary. Of 56 stocks that moved up on news of a proposed merger, 40 fell by 25% or more within the next nine months.

Sell quickly because most of the declines occur in the first three months. Of course, if you have reason to believe the takeover will be completed and then result in a much stronger organization, you will make your judgment on a different, sounder basis. *But get all the facts first. That's more than most of the people who boosted the price of your stock will have done.*

15. Get ready to sell when the stock moves up fast. If you're lucky enough to pick a stock that jumps up 50% or so in a couple of months, sell or set up a stop-loss order. The records shows that a sale is best: of 55 NYSE stocks that achieved a 50% gain in a short period, 39 fell 25% or more in the next six months.

Always sell too soon. When a stock becomes overpriced, the risks of a severe decline are far greater than the rewards of further gains. Take your profits and run to another stock that will provide similar profits in the future.

Remember: Very few securities reach prices reflecting P/E ratios beyond their average parameters. When they do, it's usually wiser to let others test the unfamiliar ground. Or set stop prices to protect your profits.

16. Watch insider transactions. When there are twice as many sellers as buyers, something unfavorable may be coming up. Get out before the bad news hits the wires.

Conversely, when there are purchases by a number of officers or directors, this could be a bullish signal. (See Chapter 23.)

17. With stocks that you own, ask yourself "If I were making a new investment, would I buy these shares at this price at this time?" If the answer is an unqualified YES, hold. If you're undecided, get ready to sell at a target price on both the up and downside. If the answer is NO, sell at once.

18. Stick with the up-moving groups. Note how fickle the stock market is. Not one of the strongest groups in 1982 was among the 1981 leaders! With the weakest groups, the changes came more slowly because a trend in motion will continue far longer than most people anticipate. Note, too, that there will always be one or two industries that bounce back fast: savings and loans were down 30% in 1981 but, with lower interest rates, soared twice as much in 1982.

Short Selling as Aid to Timing

Information on short sales can be useful in timing buying and selling but is not easy to interpret correctly. These are the most widely used checkpoints:

Total short sales. The short interest of all stocks traded on the NYSE and AMEX is published about the fifteenth of the month in financial publications. It shows stocks in which: *(a)* there has been a month-to-month change of at least 2,000 shares sold short; *(b)* 5,000 or more shares have been sold short.

The data also reports the total number of the company's outstanding common shares, the short interest of the previous month and those stocks that are involved in arbitrage because of a merger/acquisition.

FASTEST-MOVING GROUPS

1982 ADVANCES		1981 STRONGEST		1980		1979	
Automotive	+176%	Sulfur Producers	+134%	Gold	+ 90%	Oil Refiners	+ 40%
Brewers	+ 93	Scientific Equip.	+ 55	Construc/Engin.	+ 85	Steamship Lines	+ 33
Drug Stores	+ 88	Plumbing/Heating	+ 46	Oil: Internat.	+ 67	Copper Producers	+ 31
Paints & Resins	+ 80	Apparel: Shoes	+ 45	Railroads	+ 62	Aircraft	+ 30
Rubber & Tires	+ 72	Retail Drug Stores	+ 41	Electronics/Meters	+ 60	Auto/Diver.	+ 25
Nat. Food Chains	+ 67	Food: Confectionery	+ 39	Electronics/Defense	+ 57	Aerospace	+ 23
Dept. Stores	+ 64	Trucking	+ 33	Conglomerates	+ 54	Machine Tools	+ 22
Savings & Loan	+ 64	Food: Bakers	+ 33	Electronics/Diver.	+ 53	Aluminum Prod.	+ 22
Airlines	+ 64	Radio & TV Broad.	+ 28	Crude Oil	+ 48	Conglomerates	+ 19
Motion Picture	+ 63	Utilities: Commun.	+ 24	Gas Pipelines	+ 45	Electronics/Def.	+ 17
DECLINES		**WEAKEST**					
Construct. Mach.	−39%	Oil Refiners	− 47%	Discount Stores	− 24%	Office Equipment	− 19%
Electronic Syst.	−38	Auto: Trucks	− 41	Auto: Trucks	− 24	Utilities: Electric	− 18
Steamship Lines	−28	Steamship Lines	− 40	Auto: Diver.	− 22	Auto: Diver.	− 18
Nat. Gas Pipe Lines	−26	Construct/Engin.	− 37	Food: Confectionery	− 20	Electronics/Radio-TV	− 18
Sulphur Producers	−24	Machinery/Diver.	− 35	Plumbing/Heating	− 17	Chemicals: House	− 15
Engineering Ser.	−23	Gold	− 34	Steel/Non-Integ.	− 14	Airlines	− 14
Indust. Machinery	−23	Electronics/Diver.	− 32	Electronics Syst.	− 14	Retail: Apparel	− 13
Oil Refiners	−22	Distillers	− 31	Distillers	− 11	Chemicals: Rubber	− 10
Metal Producers	−21	Savings & Loan	− 30	Utilities: Electric	− 9	Steel: Integrated	− 9
Machin. & Equipment	−19	Discount Stores	− 29	Personal Loan	− 8	Soft Drinks	− 8

GROUP AVERAGES

Number Advances	73		58		75		77
Number Declines	27		42		23		20
Number Unchanged	0		0		2		3

SOURCE: Wright Investors' Service

According to technical theory, a large short interest is bullish because this provides a cushion for the market. Eventually, short sellers will have to cover their positions. This demand will boost volume and prices. Stocks with large short positions often show the greatest gains.

Similarly, a low and shrinking short interest warns that speculators are becoming bullish and that a market top may be approaching.

Maybe so. But the information is two weeks late, traders have different objectives and institutional investors seldom sell short. So, in effect, short selling represents the actions of a small group of professionals and cannot always be considered an accurate predictor. Still, when enough people believe something, it can become self-fulfilling.

In reality, short positions arise in a number of ways and many of them are complicated and of little value to the small investor. Arbitragers may hedge their dealing by buying takeover stocks while at the same time shorting the shares of the company doing the buying. This can bring sharp rises in the short interest but means little.

Short-interest ratio (SIR). This shows the short interest as a percentage of average trading volume for the preceding month. The potency of any short-interest total depends on how it compares with the total volume of trading. If the average volume is 30 million shares daily and the short interest is 30 million shares, the ratio is 1.00. Generally, it takes a ratio of 1.70 or higher to act as a bull-market prop.

When the ratio falls below 1.00, it's usually a bear-market signal. In most cases, a falling ratio is unfavorable and bull markets often start when the ratio is 2.00 or higher. Many technicians start buying when the SIR hits 1.7. In fact, since 1932, no *sustained* market rise has taken place without the short-interest ratio moving above 1.7.

The time to heed the short interest, directly or by ratio, is when the short interest of a stock that has declined for some time starts to increase. This is often an indication of psychology more than of fact. The stock may have come down so far that it may be time for it to go up again. This is a decision that is tough to interpret and should be made only with the help of an experienced trader.

Specialist short sales. These are made by professionals who have intimate knowledge of the market and specific stocks. When they risk their own funds to go short, they believe that the prices of certain stocks are going to decline. When their short sales are high (over 67%), it's a bearish indicator. When they reduce their short positions (under 40%), an improved market can be expected. These data are reported by several financial services and major financial publications. These are reliable for timing both sales and purchases but they must be followed carefully and interpreted correctly. They should never be used alone.

These are all better theories than practice. Studies show that *(a)* the short position must be of some magnitude to have any effect on the price action of the stock; *(b)* certain stocks seldom attract much short selling even after massive moves; *(c)* some short sales are artificial in that they represent arbitrage because of a proposed merger when the shorted shares will never be repurchased.

There is some evidence that the short-interest theory affects the overall market, but there are doubts as to its validity with individual stocks. An analysis by Randall Smith found that a high and rising short interest does not have an upward impact on a specific stock. But these same stocks do show greater volatility both up and down than the overall market.

Conclusions: (1) If you have a strong opinion that stocks are going to rise in price, buying short-interest stocks will give you more bang for the buck; conversely, if you are bearish, the fact that a stock has a high short interest is no reason to short it. (2) Stocks that make big moves in bull markets or that do not go down much in bear markets and which show a short interest beginning to decline from a high level often have a final, climactic upward spurt.

Watching these factors could improve the timing in a profitable sale of long stock. But analyst Barton Biggs says, "Read the short-interest tables to find out what the volatile stocks are. They do not prove anything else."

7

How to Use Technical Analysis Profitably

Technical Analysis (T.A.) is not as complex nor as esoteric as many people think. It's a tell-it-as-it-is interpretation of stock market activity. The technician glances at fundamental values of securities and concentrates on the behavior of the market, industry groups and stocks themselves: their price movements, volume, trends, patterns: in sum, their supply and demand.

Basically, T.A. is concerned with what *is,* not with what *should be.* The dyed-in-the-wool technician pays minimal attention to what the *company* does and concentrates on what its *stock* does. He recognizes that, over the short term, the values of stock reflect what people *think* they are worth, not what they are really worth.

The technical analyst operates on the basis that (*a*) the action of the stock market is the best indicator of its future course; (*b*) 80% of a stock's price movement is due to factors outside the company's control and 20% to factors unique to that stock; (*c*) the stock market, over a few weeks/months, is rooted 85% in psychology and only 15% in economics.

Broadly speaking, T.A. is more useful for trading than for investing, but even die-hard fundamentalists pay attention to T.A. in timing their purchases and sales. When properly used, T.A. can be a valuable tool to improve stock-market profits. *Everyone who wants to be a successful investor should understand technical analysis.* And, based on experience, I believe, can use it to enhance profits.

The Dow Theory

There are a number of technical theories but the granddaddy is the Dow Theory. It is the oldest and most widely used. As with all technical approaches, it is based on the belief that stock prices cannot be accurately forecast by fundamental analysis, at least not for the short term. But there are trends, indicated by price movements and volume, that can be used successfully. And they can be recorded, tracked and interpreted because the market itself prolongs movements—investors buy more when the market is rising and sell more when it's dropping.

This "follow the crowd" approach is essential for traders. It enables them to buy when the market is going up and to sell, or sell short, when it turns down. For amateurs, such quick trading can be costly because of the commissions and the need for accurate information. But when properly used, T.A. can be valuable in timing.

The Dow Theory is named after Charles H. Dow, one of the founders of Dow Jones & Company, Inc., the financial reporting-publishing organization. The original hypotheses have been changed somewhat by followers, but, broadly interpreted, the Dow Theory signals both the beginnings and end of bull and bear markets.

Dow believed that the stock market is a barometer of business. The purpose of this theory is not to predict movements of security prices but, rather, to call the turns of the market and to forecast the business cycle or longer movements of depression or prosperity. It is not concerned with ripples or day-to-day fluctuations.

Basically, the Dow Theory states that once a trend of the Dow Jones Industrial Average has been established, it tends to follow the same direction until definitely canceled by *both* the Industrial and Railroad (now Transportation) averages. The market cannot be expected to produce new indications of the trend every day, and unless there is positive evidence to the contrary, the existing trend will continue.

Dow and his disciples saw the stock market as being

made up of two types of "waves": *the primary wave,* which is a bull or bear market cycle of several years' duration, and the *secondary* (or *intermediary*) *wave,* which lasts from a few weeks to a few months. Any single primary move may contain within it a score or more of secondary waves, both up and down.

The theory relies on similar action by the two averages, which may vary in strength but not in direction. Robert Rhea, who expanded the original concept, explained it this way: "Successive rallies penetrating preceding high points with ensuing declines terminating above preceding low points, offer a bullish indication . . . (and vice versa for bearish indication). . . . A rally or decline is defined as one or more daily movements resulting in a net reversal of direction exceeding 3% of either average. Such movements have little authority unless confirmed by both Industrial and Transportation Averages . . . but confirmation need not occur in the same day."

Dow did not consider that his theory applied to individual stock selections or analysis. He expected that specific issues would rise or fall with the averages most of the time but he also recognized that any particular security would be affected by special conditions/situations.

Dow made the point that "the business community has a tendency to go from one extreme to the other. It is either contracting business under a belief that prices will be lower or expanding under a belief that prices will be higher. It appears to take five or six years for public confidence to go from the point of too little hope to the point of too much confidence and then five or six years to get back to the conditions of hopelessness." READ THAT OVER AGAIN AS YOU PLAN AHEAD.

The key indicators of the Dow Theory are:

1. A bull market is signaled as a possibility when an intermediate decline in DJIA stops above the bottom of the previous intermediate decline. A bull market is *confirmed* after this has happened, when the next intermediate rise in the DJIA goes above the peak of the last previous intermediate rise.

2. A bull market is in progress as long as each new intermediate rise goes *higher* than the peak of the previous intermediate advance, and each new intermediate decline stops *above* the bottom of the previous one.

3. A bear market is signaled as a possibility when an intermediate rally in the DJIA fails to break through the top of the previous intermediate rise. A bear market is *confirmed* after this has happened, when the next intermediate decline breaks through the low of the previous one.

4. A bear market is in progress as long as each new intermediate decline goes *lower* than the bottom of the previous decline and each new intermediate rally fails to rise as high as the previous rally.

A pure Dow theorist considers the averages, alone, to be quite sufficient to use in forecasting. He sees no need to supplement them with statistics of commodity prices, volume of production, carloadings, bank debts, exports, imports, etc. The course of the stock market is clear when one of the averages shifts from a bear market pattern . . . or vice versa . . . IF this is confirmed by another average: DJIA plus DJTA, for example.

Interpreting the Dow Theory

The Dow Theory leaves no room for sentiment. A primary bear market does not terminate until stock prices have thoroughly discounted the worst that is apt to occur. This decline requires three steps: (1) "the abandonment of hopes upon which stocks were purchased at inflated prices"; (2) selling due to decreases in business and earnings; (3) distress selling of sound securities despite value.

Primary bull markets follow an opposite pattern: (1) a broad movement, interrupted by secondary reactions averaging longer than two years, where successive rallies penetrate high points with ensuing declines terminating above preceding low points; (2) stock prices advance because of demand created by both investors and speculators who start buying when business conditions improve; (3) rampant speculation as stocks advance on hopes and expectations.

These broad swings may take years (1970–74) or happen quickly (1977–78). Markets do not normally go straight up or straight down but, according to Dow, "are subject to periodic interruptions by countermoves that are likely to retrace one third to two thirds of the original move before starting again in the primary direction. Thus, a bull market that rises 30 points will probably lose 10 to 20 points of its gain before resuming its ascent."

There are analysts who scoff at the Dow Theory. They point out that the stock market today is vastly different than in the early years of the century when Dow formulated his theory. The number and value of shares of publicly owned corporations have increased enormously: in 1900, the average number of shares traded *annually* on the NYSE was 59.5 million. Now, that's a slow *day's* volume.

The sharpest criticism is leveled against the breadth, scope and significance of the averages. The original Industrial Index had only 12 stocks and, today, the 30 large companies (despite recent substitutions of IBM, Merck and American Express) do not provide a true picture of today's broad, technologically oriented economy. They point out that the Transportation Average is also unrepresentative as some of the railroads derive a major share of their revenues from natural resources and the airlines and trucking companies are limited in their impact. Add the geographic disbursement of industry and transportation is no longer a reliable guide to the economy.

Maybe so, counter the Dow followers, but Pennsylvania still produces the steel used in nuclear submarines in Connecticut and Kansas wheat is shipped to New Orleans.

Finally, the "purists" argue that Government regulations and institutional dominance of trading have so altered the original concept of individual investors that the Dow Theory can no longer be considered all powerful and always correct.

To most investors, the value of the Dow Theory is that it represents a sort of "think for yourself" method which will pay worthwhile dividends for those who devote time and effort to gain a sound understanding of the principles involved. Whether or not you agree with its conclusions, it is a strong force on Wall Street. When enough people believe a particular theory, their own actions will make the theory come true—partially, anyway.

London Stock Market Index

This is a rather reliable indicator of what is likely to happen in the U.S. market in the following two weeks to two months. It is the London *Financial Times* Index, sort of a British Dow Jones Industrial Average. Its closing price, for the previous day, is published in the financial pages Tuesday through Saturday.

There are, of course, aberrations due to local, usually temporary, situations, but, overall, this Index has a winning record of forecasting. It reflects worldwide conditions which, often, affect the U.S. soon. Many analysts use the London Index to improve timing: to buy when it moves up; to sell when it declines. When they use charts with channels and trendlines, the signals are clear. As London is five hours ahead of New York, the early riser can benefit the most.

Volume and Velocity

Joseph E. Granville, still a skillful technician despite a couple of recent strikeouts, is convinced that volume is always a key indicator. He has developed a special system based on cumulative net volume which he calls On-Balance Volume.

In his calculations, every time the stock under study closes at higher prices, Granville adds the daily trading volume to the cumulative total. When the stock closes lower, he subtracts the daily trading volume from the running total. When there's no price change, no volume is recorded.

His reasoning: When volume rises with price, smart money is buying; soon others will follow and there will be a strong upmove.

Granville also relies on *Velocity:* the cumulative volume as a percentage of corporate capitalization. This measures turnover and thus demand. If a stock has 10 million shares, and records cumulative volume of 10 million shares, the velocity is 100%.

Says Granville, "Every time the stock turns over its entire capitalization in a relatively short period of time, it's like a giant spring getting tighter and tighter. When the velocity approaches 100%, the spring will snap and the price will break out. If the stock is in an uptrend, there will be a sharp advance."

Granville is a master showman and, with complete self-confidence, does not hesitate to make strong recommendations, usually to *sell* (or sell short) or to *buy* with equal enthusiasm. Usually, his "advice" demands fast action so is better for traders than fundamentalists. One thing is sure: this guru may not always be right but he can be exciting!

Buying-Power Indicators

Since T.A. is designed principally to measure the flow of money into and out of the market, those with special knowledge or interest place considerable importance on the quantity and quality of trading as an indicator.

Market strength is shown by:
• Rising volume in rallies. Investors are eager to buy, so the demand is greater than the supply, and prices go up.
• Shrinking volume on market declines. Investors are reluctant to sell.

Market weakness is indicated by:
• Rising volume on a market decline. Investors are getting nervous and fear still lower prices.
• Declining volume on market rallies. Investors have little faith in the higher prices.

With this technical approach, volume is the key indicator: it rises on rallies when the trend is up, and rises on reactions when the trend is down.

Note: Volume trends are apt to reverse before price trends. Shrinking volume almost always shows up before the top of a bull market and before the bottom of a bear market.

Full information on daily upside and downside volume on both the NYSE and AMEX is provided by Quotron, Financial Information Service and *Barron's*.

Most Active Stocks

This table is usually found at the top of the daily report of the stock market. In major financial publications the tables cover the NYSE, AMEX and OTC. Use these as base points to discover popular and unpopular groups and, occasionally, companies.

What you should look for is **repetition**: the same corporations or groups listed several times over two or three weeks. This indicates that something is happening. Major investors are on the move, so watch the trend. If the stock prices of one group keep moving up, find out why and get ready to buy IF other factors are favorable. Vice versa with a decline.

Forget about big name corporations: Exxon, GM, IBM, etc. These giants have so many shares outstanding that they are almost always among the Most Actives. Keep an eye out for:

Newcomers, especially small/medium size corporations. When the same name pops up, major shareholders are worried (price drop) or optimistic (price rise). Since volume requires substantial resources, the buyers must be big

MOST ACTIVE STOCKS ON NYSE

STOCK	OPEN	HIGH	LOW	CLOSE	CHG.	VOLUME
GulfWest	24	25 5/8	29 3/4	29 3/4	+1 1/2	3,484,000
Exxon	30	30	29 3/4	29 3/4	+ 1/2	1,689,500
Goodyear	30 3/8	31 3/8	30 3/8	31 3/8	+1 1/4	1,399,800
A. T. & T.	69	69 3/8	68 1/4	68 3/8	− 1/8	1,173,200
IBM	101 1/8	101 1/4	100	100 3/8	− 1/2	1,052,100
Inco, Ltd.	13 3/4	14	13 1/4	14	+ 1/2	977,600
Stan.Oil(Cal.)	37 1/4	37 1/2	36 1/2	36 3/4	+ 3/8	913,400
Sears Roeb.	31 5/8	31 3/4	31 1/8	31 3/8	+ 3/8	791,300
Mer. Lynch	75 3/4	76 1/2	74 3/4	76 1/8	+2 7/8	782,600
SuperOil	33 3/4	33 7/8	32 3/4	33 1/4	− 1/8	755,500
Sterling Drug	25 1/8	25 5/8	24 7/8	25 3/8	+ 3/4	723,700
Gr.West Finan.	21 3/4	22 7/8	21 3/4	22 7/8	+2 1/4	712,500
Dow Chem.	32	32	31 1/8	31 1/4	. . . . .	671,800
Phila. Elect.	18	18	17 3/4	17 3/4	− 1/8	661,800
Mesa Offshore	2 1/8	2 1/8	2	2 1/8	+ 1/8	660,800

SOURCE: New York Stock Exchange

money organizations that have set a course. Once they have provided the blocking, take the ball and move up the field to quick gains.

Companies in the same industry. Stocks tend to move as a group. Activities in retailers such as Sears and K-Mart *could* signal interest in this field. But wait for confirmation.

Technical services provide quick summaries of the most-active stocks. The one prepared every other week by *Indicator Digest* shows the trend in terms of *up* stocks and *down* stocks. It can be easily plotted: on a daily basis, set down the net difference between the number of stocks *up* and the number *down*. If 9 are up, 5 down and 1 unchanged, the net is +4. Total the results for the last 30 market days, then divide by 30. On the 31st day, remove the oldest data, add the newest. Record the results on your chart. According to *ID*, the time to *buy* is when the indicator is +3 or higher; to *sell* when the indicator falls below −3. Readings in between are neutral.

Advances/Declines (A/D)

These are published, in various groupings, in the financial press, usually on a weekly basis. They are an excellent guide to the trend of the overall market and, occasionally, to special groups or even stocks. The best way to utilize the data is by a chart(s). These are plotted to show the cumulative total of the difference between advances and declines on the NYSE, or for more speculative holdings, on the AMEX. The total can cover one week, 21 days or whatever period you choose.

The table shows a fairly stable week after a sharply down Monday. Tuesday showed a slight edge for ups but this was reversed on Wednesday, widened a bit on Thursday and even more on Friday. But the pattern was fairly uniform . . . on the down side. Still, on the last trading day, the number of advances rose substantially so might be signaling a brighter week ahead.

NYSE: ADVANCES/DECLINES; HIGHS/LOWS

	MON.	TUES.	WED.	THURS.	FRI.
Issues Traded	1,971	1,985	1,988	1,976	1,937
Advances	545	840	753	672	865
Declines	1,016	730	865	911	693
Unchanged	410	415	370	393	379
New Highs	76	83	120	92	126
New Lows	5	7	9	9	7
Sales (000 shares)	72,250	72,811	97,583	85,259	87,478

SOURCE: Barron's

Many analysts use a weekly chart to plot a moving average (MA). Thus, with the example, the net change would be −540: 3,675 advances and 4,215 declines. To make plotting easy, add this to an arbitrary base, say 10,000, to get an accumulated A/D of 9,560. The following week, there was a net advance of 712, so that week's total is 10,272, etc. If you are charting a 20-week MA, divide the cumulative figure by 20. When you add week 21, drop week 1. The chart will give you a visual review of what's

happened in the market in terms of optimism and pessimism.

To make comparisons with price-based averages, plot the A/Ds against the DJIA to spot significant differences in trends. Near market peaks, the A/D line will almost invariably top out and start declining well before the popular blue chip averages. This is a signal that all is not well with the overall market because investors are, generally, becoming wary or even pessimistic.

At market bottoms, the A/D line is not always so far advanced and, usually, will precede an upturn only by a short period. Still, A/Ds can be an excellent confirming indicator.

New Highs and Lows

The table (which reflects the data available in the press) also lists new highs and new lows which, in broad terms, indicates hope or despair.

Note that, while the overall market was gloomy, there were a significant, and, generally, increasing number of new highs and only a handful of new lows. These figures are not quite as useful as they seem because they record many of the same stocks day after day: "A trend in motion . . ."

Again, these figures are most effective when converted to a chart and compared to a standard average. As long as the high-low indicators stay more or less in step with the DJIA or S&P 500, they are just a handy confirmation. But when the high–low line starts to dip while the averages move up, WATCH OUT: internal market conditions are deteriorating.

Conversely, an upturn in the high-low line while the DJIA is still declining probably indicates impending market strength.

This index exposes the underlying strength or weakness of the market, which is too often too easily masked by the action of the DJIA. In an aging bull market, the DJIA may continue to rise, deceptively showing strength in a mere handful of stocks while most stocks are too far below their highs for the year to make new ones. Thus, a small total of new highs at such times is one of the most significant manifestations of internal market deterioration. The reverse is the telltale manner in which the total of new lows appears in bear markets.

Broad-Based Indicators

As defined at the end of this book, the major indices—the Dow Jones Averages, Standard & Poor's Indexes and New York Stock Exchange Composite Index—are either limited or weighted, so do not reflect what's really happening. The two most accurate indicators are those of *Value Line* and *Indicator Digest*, which report the price movements of all stocks traded on the Big Board.

One of the most accurate and easiest to follow is the **Indicator Digest Composite Index.** The core is the Indicator Digest Average (IDA) that is compiled so that each NYSE stock has the same weight (unlike the DJIA and S&P averages). Thus, the percentage changes are equal, without distortion due to the number of shares outstanding or the market price.

By and large, the IDA has moved more or less with the standard averages but note its greater stability—few of the big ups and downs of the Dow and a much more positive trend. This is a good guide for those whose emotions move to extremes.

The best part is at the bottom: the Composite Index with lines indicating points of unfavorable and favorable prospects. In most cases, this bottom line signaled future market activity: more as to the trend/direction than as to the height (or depth) or duration of the activity. At this writing, the chart is well into favorable-for-the-future territory.

But be cautious and note how things can change: in 1980 from a dismal 10 early in the year to an ebullient 80 in midsummer and then down again: to about 20.

Moving Average Lines

A moving average (MA) is just what the name suggests: an average that moves with the unit of time covered. A 30-week MA of the DJIA shows the average closing price of the 30 stocks for the 30 most recent Fridays. Each week, the total changes because of the addition of the latest Friday's closing figure and the subtraction of the Friday closing figure for 30 weeks ago. Then the new total is divided by 30 to get the MA.

Technicians use different time frames: 200 days, 30 weeks (as on the IDA chart), 39 weeks (see Legend Chart Short-Term). In most cases, they compared the MA to a regular average such as the DJIA. Here's how an MA can serve as a trend indicator:

1. As long as the DJIA is *above* its MA line, the outlook is bullish.

2. As long as the DJIA is *below* its MA, the outlook is bearish.

3. A confirmed downward penetration of the MA is a *sell* signal.

4. A confirmed upward penetration of the MA is a *buy* signal.

But always beware of false penetrations and delay purchases or sales until a substantial penetration (2% to 3%),

INDICATOR DIGEST COMPOSITE INDEX

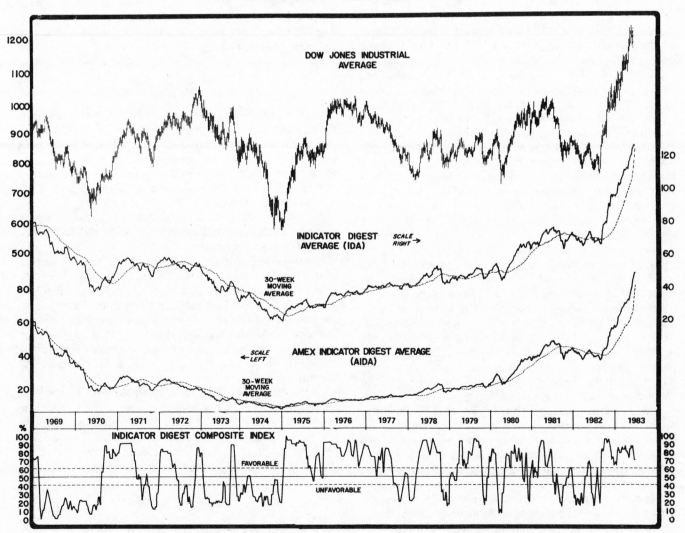

upward or downward, has been confirmed within a couple of weeks.

More cautious technicians look for comparable action with a second MA line, which is frequently plotted for a 10-week period.

Professional money managers, more concerned with long-term performance for pension-fund investments, believe that the most reliable and effective way to measure their results is by a three-year moving average. This period is long enough to compensate for stock-market fluctuations and to enable clients to judge the true capability of the investment adviser.

MAs are vulnerable to swift market declines, especially from market tops. By the time you get the signal, you may have lost a bundle because prices tend to fall twice as fast as they rise.

If you enjoy charting, develop a ratio of the stocks selling above their 30-week MA. When the ratio is over 50% and trending upward, the outlook is bullish. When it drops below 50% and/or is trending down, there's trouble ahead. Like many technical indicators, this is a hybrid: part price index and part a breadth indicator.

Psychological Attitudes

Keeping in mind that "the stock market is rooted 15% in economics and 85% in psychology," here's how to check how investors view the future:

***Barron's* Confidence Index** (*BCI*). This is published weekly in the financial news magazine. It shows the ratio of the yield on 10 highest-grade bonds to the yield on the broad Dow Jones 40-bond average. The ratio varies from the middle 80s (bearish) to the middle 90s (bullish).

The theory is that the trend of "smart money" is usually revealed in the bond market before it shows up in the stock market. Thus, *Barron's* Confidence Index will be *high* when shrewd investors are confident and buy more lower-grade bonds, thus reducing low-grade bond yields: *low* when they are worried and stick to high-grade bonds, thus cutting high-grade yields.

Many market technicians use the BCI as a *primary* indicator. If you see that it just keeps going back and forth aimlessly for many weeks, you can probably expect the same type of action from the overall stock market.

Overbought-Oversold Index (OOI). This is a handy measure of the short-term trend's anticipated duration. Minor upswings or downturns have limited lives. As they peter out, experienced traders say the market is "overbought" or "oversold" and, presumably, ready for a near-term reversal. But remember, the definitions are set by the technician and are not always uniform.

Indicator Digest constructs its OOI with a 10-day accumulation of net advances and/or net declines. On the average, a 10-day total of 1500 signals overbought conditions when on the "plus" side and an oversold condition when on the "minus" side. But there can be adjustments to the activity of the overall market.

Glamour Average (another *Indicator Digest* special). This shows what is happening with the institutional favorites, usually trading at high multiples because of their presumed growth potential and current popularity (in a bull market). By and large, this is a better indicator for speculators than investors.

Speculation Index. This is the ratio of the AMEX/NYSE volume. When trading in AMEX (generally more speculative) stocks moves up faster than does that of the NYSE (quality) issues, speculation is growing. It's time for traders to move in and for investors to be cautious.

233 Key Stocks. This indicator is one of the most useful tools because it measures the market movers from the solid, old-time blue chips to the proven growth favorites. Since these generate a large proportion of the market's capitalization and volume, no major market move would be worth its salt without their support. The batting average of this index has been high.

When the five-week moving average of this stock group rises to over 60%, the outlook is promising; over 70%, look for a durable advance.

Odd-Lot Index. This shows how little investors view the market because it concentrates on trades of less than 100 shares. Presumably the small investor is "uninformed" (a somewhat debatable assumption) and so tends to follow established patterns: selling as the market rises; jumping in to pick up bargains when it declines. The signal comes when the odd-lotter deviates from this "normal" behavior.

When the little man distrusts a rally, after a long bear market, he gives a bullish signal. His initial selling is normal but when this continues, it's abnormal and a signal, to the pros, to start buying.

Other Guides

An easy-to-follow (and usually well-publicized) indicator is the amount of cash held by mutual funds. When their cash reserves mount for a period of time, less money is being invested so that demand lessens and stock prices tend to weaken. As a rule, when the cash reserves rise above 9.5% of total fund assets, this is a bullish indicator in that major buying usually starts soon.

Conversely, when the level of cash falls to the 5% range, buying will dwindle and stock prices will tend to decline, probably into a bear market.

Short-Term Guide (SGA) is one of the most respected charts to follow relatively short-term action. The base line reflects the price swings of hundreds of stocks divided into 26 industry groups. Each group is rated from +2 to −2 on the basis of the relationship of the group's average price to a five-week moving average (MA). As long as the SGA stays ahead of the MA, things are favorable. For further reference, the Indicator Digest Average is shown at the bottom.

At this time, the SGA is at a favorable +43 versus +42 on the MA. "That's not robust but we think the lagging action of SGA reflects the market's somewhat selective character rather than any major deterioration . . . be selective and cautious . . . but real evidence is still lacking for the major correction so many people are expecting."

Rely on Consensus

Until you are very experienced, never rely on one technical indicator (and even then, buy a rabbit's foot). Only rarely

SHORT-TERM TRADING GUIDE (SGA)

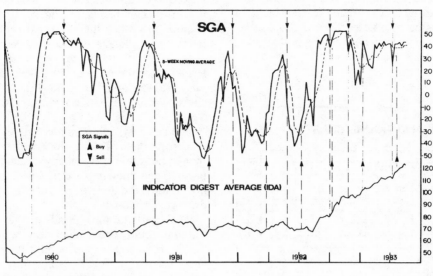

SOURCE: Indicator Digest

can a single chart, ratio, average or index be 100% accurate. There can be false signals or no signals at all (that you can discern). When an indicator breaks its pattern, look for confirmation from at least two other guidelines, preferably those involving other information. Then, wait a bit: at least two days in an ebullient market, a week in a more normal one. This should be long enough for the original indicator to continue its signal and to be joined elsewhere.

There will be times, especially when trading, when such delays will reduce or eliminate profits. But such cases are rare except in very erratic markets with volatile stocks. Significant changes, for a stock, an industry group or the overall market, seldom come rapidly and, in most cases, are clearly forecast by technical indicators. All you have to do is heed the facts, not your emotions.

This same consensus counsel applies to advisory services. If you can afford to do so, subscribe to more than one service. If you select just one, look for a publication that provides a series of indicators. And, as explained later, pay attention to the statistics, not the opinions. *The majority of commentaries are wrong more often than they are right.*

Charts: To Maximize Profits, Minimize Losses

Most chart readers believe that "one picture is worth a thousand words." They are convinced that charts, when properly prepared and interpreted, reveal the technical factors, and, thus, clues to future action more clearly than another means. They do convey the "net current verdict of the market place" but this reveals the past and, only indirectly, the future.

When combined with statistical data, charts can become an important factor in the analysis of stock market action.

Most investors and ALL speculators should understand and be able to use charts.

Charts are a graphic ticker tape. They measure the flow of money into and out of the stock market, industry or specific stock. They spotlight the highs and lows, how volume rises and falls on an advance or decline and, in summary form, show the long-term patterns of the market and individual stocks. They are an easy way to follow "smart money" which, usually, has inside information. If better earnings are imminent, these investors buy aggressively and cause a clear uptrend in the chart formation. If future profits will be flat or lower, these professionals will slow or cease buying and the chart lines will drop.

Charting is simple; interpretation can be complex. Even the strongest advocates of T.A. disagree as to the meaning of various formations but they all start with two premises: (1) What happened before will be repeated again; (2) a trend should be assumed to continue in effect until such time as the reversal has been definitely signaled; (3) a chart pattern that varies from a norm (be it a past configuration or an average) indicates something unusual is happening.

Broadly speaking, charts are most valuable to provide corroboration. Once you have more or less made up your mind to buy, sell or hold a stock, check the charts. But be careful. Charts are like fire or electricity. They are brilliant tools if intelligently controlled or handled. But they can also be dangerous.

Keeping in mind that charts are not infallible, use them to:

1. Help determine when to buy and when to sell by indicating probable levels of support and supply, and by signaling trend reversals.

2. Call attention, by unusual volume or price behavior, to something happening in an individual company that can be profitable to investors.

3. Help determine the current trend: up, down, or sideways, and whether the trend is accelerating or slowing.

4. Provide a quick history of a stock and show whether buying should be considered on a rally or a decline.

5. Offer a sound means for confirming or rejecting a buy or sell decision that is based on other information.

Remember: charts are history. By studying past action, it is often possible to make a reasonably valid prediction of the immediate future.

POINT AND FIGURE CHART

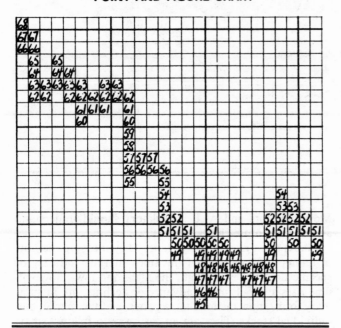

Widely Used Types of Charts

The most commonly used types of charts are Point and Figure (P&F) and bar charts. For best results, they should be constructed on a daily or weekly basis, but, with experience, you may want to supplement these with those covering months or even years. Printed charts are available for almost every purpose (see Bibliography).

If you have time, charting can be fun and highly educational. All you need is a pad of graph paper: plain squares for P&F charts; logarithmic or standard paper for bar charts.

P&F charts are one-dimensional graphics. They show only price changes in relation to previous price changes. There are no indications of time or volume. The key factor is the change in price direction.

Some professionals think that P&F charts are oversimplified and consider them useful only as short-term guides and as a quick way to choose between two or three selections.

In making a P&F chart, the stock price is posted in a square: one above or below another, depending on the upward or downward movement of the price. As long as the price continues in the same direction, the same column is used. When the price shifts direction, the chartist moves to the next column.

In the chart here, the stock fell in a downward sequence from 68 to 67 to 66. Then it rose to 67 so the chartist moved to column 2. The next moves were down to 62, up to 63 (new column) and so on. Most chartists start the new column only when there is a distinct change, typically one point, but for longer projections, two or three points.

Note how a pattern is formed with various resistance levels where the price of the stock stayed within a narrow range (57–56 and, later, 48–47). The chart signals each shift from such a base: down from 56 to 51; up from 47 to 52.

The best way for an amateur to learn about P&F charts is to copy them. Take a stock which has been plotted for many years and slowly recopy its action on a piece of graph paper. Then draw in the trendlines: the uptrendline on the high points, the downtrendline along the low points. Then draw your channels.

P&F charts do have disadvantages: they do not portray intraday action or consider volume. The information on the financial pages reports only the high (62), low (59¼) and close (61½). This does not show that the stock might have moved up and down from 60 to 62 several times during the day.

Despite the omission of volume on P&F charts, many technical analysts feel that volume should always be checked once there is a confirmed trend on the chart. Usually, rising volume on upside movements and dwindling sales on the downside indicate that the stock has ample investor support. It's always wise to be on the same side as volume.

Bar charts are described in greater detail later. The example here is simplified to show how these graphics record changes in relation to time. The horizontal axis represents time—in a day, week or month; the vertical coordinates refer to price. To follow volume on the same chart, add a series of vertical lines along the bottom. The higher the line, the greater the volume. On printed charts, adjustments are made so that everything fits into a convenient space.

In plotting a bar chart, enter a dot to mark the highest price at which the stock was traded that day; then another dot to record the low. Draw the vertical line between the

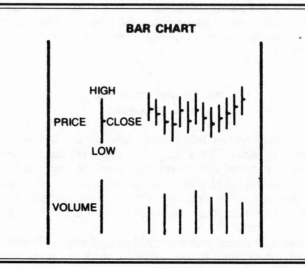

BAR CHART

dots to depict the price range and add a short, horizontal nub to mark the closing price. After a few entries, a pattern will begin to emerge.

Unusual Charts

Almost every chartist has his favorite configurations. They include such descriptive titles as: the rounding bottom, the flag, the pennant, the tombstone top, the Prussian helmet formation, the megaphone top, the latice formation, etc. One of the most popular formations is *Head and Shoulders* (H&S).

Oversimplified, the Head and Shoulders chart portrays three successive rallies and reactions, with the second reaching a higher point than either of the others. The failure of the third rally to equal the second peak is a warning that a major uptrend may have come to an end. Conversely, a bottom H&S, formed upside down, after a declining trend, suggests that an upturn lies ahead.

Left shoulder. This forms when an upturn of some duration, after hitting a climax, starts to fall. The volume of trading should increase with the rally and contract with the reaction. *Reason:* people who bought the stock on the uptrend start to take profits. When the technical reaction takes place, people who were slow to buy on the first rally start buying on the technical reaction.

HEAD AND SHOULDERS CHART

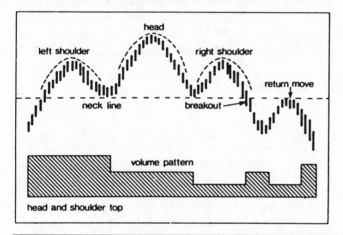

Head. This is a second rally which carries the stock to new highs and is followed by a reaction that erases just about all the gain. Volume is high on the rally, yet lower than when forming the left shoulder. *Reason:* investors who missed both the earlier actions start buying and force new highs.

This is followed by another drop as those who hesitated earlier see the second reaction and start acquiring the stock as it is sold by early buyers.

Right shoulder. The third rally fails to reach the height of the head before the reaction. This is a sign of weakness. Watch the volume. If it contracts on a rally, it's likely that the price structure has weakened. If it increases, beware of a false signal.

Breakout. This occurs when the stock price falls below the previous lows. At this point, most of the recent buyers have sold out—many of them at a loss.

No H&S should be regarded as complete until the price breaks out below a line drawn tangent with the lows on the left and right shoulders. This is called the neckline.

Reading Charts Is an Art

More than almost any other area of T.A., chart reading is an art and a skill rather than a solid body of objective, scientific information. It is an aid to stock analysis, not an end. It is especially valuable to speculators to catch short-term movements and to investors to reveal an overview of the market action of a particular stock or, when dealing with industry groups, to make comparisons.

Charts are not surefire systems for beating the market but they are one of the quickest and clearest ways to determine and follow trends. But all charts are after the fact. They may not work at precisely the times they are needed most—when the market is putting the finishing touches to a major top or bottom. At most depths, the chart pattern will be bearish and point to a much lower level of prices. At market tops, it's the reverse.

The best combination, for maximum profits and minimum losses, is fundamental analysis supplemented by graphic technical analysis. Charts report what volume and price changes occur. Proper interpretation can predict the direction and intensity for change because every purchase of every listed stock shows up on the chart.

Watch the bottom of the chart as well as the progress lines. This shows volume, and *volume precedes price.* A strong inflow of capital eventually pushes up the price of the stock; an outflow of dollars must result in a decline. To the charted results, it makes no difference who is doing the buying or selling.

Interpreting Charts

These legend charts are typical of those available from technical services. They provide valuable tools to improve timing of purchases and sales. The first figure is used for the long-term, 12-year charts; the second for 21-month movements. By using both, you get a better idea of the character and probable performance of the stock.

Top center: Information on the corporation: capitalization, dollars of preferred stocks, number of common stocks, number of common stocks and book value per share.

Left side: Per share earnings and dividends scaled from 0 to $5.50.

Monthly ranges: solid vertical bars showing the highest and lowest points of each month's transactions. Crossbars indicate the closing price.

Earnings: On a per share 12-month-ended basis as shown by the solid black line. Dots indicate whether the company issues quarterly, semiannual or annual earnings reports.

Dividends: Showing the annual rate of interim dividend payments. The small circles mark the month in which the

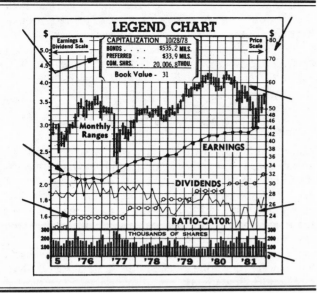

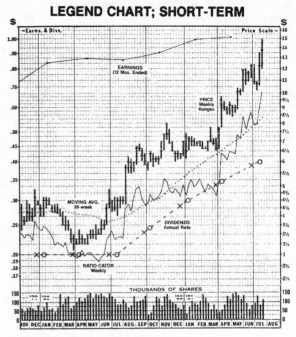

SOURCE: Securities Research Company

dividend payments are made. Extra or irregular payments are shown in typed figures.

Ratio-cator: This is a guideline used by this service. The plottings are obtained by dividing the closing price of the stock by the closing price of the DJIA on the same day. The resulting percentage is multiplied by a factor of 4.5 to bring the line closer to the price bars and is read from the right-hand scale. The plotting indicates whether the stock has kept pace, outperformed or lagged behind the general market.

Price scale (right side): This is equal to 15 times the earnings and dividends scale at the left, so when the Price Range bars and the Earnings line coincide, it shows the price is 15 times earnings. When the price is above the earnings line, the ratio of price to earnings is greater; when below, less.

Volume (bottom): the number of shares traded each month on an arithmetic scale. Watch when there are extremes: high volume with rising prices; low volume with falling values. Volume comes before price.

This provides similar information for 21 months:

Earnings line: per share profits on a 12-month-ended basis, separated by the dots. Read from left-hand scale. Earnings off the range of the chart and deficits are shown by typed notations.

Dividend line: from left, on annual rate basis. Extras and special payments are typed in. X denotes exdividend date; O shows dividend payment date.

Ratio-cator Line: shows the relative performance, obtained by dividing the closing price of the stock by the closing price of the DJIA on the same day. The result is multiplied by a factor of 7.0 to bring the line closer to the price bars. Read from right-hand scale. The plotting (solid line) indicates whether stock has kept pace, outperformed, or lagged the general market.

39-Week Moving Average. Each dot represents the average of the closing prices of the 39 most recent weeks. With the line chart, this can be a useful tool to determine trends and when to buy or sell.

Volume (bottom): vertical bars on arithmetic scale in thousands.

Trendlines

To repeat the key to technical analysis: *A trend should be assumed to continue in effect until the time its reversal has been definitely signaled.* To discern this trend, the chartist draws lines connecting the lowest points of the stock move when there's an upmove (A); its higher points when there's a decline. This trendline is reliable about 80% of the time because its predicts the immediate action of the stock or market. The shrewd trader/investor rides with the trend: buying when there's a confirmed upmove; considering selling when there's a definite downswing. There are, of course, other factors but once a trendline is formed, the stock tends to move along that line. There may be interim bounces and dips but most stocks hold to that pattern until there is a clear change.

By spotting the trend, you can get an edge in determining your tactics. By keeping your charts up to date, you can project where and, to a degree, how soon/late the market/industry/group/stock goes.

Trendlines establish bases. The uptrendline becomes a support level below which an upmoving stock is not likely to fall. The downtrendline marks a resistance level above which the stock is not likely to rise.

Before you invest—or speculate—in any stocks, check the chart and draw trendlines. Buy when the trend is up; hold or do not buy when it is moving down. The best profits always come when you buy an UP stock in an UP industry in an UP market—clearly evident with trendlines on charts. And, of course, when you sell short, it's the opposite.

A more sophisticated form of trendlines is the channel where the line is drawn parallel to the basic trendline, up or down: between A[1] and B on the short-term Ralston Purina chart in May–June 1982. These are most valuable for

SHORT-TERM CHART
RALSTON PURINA CO. (RAL)

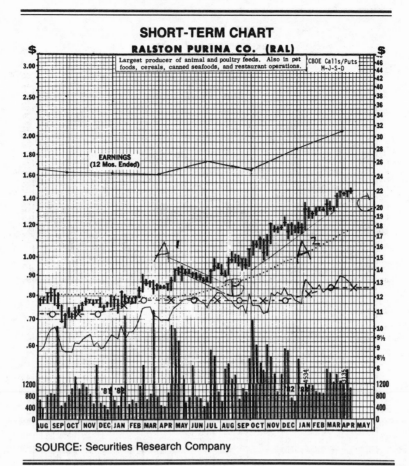

Largest producer of animal and poultry feeds. Also in pet foods, cereals, canned seafoods, and restaurant operations.

CBOE Calls/Puts M–J–S–D

EARNINGS (12 Mos. Ended)

SOURCE: Securities Research Company

trading. The speculator moves in and out quickly for a quick profit: buying when the price hits the bottom of the channel and selling, or selling short when it bounces back from the top of the channel. And, of course, when there's a break through the line, as in July 1982, the trader loads up. For amateurs, channels are more educational than profitable. The commissions eat up most of the gains. But professionals rely on them as points of action.

Using Charts

Once you have selected a quality stock, take a look at both the short- and long-term charts. There are a number of services but the examples are from Securities Research Company: for Ralston Purina Co. (RAL): 20 months and 12 years. Both are valuable.

RAL, the food, feed, and agricultural products firm, is a quality corporation, rated ABB7 by Wright Investors' and A+ by Standard & Poor's. Its stock has been a worthwhile

Patterns

There's not space to explain the importance of patterns to the technician. Briefly, he predicates that what has happened before, with a stock, will happen again . . . perhaps not exactly the same but close enough to provide extra profits.

investment as well as an excellent trading vehicle. The long-term chart shows a general up-trend; the short-term one indicates the short, rapid moves that delight speculators.

Since you are concerned with the immediate future, start with the short-term chart. Note that the stock dawdled around 12 in late 1981, moved up slowly and erratically until October when, with huge volume, the price broke 15.

One of the most reliable patterns is the 50% rule: that when a stock moves up significantly, there is likely to be a technical reaction that will lose a good share of the move: i.e., when a volatile stock jumps from 30 to 50 without serious interruption, the chances are good that it will back off to 40 (50% of the original advance).

What happens is that traders move in: taking profits with the rise, picking up bargains at the dip. Usually, they utilize channels.

The rule applies to downswings, too, but, usually not to the same degree or with as much probability. It's easy for temporary enthusiasm to push up a stock price too high but when a decline comes from a more or less stable level, there will usually be problems in the company or its industry.

Another pattern is the length of the accumulation period. Usually, the longer the stock holds within a narrow range, the greater the price rise when it comes. But the best guide, to technicians, is similar action in the past. With some stocks, the takeoff comes almost automatically . . . after 12–15 months, for example, up she goes . . . assuming the company keeps making money.

About this time, the investor drew a trendline (A²), con-

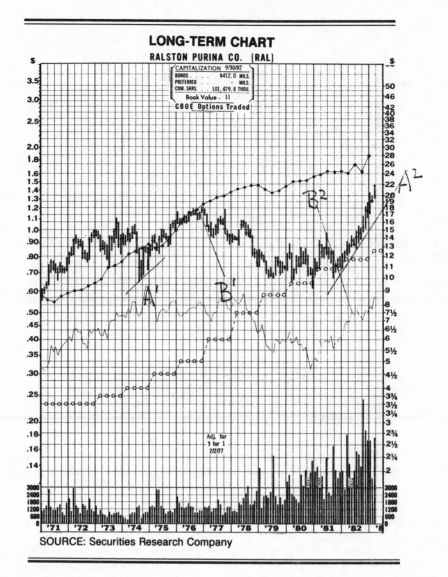

LONG-TERM CHART
RALSTON PURINA CO. (RAL)

CAPITALIZATION 9/30/82
BONDS . . . . $412.0 MILS.
PREFERRED . . - MILS.
COM. SHRS. . . 101,479.8 THOU.
Book Value - 11
CBOE Options Traded

Adj. for
3 for 1
2/2/77

SOURCE: Securities Research Company

necting the lows of 14–15. A projection (remember this was late 1982), the trendline pointed to a price potential of at least 18. By updating these data in the spring of 1983, the goal was close to 24. Those who bought RAL around 12 could expect to double their money—plus modest dividends.

If you were the nervous type, you might consider selling in the spring of 1982 when the trend reversed (Channel B) and the stock price fell from 14½ to 13. But this was such a modest decline, and the volume so small, that this dip could not be considered a true reversal of the uptrend.

On the other hand, the long-term chart indicated possible problems when the price of RAL reached 18 . . . in late 1982. Looking back, you see that 18 was the highest point reached over the 12-year period, in late 1976. Some investors who bought at that peak will want to bail out to break even. If these sales are substantial and there are not enough eager buyers, the extra supply will force down the price of the stock.

But the chart shows that, at around 18, the volume soared because institutional investors felt that the stock

would break through its old high and move to reach peaks . . . which RAL did.

As shown by lines B^1 and B^2, the trend was not always favorable and there were times when the stock should have been sold. The trend was reversed and the chart gave the signal.

Obviously, no stock moves in a vacuum. Its action is influenced by the overall market and corporate performance. RAL plugged along with profits rising 10% to 25% in the early 1970s (stock rose modestly), then ran into trouble in 1979 when its per share earnings fell to $1.24 from $1.45, bounced back to $1.71 in 1982, then plummeted to $1.08 after heavy write-offs.

Note that the stock wavered a bit but held fairly steadily because major investors felt that management bit the bullet and was building for the future.

The upsurge in profits came in the last quarter of 1982—to 74¢ per share vs. 21¢ the previous quarter—and to 63¢ in the first three months of 1983—with predictions of $2.22 per share earnings for the year. That meant that the high of 22 was only 10 times projected profits and that trendline projection to above 24 was realistic.

But with such rapid gains, isn't there danger that the price of the stock will rise too high and will be dumped soon? The chart cannot tell you that but fundamental analysis can give you a clue. If RAL scored a more normal 10% increase in profits in 1984 and 1985, its earnings, according to Wright Investors' Service, would be $2.66 in 1985. With a traditional price/earnings ratio of 12, this would mean a market value of about 31 ... about a 40% rise. This is nothing to be sneezed at but would be less than achieved in the last 18 months.

And a realist will recognize that there could be problems especially since food prices are subject to forces outside management's control. Hold and watch carefully for a confirmed reversal of the uptrend!

Technical analysis, especially charts, can be a valuable aid to timing. Unless you are extremely optimistic and can afford to tie up your money for a while, *never* buy any stock until its chart is pointing up. And *always* check the chart action before you sell. You may think the high has been reached but the chart may disagree and make possible greater gains.

On the other hand, if the chart shows a downtrend, consider selling. If it's a good investment, you can buy the stock back later at a lower price. If it's not, you'll save a lot of money.

Properly utilized, Technical Analysis can be an important adjunct to fundamental investing and, more often than not, it will keep you humble!

For Extra Profits

Watch the last hour of trading on the NYSE. With the net change in the DJIA between 3 and 4 P.M., construct a cumulative average, adding today's figure to yesterday's total.

If the market is +12 points at 3 P.M. and only +6 points at close, that's a disappointing day and not bullish for tomorrow. What happens is that, in that last hour, the specialists try to position themselves for the next day's business and the traders make their moves.

• **Discover the Coppock Curve.** This has been an accurate indicator of the market's emotional state. It applies only to BUYING and has been bullish only 10 times in the last 34 years.

The curve is based on a 10-month weighted MA of the closing DJIA. The calculations are as follows: (1) Determine the percentage change of the Dow Industrials over the past 14 months and then find out what percent this month's close is above or below the final average 14 months ago; (2) calculate the percentage change in the DJIA in the past 11 months; (3) add both of these percentage changes; (4) prepare a 10-month weighted average MA chart of these sums; (5) plot a curve on a chart; (6) when the trend starts up, BUY.

Well, you can't say that Technical Analysis is always simple!

8

How to Read an Annual Report

The single best source of information about any public corporation is its annual report (and, to a limited degree, its quarterly financial statements). In a few minutes, you can learn whether to buy, hold or sell a stock or bond. With a little more study, you can decide whether the security is an investment or a speculation.

When you're investing for income this report will tell you whether the interest or dividends are amply covered by earnings. If you are seeking growth, zero in on the basic investment criteria: profitability, growth and character (which, in a sense, is a synonym for competence of management).

These days, with pressure from the accounting profession and the Securities and Exchange Commission, annual reports are more revealing than ever before. The report of every publicly traded corporation must contain an amazing amount of detailed information presented in comments by management; figures; source of revenues/earnings of major segments; foreign and domestic activities; off-balance sheet financing such as store/plant/equipment leases; sales of tax credits; depreciation and special tax credits; effects of inflation; allocations of expenditures for interest, research and on and on. Almost all the data a conscientious investor needs to know are available in these yearly summaries of corporate activities. But always recognize that management is trying to present the best possible interpretation within legal/accounting limits.

Here's what to look for in all areas:

Trends: in sales, earnings, dividends, accounts receivable and debts.

Information: *from the tables:* corporate financial strength and operating success or failure; *from the text:* explanations of what happened during the year and what management expects in the future.

Positives: new plants, products, personnel and programs.

Negatives: plant closings, sales of subsidiaries, discontinuance of products and future needs for financing.

Do not rely on highlights trumpeted in the president's message or emphasized, with dramatic photos, in the early text. These are designed to be sales pitches rather than factual commentaries.

Always read the report Chinese style: from back to front. Start with the auditor's report. If there are hedging phrases such as "except for" or "subject to," be cautious. These phrases can signal future problems and/or write-offs.

Then, study the footnotes to see if there are any pending situations that could hamper prospects: a major lawsuit; new or proposed legislation that could have an impact on operating costs or marketing practices. Wall Street hates uncertainty and some analysts will shudder when they read some possibilities.

Next, glance at the balance sheet to see whether cash/liquid assets are diminishing and whether accounts receivable/inventories/total debt are rising. This will usually be more of a yellow than a red signal.

Finally, study the financial summary of the past five or 10 years (usually toward the end). This will provide an overall view of corporate performance and set the stage for an analysis of the most recent data.

In the stock market, past is prologue. Few companies achieve dramatic progress or fall on hard times suddenly. In most cases, the changes have been forecast. The corporation with a long, fairly consistent record of profitable growth can be expected to do as well, or better, in the years ahead and thus prove to be a worthwhile holding. The erratic performer is likely to move from high to low profits (or losses). And the faltering company will have signs of deterioration over two or three years.

Reading the Report

When you review the text, you can get an idea of the kind of people who are managing your money, learn what and why they did, or did not, do, and some idea of future prospects. If you save previous annual reports, compare what was predicted and what happened.

Always read the president's message and look for possible danger signals such as:

Unfulfilled promises. If there were failures, there should be logical explanations. Management is not always right in its decisions but, in financial matters, frankness is the base for confidence. If you cannot believe the chief executive officer, do not hold the company's stock.

Double-talk. Clichés are integral parts of business writing but they should not be substitutes for proper explanations. If you find such meaningless phrases as "a year of transition" or "we have identified the problem and are taking corrective steps," start getting ready to unload.

Inadequate information. For competitive reasons, no president can reveal everything but he should not neglect to mention important problems such as a major lawsuit, governmental litigation, delays in operation of a new plant, etc. These subjects are too important for footnotes alone.

Quality/source of earnings. When profits are entirely from operations, they indicate management's skill; when they are partially from bookkeeping, be wary. Even the best of corporations may utilize "special" accounting.

Examples: With inventories, LIFO (Last In, First Out), current sales are matched against the latest costs so that earnings can rise sharply when inventories are reduced and those latest costs get older and thus lower. When oil prices were at a peak, Texaco cut inventories by 16%. The LIFO cushion, built up over several years, was a whopping $454 million and transformed what would have been a drop in net income into a modest gain.

Such "tricks" are one reason why stocks fall or stay flat after annual profits are reported. Analysts are smart enough to discover that earnings are more paper than real.

Another "area of opportunity" is reporting foreign currency transactions. Under recent revisions, it's possible to recast them retroactively—when, of course, they can be more favorable. Xerox altered earnings back four years to $7.08 compared to what would have been $6.67 per share!

More recently, with high interest rates, one of the favorite ploys is to raise the *assumed returns on pension funds.* General Motors boosted its calculations to 7% from 6% a year and added 69¢ a share to its earnings!

Conglomerates take another approach: *equity accounting.* This allows companies to show, as regular earnings, a percentage of the profits of other companies in which they own 20% of the stock. The parent corporation never gets any noncash dividends so cannot use these reported dollars for expansion, etc. But this maneuver sure tidies up the profit picture: Teledyne reported $19.96 per share earning but $3.49 of this was from equity accounting and was 17% of its annual earnings: $72 million on the books but only $18 million in cash dividends.

Projections. Be wary when any chief executive promises "a 25% increase in sales" or "earning of $3.00 per share." Modern business is too competitive and too subject to unexpected pressures for such assurance. Make your own calculations on the basis of past performance and never be as optimistic as your broker.

In much the same way, denigrate overenthusiasm about new products, processes or personnel. Usually it takes at least three years to translate new items into sizeable sales and profits, to get new plants running smoothly and to find out whether the reputation of the new marketing vice president is deserved.

Be skeptical of words and impressed with figures. When you buy and hold any stock, you are (or should be) doing so on the basis of financial facts and logical projections, not on the suavity of the words or appearance of corporate executives. With money, be tough minded.

New Rules

In 1982, the SEC made, or proposed, several changes regarding directors and officers:

• *More disclosure* of company transactions with directors, managers and their families so that shareholders could be aware of possible "self-dealing."

• *Less disclosure* of personal dealings with customers, suppliers and law firms. Under the old rules, if a director sat on the boards of two different companies doing business with each other, he had to disclose this when the transactions involved more than 1% of corporate revenues of either corporation. Now, there's no need for disclosure unless the director is also an officer of one of the companies or owns 10% of the stock and the companies are doing business in excess of 5% of their separate revenues.

• *Less reporting* of noncash compensation such as stock options, "golden parachutes" (compensation agreements that "protect" officers after a takeover) and other special benefits: i.e., an executive using a company plane does not have to report this if the cost is under $10,000 a year or less than 10% of his salary and cash bonuses.

Follow Up

Once you have read several annual reports and made notes, take advantage of what you have learned, make your own calculations and then decide whether to sell or hold the shares you own or buy more. If you feel uncomfortable in any area, check with your broker and get comments/analyses from his firm's research department. If this information doesn't calm your fears, sell unless there are very strong reasons for optimism. There are always other opportunities that can be more rewarding and make you, and your spouse, sleep better.

In finding those new stocks, ask your broker for recommendations (if you do not already have a "future" list). When you have narrowed your list to three, or possibly five, companies, get their annual reports (by writing to the Secretary of the corporation) and start your homework over again. This should be easy because you will know what to look for, and, presumably, the professionals have done some checking on their own.

Finally, review your final choices against the stocks you continue to hold. You may prefer to add to your present portfolio as long as you maintain a balance.

Do not become too enthusiastic about any new holdings until management has proven itself by continuing to boost sales and earnings. The successful investor relies on information and the best single source is the annual report ... with checking by means of the quarterly statements. If your original review turns up any questionable areas, mark that item with a red pencil and take a look at those pages every six months or so. These days even the best of companies can run into trouble in a short time but, usually, such

---

What They Say May Not Be What They Mean

As an old PR man, I can testify to the techniques used in writing annual reports: to phrase comments in terms that tend to divert the reader's attention away from problems:

They Say: "The year was a difficult and challenging one."

They Mean: "We blew it. Sales and profits were down but expenses (and, of course executive salaries) were up."

They Say: "Your management team worked hard to preserve the company's strong financial position."

They Mean: "We were lucky and did not have to float new debt."

They Say: "Management has identified the problems and is taking constructive steps to assure their elimination."

They Mean: "We have tried half a dozen solutions without success. Now, we'll let things take their natural course ... and pray."

They Say: "Your company is proud of the dedicated service and talent of its employees."

They Mean: "Despite the loss of several key executives and a score of able middle managers, the company continues to pay marginal salaries and most workers should be happy to still have a job."

INFLATION-ADJUSTED ACCOUNTING: GREAT WESTERN FINANCIAL

($000 omitted, except per share)	1982	1981	1980	1979	1978
Income					
—Historical	$1,387,146	$1,381,949	$1,187,093	$1,045,112	$849,623
—Adjusted for inflation	937,239	991,673	939,868	939,347	849,623
Net earnings (loss)					
—Historical	(76,458)	(30,828)	42,781	110,083	107,584
—Adjusted for inflation	(55,117)	(24,912)	30,983	96,978	105,998
Earnings (loss) per share					
—Historical	(2.75)	(1.11)	1.55	4.01	3.94
—Adjusted for inflation	(1.99)	(.90)	1.12	3.54	3.88
Cash dividends per share					
—Historical	.52	.88	.88	.84	.67
—Adjusted for inflation	.35	.63	.70	.75	.67
Stockholders' equity at year-end					
—Historical	642,713	731,616	781,148	760,260	671,525
—Adjusted for inflation	519,768	597,456	678,544	722,561	709,723
Loss in general purchasing power on net monetary items	(14,235)	(37,062)	(56,388)	(63,254)	(40,031)
Market value per share at year-end					
—Historical	27.38	14.50	18.63	22.00	17.75
—Adjusted for inflation	18.50	10.41	14.75	19.77	17.75
Average Consumer Price Index (U.S. Department of Labor, Bureau of Labor Statistics: 1967 = 100)	289.2	272.3	246.8	217.4	195.4
Index of general purchasing power: 1978 = 100	67.6	71.8	79.2	89.9	100.0

situations will be forecast, or, at least, hinted at in the annual report.

Inflation Accounting

A couple of years ago, the big thrust in corporate accounting was to show the impact of inflation in annual reports. The concept was to list standard, historical data and then adjust the figures—for income, earnings, dividends, equity, etc.—for inflation. This new approach was widely hailed as an aid to interpreting what was actually happening within the corporate structure: whether profits were increased or decreased because of the erosion of purchasing power.

In most cases, the comparisons were negative: what appeared to be a profit of $2.75 per share (as shown in the table for Great Western Financial) was really only $1.99, etc.

To the professionals, this was a more honest and more honorable recitation of financial results. But whether because of the slowing of inflation or just general confusion, the public was unconcerned. All that interested them was the normal data. As a result, this entire subject is being reviewed by accounting experts.

If you are a VERY serious investor, you will find inflation-adjusted accounting valuable in determining the progress of your holdings but, to most folks, it's just another set of statistics that are difficult to analyze and of little real impact on investment decisions.

9

Preferred Stocks: Better for Corporations Than for Individuals

A preferred stock is just what the name implies. It has preference on all income available *after* the payment of bond interest and amortization and *before* dividend payments on the common stock. It is a "middle" security: halfway between a bond and a common stock. In most cases, the dividend is secure but will remain unchanged over the life of the issue. Usually, the dividends are cumulative so if they were skipped because of corporate losses, they will be paid later when profits are available.

Compared to common stocks, preferreds are safer, but unless they are convertible to common, they cannot provide the ever-higher income of equity investments in growing, profitable companies. In addition, the market value of preferreds moves opposite to the interest rate: UP when the cost of money declines; DOWN when it increases. And, unlike bonds, where the accumulated interest is added to the sales price, preferred stocks are traded at the quoted price and the dividends are paid only to those who own the shares on the record date as set by the terms of the original issue.

Preferred stocks are suitable for portfolios of individuals or fiduciary funds when the objective is modest income and, when the shares are bought at a discount, income plus appreciation. Their cost is low: typically $25 or $50 per share but occasionally $100, and dividends are paid quarterly.

Their best use, however, is as corporate investments because they offer an excellent tax shelter: only 15% of the dividends are taxable. Thus, a corporation in the 46% tax bracket can enjoy an after-tax return of 93.1%.

Example: In their professional corporation, Drs. P and Q set up a deferred compensation program by allocating $10,000 each in a diversified portfolio of preferred stocks currently paying 12%. At the 6.9% corporate tax rate, the $1,200 annual income incurs only $82.80 taxes. But there is one drawback: that investment losses cannot be written off against other corporate income/earnings.

To calculate whether it's worthwhile to buy preferred

CALCULATING BENEFITS OF PREFERRED STOCK INVESTMENTS

Assumptions: 12% preferred stock dividend rate; 85% corporate tax exclusion on dividends; 46% corporate tax rate.
1. What is the effective after-tax rate of the dividend?
   12% dividend − 12% (1 − .85 [.46]) = 11.31% after-tax return
2. Should you borrow to invest?
   Borrowing cost: 16% (1 − 46) = 8.6%
   Effective yield − borrowing cost =
      11.31% − 8.60% = 2.71%
3. How much after-tax yield improvement can I expect?
   Money market investment after-tax rates:
         12% (1−46) = 6.48%
      11.31 /7.56 − 1 = 74.5% after-tax yield improvement

SOURCE: Based on Donoghue's MONEYLETTER

stocks for your corporation, see the table. You may find that it will be worthwhile to borrow to do this.

Checkpoints for Preferred Stocks

In selecting preferred stocks, look at these factors:

Quality: those rated BBB or better by Standard & Poor's. The difference in yield between a well- and not-so-high rated issue is small or nil. With Beneficial Corp. $2.50 preferred, rated A−, and Ohio Edison $3.92, rated BB, the recent yields were both 13%. Choose safety over yield.

Low debt: capitalization that is not overloaded with bonds. Since bond interest must be paid first, the lower the debt ratio, the safer the preferred stock. This is especially significant with utilities.

Call provision: the time at which the shares can be redeemed, usually at a few points above par and, typically, after five years. When the original issue carried a high dividend, over 12%, the company will find it advantageous to exercise the call when it can float new debt/preferred at a lower coupon, say 9%.

With large, established companies, there's little need to worry about shenanigans but watch out with: (*a*) preferreds of small, struggling corporations where there may be special call/conversion provisions in small type; (*b*) utilities that take advantage of obscure provisions in their charters to save interest costs. What they do is to use other assets to call in the preferred prior to that five year date. You may still end up with a modest profit but, chances are, the redemption price will be less than that at which it was selling earlier . . . so the investor loses.

STRAIGHT PREFERRED STOCKS

COMPANY	DIVIDEND	S&P RATING	RECENT PRICE	RECENT YIELD
American Brands	$2.75	A−	25 5/8	10.7%
Beneficial Corp	2.50	A−	19 1/2	12.8
Commonwealth Edison	7.24	BBB−	57	12.7
GTE	2.48	BBB+	21 1/2	11.5
Iowa-Illinois G&E	2.31	A	20	11.6
Niagara Mohawk	4.10	BBB	32 1/2	12.6
Penna. P&L	4.50	BB−	28 1/2	11.7
Public Service E&G	1.40	A+	12 5/8	11.1
Utah P&L	2.80	A+	24 3/8	11.5

SOURCE: Standard & Poor's; New York Stock Exchange

Sinking fund. This permits the corporation to buy up a portion of the outstanding preferred shares each year so that the entire issue is retired before the stated maturity date: i.e., starting five years after the original sale, the company buys back 5% of the stock annually for 20 years. Usually, the yields of such preferreds will be slightly less than those where there is no such provision.

Corporate surplus. When this becomes substantial, there will be pressure to retire some of the preferred. For the common stockholder, this means less interest to be paid and thus a chance for higher dividends. For the preferred shareholder, prospects of redemption tend to raise the market price if the stock is selling below par.

Junior preference issues. Many of these permit refund-

ing prior to the stated date through the issue of common stock. These carry a lower rating and tend to be more volatile than their senior companions.

Marketability. Preferred stocks of major corporations listed on stock exchanges are actively traded, but their prices may shift quickly—as much as 2 or 3 points a day. Those of smaller companies, especially when traded OTC, may fluctuate even more because of their thin markets. As a general rule, place your orders, to buy or sell, at a set price or, if you are really anxious, within narrow limits.

Full voting rights. Preferred stockholders should not be shut out from having a say in the management of the company. The NYSE lists only preferreds with the right to vote if the company gets into trouble.

Restrictions on common dividends. Adequate working capital and a satisfactory surplus should be required before dividends on the common stock can be paid. This helps protect you against a dip in earnings.

Restrictions on new preferreds or bonds. There should be some workable provision to limit management from issuing new preferred shares or bonds—preferably only by approval of at least two-thirds of the preferred shareholders.

Premiums. As a rule of thumb, the yields of preferred should be 20% greater than those of corporate bonds of the same or similar company. These are not always easy to locate but the results will justify the extra research.

· Heed the counsel of fundamentalist Benjamin Graham; "The preferred holder lacks both the legal claim of the bondholder and the profit possibilities of a common stockholder. All investment grade preferreds should be bought by corporations, not by individuals."

Experienced broker. If you plan substantial investments in preferred stocks, deal with a brokerage firm that has a research department that follows this group. Many registered representatives neither understand nor like preferred stocks!

Higher fees for brokers. Because preferreds are more difficult to sell and have a more or less limited clientele, the commissions on the original underwriting are usually higher. With one utility company, Wall Street received $1.34 million to market a $40 million preferred stock issue but only $890,000 to float $100 million in bonds.

And commissions for low-par preferreds are often double those of $100 par value transactions.

New Types of Preferreds

With their ever-sharper marketing skills, financial officers, with a nudge from Wall Street, have developed special types of preferred stocks to attract new capital:

• **Convertible, redeemable preferreds.** These were introduced by Wells, Fargo & Co., a bank holding company, to raise additional capital. The shares, offered at $50 each, pay a regular dividend for the first five years. Then, the investor can swap for common stock at a price 5% below the market value. And to sweeten the deal, the bank will redeem 4% of the 700,000 preferred shares annually. This has helped to hold the market price above that of comparable issues and if the common shares continue to appreciate, there will be an extra bonus from capital gains.

• **Floating rate issues** where the yield is reset quarterly at ½ of 1% above the highest of: (1) the current yield of three-month T-bills; (2) the maturity rate of 10-year U.S. Treasury notes; or (3) the yield to maturity rate of 20-year Treasury bonds. There's usually a floor, typically 7.5%, and a ceiling, recently 16.4%.

Here's how Donoghue's MONEYLETTER calculates the benefits from these variable payers:

Assumptions: 12% preferred stock dividend rate; 85% corporate tax exclusion on dividends; 46% corporate tax rate.

1. *What is the effective after-tax rate of the dividend?*

12% dividend—12%−[(1 − .85) (.46)] = 11.31% after-tax return

2. *Should you borrow to invest?*

Borrowing cost = 16% (1 − 46) = 8.6%
Effective yield—borrowing cost =
11.31%−8.60% = 2.71%

3. *How much after-tax yield improvement can I expect?*

Money market investment
after-tax rates =
(11.31/6.48)−1 = 74.5% after-tax
yield improvement

How to Make 36% a Year

Sharp traders can get as many as 12 dividends a year by rolling over preferred stocks. By buying shares just before the dividend date, they get the full payout. They sell the next day and buy another preferred with an upcoming dividend payment date. Because of commission costs, this is difficult and expensive for amateurs but can work out well when deals involve 500 shares or more and you get a hefty discount on transactions.

In theory, these 12 annual dividends could yield 36%. Realistically, of course, most people will have to settle for about eight checks annually. Still, with a 12% yield, that will total a 24% annual rate of return.

To win with such machinations, you must watch the timing. After the payout date, the preferred will drop, typically almost as much as the dividend. Thus a 12% preferred might trade at 100 before the dividend date and drop back to 96 the next day. If you sell, you take a small loss and dent your total income. If you wait a week or so, you may be lucky and be able to get that 100 per share. But, over the year, you won't be able to roll over your holdings as often.

Unique Mutual Fund for Tax Benefits

The 85% tax deduction allowed corporations on dividend income has triggered new types of investment companies: Qualified Dividend Portfolio I (common stocks) and Qualified Dividend Portfolio II (preferred stocks). Their objective is to provide income that qualifies as dividends and is therefore eligible for the tax deduction.

The structure of these funds has been changed as a result of an IRS ruling that short-term capital gains realized on securities purchased before 1981 are considered "gross income" in calculating income for that 85% corporate dividend deduction.

The Vanguard Group, which sponsors the QDP funds, now limits short-term gains to 25% of gross investment income (dividends, interest and short-term gains), so that 100% of this income meets the IRS standards. Under Federal tax law, both short-term gains and interest income can be treated as dividends as long as they pass through a regulated investment company. To maintain this advantage, the QDP funds sell holdings in which they have capital gains within 12 months and, if the securities look good, buy them back.

The tax savings are dramatic. A corporation that invests $4 million in a diversified portfolio gets a total return of $680,000: $260,000 in dividends; $34,000 in interest; $86,000 in short-term capital gains and $200,000 in long-term capital gains. Normally, these would be subject to total taxes of $119,770. But when the same sum is invested with a QDP and achieves the same returns, the taxes will be cut to $72,120 so the net gain will be $47,650. BUT there could be a substantial difference if the performance of the QDP was less rewarding than that of the managed holdings.

ACCOUNT MANAGED INTERNALLY (AMI) vs. INVESTMENT IN QDP FUND

TYPE INCOME	FUND	GROSS	TAX RATE	NET
Dividends	AMI	$360,000	6.9%	$335,160
	QDP	360,000	6.9	335,160
Interest	AMI	34,000	46.0	18,360
	QDP	34,000	6.9	31,654
Short-term gains	AMI	86,000	46.0	46,440
	QDP	86,000	6.9	80,066
Long-term gains	AMI	200,000	20.0	160,000
	QDP	200,000	20.0	160,000

SOURCE: Vanguard Group, Valley Forge, PA 19482

10

Convertibles: Income Plus Potential Appreciation

Convertibles combine the fixed income of senior securities with the growth potential of common stocks. They are debt issues that can be converted into shares of common stock, usually of the same company but, occasionally, of a subsidiary/affiliate. In theory, convertibles are the best possible investments: sure interest/dividends plus capital gains when the value of the common shares rises as the result of higher corporate profits. In practice, it's not that easy and, as demonstrated in the recent erratic markets, CVs can involve the failings of both debt and equity: lower values when interest rates rise and slower gains when earnings falter.

There are two types of CVs: *debentures,* which are secured by the overall assets of the corporation, usually priced at $1,000 each; and *preferreds,* which in case of corporate liquidation will be secondary to bonds but ahead of the common stock. Their big plus is their low price: $25 to $100 each. All CVs can be converted into common stock, usually at a fixed-in-advance ratio but, sometimes, at varying rates. In most cases, CVs are callable prior to maturity, typically after the first five years.

Note: for convenience, when the term *convertible* (CV) is used, it refers to both debentures and preferred stocks.

Broadly speaking, CVs are a conservative way to play the equity market and an aggressive way to play the fixed-income market. Investors like the fair-to-good yields; speculators become excited about the possible gains from a rise in the price of the related common stock. CVs are best in strong markets but, with careful selection and sharp timing, can be profitable in bear markets. The key is always the ability of corporate management to make more money. *All CVs are more closely related to equity than to debt.*

Value Determinants

According to Wall Street lore, CVs permit the investor "to have his cake and eat it too." This optimism is based on the fact that there are two value determinants:

Investment value: the estimated price, usually set by a statistical service, at which the CV would be selling if it had no conversion feature. This is supposed to be a floor price under which the CV will not decline regardless of the price action of the related stock. This value reflects the interest rate so that the price of the CV will drop when interest rates rise and go up when they fall. Thus, when the stock is selling well below the conversion price, an 8% CV

issued at par ($1,000) will trade at around 66 ($660) when the yield on straight bonds is about 12%. Similarly, a CV with a high 11% coupon might sell at 110 ($1,100) when bond yields are 10%.

Conversion value: the amount the CV is worth if exchanged for shares of the common stock. A bond convertible into 40 shares of common stock has a conversion value of $1,000 when the stock is at $25 per share (40 × 25). If the price of the stock soars to $60, the conversion value will be $1,500, probably higher because of the ever-present element of hope.

A CV will usually sell at the higher of the two values and, in a strong market, at a premium. But don't kid yourself. Despite what some "experts" insist, CVs are no sure road to financial success. Their values can fall fast and, often, well below that "investment" floor.

Historically, CVs have been issued by companies that cannot get the lowest interest rate on straight bonds. To attract investors, there has to be an extra inducement. In recent years, however, CVs have been used in takeovers to keep all types of selling shareholders happy: fixed income for the hesitant; hopes of appreciation for the more aggressive.

CVs are also a favorite with small firms seeking capital for expansion. They add an element of security to the financing. But they can be dangerous because, as debt, they require regular payments of interest or dividends when the company is struggling to show a profit and, when they are converted, they will dilute shareholders' equity. Just as with common stocks and straight bonds, the key factor is *quality.*

Definitions

Company/issue. The name of the issuing company, the interest rate of the CV and the date of maturity when the CV will be redeemed, generally at par. Some securities have a deadline for conversion. After that date, you get fewer shares of stock.

Rating: the company's financial strength as determined by a financial service. As with bonds, the top rating is Aaa, then Aa, A, Baa, etc. Never *invest* in any CV of any corporation rated Ba or lower. Continued payment of the interest is uncertain and there will be little chance of appreciation of the common stock.

Call price: the dollars you will receive if all or part of the

SOME CONVERTIBLE PREFERREDS

COMPANY/DIVIDEND	NO. SHARES CONVERSION	PRICE STOCK	PRICE CV
Armco, Inc. $2.10	1.275	19	30
Arvin Industries $2.00	1.600	22	33
Brunswick Corp. $2.40	1.720	25	45
Champion Inter. $4.60	1.667	25	51
Chromalloy $5.00	3.888	11	50
General Dynamics $4.25	2.273	42	92
IC Industries $3.50	1.500	40	60
I.T. & T. $5.00	1.447	35	55
Kidde (Walter) $1.64	1.574	26	62
RCA Corp. $2.12	0.714	25	24
Reynolds Metals $4.50	2.080	32	66
Scovill, Inc. $2.50	2.44	26	60
Time, Inc. $1.57	1.44	57	80
United Technol. $3.87	1.250	68	85

SOURCE: Standard & Poor's; New York Stock Exchange

SOME CONVERTIBLE DEBENTURES

COMPANY/INTEREST	RATING	NO. SHARES CONVERSION	PRICE STOCK	PRICE CV
Allied Stores 9½,'07	A−	25	46	125
Becton-Dickinson 5,'89	A	20.48	49⅛	87
Ford Credit 4½,96*	A−	18.04	49⅞	85½
Greyhound Cp. 6½,'90	BBB−	54.42	23⅞	130
Jim Walter 8,'07	BB−	26.85	43⅛	123½
National Dist. 4½,'92	A−	39.97	26⅞	110
Xerox 6,'95	A	10.87	45	74½

SOURCE: Standard & Poor's; New York Stock Exchange

CV issue is redeemed in advance of the stated maturity date.

Amount outstanding: the dollar value of the CVs publicly traded. As a general rule, stay away from small issues—less than $20 million. Their market will be limited.

Conversion ratio: the number of shares of common stock the CV will convert to. With each $1,000 CV debenture and a conversion ratio of 25, you'll get 40 shares of common. Your broker has printed material to save you the arithmetic.

Price: the recent market values of the stock and CV.

Yield to maturity: the rate of interest plus the appreciation when the CV is selling below par or minus the appreciation when trading at a higher-than-issued price.

Stock Value of CV: price at which the CV must sell to equal the price of the stock: i.e., number of shares received on conversion times price of stock.

Premium: percentage difference between the conversion value and the market price of the CV. To calculate, use this formula:

PC = price of the common stock
SC = number of shares by conversion
PV = par value of the convertible
$P = dollar premium you pay
CV = present value of the convertible
P = percentage of premium

$$CV = PC \times SC$$
$$PV - CV = \$P$$
$$\frac{\$P}{CV} = P$$

Example: Tall timbers convertible debenture 8% due in 1996, rated A, is selling at 100 ($1,000). Each bond is convertible into 32 shares of common stock, which is trading at 30. To find the percentage of premium:

$$CV = 30 \times 32 = 960$$
$$1000 - 960 = 40$$
$$\frac{40}{960} = 4.16\%$$

This is a low premium for a CV of such a well-rated corporation. If corporate prospects are good and the stock is attracting investor interest, such a CV could be a worthwhile investment.

N.B.: In prosperous times, new issues of CVs often carry high premiums because of the hope that the company will prosper and the value of its stock will rise sharply. But remember that CVs are issued when the underwriter feels they can command the maximum price. As guidelines for suitable premiums, follow these criteria:

• *Premium under 15%:* risk is modest with quality companies. Typically, this is the percentage spread of a new issue. It will narrow when the price of the common stock rises or that of the CV falls.

• *Premium of 15% to 25%:* getting risky unless the yield of the CV is close to that of similarly rated bonds. It will take quite a jump in the stock price to have an impact on the value of the CV.

• *Premium above 25%:* a speculation that will probably take time to work out; more or less typical of junk CVs.

CVs Benefit the Issuer

In judging the merits of any new investment, it is wise to consider the benefits to the issuer. With common stock, shareholders are partners; with bonds, they are creditors. With CVs, they are in between: potential shareholders with hopes sustained by a promise of steady income. CVs are a call on the stock so no gains can be achieved unless the corporation grows profitably.

Generally, CVs enable the corporation to:

1. Sell stock at a higher price than could be obtained with a straight issue. To raise $10 million through an equity offering, a company would have to sell 100,000 shares of common at $100 (disregarding financing costs). Since CVs usually command a premium of about 15%, the $10 million could be raised by selling CVs at 115. When converted, they would require only 85,000 shares of common! In effect, the corporation is selling common stock at higher than current prices, and without presently diluting equity.

2. Obtain a lower interest rate. There's usually a substantial savings in the interest rate of CVs as compared to straight bonds. Depending on the caliber of the issuing company and market conditions, CVs bear interest rates as much as 2% below those of regular bonds. On a $10 million issue, that means a savings of $100,000 to $200,000 a year.

3. Achieve gradual dilution of the common stock. The company hopes the funds obtained from the CVs will enable greater and more profitable growth. When the price of the common stock rises above the conversion point, some

CV holders will convert and the dilution will be largely offset by higher earnings. At the end of the option period, all CVs become stock, so the debt, if debentures, will be wiped out. Almost all CV debentures are unsecured and usually subordinate to other debts of the issuing corporation.

4. Secure tax benefits. Financing by CV bonds rather than by preferred or common stock has tax benefits: bond interest is tax deductible as a cost of doing business; dividends are paid with after-tax dollars.

And before you go overboard on a CV issue of an exciting growth company, read the fine print to learn whether the major beneficiary is the corporation or the investor. Some corporations used CVs to borrow millions of dollars with no, or little, interest:

In May 1980, when yields of new corporate bonds were 14%, Wang Laboratories floated $50 million of 8% debentures with a conversion price of 38⅝ when the common stock was at 33. For such a fast-expanding computer company, this 17% premium was in line so the issue sold out quickly. Investors were happy with the modest yield and prospects of long-term appreciation.

But in October, before the first interest date, Wang called the entire offer. Since the stock was selling between 51 and 64, investors averaged gains of 47%. But this was far below the 72% profit that they would have made if they bought the stock directly. The big winner was Wang because the company had the use of the $50 million for 4½ months without paying one cent of interest. This saved the company about $2.6 million!

Similar "opportunities" have not been so rewarding. When Digital Equipment tried to force an exchange, a few months after the new issue of 8⅞% CVs, investors balked. They pointed out that this would dilute the number of shares of common stock by 12% and dumped their shares. When the stock price fell 10 points, the swap was canceled.

Now that Wall Street is wary of trick deals, they are not likely to be repeated with listed corporations but they may be used by small companies, especially when underwritten by swinging brokers/syndicates. After all, they are legal . . . and can be very profitable!

Checkpoints for CVS

The common stock. This is *always* the key. When you consider any CV, work backward: start with the common stock and the probability of a not-too-distant rise in its value. The CV should be considered primarily as an income-yielding parking place for your savings until they can be swapped for the common shares with a modest gain in income and a hefty rise in price.

If a stock is speculative, the CV will be risky, too. If it's stock of a stodgy company, the conversion privilege of the CV won't make the corporation grow faster or more profitable.

Buy CVs only of companies whose common stocks you want to own on the basis of quality and value.

Trade-off. With profitable CVs, the investor faces a trade-off between the premium and the yield: the difference between the income of the CV and the dividend of the related stock. The calculation is based on how quickly the premium will be paid back:

Example: A $1,000 CV paying 9% can be exchanged for 20 shares of common stock now selling at 42. The difference is $160 ($1,000 − $840). That's a 19% premium.

The stock pays a $2 per share dividend or a total of $40 if the swap were made. The difference between the $90 annual interest and $40 dividends is $50 a year. Divide $160 by $50 to get 3.2 years—the time needed for the extra income from the interest to make up the conversion premium.

Professionals use these guidelines: payback in three years or less: buy the CV; for a longer time-frame, the stock is probably better.

Duration of the conversion privilege. If the conversion period is short, the company may not be able to show growth and profits fast enough for the common stock to appreciate to the point at which the option will be valuable. If you are looking for long-term gains, you may be better off with the common stock than with the CV, especially if there is a chance of an early call at a price which is below the current market value.

Do not assume that the conversion period runs for the life of the CV or that the terms of the swap will be unchanged. These days, in their zeal to attract capital, underwriters come up with some deals that may make the original sale easier but may be dubious, if not detrimental, in the future.

New vs. Old Issues. New CVs are usually offered in strong markets when the company can take advantage of investor optimism. They will be pushed by sales representatives who will emphasize their dual potential and the no commissions cost. You may save a few dollars on the purchase but, in most cases, the gains will be slow and modest until the corporate management has proven its ability to earn extra profits with the proceeds of the loan.

It's wiser, safer and usually more rewarding to buy older CVs that are trading at below issue prices and premiums. With a sound corporation, you'll be getting a bargain and, in bear markets, the relatively high yield will ease the pain of what you hope will be a temporary paper loss.

Trend of interest rates. The toughest time to own CVs is when the cost of money is rising. Then the interest rate/investment value takes precedence and a small upmove of ½% can cause a drop of 5 points in the market value.

Comparable yields. As a rule of thumb, the yield of the CV should be no more than 25% below that of a nonconvertible issue of comparable quality.

When you do spot a bargain, be cautious. Once in a while, you can pick a winner but, usually, there's a reason (logical or not) for the low price. Ask your broker for a list of CVs in his firm's inventory and, with odd lots, you may save a few points.

Timing. The investor should make the swap when the income from the dividends on the common stock is greater than the interest of the debentures or the dividends of the preferred.

Example: PDQ $4.00 preferred is convertible to 1.05 shares of common stock. The owner of 100 shares of preferred is sure of $400 annual income. By converting, he can own 105 shares of common that, with a $5.00 per share dividend, brings in $525.

The speculator must stay alert. When the price of the CV moves above its conversion value or call price, he should act immediately: sell or set a stop-loss order. The company may start redemption to improve its balance sheet, or the price of the stock may drop.

Example: Back in 1978 when airlines were making money and their stocks were popular, Pan American 9⅞s, '96s, convertible into 166.67 shares of stock, were trading at $1,791.70 when the stock was at 10¾. The bond redemption price was $1,086.20. This was the time to take a profit. A few months later, when Pan Am stock fell to 6, the CVs were down to $1,000, so some folks missed the boat.

Pros: According to a Broker

Most registered representatives are not skilled with CVs but those who are become quite enthusiastic because, they feel, CVs offer these advantages:

Floor but no ceiling: the investment value sets a floor; the conversion value can soar if the company prospers or becomes a takeover target. This may be true with CVs of high-quality corporations but not with marginal firms whose securities bounce up and down with their popularity. In bear markets, the values of CVs can fall just as far and fast as those of the common stock and when interest rates rise, their declines are almost certain. Be skeptical!

Lower commissions. As bonds, CVs are traded for commissions that are below those for an equal dollar amount used to buy stock. To purchase five CVs selling at 80 might cost $25. The same $4,000 used to acquire 200 shares of stock at 20 would cost nearly twice as much.

On the other hand, that $25 will be a minimum charge for two CVs and, when the purchase is over five bonds, the per unit cost may be as low as $2.50 each. If you trade in listed CVs, you can check the price. If you speculate with OTC issues, you can never be sure that you paid a fair price.

Worthwhile investments for your children and grandchildren. While you live, the income is ample and after you're gone, your heirs can hope for appreciation.

Sinking fund obligation. When CVs have provision for a sinking fund, this is a guarantee that the company will retire a portion of the issue annually: at par or, when the price is low, by buying in the open market. Either way, this assures market support and, usually, a higher price. Once in a while, a cash-shy company may swap a sinking fund issue for one that won't be redeemed for some years. In such a switch, there can be a welcome premium: with Lockheed 4¼, '92, the exchange called for a new issue at 75, for the old debt trading at 56.

Easy swaps for higher yields. When the premium gets high, the yield may lessen so that it will pay to swap. Recently, with the enthusiasm for brokerage stocks, Merrill Lynch 9¼s, 20005 sold at a 10% yield and a 22% premium. A sharp investor could have swapped—at almost the same price—for Enserch CVs with an 11.5% yield and about the same premium.

Cons: Based on Experience

Specialized analysis. To pick profitable CVs requires more research than needed for bonds or common stocks. You have to study the terms of the CVs, the comparative market values, the projections for interest rates and, of course, the issuing corporation. Large brokerage firms have special research analysts for CVs but smaller organizations rely on outside services that rely on mechanical ratings/projections by computers. This approach works well with CVs of major corporations but is seldom useful with those of small companies. *Alternative:* special reports issued by investment advisory firms.

Limited marketability. Both CV debentures and preferreds have limited investor acceptance. As a result, their trading volume is modest and prices can swing substantially. That's an important consideration if you have to sell in a hurry. Take a look at the daily quotations and you'll see that, with many CVs, prices can fall (and, occasionally, rise) rapidly: 2 or 3 points a day.

If you plan to speculate with CVs, check the trading volume and price movements over a couple of months. With investments, of course, temporary fluctuations are not important.

Projecting Returns with CVs

To give you an idea of how to project profits (or losses) with CVs, refer to the table. This shows what might happen with a $1,000 debenture, convertible to 25 shares of common stock, now trading at 32. At issue, the conversion value is $800 because this reflects the $32 price multiplied by the 25 conversion ratio.

If the stock goes up:

By the second year after the issue of the CV, the company reports a hefty rise in profits and continuing good prospects. As a result, the price of the common stock jumps 25% to $40 per share. The CV goes up too, but at a slower rate, say 20%, from 100 to 120. There is good reason for this. As the bond price increases, the CV acts more like a stock and less like a bond. The investment value is of diminishing importance, the risk increases and the yield declines—all factors which tend to hold back the price of the senior security. *Conversion is unrealistic but some holders might want to sell the CV and take their profits.*

XYZ continues to do well, and with a buoyant stock market, the price of the common stock hits $60 per share: an 87½% gain. But the CV price goes up only 50% to 150. At this point, virtually all the bondlike characteristics are lost and the CV is interchangeable with the stock—as indicated by the disappearance of the conversion premium.

When a CV's conversion value and market price become the same, the stock and the CV should move up and down together.

When a CV sells with a negative conversion premium (that is, below its conversion value), professional traders move in for arbitrage. They buy the CV and simultaneously sell the stock short. Converting the CVs enables them to replace stock borrowed for the short sale.

Example: If the XYZ CV is priced at 145 while the conversion value is $1,500 the trader will buy 10 bonds for $14,500. He will then sell short 250 shares of XYZ common for $15,000 for a quick profit of $500!

If the stock goes down:

The other possibility is that XYZ runs into trouble and its profits dwindle, so that the price of the common stock is cut in half to 16. The price of the CV will fall but will be cushioned by its investment value of 75: a 25% dip.

The price of the CV might go lower, as the investment value would be adjusted with the interest rate. If the cost of money went down, the value of the CV would rise a bit; if interest rates rose, the price of the CV would fall further.

CV Preferreds

In addition to their low prices (par values of $25 to $100), CV preferreds are excellent investments for corporations because 85% of their fixed dividends is tax-exempt. Other advantages:

• No retirement date unless so specified under a sinking fund agreement. The income and conversion value will continue for a long time, often long after it's smart to swap. Some folks want the security of a quarterly dividend.

• Lower capital gains tax since the 12-month holding period includes the time of ownership for both securities. In January, you buy 100 CV preferreds at 35 ($3,500). In June, when their price has risen to 40, you convert for 150 shares of common stock. The following February, you sell the stock at 30 ($4,500). This $1,000 is a long-term capital gain, so taxed at a low rate: for the investor in the 50% tax bracket: 20%. This example does not count commissions/fees.

Hedging with CVs

For sophisticates, CVs offer excellent vehicles for hedging: buying one security and simultaneously selling short its related security. The hedge is set up so that, if the market goes up, you make more money on the purchase than you lose on the sale, or vice versa if the market goes down. Such trading works best in volatile markets.

Here's an example cited by Thomas C. Noddings, CV specialist: The CV debenture carries a 10% coupon and is convertible into 40 shares of common stock. The CV trades at 90; the common at 20.

| Buy 10 CVs @ 90 | $9,000 |
| Sell short 150 common @ 20 | 3,000 |

Since the short sale requires no investment, the cost is $9,000 (not counting commissions).

CALCULATING WHAT A CV IS WORTH

	At issue	Stock Goes Up	Stock Goes Way Up	Stock Goes Down
Market price CV	100 ($1,000)	120 ($1,200)	150 ($1,500)	75 ($750)
Yield	8%	$\frac{80}{120}=6.6\%$	$\frac{80}{150}=5.33\%$	$\frac{80}{75}=10.66\%$
Conversion ratio	25			
Conversion price	$\frac{1,000}{25}=40$			
Market price: stock	32	40	60	16
Conversion value	$25\times32=\$800$	$25\times40=\$1,000$	$25\times60=\$1,500$	$25\times16=\$400$
Conversion premium	$\frac{1,000-800}{800}=25\%$	$\frac{1,200-1,000}{1,000}=20\%$	$\frac{1,500-1,500}{1,500}=0\%$	$\frac{750-400}{400}=87\frac{1}{2}\%$
Investment value	75 ($750)			
Premium over investment value	$\frac{1,000-750}{750}=33\%$	$\frac{1,200-750}{750}=60\%$	$\frac{1,500-750}{750}=100\%$	0%

SOURCE: New York Stock Exchange

RISK-REWARD ANALYSIS

Common stock: 20; debenture, 10% yield, convertible to 40 shares common.
Stock Price in 6 Months

Hedging with Common Stock	10	15	20	25	30	40
Estimated bond price	72	80	90	104	122	160
Profit (loss): CV	(1,800)	(1,000)	0	1,400	3,200	7,000
Stock	1,500	750	0	(750)	1,500	(3,000)
Interest received: CV	500	500	500	500	500	500
Profit (loss)	200	250	500	1,150	2,200	4,500
Annualized rate of return	+4%	+6%	+11%	+26%	+49%	+100%
Hedging with Call Options						
Estimated bond price	72	80	90	104	122	160
Estimated call price	0	0	0	5	10	20
Profit (loss): CV	(1,800)	(1,000)	0	1,400	3,200	7,000
Calls	600	600	600	(900)	(2,400)	(5,400)
Interest received: CV	500	500	500	500	500	500
Profit (loss)	(700)	100	1,100	1,000	1,300	2,100
Annualized rate of return	−17%	+2%	+26%	+24%	+31%	+50%

SOURCE: Noddings, Calamos & Associates, 444 No. Michigan, Chicago, Ill. 60611

Now refer to the Risk-Reward Analysis to see what can happen in six months.

• *If the price of the stock falls to 10,* the CV's estimated price will be 72, so there will be a loss of $1,800 ($9,000 minus $1,800). But the 150 shares of stock can be acquired for $1,500 for a profit of $1,500. Add $500 interest (10% for six months) and the net profit is $200.

• *If the price of the stock dips to 15,* the CV will sell at 80 for a $1,000 loss but this will be offset by the $750 profit on the stock plus $500 interest for a return of $250.

• *If the price of the stock holds at 20,* the CV will stay at 90. There will be no profit on either but the $500 interest will represent an annualized rate of return of 11%.

• *If the stock rises to 25,* the CV will be worth 104 for a $1,400 profit but there will be a $750 loss on the shorted stock. With the $500 interest, there'll still be a $1,150 profit.

• *And if the stock soars to 40,* the CV will trade at 160 for a whopping $7,000 gain which will be offset by a $3,000 loss on the stock but enhanced by the $500 income for a total of $4,500 on that $9,000 investment... all in six months!

Says Noddings: "Selling short stock against undervalued CVs can eliminate risk while offering unlimited gains if the stock advances."

Best bet with hedges of CVs: Try out the "if projections" on paper until you are sure you understand what can happen. There's no guarantee that the gains or losses will follow this pattern, but that's one of the risks of speculating.

Writing Calls with CVs

Noddings also recommends that aggressive, experienced investors write calls against CV debentures. Since these are convertible to stock, they represent a viable base. Let's say that a $1,000 par value CV can be swapped for 45 shares of common stock. The CV is at 90; the stock at 20; the calls, exercisable at 20, are due in six months and carry a premium of 2 ($200) each.

Buy 10 CVS for $9,000 and sell three calls (since the CVs represent 400 shares of stock, this is no problem). The

$600 premium will reduce the net investment of $8,400.

To summarize the table, here's what can happen:

• *If the stock falls to 10,* the CV will trade at 72. The $1,800 loss will be offset by the $600 premium and $500 interest for a full loss of $700.

• *If the stock stays at 20,* the sure return will be $1,100 ($600 premium plus $500 interest) for a $1,100 profit or an annualized rate of return of 26%.

• *If the stock jumps to 40,* the CV will sell at 160 for a $7,000 gain. Add $500 interest to get $7,500 income. But there will be a $5,400 loss because the calls will have to be repurchased at 20: $1,800 each. Thus the net profit will be $2,100.

Warning: Writing calls on CVs is *not* for amateurs. To be worthwhile, this technique should: (1) involve a substantial number of shares of stock (at least 300); (2) be done with the aid of a knowledgeable broker who watches for sudden aberrations in price spreads; (3) be initiated with adequate cash or margin reserves that may be needed to buy back the calls; (4) be followed by an individual in a high enough tax bracket to benefit from the short-term losses.

SOME CV DEBENTURES WITH LISTED OPTIONS

COMPANY/SECURITY	CONVERSION RATIO	PRICE STOCK	CV
Becton Dickinson 5, '89	15.41	42	65
Citicorp 5 3/4, '00	24.39	37	94
Ford Credit 4 1/4, '98*	18.04	40	81
Grace (W.R.) 4 1/4, '90	17.45	42	83
Greyhound 6 1/2, '90	54.42	24	129
Inter. Paper 4 1/4, '96	26.32	57	136
K-Mart 6, '99	28.17	27	89
Lockheed 4 1/4, '92	13.79	84	116
National Medical 9, '06	32.26	30	112
Pfizer, Inc. 4, '97	21.05	70	147
Ralston Purina 5 3/4, '00	65.23	20	128
RCA 4 1/2, '92	16.95	23	65
Xerox Corp. 6, '95	10.87	39	69

* To stock Ford Motor Co.

SOURCE: New York Stock Exchange; Standard & Poor's

11

Bank Savings/ Investment Accounts

Banks are battling for your investment dollar by stressing safety, convenience and variety. They offer fixed asset investments: insured, up to $100,000 per individual, by an agency of the federal government; with different yields for different maturities; with varying methods of compounding interest; and, when deposits are substantial, free gifts. These benefits are widely promoted but only in the small type (usually asterisked at the bottom of the page), can you discover the real situation; that the yields are modest, the projections optimistic, the minimum deposits substantial and, in many cases, there are penalties for early withdrawal.

According to the promotional claims, each institution and each account is unique but, realistically, they are similar because all banks and thrift institutions are subject to federal supervision . . . until 1986 when there will be no more ceilings on interest rates.

In recent years, the distinctions between banks and thrift institutions have narrowed so that it's hard to tell one from the other (or from brokerage houses, for that matter). These shifts will continue and, probably, accelerate but the ultimate changes should benefit the individual.

No matter how they are named, deposits in accounts or certificates of banks and thrift institutions are SAVINGS rather than investments. You will always get back the same number of dollars you put in (unless you make an early withdrawal) plus interest but the income is taxable at the highest rate and, with inflation, the purchasing power of both the principal and income will decrease every year.

Savings are essential for financial security but the portion of your assets to be allocated to static, fixed assets/ income holdings depends on your sleep-well level. If safety is paramount, buy and hold nothing else.

But for those who want high total returns or growth, these fixed asset bank accounts are best for reserves—for emergencies and for a parking place—except in periods of high interest, such as 1979–81. As a rule of thumb, the yields of bank accounts will be 1% to 1.5% below those of money market funds and 2% to 3% less than those of quality bonds. But you have safety and convenience.

In broad terms, these are the major types of bank-sponsored accounts:

• *Certificates of Deposit (CDs):* both the principal and the interest rate are specified to a set date of maturity. With a 30-month $1,000 CD, you are sure of getting back your investment plus interest, usually compounded daily.

• *Savings accounts* where the yields are fixed by law.

• *Investment accounts* where the yields and maturities

vary but, generally, are related to the returns on Treasury bills/notes. These are primarily controlled by the institution but also include special debt issues of the bank/S&L.

Specifically, here are the most widely available accounts:

Passbook savings. This is the traditional account that is widely used for initial savings and emergency funds. There's no minimum deposit and the interest rate, set by federal authorities, is 5.25% for commercial banks; 5.50% for thrifts. There can be differences in total yields because of the data on which interest is paid (an account started on January 19 might not pay interest until February 1) and the method of compounding (savings will double, with daily compounding, 11 days faster than with monthly compounding and 31 days faster than with quarterly compounding).

NOW (Negotiable Orders of Withdrawal) account. This is an interest-bearing checking account where the rate of return is the same as with passbook accounts. At the outset, most banks had no minimum balance but now, many require $1,000 for full services. Usually, there's a monthly service charge and a computerized printout rather than a return of cancelled checks.

A new variation is the SuperNOW account that pays

BANK ACCOUNTS

TYPE/MATURITY	MINIMUM	INTEREST RATE*	PENALTIES
Passbook Savings	None	5¼-5½%	None
Regular checking	None	0	None
NOW checking	None	5¼%	Fees when below minimum
SuperNOW checking	$2,500	6.2-9%	Drop to 5¼% for month when balance below minimum
Money Market Account	2,500	8.9-11.2%	
7-31 day account	2,500	7.7-8.5%	Loss of all interest for early withdrawal
91 day account	2,500	7.8%	
Money Market CDs 6 mo.	2,500	8.3%	Loss of 3 months interest early withdrawal
18 month CDs (IRA/Keogh)	None	9.2-10.5%	Loss of 6 months interest for early withdrawal
30 month CD	None	9.4%	
42 month CD	None	9-10%	

N.B. These are subject to change as, generally, they are keyed to yield of T-bills which have been declining.

more, usually about 7%, but mandates a minimum balance of $2,500 with a return to the low passbook yield if this is not maintained. Monthly service fees range from $3 to $10 plus as much as 35¢ per check plus charges for deposit tickets and use of automatic teller.

Money market accounts. These require a minimum deposit of $2,500 and limit third party checks to three a month. The sponsor may set the interest rate but also the minimum balance, in most cases, $2,500.

The yields will be lower than those of straight money market funds because banks are required to keep, with the Federal Reserve, deposits of up to 12% of the balance . . . and this also applies to certificates of deposit such as:

• 7–31 day account: interest rate tied to that of a 13-week T-bill.

• 91-day CD: interest tied to that of 13-week T-bill.

• 6-month CD: yield can be ¼% above that of the average T-bill rate for the most recent four-week period.

There's no compounding, and, by law, thrifts can pay ¼ of 1% more than commercial banks.

Federal Insurance

With all bank/savings accounts, there is $100,000 insurance: for commercial banks through the Federal Deposit Insurance Corporation (FDIC); for thrifts, by the Federal Savings and Loan Insurance Corporation (FSLIC).

In any one institution, including branches, the maximum coverage for one individual is $100,000 but you can exceed this when accounts are held in different capacities: your own, with spouse, as trustee for children, etc.

HOW MORE FREQUENT COMPOUNDING BOOSTS RETURNS
YEARS TO DOUBLE

Interest Rate	Daily Compounding	Monthly Compounding	Quarterly Compounding
6.0%	11.553	11.581	11.640
7.0	9.903	9.931	9.981
8.0	8.665	8.693	8.751
9.0	7.703	7.731	7.788
10.0	6.932	6.960	7.018
11.0	6.302	6.330	6.388
12.0	5.777	5.805	5.862

SOURCE: Donoghue's MONEYLETTER

Repos: These are repurchase agreements with which a bank or thrift invests a certain amount of money (usually $1,000 to $5,000) for a short period of time (8 to 89 days). At maturity, the investor gets back the money with interest. The investment must be collateralized with U.S. Government securities owned by the institution. They are not insured.

There are still traditional accounts/certificates with one- to eight-year maturities and different methods of compounding. These are most useful when you want to be sure of money at a set future date.

With all special CDs, there are penalties for early withdrawal: for those held less than one year, the loss of three months' interest. If the penalty is greater than the interest, you get back less than you deposited. For those held more than one year, there is a loss of six months' interest.

The penalty is waived when:

• The owner dies or is found mentally incompetent.

• The time deposit is in a Keogh or IRA retirement plan and the depositor is over 59½ years old.

Zero coupon CDs. These are sold at deep discounts, pay no interest and are redeemed at face value at some distant date, typically 8 to 14 years hence. In Florida, one S&L sold $1,000 zeros for $250 and $500 each. The yields to maturity, compounded semiannually, were 11.747% and 11.998% respectively.

But watch out for these with personal savings: taxes must be paid annually on the imputed interest and, if sold early, the calculations for tax purposes can be tricky.

Floating rate notes. With these, the interest rate shifts with that of six-month T-bills. Usually, there are minimum and maximum returns: from a guaranteed low of 6% to a high of 19%. Continental Illinois has six-year notes with a yield of .5% above that of six-month T-bills plus convertibility into 8.5% debentures.

Bank Accounts vs. Money Market Funds

To a degree, there's still competition between money market funds and bank savings accounts, but, increasingly, the emphasis (thanks to clever marketing by the institutions) is shifting to using these accounts as a means to build profits with other, more-or-less traditional services: unlimited checking, securities brokerage, no fee credit cards, extended line of credit, bill-paying by phone, 24-hour banking via automated tellers, interstate banking, direct deposit of pension and dividend checks, and so on and on . . . all next door to home or business.

There are still legal limits—on minimum accounts, interest rates, etc. and, in some cases, penalties for early withdrawal but, generally, there's considerable flexibility. With the help of your "Friendly First" representative, you can tailor your savings accounts to your own and family needs and deal with that pretty blonde teller rather than some sepulchral voice over the phone.

Compared to regular money market funds, bank accounts also have these advantages:

• A new deposit is credited immediately. With funds, it takes a couple of days for the mail to be received and seven to 10 days more for the check to clear, so you can lose as much as one-third of your interest on that money.

• Local merchants will accept checks drawn against your local bank account but not on the funds deposited in State Street Trust Company for Big Money Market Fund.

• In Connecticut and New Hampshire, income from money market funds is taxed as dividends. But there's no tax on bank savings/investment accounts.

Checkpoints for Choices

In most cases, you'll pick the financial institution that's close by or run by friends or neighbors, but if you want to get the most for your money, get information in these areas:

Bank CDs/Accounts vs. T-Bills

When you can afford to invest $10,000, compare the six-month money market certificates with Treasury bills. In most cases (especially in states where there are income taxes), the T-bills will be a better deal. Here's the calculations:

1. Since T-bills are sold at a discount, use this formula:

$$D = \frac{L \times SY}{360}$$

D = discount per $100 face value
L = life span of security
360 = number of days in financial year
SY = stated yield

With a 180-day T-bill and a 9% yield,

$$D = \frac{180}{360} = 5 \quad 5 \times 9 = 4.50$$

Subtract the 4.50 ($450) from $10,000 to get $9,550 cost.

2. The true yield of the T-bill is more because T-bill trading uses a 360-day year but your money works 365 days and the stated yield is based on the cost.

$$TY = \frac{D}{C} \times \frac{365}{L}$$

TY = true yield
D = discount
C = cost
L = life span of security

With that 180-day T-bill, a yield of 9% and a cost of $9,550, the true yield is 9.56%.

$$TY = \frac{4.50}{9550} = 4.71$$

$$\frac{365}{180} = 2.03 \quad 4.71 \times 2.03 = 9.56\%$$

3. Interest on T-bills is exempt from state and local income taxes. That on the certificate is fully taxable.

4. If the certificate is cashed in early, there's a penalty. With T-bills, there's an active after-market so you will get more than you invested since the sales price includes accumulated interest—unless there's a sharp rise in interest rates.

Read the fine print . . . whether there are service fees for low balance accounts; charges for extra checks; higher than normal fees for overdraft privileges.

Be skeptical of the compounding projections. The advertisements make the not-so-certain assumption that current conditions will continue: that compounding will be daily, that the same rate of interest will hold and that the terms will be unchanged.

Costs of extra checks: $5 per check for each check above the minimum is a hefty charge.

Are fees tiered: no fees for anything when the balance is over $10,000; when below $5,000, $5 monthly charge plus 25¢ per check. This can add up. With a $4,000 (vs. $5,000) minimum balance, and a 7% annual yield with 10 checks, the cost is $90 a year so the next yield is 4.65%—under the passbook rate.

Do you get a break on personal loans: for a new car, appliance, etc? This could be a welcome plus.

Is the T-bill rate used for calculations: the coupon or discount figure? If coupon (which it seldom is), the rate will be ½ of 1% higher.

How is the minimum balance calculated? On any one day? Average daily balance? The average will work out better and avoid extra costs if there's a one-day drop.

Here are some guidelines to help you choose between a 91-day bank certificate and a 91-day Treasury bill, according to Donoghue's *MONEYLETTER:*

• If you have $25,000 or more, you will earn more with the T-bill, in spite of the $35 or so transaction costs.

• If you have less than $25,000, you'll earn more with the bank CD.

• If you buy a CD, patronize a thrift institution (savings & loan or savings bank) because they can pay 25 basis points more than commercial banks.

• If the discount on the T-bill rises 100 basis points (1%) or more one week following your purchase of the CD, you will make more money by turning this in immediately, forfeiting seven days' interest and buying a new CD at the higher rate.

• If you believe that interest rates will average more in the next three months than the fixed-rate T-bill or CD, invest in a money market fund. You will earn more.

12

Money Market Funds:
For Convenience, Not Profits

From the first mention of money market funds, *Your Investments* has viewed them as "profitable parking places for temporary funds," not as wise investments. For a couple of years, when interest rates were at record peaks, they were rewarding but today, they are more convenient than profitable and even that convenience is equalled or surpassed at the local bank/thrift institution. For most investors, money market funds are useful primarily in connection with other investments: *with the broker:* for holding proceeds of sales of securities while deciding on new commitments; *with an investment company:* for deposits of new savings, again while waiting before choosing a specific fund. Money market funds are no longer another of Wall Street's fads but they are still less attractive than properly selected stocks or bonds.

Money market funds are investment companies that invest your money in liquid assets: Treasury bills and notes, CDs, commercial paper, repurchase agreements, bankers' acceptances, etc. Recently, some funds have expanded their portfolios to include foreign debt, tax-exempt securities and special packages of longer-term bonds. All of these funds pay daily interest and thus compound income for higher returns. Their yields always reflect the cost of money, with a slight lag when rates shift. Recently, their stated rates of return were about 8%—far below the 15% (or more) paid in 1980. And, say some analysts, future yields will be lower!

In their heyday, money market funds were hailed as "a sure way to fight inflation" but now that public enthusiasm is fading, their assets have declined sharply. Still, they represent some $170 billions in savings. Part of the drop has been due to investments in the stock market but a rising portion has reflected in switches to local institutions that now offer comparable yields and that all-important convenience. William E. Donoghue, publisher of *MONEY-LETTER* has shifted his focus to No-Load Mutual Funds (the title of his latest book) but his comments on money market funds are still valid:

• Your money is always at work because interest is compounded daily.

• There are no loads on purchase so all of your money goes to work immediately. With T-bills, bought through a bank, the cost is about $15 and you lose three days of interest and four days discount on the discount. If you deal direct and mail in your check on Thursday to the Federal Reserve Bank, you lose a week's interest and, at maturity, get no interest for five more days.

• Small investment: as little as $500 to open an account compared to a minimum investment of about $9,200 for a $10,000 T-bill.

• Safety. Your money is used to buy prime debt of well-rated corporations or of the U.S. Government or its agencies. If you choose a fund that invests only in U.S. securities, your yield will be ½ of 1% lower but you can count on Uncle Sam's guarantee.

And, for super safety, there are special funds that team with a bank so that accounts are insured for up to $100,000 or that are insured by a consortium of insurance companies.

• Continued high yields when interest rates drop: for about a month until the high-yielding securities are redeemed. With a bank, the yield may change weekly. And, if interest rates rise, you will get the extra return immediately rather than having to wait until you make new investments.

• Check-writing privileges: (1) for convenience, customers of funds managed by major bank holding companies and/or brokerage firms can cash checks in many places that accept credit cards of the same sponsor (but your local supermarket may refuse checks on an out-of-area institution); (2) for income by taking advantage of the float—the

INTEREST RATES

YEAR	TREASURY BILLS	PRIME RATE	CORPORATE BONDS	MUNICIPAL BONDS
1934	0.3%	1.5%	3.4%	4.2%
1939	0	1.5	2.3	2.8
1944	0.4	1.5	2.1	1.6
1949	1.1	2.0	2.0	2.2
1954	1.0	3.1	2.6	2.4
1959	3.4	4.5	4.4	3.6
1964	3.6	4.5	4.4	3.2
1969	6.7	8.0	7.5	5.7
1971	4.3	5.7	6.9	5.5
1973	7.0	8.0	6.7	5.2
1975	5.8	7.8	9.0	7.0
1976	5.0	6.8	8.5	6.6
1977	5.3	6.8	8.2	6.1
1978	7.2	9.1	9.2	6.8
1979	11.9	15.0	10.9	7.6
1980	11.6	15.3	12.0	8.15
1981	14.0	18.8	14.0	12.20
1982	7.9	11.5	12.0	8.85

SOURCE: Wright Investors' Service

week or more needed for the check to clear.

Example: A New York shareholder, using checks supplied by a California-based fund, pays his $1,000 monthly rent. It takes seven days for clearance so he picks up 84 days of "free" interest a year.

• The privilege of quick switches into other types of mutual funds under the management of the same advisory firm. Thus, you can use the money market funds as a parking place while you decide whether to invest for income or growth. Usually, there's no charge.

Caveats

All of these advantages are exciting and may be useful but, with the relatively low yields today, all money market funds are better for convenience than for investment returns because:

• All income (except that from tax-exempt funds) is taxed at the highest rate. In the 50% tax bracket, that 8% return nets only 4%. With discount bonds and stocks, the appreciation is taxed at the low capital gains rate when securities are held for more than 12 months.

• Most money market funds are not insured. CDs in bank and thrift institutions are covered, up to $100,000 per individual investor, by an agency of the U.S. government. As noted, there are funds that provide such protection by investments through a bank or by insurance. Usually, their yields will be slightly less than generally available.

• In an effort to beat competition, some fund managers are taking extra risks: buying European securities, commercial paper of lower-rated corporations, etc. That's why the supercautious investor checks the quality of the fund holdings available from statistical services.

• There can be a temporary loss if the money market managers guess wrong on the trend of interest rates.

How These Funds Operate

Money market funds invest in short-term, fixed-income holdings, so the interest rate is always the key factor. When the manager anticipates that the cost of money will fall, he believes that he will have to invest new money for a lower yield, so he tries to extend current maturities . . . occasionally as long as 60 days. When he feels that the cost of

money will rise soon, he expects to make new investments at a higher rate so he shortens maturities. This strategy was effective when interest rates were swinging but now that they are relatively stable, there is only a small difference between the 7-day and 30-day yields.

How Fund Assets Are Valued

All money market funds price their shares at $1.00 each. The stated yield, as reported weekly in the financial press, reflects the interest earned on investments. But the methods of calculating the value of the underlying assets and the earned income varies. The base is the net asset value (NAV) per share. This is determined by subtracting all liabilities from the market value of the fund's shares and dividing the result by the number of shares outstanding. Here are the most widely used systems of calculation:

Amortized cost. This technique values each security at cost at the time of purchase and assumes a constant rate of amortization, to maturity, of any discount or premium. It does not take into account the impact of fluctuating interest rates on the market value of the holdings. The concept is that, since the securities will be held to maturity, price is not important.

Example: DD Fund invests $10 million in 8.75% six-month commercial paper. It expects to get the money back plus interest. But if the cost of money should rise to 9.75% in the next month, the market value of the $10 million holdings will decline. A new investor might pay $1.00 for a share worth 99¢.

To keep the share value at a constant $1.00, the fund must lower the daily dividend by the amount of the change in the underlying values. With a large fund, the effect is minuscule. A one-day drop in the NAV might decrease the dividend rate by only 1/200 of 1%.

But other funds, investing at a higher rate, will report a better yield so some DD shareholders will redeem their shares and, with new investors, buy shares of the higher-yielding funds. If this continues, the DD fund will be in trouble.

Mark to market. This is like an equity mutual fund. At the end of each day, the managers value the shares. The "pure interest" yield is computed to reflect the interest income earned on the portfolio. Then they (1) mark their holdings to the day's closing market prices; (2) figure the

MONEY MARKET FUNDS

FUND	U.S. 30 day	U.S. 12 mos.	AVERAGE MATURITY (Days)	U.S. Treas.	U.S. Other	PORTFOLIO HOLDINGS REPOS	CDs	BA	CP	EURO	YANKEE	NON-PRIME
Capital Pres.	7.5%	11.5%	4	100%								
CMA Government	7.2	11.8	46	100								
AARP Government	7.8	11.6	39	31	31%	37%						
Dean Witter Govt.	7.5	11.1	11	14	65	21						
Fidelity Cash	8.3	13.0	34				7%	6%	14%	12%	61%	
Hutton Reserve	8.1	12.9	35	∶3			5	7	62	13		
Lexington MM	8.3	13.0	31				4		43	0	40	17%
Price Prime	8.3	12.9	33				4	3	36	29	12	16

SOURCE: Donoghue's MONEYLETTER

per share capital appreciation or depreciation; (3) add or subtract the gain or loss from the pure interest yield to arrive at an "actual yield."

A variation of this is to mark to market on a variable NAV basis. This does not factor capital gains or losses into the interest figure but adjusts the NAV (the price of the fund shares paid by investors).

Straight line accural. This recognizes pure interest income only and does not reflect market value fluctuations, so provides stability of principal and yield.

Advice for all investors: Do not worry about the seven-day figures. By the time you act, they will be out-of-date. Heed the 30-day average yields. Once in a while, there may be significant variations but, over a period of time, the yields of most funds will average out about the same. It is foolish to switch for a small higher yield that may last only a week or two. Yet, too many people get overly excited and when they read of the possibility of ½ of 1% more, switch their account. In most cases, the costs of phone and postage will be greater than the benefits!

Cash Management Accounts

These are a special type of money market fund pioneered by Merrill Lynch (which copyrighted the name and abbreviation CMA). Similar funds are now offered by almost all major brokers and investment companies. Here's how a CMA operates as digested from an article I wrote for *Physician's Management:*

In January, Dr. Blake sold 100 shares of IBM for a net of $5,600. In February, Mrs. Blake, vacationing in Paris, used a special VISA card to pay the equivalent of $1,600 for a painting. In March, Dr. Blake wrote a check for $4,080 to complete the purchase, with a trade-in, of a new car. In April, the Blakes paid $10,000 as a down payment on a summer cottage.

All of these transactions were made from one source: a Cash Management Account®(CMA™)(trademark for this unique service). And, except for the $10,000 that was a short-term interest-bearing loan, there were no extra costs for such convenience. The $80 of the car purchase represented interest earned, at a 12% yield, on the $4,000 balance when automatically invested in a money market fund.

Here are the details, as explained by Michael J. Foley, vice president and director of Merrill Lynch's CMA:

With a minimum of $20,000 in cash and/or securities, the investor can open an account that involves these elements:

• A standard brokerage account in which securities can be bought and sold with regular commissions and normal five-day clearance.

• A checking account with free checks cashable at some 100,000 bank branches in 55 countries.

• A VISA card that can be used for purchases, loans or cash at 3 million locations around the world.

• Prompt reinvestment of all cash—from sales, dividends, interest and new deposits—in one or more of three money market funds:

1. CMA Money Fund, which invests in a diversified portfolio of short-term liquid assets.

2. CMA Tax-Exempt Fund, which buys short-term, high-quality municipal debt, so the income is tax-exempt.

3. CMA Government Securities Fund, which invests in short-term obligations of the U.S. Government or its agencies.

• Quick loans secured by the margin value of the securities held in the CMA with interest charged at the current broker's loan rate.

• One comprehensive monthly statement of each purchase/sale of securities: checks written; interest earned; dividends received; debit card transactions and interest charged on loans.

Other firms have similar arrangements:

• Bache Command Account: minimum $20,000; VIA tax-coded checks; complete year-end state, emt; insured by Prudential up to $10 million; free enrollment in a national discount shopping club; and travelers' checks by mail or phone. Annual fee: $50.

• Financial Management (Shearson/American Express): minimum $10,000 cash or $20,000 securities; American Express Gold Card; canceled checks and charge slips returned. Annual fee: $100.

• Active Assets Account (Dean Witter Reynolds): minimum $20,000; VIA checks coded to keep track of 20 different types of expenses; monthly statement and year-end summary; checks up to $250 can be cashed in any Sears Roebuck store. Annual fee: $30.

Checkpoints for Selection

Know the management firm. Look for a well-known, established organization that has been actively involved with fixed income investments for many years. No major brokerage firm, insurance company or mutual fund group will endanger its reputation by risky investments or trick accounting.

Look for low average maturities: 40 days at the most. This assures flexibility and the opportunity to move with interest rate changes. These maturities are published weekly in the financial press or you can get the information from the fund by calling its toll-free number.

TOTAL/ANNUALIZED RATE OF RETURN

Mutual fund shares bought at $10; held for 9 months; received 50¢ dividends and 75¢ capital gains distribution. At end, share price at $9.90.

TR = Total Return

$$TR = \frac{\text{Div. Inc.} + \text{Cap. gains} - \text{per share decline}}{\text{original price share}}$$

$$TR = \frac{.50 + .75 - .10}{10.00} = 11.5\%$$

ARR = Annualized Rate of Return

$$ARR = \% \text{ return} \times \frac{\text{year}}{\text{period held}}$$

$$ARR = 11.5\% \times \frac{12 \text{ months}}{9 \text{ months}} = 15.3\%$$

SOURCE: WILLIAM E. DONOGHUE'S NO-LOAD MUTUAL FUND GUIDE (New York: Harper & Row, 1983.)

In the week for the figures in the table, the average yield of the listed funds was 39 days and had held steady for some time. If this drops, this will be a signal of anticipation of rising short-term rates. Vice versa if it lengthens.

After you follow tables like these for several months, you'll see that there are other signals:

• When the average rate of maturity moves within a narrow range, interest rates are likely to remain stable.

• When the maturity jumps, say from 30 to 34, there will probably be a sharp decline in returns.

Check the 7-day data but focus on the 30-day figures. These funds are so huge that it takes time to make shifts.

This table also shows how to check the composition of the portfolios. The most conservative funds are those that buy primarily U.S. Government obligations; the most aggressive are those which hold European instruments and Yankee dollar CDs. If you invest a large sum, always ask for the minimum standards for Commercial Paper and watch out for any fund that OKs ratings under A.

And one timing tip: Buy new shares after 3 P.M. You will pay the closing price and get interest for that day.

SUMMARY OF MONEY MARKET FUNDS

FUND	AVERAGE MATURITY (Days)	YIELDS 7 Day	30 Day	YIELD TO MATURITY 12 Months
Taxable				
U.S. Treasury	37	7.34%	7.33%	11.31%
U.S. Gov't & Agencies	31	7.62	7.77	11.47
Domestic Prime	41	7.79	7.87	12.31
Domestic & Euro $	40	7.97	8.05	12.6
Domestic & Euro & Yankee $	36	7.92	8.02	12.70
Aggressive	29	8.09	8.17	12.99
Special Purpose	36	7.91	7.91	12.53
Tax-Free				
General purpose	89	4.62	4.72	6.86

SOURCE: Donoghue's MONEYLETTER

Cash Mismanagement Accounts

In their efforts to develop new, and more profitable to the sponsor packages, some fund managers are offering special deals that involve unusual activities: moving part of their portfolio into debt investments by short-term loans, to shareholders, based on home equity. These are really second (or third) mortgages so dangerous to the borrower as well as to other shareholders. The interest charges are high, the paperwork substantial and the rationale questionable.

Whenever you are offered such special "opportunities," check the costs and terms yourself and do not rely on the salesman's explanation. In most cases, you will find that the costs are higher than those readily available elsewhere and that the services will be provided by an outside organization that will be difficult to monitor and almost impossible to control.

Money market funds are convenient and can keep your money working but they are no longer the best investments for income.

SLY System

This is an indicator, developed by Donoghue, to predict the trend of interest rates. It is an acronym for Safety, Liquidity and Yield, which, he believes, are the key characteristics of all money market funds. The probable future trend of yields is forecast by the average maturity of the underlying securities, which, in turn, reflects the opinions of the professional money managers. When the average maturity of a fund, or groups of funds, shortens, it's a good bet that interest rates will rise. The pros are getting ready to take advantage of higher yields.

Conversely, when the average maturity lengthens, it's a sign that the fund managers believe interest rates will decline, so they strive to lock in the current high yields. But these days, with fluctuating yields, projections are not always correct.

This was good advice when yields were high but, as even Donoghue admits, when average returns fell below 12%, greater rewards, with comparable safety, could be obtained elsewhere. What he means, of course, is that, these days, money market funds are back to their original role: convenient parking places for cash while you choose new investments.

13

Taxable Debt Issues: Corporate and Government

Traditionally, taxable debt issues were primarily bonds of corporations and the federal government. They were conservative investments that provided modest income, secure principal (at maturity, you were sure of getting back the face value) and relatively stable market prices. But the value of your dollars—both principal and interest—was eroded by inflation and the net income decreased by taxes at the highest rate.

But when interest rates soared in the late 1970s, bond prices fell and, in many cases, these debt issues became better speculations than investments.

Now, however, bonds are busting out all over and can be rewarding holding for almost every type of portfolio:

• High yields with new issues.

• Excellent total returns, from interest plus appreciation with old issues selling at discounts.

• A variety of new packaging that offers bonds for almost every purpose and for almost every purchaser.

To get the best results, you can seldom buy and hold. You must be willing to trade when justified, stay flexible enough to take advantage of special situations and to manage your holdings rather than lock them in a safe deposit box.

Bonds are debt. When you buy a bond, you are loaning money to a corporation or government. In return, you receive a certificate that states the issuer will pay interest at a specified rate, usually twice a year, until the debt is repaid, at a specified date, 5, 10, up to 40 years hence.

For corporations, bonds are a relatively inexpensive way to obtain funds for capital improvements and expansion. The interest is a tax-deductible business expense, so the cost of a 12% bond for a firm in the 46% tax bracket is 6.48% (.12 × 54%).

As with all long-term debt securities, there are disadvantages.

• **Limited appreciation** because the value of all debt issues, unless of inferior quality, moves with the cost of money: UP when interest rates fall; DOWN when they rise.

Example: When first sold, Pacific Telephone 15½s, '20 were priced at 100 ($1,000). When interest rates soared, their price dipped to 85½ ($855); when the cost of money fell, they traded at 118 ($1,180). The profitability of the company made no difference.

• **Erosion by inflation.** The purchasing power of the debt assets is reduced every year: with 5% annual inflation, from $1,000 to about $614 in 10 years. Or, to put it another way, to buy the same goods and services 20 years from now, you'll need $2,650.

• *High taxes:* All interest (except that of tax-exempt bonds) is taxable at the highest personal income tax rate. With long-term capital gains (when the property is held over 12 months), only 40% of the profit is taxed. Thus, for those in the 50% tax bracket, the $100 interest ends up as $50, but the $100 realized appreciation, after one year, means $80 in your bank account.

• *Difficulty of compounding.* Unless you buy shares in a bond fund or zero coupon bonds, there can be no automatic reinvestment of interest as with stock dividend reinvestment plans. *One partial solution:* instead of depositing interest checks in a low-yielding savings or NOW account, add to your shares of your money market fund. As long as the fund yields a return close to that of the bonds you'll be OK but when the fund pays 8% vs. 11% for the bonds, try to add some savings.

Price and Yields of Bonds

The interest rate is the important factor in the price of bonds, not supply and demand as with common stocks. Bond values rise when interest rates decline; conversely, bond values fall when interest rates go up.

But that does not mean that the prices of all bonds move in unison. Yields and market values reflect the time to maturity and coupon rate. *Yields* on short-term issues tend to fluctuate more sharply and more quickly than those of longer-term debt. In tight money periods, short-term interest rates are usually much higher than those of issues due in 20 years or so. In more normal markets, short-term issues yield less than long-term ones, but, as has been evident in recent years, the swing back to traditional patterns takes time, often as long as two years.

By contrast, *prices* of long-term bonds fluctuate more than those of short-term issues. *The reason:* time is money. A change in interest rates calculated for a few weeks or months involves a lesser change in price than the same change projected for years ahead.

A rise of 1% in the interest rates will mean a drop of about $10.00 for a $1,000 short-term T-bill but it can force a decline of $100 or more for a bond with 20 years to maturity.

What to Look For in Bonds

Quality. This is essential in choosing bonds for investment. Since you buy bonds for safety, stick to quality and forget the small extra interest ($5 to $10 per year per bond) which can be obtained with the debt of a secondary corporation.

Most corporate and municipal (but not federal government) bonds are rated by statistical services in nine categories from gilt-edged to extremely speculative. These ratings represent carefully calculated estimates of the degree of protection for both principal and interest. They are based on past performance, current financial strength and future prospects. By and large, the two top services, Moody's and Standard & Poor's, come up with about the same opinion.

HOW BONDS ARE RATED

General description	Moody's	S&P
Best quality	Aaa	AAA
High quality	Aa	AA
Upper medium	A	A
Medium	Baa	BBB
Speculative	Ba	BB
Low grade	B	B
Poor to default	Caa	CCC
Highly speculative default	Ca	CC
Lowest grade	C	C

Ratings may also have + or − sign to show relative standings in class.

Prices for high-grade bonds reflect money market conditions and interest rates. Farther down the quality scale, however, bond prices are more closely attuned to business conditions and the financial prospects of the corporation. Medium-grade Baa and BBB bonds are the lowest category that qualifies for commercial bank investments. With lower ratings, you are speculating: Petro-Lewis 11s, '97, rated B or junk bonds of Rapid-American, rated CCC.

Watch for changes in ratings of all types of bonds. Upgrading is beneficial so the market price will probably rise (and the yield dip) a bit; downgrading signals possible trouble so the value will decline. Shifts are not too important as long as the rating is A but with any B category, be wary.

CHANGE IN BOND RATINGS

UP:	Alabama Power	from BBB to BBB+
	Kroger Co.	from A to A+
DOWN:	Beatrice Foods	from AAA to AA
	St. Regis Paper	from A to A−

SOURCE: Standard & Poor's BOND GUIDE

Terms: Most debt issues of both the federal government and corporations carry a fixed coupon with a fixed date of maturity. But, occasionally, there will be serial bonds where a portion of the issue will be paid off periodically. Usually, the earlier the redemption date, the lower the interest rate—¼ to ½% or so. These can be useful when you have a target date when you will need money: in seven years when daughter Delphinium enters college, etc. Serial bonds are widely used with tax-exempt issues.

Corporate collateral. This is the property behind each bond. *Secured bonds are:* (1) first mortgage bonds backed by the company's real estate, plants, trucks and so on *or* equipment trust certificates secured by railroad equipment—locomotives, freight cars, etc.; (2) bonds guaranteed, as to principal and interest, by another corporation or by the government or a government corporation or agency. Examples of the former are foreign bonds offered for sale abroad by foreign subsidiaries or affiliates of U.S. corporations and guaranteed by the parent company.

Unsecured bonds or debentures are backed only by the general credit standing of the issuing company. The investor should translate this credit into the company's ability to pay annual interest and amortization plus the principal sum when due. The projection should consider recent historic ratios and trends and should apply to the *total* debt.

In practice, for most bonds, the ability of the corporation to pay is much more important than theoretical security because legal obstacles to investors collecting a bond's security in the event of insolvency are often formidable and time-consuming, quite possibly requiring litigation.

A handy formula for determining investment-grade bonds (interest charges should be covered over a period of five years):

	Before Federal Income Taxes	After Federal Income Taxes
Industrial Bonds	5x	3x
Public Utility	3x	2x
Railroad	4x	3x

Type. Bearer or Registered. Historically, there have been two types of bonds:

Bearer with interest coupon attached. To get interest payments, the owner has to detach (clip) the coupons and send them to a bank or paying agent. These are vulnerable to loss and theft but easy to trade and an excellent way to retain anonymity (and, in some cases, to avoid taxes). Old issues are still available in bearer form but, by congressional mandate, are being replaced by:

Registered bonds where the issuer, or its agent, must keep a record of ownership. Interest checks are mailed semiannually and since the names of the owners are recorded, holders have protection against theft, fire or loss and will receive prompt notification of redemption calls.

You may be able to save a point or so ($10 per $1,000 face value) by buying registered bonds because large institutions prefer bearer issues that are easier to trade and that avoid the usual four business days transaction time.

Bond Interest Payments

Interest on bonds is added to the sales price but does not include the day of delivery. It is calculated on a daily basis. For U.S. Government issues other than Treasury bills, the base is the exact number of days in a 365-day year. With

From the:	
1st to 30th of the same month	29 days
1st to 1st of next month	30 days
1st to 28th of February	27 days
If interest is payable on the 30th or 31st, from the:	
30th or 31st to 1st of next month	1 day
30th or 31st to 30th of next month	30 days
30th or 31st to 1st or 2nd of next month	1 month, 1 day

other bonds, it's a 360-day year or twelve 30-day months.

To figure the yield superiority of 360-day bonds versus 365s, divide the interest rate by 360 to get the daily return, then multiply the result by 365. With a 12% interest rate, the daily rate works out to 0.333%, so the annualized rate, for 365 days, would be 12.16%.

How to Read Bond Quotations

These quotations, for a week of trading, are typical of the gyrations that have dominated the bond market in the last year: swings of almost 50% and daily changes of 2 or 3 points ($20 to $30 per bond).

The first line shows AAA-rated Telephone debt, with a coupon of 3⅞ and maturity date in 1990. The last quotation was 74 ($740) and, during the day, the high price was 75¾, just below the 52-week peak of 75⅞. There were 399 trades with a low price of 73⅝ and the last transaction was at 74, for a loss, from the close of the previous week, of ⅝ ($6.25 per bond).

Each bond paid $37.85 annual interest so the current yield was 5.2%. Investors were willing to accept this modest rate of return because they know that, in about seven years, each bond will be redeemed at $1,000 for a long-term capital gain of $260 per bond. The yield to maturity was competitive with that of new issues.

The Bell Penna. bond was selling at a couple of points higher than the Ma Bell debt; its current yield was 11%—about double that of the ATT bond. *Reason:* the Penna. bond will not be paid off until 16 years later. People want to be paid for waiting for their money . . . as they will be because, by 2006, there will be a capital gain of $216.25.

Note that: (1) the Bell Penna. bond price ranged a bit higher but fell only a fraction lower than the senior issue. The interest paid made the difference; (2) the 2⅝ point drop, for the week, was a big one, reflecting the modest volume of 99 bonds for the week.

The Philadelphia Electric bond, rated a not-so-good BBB−, paid the highest yield. Investors were not too con-

fident that the company would be able to continue to pay interest and redemption. With the high 18% coupon, the price of the bond had risen sharply to a high of 124½ and a last sale of 120¾. That means that those who bought at around 100 could count on excellent income plus 20+ appreciation: an annual rate of return of over 30%!

Here again, the quotations were volatile as the price dropped 1¾ from the previous week. Investors who want income should hold but keep an eye on the calendar because, in March 1987, this issue can be called, at 117.

Government debt issues, traded OTC, are quoted in thirty-seconds (3.125) with similar price/volume, yield data. Here, the quotations are for $1,000 face value. The first line shows notes due in the near future with a coupon of 9¼%, a high price of 100, and a low and close quotation of 99²⁶⁄₃₂ for a yield of 9.37%. For the week, the change was minus ¹⁵⁄₃₂s.

With a low 3½% coupon, the 1990 debt yields only 4.71% but will provide sure appreciation of about $75 per bond.

GOVERNMENT NOTES/BONDS

RATE	MATURITY	HIGH	LOW	LAST	CHG.	YIELD
9 1/4s	Jan. 1985n	100	99.26	99.26	−.15	9.37
3 1/2s	Feb. 1990n	93.14	92.16	93.4	−.6	4.71
15 3/4s	Nov. 2001	141.9	138.28	138.28	−3.25	10.84

n = Note

SOURCE: Barron's

The 15¾s, due in 1001, were popular: a high of 141⁹⁄₃₂ and a close/low of 138²⁸⁄₃₂ for a sharp drop of 3²⁵⁄₃₂. The current yield is 10.84% but will soon rise because the 15¾% payment will continue while the value of the bonds will gradually decline toward 100 at maturity. There is no early call with government debt!

Bond Yields

Yield is a matter of definition and objective.

The nominal or coupon yield. This is the interest rate stated on the bond: 10%, 11.25%, etc. It depends on the quality of the issuing corporation and the prevailing cost of money at the time the bond is issued.

The actual yield on the purchase price. This is the rate of return per year that the coupon interest rate provides on the *net* price (without accumulated interest) at which the

HOW CORPORATE BONDS ARE QUOTED

52 Week High	Low	Issue	Cur. Yld.	Sales 1000s	High	Low	Last	Chg.
75 7/8	58 1/2	ATT 3 7/8s90	5.2	399	75 3/4	73 5/8	74	−5/8
81 5/8	57 3/8	BellPa 8 5/8s06	11	99	81 5/8	76 5/8	78 3/8	−2 5/8
124 1/2	97 1/2	PhilEl 18s12	15	99	122 7/8	120 3/4	120 3/4	−1 3/4

SOURCE: New York Stock Exchange

bond is purchased. It is *higher* than the coupon yield if you buy the bond below par, *lower* if you buy the bond above par.

The current yield. This is the rate of return on the current market price of the bond. This is *higher* than the yield on the purchase price if there has been a decline in the price, *lower* if there has been a rise in the market value of the security.

The yield to maturity (YTM). This is the rate of return on a bond held to redemption. It includes the appreciation to par from the current market price when bought at a discount from par, or the depreciation to par when bought at a premium.

To approximate the YTM for a discount bond:

1. Subtract the current bond price from the face amount.

2. Divide the difference by the number of years to maturity.

3. Add the annual interest.

4. Add the current price to the face amount and divide by two.

5. Divide (3) by (4) to get the YTM.

Example: A $1,000, 5% coupon bond, due in 10 years, is selling at 57 ($570). The coupon yield is 5%; the current yield is 8.8% (5 ÷ 57); the YTM is 11.8%.

$$\$1,000 - 570 = 430$$
$$430 \div 10 = 43$$
$$43 + 50 = 93$$
$$570 + \$1,000 \div 2 = 785$$
$$93 \div 785 = 11.8\%$$

This is approximate, as an exact figure would have to include the accrued interest and number of days to maturity.

The discount yield. This is the percentage from par or face value, adjusted to an annual basis, at which a discount bond sells. It is used for short-term obligations maturing in less than one year, primarily Treasury bills.

Roughly, this is the opposite of **YTM**. If a one-year T-bill sells at a 12% yield, its cost is 88 ($8,800). The discount yield is 12 divided by 88 or 13.64%.

The importance of various calculations on yields is shown in the table, *How Bond Values Have Changed.* These rises in prices and declines in yields took place in about 18 months, a very short period for most debt investments. And, many analysts predict, there is more to come, perhaps not as far nor as fast, but, in the next couple of years, discount bonds can continue to be profitable investments.

U.S. Government Bonds

These are the principal types of U.S. Treasury securities bought by individual investors. In order of maturity, they are:

U.S. Treasury bills. These mature in 91 days, six months, nine months and one year. The first two maturities are issued weekly; the latter two once a month. They come in bearer form with a minimum face value of $10,000 but are sold at a discount. Smaller units can be traded in the after market.

T-bills are at a price that reflects the yield as set by bids from major institutions. Thus, a one-year 9% bill will be bought for $9,100 and, 12 months later, will be redeemed for $10,000. This gain is interest and thus taxable at the full federal income tax rate but it is not subject to state and local income levies.

Individuals can buy T-bills via a form available from the nearest Federal Reserve Bank. This is done by a noncompetitive bid (to arrive by mail on Friday or, in person, before 1:30 P.M. on the day of the auction).

The price you pay will be the average of all competitive offers from large institutions that buy millions of dollars' worth each week. With the form, enclose a personal certified check or an official bank check drawn on a bank in the Federal Reserve district. The check should be made payable to the "Federal Reserve Bank of (District)." A third-party check endorsed by you to the Fed will not be accepted.

A few days after the auction, the Fed Bank will mail you a "discount" check, representing the difference between the purchase price and the face value of the bills. With this will be a receipt as proof of your purchase.

The details of the acquisition are entered in a government ledger, with no extra charge. This book entry reduces the risk of loss or theft, saves printing costs and eliminates delivery and clearance problems.

If you prefer to buy through a broker or a bank, charges will be $15 to $25 per transaction.

To roll over a T-bill at maturity, you can indicate your wishes at purchase or send in Form PD 4633–1 at least 20 business days before the maturity date.

For more information, request "Basic Information on Treasury Bills" from your nearest Federal Reserve Bank or Federal Reserve Bank of New York, 33 Liberty Street, New York, N.Y. 10045.

U.S. Treasury notes. These mature in from one to five years, are issued in bearer form and pay interest semiannually.

U.S. Treasury bonds: medium-term (five to 10 years) and long-term (10 to 40 years). Interest is paid semiannually.

U.S. Treasury tax anticipation bills and certificates. These are issued to mature a few days after federal income

HOW BOND VALUES HAVE CHANGED

ISSUE	PRICE Fall 1981	PRICE Recent	YIELD TO MATURITY Fall 1981	YIELD TO MATURITY Recent
U.S. Government				
9 1/4, May '84	86.4	100.7	14.8%	9.05%
8 1/4, May '88	74.0	93.5	14.3	9.98
10, May 2005-2010	75.8	93.31	13.3	10.69
Intermediate-term				
AT&T 3 7/8, '90	55 3/4	72 1/4	6.95	5.40
Avco Fin. 11, '90	88 1/2	99 5/8	12.4	11.00
GMAC 8.15, '86	79 3/4	93 1/8	10.3	8.8
Pac. Tel. 4 3/8, '88	59	76	7.4	5.8
Long-term				
AT&T 8.80, '05	69	80	12.7	11.0
Bell Pa. 8 5/8, '06	64	75 5/8	13.5	11.0
Cleve. Elec. 8 3/4, '05	61 1/4	72 3/4	14.3	11.0
S. Cal. Bell 8 1/4, '04	63 1/2	73	13.0	11.0

SOURCE: New York Stock Exchange; Wall Street Journal

tax payment dates (April 15, June 15, etc). They can be used to pay income taxes at par (or with full interest to maturity), thereby giving the taxpayer a bonus of several day's interest. They are designed for large corporations with large tax bills.

Federal Agencies' Debt

There are well over 100 series of notes, certificates and bonds issued by federal agencies as instrumentalities of the U.S. Government: Federal Intermediate Credit Banks, Federal Land Banks, Banks for Cooperatives, Federal Home Loan Banks, etc.

They are backed by the full faith and credit of Uncle Sam and carry maturities from a few months to many years. They are among the highest quality securities available. Their yields are as high as, and often higher than, those of most Aaa- or Aa-rated industrial bonds.

Problems: In odd lots, Government agency bonds may be less liquid than corporates, so you could take a small loss if you have to sell quickly. The point spread between bid and asked prices has been as high as ½ of 1% versus a normal spread of ¼ of 1%. *But most people buy bonds for long-term holdings.*

Some of these difficulties have been overcome by a new market on the AMEX, dealing in odd lots of T-bills and federal notes and bonds. This reduces commission costs and makes it possible to buy in comparatively small units. You do not get possession of the certificates, which are held in trust in a bank. Credits for interest and transactions are made to the account, with copies to you and your broker.

Profits with Bonds

Broadly speaking, the mechanics of buying and selling listed bonds (those traded on the NYSE and AMEX) are similar to those of stocks. You enter an order with your broker who arranges for it to be executed at the best price. With small lots (less than 10 for active issues, 25 for others), it's best to set a price that you are willing to pay or accept. As the tables show, bond prices can shift sharply so if you give a market order, you may lose money.

Unless your spouse is determined to own a specific issue, buy from your broker's inventory. Tell him the quality rating, the approximate maturity and the amount of money you have to invest and let him give you suggestions. This can save you as much as $20 a bond in buying and if you are a good customer, nearly as much in selling.

Accrued interest. With both government and corporate bonds, the accrued interest must be taken into account. The holder of the bond on the stated interest payment date is entitled to collect the entire amount of the interest since the previous coupon date. Thus, the buyer will have to pay the seller extra. *Example:* 10 corporate bonds are sold at 79¾. The seller receives $8,046,67: the $7,975 price plus $71.67 interest (not counting commissions).

Since most investors buy bonds for income, the compounding of interest, over a period of time, will provide more than half of the total return. It's easy for professionals to reinvest the interest but difficult for amateurs to do

HOW BOND INTEREST COMPOUNDS
at 12% Annually for $10,000 Investment

Time	Semi-Annual Interest	Cumulative Growth
6 mos.	$ 600	$10,600
1 year	636	11,236
1½ years	674	11,910
2 years	715	12,625
2½ years	758	13,383
3 years	803	14,186
3½ years	851	15,037
4 years	902	15,939
4½ years	956	16,895
5 years	1,014	17,909
5½ years	1,075	18,984
6 years	1,139	20,123
6½ years	1,207	21,330
7 years	1,280	22,610
7½ years	1,357	23,967
8 years	1,438	25,405
8½ years	1,534	26,929
9 years	1,616	28,545
9½ years	1,713	30,528

SOURCE: Robert Lawrence Holt, THE COMPLETE BOOK OF BONDS

so because of the small sums involved. With 10 bonds at a 10% yield, the semiannual interest is $500—just enough to buy one deep discount bond. *Alternatives:*

1. Schedule your savings so you will have extra money to add to the interest.

2. Buy shares of bond funds that provide automatic reinvestment.

Still, as shown by the table, compounding with a pension or trust fund can be a powerful force over the years.

Caveats. Always remember that, as debt, bonds are little influenced by the growth and profitability of the issuing corporation except as to the rating. The key factor is always the cost of money. The higher the interest rate, the lower the market price of the outstanding bond . . . until the approach of the redemption date. Thus, a 4⅝% U.S. Steel bond, issued at $1,000 in 1965, maturing in 1996, sold at 55 when the interest rate was 8%, below 40 in 1980, when new issue coupons were 14% and bounded back to 54 in 1983 when interest rates were around 10%. The values of bonds move opposite to the trend of interest rates: *UP when the cost of money drops; DOWN when it rises.*

• Watch out for wash sales: where the same or nearly identical security is repurchased within 30 days (Chapter 20). Losses are not tax deductible. There must be a significant difference in one of these criteria: issuer, coupon and maturity. Thus, you can sell Philadelphia Electric and buy U.S. Steel but not other PE bonds.

• Maintenance fees, levied by a custodial bank, can cut into your income. Typically, the charge will be about $5 per month: $60 a year—a hefty bite into your return. They are tax deductible but, unless you are nervous, leave them with your broker or in your safe deposit box.

Yield Curve

A yield curve is a diagram that illustrates the relationship between rates of return and maturities of similar fixed-income securities. Analysts use the different patterns to decide which type of bond to buy at certain periods.

To draw a yield curve, the professional sets out the maturities on graph paper on a horizontal line, from left to right, starting with the shortest maturities (30 days) and continuing over days/years to the most distant (30 years). Then he plots the yields on the vertical axis and connects the dots with a line that becomes the yield curve.

The shape of that curve is affected by how investors *expect* interest rates to change. If they think interest rates are going to climb, they put their money in short-term securities while they wait. At the same time, borrowers get their dollars before the cost of money rises. Both responses tend to push short-term interest rates down and long-term rates up—not always immediately but always over a reasonable time span.

The illustration shows the yield curve as of late May 1983: the short-term yields (on the left) hit a high in December 1980—over 18%, dropped fairly sharply, forecasting lower yields (which came in the spring of 1982).

Note that, for a while, the short-term yields were higher—and forecast higher—than long-term returns but by May 1983, the spread shifted and began to return to the historical pattern where short-term yields were well below those with longer payout.

Let's suppose you want to invest $10,000 in debt issues for 10 years. You have these choices:

• A six-month T-bill that will be rolled over at each maturity—probably at a slightly higher rate of return.

• A two-to-three-year Treasury note which, at maturity will be turned into a seven-to-eight-year note, at a somewhat more rewarding yield IF the projection proves out.

• A 10-year bond to be held to redemption. This would be best if you expect interest rates to decline or stay about the same.

• A 15–20 year bond to be sold at the end of 10 years, best if you project lower costs of money. But the longer out the maturity, the greater the risk. The yield curves are most useful when they are kept up to date and checked to find the trends.

If you are not chart minded, ask your broker for copies from his research department.

U.S. Savings Bonds

Before getting into the various types of debt issues that are available, let's review U.S. Savings Bonds—those old favorites that date back to WWII and, frequently, are pushed as investments (by major executives of major corporations that do business with Washington). About the best that can be said for them is that they are safe and better than in the past. Buy them as a patriot, not as an investor.

The old Series E and H savings bonds are being replaced by EEs and HHs. There are still no taxes on accrued interest until redemption but no interest will be paid for E bonds issued before April 1952 and held for 40 years. (Those bought after that date get one 10-year extension and then stop paying interest.) For H bonds purchased before May 1959, no interest will be paid after 40 years. When acquired later, there's 10 more years of income but maturity will take place 20 to 30 years after the original

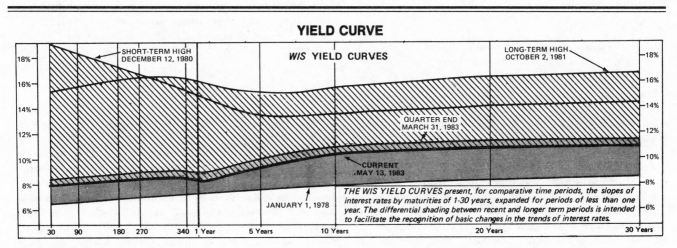

YIELD CURVE

WIS YIELD CURVES

SHORT-TERM HIGH DECEMBER 12, 1980

LONG-TERM HIGH OCTOBER 2, 1981

QUARTER END MARCH 31, 1983

CURRENT MAY 13, 1983

JANUARY 1, 1978

THE WIS YIELD CURVES present, for comparative time periods, the slopes of interest rates by maturities of 1-30 years, expanded for periods of less than one year. The differential shading between recent and longer term periods is intended to facilitate the recognition of basic changes in the trends of interest rates.

SOURCE: Wright Investors' Service

purchase. *DO NOT HOLD E or H BONDS. Cash them in or roll them over.*

EE bonds are sold at 50% of face value: $25 for a $50 bond; $50 for a $100 one, etc. The maximum investment is $15,000 face value. Bonds issued after November 1982, when held for five years, will pay interest at the *higher* of 7.5% or 85% of the average return of U.S. Treasury notes with five years to maturity. This is compounded semiannually.

EEs can be redeemed six months after issue at a local financial institution, Federal Reserve Bank or Bureau of the Public Debt.

DEADLINES FOR INTEREST ON E BONDS

Date of Issue	Date of Maturity
May 1941–April 1952	May 1981–April 1992
May 1952–January 1957	January 1992–September 1996
February 1957–May 1959	January 1996–April 1998
June 1959–November 1965	March 1997–August 2003
December 1965–May 1969	December 1992–May 1996
June 1969–November 1973	April 1995–September 1999
December 1973–June 1980	December 1998–June 2005

No interest will be paid after maturity. The bonds may be exchanged for Series HH bonds within one year after maturity.

HH bonds, in denominations of $500 to $10,000, mature in 10 years, pay 7.5% interest semiannually (down from 8.5% in 1982). At maturity you get back your purchase price only. There's a penalty for early redemption when bought for cash but not when exchanged for E bonds. *Maximum investment: $20,000.*

When Es and EEs are swapped for HHs, the minimum redemption value must be $500 and there can be no further deferral of interest. You pay Uncle Sam when you cash in the HHs. At the time of the swap, the amount of the accrued E or EE interest is stamped on the face of the HH bonds.

N.B. Do not exchange old EEs for new EEs when held for less than five years. The yield of the old issues will be higher.

Added plus: Interest on all types of savings bonds is free of state and local income taxes.

Government Retirement Bonds

These are issued in denominations of $50, $100 and $500 through Federal Reserve Banks and the U.S. Treasury. They are designed for investment of funds in Individual Retirement Accounts. They pay 9% interest, compounded semiannually. (See Chapter 27.)

Locating Lost Savings Bonds

If you've lost your savings bonds, get form PD 1048, an Application for Relief, from the U.S. Treasury. Write down as much information as you have: serial number, issuance date; name, address and Social Security number of the original owner. Mail the form to Bureau of Public Debt, 200 Third Street, Parkersburg, W.Va. 26101. Even with the partial data, they may be able to locate/replace the bonds.

Corporate Notes

Investors who want competitive yields and flexibility should find out about corporate notes. These are debt issues by major corporations that, in many cases, tailor the maturities to meet your time schedule: 133 days, two years and three months, etc.

General Motors Acceptance Corporation (GMAC) offers both short- and medium-term notes. The short-term debt is bought at a discount (interest is deducted on issue and the investor receives face value at redemption). Longer-term debt is on an interest-bearing basis.

At maturity, the notes can be rolled over or collected through your local commercial bank. For information, check with your GM dealer or the yellow pages. GMAC offices are in major financial cities. Recently:

• For minimum investments of $50,000: 30–179 days, 8¾%; for minimums of $25,000: 180–270 days, 8¼%.

• For minimum investment of $5,000: medium-term notes: 9 to 12 months, 8¾%; 12–18 months, 9%; 18–24 months, 9⅜%; 24 to 36 months, 9⅝%; 37 to 48 months, 9⅞%; and 4 to 5 years, 10⅛%.

Check your local bank for similar opportunities with local businesses.

Tax Certificates

For shrewd, locally savvy investors, delinquent tax certificates provide high return in a short time. These represent unpaid property taxes. They are sold, by auction, at local country courthouses. Typically, bidding starts at discounts of 20% and often drops to 15%.

The buyer pays off the taxes and collects from the property owner. If the payment is made within three months (as 80% are), the investor makes out well. If the property owner fails to redeem the certificate, the buyer can apply for a tax deed and, ultimately, take possession of the property. These special certificates can be highly profitable if you know what you're doing, work with a knowledgeable attorney and can take abuse from dispossessed property owners.

Special Debt Issues

The old days when a bond was a bond are gone, replaced with an amazing variety of special issues involving extra inducements, flexible rates, indexing and no interest. At the outset many of these were offered by secondary corporations (with the aid and advice of friendly underwriters) but, increasingly, these "opportunities" are offered by well-known, well-rated companies. In most cases, they are best suited to wealthy investors but, on occasion, they can be rewarding for those with modest savings. But always check all details in the prospectus.

Equipment certificates. These are floated by airlines and railroads to finance the purchase of new planes or rolling stock. Their yields are excellent and there's little chance of a default because the company would then be out of business. Certificates are issued in serial form so they mature at different dates.

Optional maturity. These are bonds that can be redeemed anytime after the first five years or so. This provision protects the investor against unfavorable shifts in the cost of money by setting a floor on the value of the debt.

Example: In 1979, Beneficial Corporation, the big finance firm, issued an 8% bond redeemable in any year after 1983 through 2001. Thus, in 1984, if interest rates rise (and the price of the bonds falls below 100), the investor can get back his $1,000 and reinvest the money in more rewarding situations. But if, starting in 1984, interest rates fall well below 8%, the investor is locked in with a better-than-average yield and, probably, a higher market value.

FHA-backed bonds. These are private debt issues 90% guaranteed by the Farmers Home Administration. The proceeds are used to finance business acquisition, plant expansion or equipment purchases when the project is in a rural area and shows promise of providing permanent jobs.

For investors, these bonds provide longer maturities and the assurance that Uncle Sam will make good on any loan in default. To the borrower, they offer a lower interest rate than could be obtained on its own credit. Typical issue: $15.25 million, 20-year, 8.9% bonds for Perdue, Inc., a poultry processing firm.

Eurobonds. These are issued by foreign subsidiaries of U.S. companies. They pay 50 to 100 basis points (0.5% to 1%) more than similarly rated domestic bonds.

Since these have heavier sinking funds than most U.S. issues, there's less risk of loss of capital when interest rates rise. Buy only in units of 10 or more because these bonds are sold in a dealer's market oriented to major investors.

Yankee bonds. These are foreign issues floated in dollars. They include debt of governments, governmental agencies and publicly owned corporations. Their yields are good, and there are possibilities of extra profits due to shifts in exchange rates, but their marketability is limited. You had better know something about the issuer or have a money-savvy adviser.

Foreign bonds. These are issued in native currencies and so are subject to the fluctuations in their value against the dollar. The stronger the dollar, the lower the real value of the bonds and the interest paid. The yields are a bit higher than those of American debt but so are the risks.

Remember, too, that, with most foreign firms, accounting practices are different and, usually, more liberal than those permitted by American agencies and CPAs.

Indexed to inflation. These are great speculations if you have some idea of the areas in which the payments are to be made. Sunshine Mining Company, a major silver producer, issued an 8.5% coupon bond redeemable for the greater of $1,000 cash or the going value of 50 troy ounces of silver (equivalent to $20 an ounce). If you want to gamble on metals, this could be rewarding . . . if you are patient.

Indexed to oil prices. These are bonds where the interest rate fluctuates with the price of oil. Petro-Lewis sold 20-year bonds with an initial coupon of 13%. This yield goes up annually if the price of "sweet crude" from West Texas rises 10%. The rate cannot drop below 13% or go above 15.5%. Apparently, investors were not overly impressed: the original bonds, offered at $1,000 each, were selling recently at $860.

Floating-rate debt. These are adjustable rate notes where the interest rate changes every two years to a level at a preset percentage of the prevailing yield of two-year Treasury notes. With BankAmerica notes, due in 1989, the yield is 105% of the base. Great when interest rates are rising but not so attractive when they are likely to decline.

A variation is the "extendable note" where the maturities can be stretched out at the option of the issuer. IBM notes permit three extensions in 12 years. At the normal maturity, the investor can cash in at par or can keep the notes with interest to be paid at the then current rate. *Good hedge.*

Zero coupon bonds. These are corporate debt, sold far below face value, that pay no interest but are redeemed at full face value at some specified future date. In effect, they assure compounding of the interest so that the average rate of return is more or less competitive.

Example: In April 1982, Allied Corporation offered $1,000 Money Multiplier notes on these terms:

Maturity Price	Maturity Date	Price to Public
$1,000	July 1, 1987	$500.00
1,000	October 1, 1992	250.00
1,000	January 15, 1996	166.67
1,000	September 15, 1998	125.00
1,000	August 15, 2000	100.00

In effect, Allied deferred interest payments to maturity so that, for the debt due in the year 2000, the company would have to come up with an additional $900: nine times what was originally paid.

But what looks like capital gains is considered interest by IRS. The investor must pay an annual tax, on the assumed income, in increasing portions so that the total tax base, in this example, will be $900. For the investor in the 50% tax bracket, this means a tax bite of $450—over the years. If the bond is sold before maturity—at a higher-than-cost price—the individual must pay a capital gains tax on the difference between the sales price and the cost plus annual amortization.

These serialists are seldom suitable for individual portfolios because of the complex tax calculations, but they can be worthwhile for pension funds where there are no taxes on income. It's a convenient way to count on automatic compounding.

With its usual ingenuity, Wall Street has developed several variations. Basically, they involve "stripping": separating the interest portion of the debt from the principal and selling the separate items to investors according to their objectives/needs.

Two of the most publicized are TIGERS (Treasury Investment Growth Receipts) and CATS (Certificates of Accrual on Treasury Securities). The unique selling proposition is that there are two sections: the coupon (interest) and the debt (principal). Each can be sold separately.

Thus, a TIGER would be a U.S. Treasury bond, sold at a low price with no interest to be paid and redemption at face value.

Example: A 20-year TIGER, bought for $1,912, would yield 11.75% compounded semiannually to return $19,125 at maturity: $1,912 return of principal; $4,495 in interest ($225 a year); plus a whopping $12,718 in interest-on-interest.

SOME ZERO COUPON BONDS

ISSUER/DATE	Maturity	Offering Price*	Recent Price	Yield	S&P Rating
Allied Corp. 5/82	7/87	$500.00	62 3/8	12.28%	A
BankAmerica 4/82	11/92	250.00	34 3/4	11.40	AA+
GMAC 6/81	7/91	252.50	41	11.67	AA+
Penney (J.C.) 4/81	5/89	332.50	53	11.50	A+
Security Pacific 11/81	12/86	526.50	68 1/2	12.21	AA+

* Per $1,000 face value

SOURCE: New York Stock Exchange; The First Boston Corporation

Automatic Bond Reinvestment

Just as with common stocks whose dividends are used to buy new shares, corporations now offer interest-reinvestment programs. Illinois Power Company permits the interest to be used to buy shares of common stock at a 5% discount from the average price of the stock on the first trading day of the month in which the interest is paid. Over a three-year period, this formula plan boosted the total return of the 8⅞, '08 bonds to 10.57%.

N.B.: To the IRS, this interest is still taxable as ordinary income whether received or converted to stock.

Flower Bonds for Old Folks

One of the best investments for affluent senior citizens is a package of "flower" bonds. These are U.S. Government obligations that carry low coupons (because they were issued years ago) and so are selling at discounts. *Their benefits:* they will be accepted at face value in paying estate taxes when they are owned by a person at death. If you are in your seventies, or are responsible for some older person, check this opportunity. The savings are not great but they can be welcome.

FLOWER BONDS TO REDUCE ESTATE TAXES

ISSUE	RECENT PRICE	YIELD
3 1/2s, Feb. 1990	89.22	5.29%
4 1/4s, Aug. 1987-92	88.26	5.79
4s, Feb. 1988-93	87.22	5.63
4 1/8s, May 1989-94	88.31	5.46
3s, Feb. 1995	87.24	4.32
3 1/2s, Nov. 1998	88.22	4.52

SOURCE: Barron's

Example: February 3½s, due in 1990, are trading at 89²⅔₃₂ ($896.87). Uncle Fred, age 81, buys 10 bonds. If he dies before 1990, his estate will get a credit of $10,000 against federal estate taxes.

Price Shifts

The exact moves depend on the quality and maturity of the bond and the tenor of the market, but here are some general figures that can be used in projections.

For bonds priced to yield 11.5% with these maturities, the percentage price gains will be:

Maturities	Interest Rate Decline	
	− 1%	− 3%
2½ years	+0.21	+0.65
7 years	+0.50	+1.16
20 years	+0.83	+2.86

Call Protection

To attract major investors for long-term commitments, corporations usually include call protection with new bond issues. This rules out redemption for the first five or 10 years and then, usually, only at an above par price: i.e., a $1,000 bond will not be called until after the fifth year when it can be redeemed at 105 ($1,050).

A call will usually be exercised when the current interest rate is lower than that of the coupon when issued. The corporation can save money by borrowing new money at, say, 10%, when the yield on the original bonds was 15%. Corporate treasurers begin to think about refunding when the current interest rate is 2% below that of the old coupon, if there are quite a few years to normal maturity.

Investors should always look for adequate call protection. It's annoying and costly to have to turn a long-term loan into a short-term one.

When the price of bonds moves above the call price, the professionals sharpen their pencils and calculate the Yield to Call rather than the Yield to Maturity. Often, this will show a favorable spread of 50 basis points. Even with a redemption below the market price, a high yield will more than compensate for the capital loss. Dupont 14s, 1991 at 111⅜ and callable at par had a Yield to Call of 11.24%, better than the Yield to Maturity of comparable issues.

Sinking Fund Provisions

When a bond issue sets up a sinking fund, it means that the corporation must make periodic, predetermined cash payments to the trustee of the debt. With this money, the trustee buys back a portion of the issue each year: in the open market when the bond price is below par; by lot when it is trading above face value.

With a sinking fund, the corporation pays less total interest. With a 25-year issue set up to buy back 3.75% of the debt annually, 75% of the bonds will be retired before maturity. This means that the average life of the bonds will be about 17 years, not the 25 years anticipated by the investor. And, again, the proceeds may have to be reinvested at a lower yield.

A similar situation to the early-call provision is the use of the "funnel." This allows the company to satisfy sinking-fund requirements for its entire mortgage debt by zeroing in on and retiring bonds of a single issue. Obviously, the called bonds will be those with the highest coupons. The same threat of early retirement applies to some preferred stocks.

Another special situation with sinking funds is "doubling the option." This allows the corporation, at the time interest payments are due, to call up twice the normal number of shares at a special call price. Thus, with a 6% sinking fund, started in the fifth year, this will amount to an annual call of 12% of the entire issue. To the investor, this would be worthwhile only if the call price were well above par.

A sinking fund adds a margin of safety in that the purchases provide price support and enhance the probability of repayment. But it narrows the time span of the loan so there will be less total income for the long-term investor. Sinking funds benefit the corporation more than the bondholder.

Watch out for:

• Corporate policy changes that may save the company money at your expense. In late 1979, A.T.&T. reduced the extra interest paid on called bonds from 12 to 6 months premium.

• Call provisions for high-coupon utility bonds. With Niagara Power 10⅝s, '85, the *big type* set the call price at 103.54 after 1981 but the *small type* referred to a replacement fund, a reserve for the repair and maintenance of mortgaged property, to be used to redeem the bonds at any time. So, four years *before* the anticipated protection date, investors had to turn in their bonds.

• Bonds selling close to their call price when the call date is near or past. Such debt issues tend to move like short-term holdings when the market is moving up; like long-term ones when the trend is down.

High-Yielding Bonds

Bonds with high yields fall into two categories:

1. Investments that provide excellent income now but are selling at premium prices so that their values will decline in the future (at call or maturity).

If you buy Alabama Power, you will get $173.75 interest on each $1,000 bond and, after 1986, may have to surrender the debt at 113.66 for a loss of about $60 per bond.

You'll be safer with Tenneco 15s, '06. The cost is 109, the current yield 14% and there's no call until 1991 when the redemption price will be $1,115 for a small gain over current cost.

Taxwise, IRS wants its share. You can elect to amortize the premium each year and take an annual deduction or take a full deduction when you sell or redeem. (See Chapter 20.)

2. Speculations which, broadly can be classified as "junk" bonds—those of financially troubled companies

where a comeback is possible or those of firms with highly leveraged balance sheets where you're shooting dice.

One corporate tactic is to swap bonds for common stock. This permits the company to record an instant earnings increase because the after-tax interest costs will be less than the earnings attributed to the acquired common stock: i.e., to cover a stock selling at five times profits, the corporation has to earn only 40% as much (before taxes). And that balance sheet looks a lot better—especially when the bonds are promoted by aggressive brokers.

Another trick is to swap new bonds, with warrants, for old bonds selling at deep discounts. International Harvester cleaned up its financial statement by swapping $1,000 in old 9s, '04 for $500 or new 18% bonds plus warrants to buy the common stock at $5 a share until 1993. Since the old bonds were trading at deep discounts, the deal lowered the debt. But the interest payments were the same and the stock was selling at about 10. You have to wait to win.

N.B. The values of many junk bonds rose sharply last year but there may still be opportunities for extra gains for those who are willing to take risks. Chances are that all but the lowest rated issues (CCC) will be able to pay interest. Why else would some of those BBB− bonds be selling above par?

Guideline: Junk bonds should yield 3.5 to 4.5% above those of similar maturity government debt. When the spread gets greater, the risks are rising.

SOME HIGH YIELDING BONDS

COMPANY/SECURITY	S&P RATING	RECENT PRICE	YIELD	CALL DATA PRICE	DATE
Alabama Power 17 3/8, '11	BBB−	119	15	113.16	1986
Baltimore G&E 16 3/4, '91	AA	119 3/4	14	104.65	1986
Caesar's World 12, '94	B	86 3/4	14	100	1984
Citicorp 16, '87	AA+	109 3/4	15	110	1985
Common. Edison 16, '90	BBB+	114	14	103	1987
Duquesne Light 16, '11	BBB+	113 1/2	14	114.23	1986
Fedders 8 7/8, '94	CCC	61 1/8	15	103.50	.....
Gelco 14 5/8, '99	BB	103 7/8	14	105	1984
Inter. Harvester 9, '04	CCC	50 1/4	18	105.58	1985
Lykes 11, '00	B+	77	14	100	1985
MCI 15, '00	BB−	108 5/8	14	112	1990
Nortek 12 1/2, '99	B	89	14	112.50	1989
Ohio Edison 15 1/2, '00	BBB−	111	14	114.36	1990
PAA 11 1/2, '94	B	80	14	105.75	1987
P. S. N. H. 14 1/2, '00	BB+	101 3/8	14	112.22	1985
Tenneco 15, '06	A	109	14	111.50	1991
Tex. American Oil 12, '99	B	80	15	108.40	1984
Valero Energy 16 1/4, '01	BBB−	111 1/2	15	......	.....
Xerox Credit 16, '91	AA	115 1/2	14	100	1988

SOURCE: Standard & Poor's; New York Stock Exchange

Monthly Checks/High Yields

For convenience, high yields and safety, Government National Mortgage Association securities are hard to beat. They are shares in pools of Federal Housing Administration (FHA) and Veterans Administration (VA) mortgages, primarily on single family homes. Payments are made to investors about the middle of *every* month at interest rates ranging from 9% to 14%. Both interest and principal are doubly protected: by the insurance of FHA or guarantee of VA plus the overall guarantee of GNMA.

These securities are called "pass-throughs" because the mortgage bank that packages the original loans "passes through" the income (minus a modest fee) to investors. When a loan is repaid or refinanced, the monthly check will be greater. At the payment of the last mortgage—typically 15–18 years—there will be nothing left.

There are two types: *Ginnie Maes,* pools of regular, level payment mortgages; and *Jeeps,* packages of graduated-payment mortgages (GPMs), where the payments start low and rise as the homeowner earns more money.

Here's how these pass-throughs work. A large brokerage firm buys a multimillion-dollar package of home mortgages at wholesale and sells at retail, usually at $25,000 each. (But you can buy shares in funds for $1,000 each with a sales load of about 3%.)

For easy figuring, let's assume that you invest $50,000 in certificates of a $1 million, 14% package of Ginnie Maes. You own 5% of the offering. The first monthly checks will be around $580, representing almost all interest minus small management fees. After a while, the interest portion will decline and the amortization will increase, but you'll still get the same amount.

At some point, a $50,000 mortgage is paid off, so you will receive 5% of this cash-in—a little less than $2,500. Thereafter, your monthly check will be smaller because there will be less interest and amortization. But the annual rate of return will be more than 14% because payments are made monthly.

QUOTATIONS FOR GINNIE MAES

INTEREST RATE	BID	ASKED	CHANGE	YIELD
7 1/2%	77-31	78-15	+ 1/4	10.83%
8	80-26	81-10	+ 1/4	10.88
9	85-23	86- 7	+ 1/4	11.11
10	90-23	91- 7	+ 1/4	11.32
11 1/2	98-20	98-10	+ 1/13	11.69
12 1/2	103-40	103-12	+ 1/25	11.88
13	105-20	105-10	+ 1/2	12.06
14	107-10	107- 9	+ 0-12	12.70
15	108	108- 8	− 0-9	13.49

SOURCE: Barron's

Quotations are based on the stated yield: as low as 77 ($770 per $1,000 face value) for old 7½% coupon pools to 108 ($1,080) for more recent packages with a 15% yield. Unlike discount bonds, there will be no appreciation to maturity.

With these mortgage pools no one knows the actual maturities. With old mortgages, at 10% or less, the quotations assume average maturities of 12 years. This is probably low because most people will hang on to these bargains. The odds are that the real payout time will be close to 18 years.

But when a prepayment is made, the investor gets a bonus: the loan is paid at the full value of the balance but the security was bought at a discount: i.e., payback of $1,000 for each $770 investment.

Similarly, when the investor pays a premium, say $1,080, he will lose 8% when a mortgage is repaid. But with high-coupon issues, the repayments will be faster. As interest rates decline, more homeowners will replace their loans. In effect, high-yield issues, at this time, are self-destructing: a 9% Ginnie Mae based on a life expectancy of 12 years, selling at 69, would yield 14.63%. If repayments slowed to 16–18 years, the yield would rise well over 15%!

With all types of pass-throughs, the first income (interest only) is fully taxable. But as amortization rises and mortgages are repaid, a larger, but not regular, portion is a nontaxable return of capital. With *Jeeps,* where the interest payments may be delayed, the early payments are tax-free. The managers of both types of pools provide detailed data for tax returns.

Pass-throughs are excellent investments for those who want regular income but are best for elderly folks over age 70. The 15-year time span for Ginnie Maes, for example, is closely related to the actuarial life expectancy of older investors: 11.2 years for a male; 14.9 for a female. But there should be other reserves because, in the late years, the payments will dwindle and, eventually, cease.

New Packages: jumbo pools of 50 mortgages from different lenders. There's one central paying agent, and, with diversification, greater consistency of prepayments. A companion deal provides for payments to be made on the 25th rather than the 15th of each month. This delay lowers the yields by about five basis points so the packages cost a bit less.

Swapping Bonds

To the serious investor, swapping bonds can be profitable: a capital loss can reduce taxes; a higher yield can boost income and a wise switch can raise quality and extend the maturity of the debt.

Example: In 1976, Dan bought 10 ARCO Pipelines 8%s, due in 1984. In September 1982, the bonds were trading at 95 ($9,500). Since Dan could use a modest tax loss, he sold them for a $500 long-term loss.

With the proceeds, he bought 10 10¾%s, '90 U.S. Treasuries at 95. Result: he (1) increased his annual income from $800 to $1,075; (2) upgraded the quality of his holdings from AA+ to AAA (and made his spouse happy); (3) extended the maturity six years to 1990.

This is oversimplified and neglects the fact that, over a period of time, the majority of income from debt issues, when interest is promptly reinvested, will come from compounding. The example assumes that the reinvestment rate would be higher for the new, higher coupon bonds than for the old ones. This is not true. The reinvestment rate would be the same for both bonds!

Counsel: When you swap a sizable block of bonds, get full projections of total returns from your broker first. My guess is that he will be surprised, too.

Bond Funds

For those with modest savings and reluctance to become involved with debt securities, there are bond funds. They

Debt for Equity

There are two types of this new development:

1. **Defeasance:** used by corporations to discharge debts without actually paying them off prior to maturity. The company arranges for a broker to buy a portion of the outstanding bond issues, for a fee. The broker then: (a) exchanges the bonds for a new issue of corporate stock with a market value equal to that of the bonds; (b) sells the shares at a profit. The corporate balance sheet is improved without harming operations or prospects.

Or, the deal can be privately controlled: Exxon turned over to a trustee bank, Morgan Guaranty Trust, $312 million of U.S. Treasuries and government securities with an overall yield of 14%. Morgan then took control of $515 million Exxon debt, paid interest on the low coupon issues and pooled the balance of income so that, by the year 2009, the date of the last maturity, the trustee will have $515 million to pay off the principal.

Exxon could no longer deduct $31.7 million in interest expenses but brightened its balance sheet and reported an after-tax gain of $130 million because the debt was discharged at less than face value.

2. **Debt for Equity.** Manufacturers Hanover, in need of additional capital, issued 10-year, 15⅛% notes with attached equity contracts mandating conversion into common stock at the lower of $55.55 per share or the 30-day average closing price prior to conversion—with a floor of $40 per share.

For the investor, this worked out well. When interest rates dropped, he sold each $1,000 note for $1,200 for a $200 profit. He then reinvested the $1,000 in other securities which he turned over to the bank as collateral to replace the now detached equity contract. He can look for profits on the new investments and, eventually, the common stock.

---

come in all shapes, sizes, packages and styles and are available as no load and loads and open and closed ends. You name it and Wall Street has it or will soon.

Shares can be purchased for as little as $1,000 with even small savings later and most funds encourage automatic reinvestment of income for compounding. The yields may be a bit less than those available by direct purchases but you get diversification, excellent reports and professional management that is more illusory than real. *The prices of all debt securities move opposite to the cost of money.* There may be situations that will be improved by shrewd administration but when interest rates soar, the values of all bond funds decline. Vice versa when the cost of money drops.

For more information, see Chapter 17 but with these special bond funds, there are extra checkpoints to help you make a choice.

Get the pedigree of the sponsor. Dealing in bonds is a special art that requires different types of analyses than with stocks. The future projections always factor in the anticipated cost of money and, in normal markets, this is difficult to forecast, almost impossible in erratic periods. Look for a backup team of experienced-on-debt-issues analysts and traders who have lived long enough to understand the vagaries of the bond market.

Evaluate the portfolio. For safety, choose funds with the most A-or-better rated holdings. For good income, look for those with lower quality (but not too low) issues. For high returns, find out about "junk" bond funds. A couple of big winners will offset the inevitable losers.

Check the performance over at least 10 years—long enough to include both bad and good years for debt securities. Choose the fund that scored highest according to your specific objectives.

Determine the average price of bond holdings (or have the fund do it for you). If this is low, it means that, when interest rates decline, the bounce-up will be greater than if the average price was higher.

Look for frequent distributions. A fund that pays monthly assures a steady cash flow. If this is reinvested, compounding will be at a more rewarding rate. Buy just before the distribution-declaration date.

Check the repurchase price. If the fund buys only at the lower side of the price spread, you will lose a few dollars when you cash in. At redemption, Nuveen pays a bid side price; Merrill Lynch pays the offering price as long as the fund is one in which the firm makes a market.

FIXED-INCOME SECURITIES

TYPE	Minimum Purchase	Maturity Range	Liquidity	Interest	Where Available
SHORT TERM					
U.S. Treasury Bills*	$ 10,000	3-12 mos.	Best	Discount*	Brokers, Banks, Federal Reserve Banks, AMEX, Banks, Brokers
Local Authorities	1,000	3-12 mos.	Average	Straight	Banks, Brokers
FNMA notes**	50,000	30-270 days	Good	Discount	Major dealers
Federal Intermediate Credit	5,000	270 days	Good	Straight	Banks, brokers
State/Local Govt. Notes	5,000	1-12 mos.	Average	Straight	Banks, brokers
Bankers' Acceptances	5,000	1-270 days	Average	Discount	Banks, brokers
Negotiable CDs	100,000	1-12 mos.	Average	Straight	Banks, brokers
CDs	10,000	1 year	Penalty/early withdrawal	Straight Compounded	Banks, S&Ls Credit Unions
	1,000	30 mos.	See above	See above	Banks, S&Ls, Credit Unions
Commercial Paper	100,000	1-270 days	Average	Straight	Dealers
MEDIUM TERM					
U.S. EE Bonds	25	9 years	Poor	Discount	Banks, U.S. Treasury
U.S. HH Bonds	500	10 years	Penalty/early withdrawal	Straight	Federal Reserve
U.S. Treasury Notes/Bonds	1,000	1-30 years	Good	Straight	Banks, brokers
Federal Financing Bank Notes/Bonds	1,000	1-20 years	Good	Straight	Banks, brokers
Farmers Home Administration notes/certificates	25,000	1-25 years	Average	Straight	Banks, brokers
GNMA Securities/Certificates***	5,000	1-25 years	Average	Straight	Banks, brokers
GNMA pass-throughs***	25,000	14-17 years	Good	Straight	Banks, brokers
Federal Land Bank bonds	1,000	1-10 years	Good	Straight	Banks, brokers
Corporate Notes/Bonds	1,000	1-30 years	Good	Straight	Brokers
Eurobond Bonds/Notes	1,000	3-25 years	Average	Straight	Foreign Banks
LONG TERM					
Housing Authority Bonds	5,000	1-40 years	Good	Straight	Banks, brokers
Federal Home Loan Mortgage Certificates	100,000	15-30 years	Average	Straight	Banks, brokers
FNMA Bonds**	25,000	2-25 years	Average	Straight	Banks, brokers
State/Local Gov't Notes/Bonds	5,000	1-30 years	Average	Straight	Brokers
Inter. Bank: Reconstruction/ Development; Asian; Inter-American notes/bonds	1,000	3-25 years	Average	Straight	Banks, brokers
Foreign notes/bonds denominated in dollars, issued by U.S. and foreign corporations	1,000	1-20 years	Average	Straight	Brokers, overseas banks
Corporate Preferred Stock	25	No maturity	Average	Quarterly Divs.	Brokers

*On discount basis: with 1 year, $10,000 bill @ 10% = $9,000.
**Federal National Mortgage Association;   ***Government National Mortgage Association

SOURCE: Based on David M. Darst, THE COMPLETE BOND BOOK

14

Tax-Exempt Bonds: Big Changes Ahead

On July 1, 1983, tax-exempt bonds started to join the broad investment market. This was the day that, by congressional action, all new municipal bonds must be issued in *registered* form with the name of the owner identified on the face of the certificate or, more likely, in a central filing system. This is expected to be the catalyst for a major transformation of the municipal bond market from a limited, relatively controlled, professional area for institutional and wealthy investors to a broad, active market for individuals: more bonds available in units of $1,000; listing on the NYSE; slightly higher yields to cover handling costs of the issuer; the eventual elimination of printed certificates and lower transfer/custody fees.

Tax-exempt bonds are still best for those in the highest tax bracket but they can be worthwhile for those whose tax rate is 35% and, with inflation and two incomes, more families will qualify.

Tax-exempt bonds (also called municipals) are debt issues of states, local governments and certain public authorities. Their interest is free of federal income taxes and when the bonds are issued in the state of residence of the investor, also exempt from local and state income levies. Debt issues of Puerto Rico, Virgin Islands and District of Columbia are tax exempt in all 50 states.

That means that, for those in the 50% tax bracket, the 8% yield of a municipal bond is equal to 16% taxable income (almost 20% for those who live in New York City and buy New York-issued bonds). The exemption applies only to interest, not capital gains.

Added plus: If you substitute sufficient tax-exempt interest for currently taxable income, you may move down to a lower tax bracket. To make your calculations, use your effective tax rate, not the one that is shown for your gross income tax bracket. In most cases, this will be the tax rate finally used after all deductions and adjustments. But keep in mind that, unless the law is changed, the tax rates will be lower in 1984 and, with indexing, will tend to remain fairly stable. *Buy tax-exempts according to two incomes: this year's and that anticipated five years hence.*

Calculating Equivalent Yields

To figure the exact equivalency between any tax-exempt and taxable yield, use these formulas:

• To determine the percent yield that a bond or other fully taxed security must provide to give an after-tax return that matches a given tax-exempt yield:

TEY = Tax-Exempt Yield
TB = Tax Bracket
TY = Taxable Yield

$$\frac{TEY}{(100) - TB} = TY$$

If a tax-exempt bond yields 7% and the investor is in the 40% tax bracket, the equivalent taxable yield is 11.67%.

$$\frac{7}{(100) - 40} = \frac{7}{60} = 11.67\%$$

• To determine the percent yield which a tax-exempt bond must pay to match the after-tax return of a bond or other security, with a given, taxable yield, reverse the formula:

$$TEY = TY \times (100) - TB$$

$$TEY = 11.67 \times (100 - 40) = 11.67 \times 60 = 7.00\%$$

TAX-EXEMPT vs. TAXABLE INCOME
Conversion Table

TAX–FREE YIELD	EQUALS TAXABLE PER CENT YIELD IN THESE BRACKETS				
	30%	35%	40%	45%	50%
5.0%	7.1%	7.7%	8.3%	9.1%	10.0%
6.0	8.6	9.2	10.0	10.9	12.0
6.5	9.3	10.0	11.0	11.8	13.0
7.0	10.0	10.8	12.7	12.7	14.0
7.5	10.7	11.5	13.6	13.6	15.0
8.0	11.4	12.3	14.5	14.5	16.0
8.5	12.1	13.1	15.5	15.5	17.0
9.0	12.9	13.8	16.4	16.4	18.0

Be Cautious

Before you start buying tax-exempts, recognize the risks, be certain there are *real* tax benefits and consider other options:

• **Weigh the alternatives:** With pension plans, you get tax deductions for the amount of the annual contribution; with common stocks, you will get slightly less income but the opportunity for growth in value and dividends can make a huge difference. You can, of course, get appreciation by buying low coupon municipals selling at discounts but, in small lots, the acquisition costs can be high and the liquidity limited.

• **Check the ratings.** These are the classifications made by statistical services such as Moody's and Standard & Poor's. They are similar to those of taxable debt: AAA, highest; AA, very strong; down to BB, speculative; and even lower (to D) for governments/agencies in financial trouble.

Just as with taxable bonds, never invest in any tax-exempts rated below BBB! Most debt issues are, and will be, safe. Their interest will be paid regularly and they will be redeemed at face value. But the chances of default are rising. Governments, like individuals, try to maintain their lifestyle even in the face of reduced income. With their citizens resisting higher taxes and cuts in federal aid, state and local governments face sharply reduced income. Many of them use debt to finance current costs. That's mortgaging the house to pay the grocery bill, and, inevitably, will signal trouble ahead. In 1982, Moody's downgraded the ratings of twice as many municipalities as it raised!

• **Anticipate fluctuating prices.** As with all debt securities, tax-exempts move opposite to the cost of money: *down* when interest costs rise; *up* when they fall. New Jersey Turnpike debt, issued with a 6% coupon and due in 2014, were selling at 70 ($700).

The price spreads become more significant with small lots when the difference between the bid and asked price can be $20 to $30 per bond.

• **Recognize the erosion of inflation.** As with all fixed-income holdings, the purchasing power of the interest and principal will be reduced by inflation. Over a 30-year life, the typical municipal bond will lose almost all of its original value.

Major Types of Tax-Exempt Bonds

There are over 100,000 issues of municipal securities issued by more than 15,000 communities/states/agencies. They range from multimillion-dollar AAA-rated state highway bonds to unrated $50,000 obligations of a local parking authority.

Traditionally, tax-exempts have been traded by professionals who regard $100,000 as a small lot. But in recent years, there has been an astonishing increase in the number of individual owners. This has been due to a combination of superhigh yields and aggressive selling by brokers attracted by the ample income from "commissions" (actually the spread between bid and asked prices), the variety of products, and unique new issues that provide excellent sales tools. And, as is to be expected, the enthusiasm is not always justified by the facts.

These are the most widely issued, and traded, forms of tax-exempt securities:

1. General obligation bonds. These are the most common and, generally, safest. They are backed by the full taxing power of the issuer. The payment of their interest and redemption is a primary obligation, so they usually have the highest ratings and the lowest yields.

A couple of years ago, some promotional-minded state/city treasurers came up with "minibonds," issued directly to the public in denominations of $100, $500 and $1,000. These made headlines but failed to catch on because of the handling costs and the issuer's need for large sums. Still, if they are available where you live, you can be a good citizen IF you are sure of the creditworthiness of the issuer.

2. Limited-tax bonds: backed by the full faith of the body but not by its full tax power. Usually, they are secured by the receipts of a particular tax.

3. Revenue bonds: based on revenues from projects built or maintained by local governments: sewers, waterworks, dormitories, etc. Their quality varies with the financial success of the underlying enterprise.

The best known revenue bonds are those secured by income from motorists: toll, roads, bridges and tunnels. Lately, this concept has been extended to housing, parking, etc.

Major projects will be rated by the services, but smaller programs should be checked carefully, preferably with the local broker involved in the underwriting and later, in the annual reports. For a good electric or water system, net revenues of 120% of annual debt-service requirements should be OK. With a new project, look for projected 200% coverage.

For extra protection, concentrate on bond issues that offer special provisions:

• Turnpike Authority of Kentucky 7½s, '09 are paid by toll revenues but also have a call on the proceeds of a "severance" tax assessed on all coal produced in the state. Thus, the true coverage of interest and principal is 3.32 compared to 1.5 for most revenue issues.

• New York State Dormitory Authority bonds are paid from rentals to students. Their acceptance has been tainted by slow payments so that several major universities have pledged their endowment-fund securities as collateral.

4. Anticipation notes: short-term obligations to raise temporary cash while waiting for funds from a bond issue; to tide over until taxes are received, etc. These are not designed for individuals but are often available from a local bank or broker. Competitive yields and short maturities.

5. Industrial development bonds: issued by states/authorities to finance construction of plants, building and facilities which are then leased to private firms such as Exxon, K-Mart, McDonald's, etc.

Because of the backing by major firms, many of these

TAX RATES SCHEDULED FOR 1984

Joint Return

TAXABLE INCOME	TAX RATE
$11,901 to $16,000	16%
16,001 to 20,200	18
20,201 to 24,600	22
24,601 to 29,900	25
29,901 to 35,200	28
35,201 to 45,800	33
45,801 to 60,000	38
60,001 to 85,600	42
85,601 to 109,400	45
109,401 to 162,400	49
162,401 to 215,400	50

SOURCE: Internal Revenue Service

issues carry top ratings (and, thus, lower yields). In some cases, the tax exemption applies only to the first $5 million, so get full details. For long-term income, these can be worthwhile.

A variation is the hospital revenue bond issued by a municipal/state agency to finance construction of hospitals and/or nursing homes. Some may be operated by nonprofit organizations but others by big corporations such as Hospital Corporation of America. The guarantee sounds better than it is because, in many cases, the credit of the state itself will not be involved.

To permit small investors to share the opportunities, Paine Webber has packaged industrial revenue bonds into a limited partnership: $5,000 per unit. The income increases with higher gross revenues from the tenant. The after-market is limited; there's little diversification; the costs are ample: off-the-top 8% commission, 5% organization expense; 3% bond acquisition cost; and the general partner gets 1% of the income plus a fee of 4% of the adjusted cash flow plus an incentive fee! Well, at least, they tell you what you're buying!

6. Authority debt: either general obligations, revenue or a combination. These can be short-term construction loans or long-term commitments for housing, plants, pollution control equipment, etc.

Typically, a short-term loan would be issued by a local housing authority to provide funds for low/middle income housing. The yields, from 8% to 9.5%, are free from federal income taxes and from local/state taxes, if applicable. Maturities run from 18 months to 4 years; units sell at $5,000 each. The bonds cannot be called and at maturity are paid off with proceeds of FHA-insured loans . . . as agreed when construction started.

A long-term loan might be issued by a local housing authority under contract with federal agencies, so is 100% safe. The yields are competitive and, in sizable units, the bonds are marketable.

Another type is debt of publicly owned utilities: Colorado's Platte River Authority, Nebraska's Omaha Public Power District or Arizona's Salt River Project: good yields, security and, when you deal with a market maker, liquidity.

7. Life-care bonds: more aptly described as retirement-community debt. In some states, they are issued, through a special authority, to build housing units for well-to-do tenants who do not qualify for government aid. Usually, the operators are nonprofit religious groups. For individuals, these are better for dedication than profit. They pay reasonably well but are difficult to sell, usually from an estate.

8. Option tender bonds. These are standard municipal bonds with a fillip to spur sales. They permit the investor to turn in the bonds, at face value, for cash, after a five-year waiting period. In effect, this is a call provision subject to your choice.

You must give six months' written notice. With such protection, these bonds sell close to par (almost regardless of the shifts of interest rates). The repurchase is guaranteed by a letter of credit issued by a bank.

Example: In 1982, Platte River Power Authority issued tax-exempt bonds maturing in 2002 and 2012 with coupons of 14% and 14⅛%, respectively. They carried 10-year call protection.

> ### Pre-refunding
> This is a trick (but often profitable) deal with high coupon bonds that cannot be redeemed for some years. When interest rates drop, the issuing authority raises cash—from reserves or a new, lower cost loan—and uses the proceeds to buy taxable securities such as Treasury notes or CDs. These are deposited as security for the original issue and their income, and eventually, principal are used to pay off the original debt.

In early 1983, when interest rates fell, the Authority issued new bonds at 9.75% and bought high-yielding U.S. notes. The new debt is held in escrow until the first call date when a portion will be sold to pay off the original bonds. Meantime, the Authority reduces the debt service by the difference between the old and new coupons.

The investor does well, too. He feels secure with the original purchase because the bonds were rated A− by Moody's and, once the refunding started and the bonds became backed by Uncle Sam, their prices rose sharply so the investor could sell out for a welcome long-term, low-taxed capital gain!

Advice from Ben Weberman of *Forbes* magazine: Take a look at high coupon utility and hospital issue, especially those with issues 200 to 300 basis points higher than the current rate. *Best bet:* revenue bonds because they are more likely to be refunded.

9. Floaters. These are tax-exempts where the principal remains static and the yields fluctuate with the cost of money;

Example: U.S. Steel #1 Environmental Improvement Revenue Bonds yield the *higher* of 67% of 13-week T-bills or 72% of 30-year Treasury bonds. Offsetting this protection is the provision that the rate of return cannot be greater than 12%, but neither can it be less than 6%. Good deal with a well-rated corporation as guarantor of the issuing agency.

10. Commercial paper: with maturities of from 30 to 270 days. These are excellent for temporary parking place for idle cash. Reasonable yields, no taxes. But they are not widely available and then only through experienced brokers.

11. Zero coupon bonds. These are debt issues that pay no interest. They are sold at a low price: for $5,000 face value, at from $250 to $2,500 depending on years to maturity. Most issues are callable in 15 years or so. Their big benefit: you don't have to worry about reinvesting the income. Sales pitch: buy them (or have a doting relative do so) at the birth of a child. By the time, he/she is ready for college, the money will be ready, tax-free. With a little help from your broker, you can probably find an issue that will come due at a specific future date.

The tax situation can be favorable in that investors who sell early may realize losses for tax purposes, even though the bonds are sold above cost. The IRS allows you to write up the cost basis faster than the prices are likely to rise in a static market. The rules also assume straight-line depreciation but accept compounding, which, of course, speeds up with time.

Example: $10,000 zero coupon bond, due in 17 years,

sells for $1,500. After 10 years, the bond will have a compounded value of about $4,600. Under straight-line depreciation, the IRS value will be $6,500 so you triple your money (on paper) and have a $1,500 write-off. But there's also a sales commission!

12. Two-fers. These are similar to zero bonds in that they are issued at a deep discount, but they pay annual interest and all income—from interest and appreciation—is tax-free. Furthermore, it's possible to chalk up a tax loss if the sale is made before the redemption date even if there's no capital gain.

Example: Public Service of New Mexico issued tax-exempt bonds, through a local government agency, 5% coupon, 20-year maturity at 50 cents on the dollar.

Charlie B. buys $100,000 worth of new bonds for $50,000. He gets $5,000 annual income (5% on the $100,000 face value). At the end of 20 years, he cashes in for $100,000 and gets a $50,000 capital gain. No taxes, but 20 years is a long-term commitment.

If Charlie sells after five years at $60,000, he can take a $2,500 tax write-off. His long-term capital gains tax is determined by accreting the cost basis from 50 to 100 on a straight-line basis over the 20-year life of the debt.

$$\text{Cost basis: } 50 + 5\,\frac{(100 - 50)}{(20)} = 50 + 12.5 = 62.5$$

Now his cost basis is $62,500. Since he sold for $60,000, he takes a tax loss of $2,500.

Insured Tax-Exempts

You can avoid the need for checking ratings by concentrating your investments on bonds whose principal and interest is guaranteed by private insurers: American Municipal Bond Assurance Corp. (AMBAC) or the Municipal Bond Insurance Association (MBIA), a consortium of major insurance firms. Usually, these are debt issues of small or middle-sized communities with not-too-high credit rating. For a premium of $10 to $20 per bond, the insurance boosts their quality and, usually, their yields.

Example: AA-rated, 10-year bonds of the State of Montana were issued at 10.3%. A similar 10-year issue of Escambia County (Fla.) Utilities Authority was rated BBB but, because of the insurance by MBIA, was upped to AAA with a yield of 11.75%.

This same technique is used with municipal money market funds. They buy commercial paper with a maximum maturity of one year (average 120 days) and, with the longer maturities and insurance, pay higher yields than competitive funds.

Checkpoints for Tax-Exempts

As with all investments, the #1 checkpoint is *quality,* best indicated by the rating set by Moody's, Standard & Poor's or Fitch's. (See Chapter 13.)

For investments, buy only debt issues whose ratings start with an "A" or "a." They are safe and, in most cases, their yields will be only slightly less than those of lower quality issues.

For speculations, a "Baa" rating involves as much risk as anyone seeking income should take. If you want to gamble, do not buy tax-exempt bonds unless you are very experienced and very rich.

Once in a while, you may be asked to buy un-rated issues: those of municipalities that are so small or have such modest debt that they have never had to bother with the paperwork of statistical services. If you personally know the community and its officials, these can be OK but keep those maturities short as you will have difficulty in selling in a hurry and may incur local criticism.

State and local tax exemption. In states that have local or state income taxes, the interest on municipal bonds issued in that state are exempt from these levies as well as the federal income tax. Thus, if you live in New Jersey, try to buy bonds issued there.

• **Maturity date.** For bonds with the same rating, the shorter the maturity, the lower the yield and the greater the price stability. Unless you plan to buy municipals regularly, it is usually prudent to stick to those with maturities of less than 10 years. In many cases, these will be older bonds selling at a discount (more on that later).

Select maturities according to your financial needs and time schedule. if you plan to retire eight years from now, pick a discount bond that will mature at that time. You will get a competitive yield plus a capital gain that will be taxed at the long-term rate, made lower by your after-65 exemptions.

• **Marketability.** The most readily salable municipals are general obligation bonds of state governments and revenue bonds of large, well-known authorities. Smaller issues have few price quotations and the cost of selling, especially in odd lots, can be more than half the annual interest income!

The most dangerous holdings are those of small municipalities or authorities. How can you expect to get a quick sale of 17 bonds of Dogpatch Septic Tank Authority? And whenever you get a phone call offering you such "bargains," hang up!

• **Call provision.** Larger issues usually permit the bonds to be redeemed, at a price above par, after the first few years. With older, low coupon issues, there's no problem as they will be selling below par. But with high coupon issues, when interest rates decline, watch out. The bond that is trading at 115 might be callable at 105 so it could pay the issuer to refinance.

Once in a while, an early call, when mandatory rather than optional, can be profitable. In January 1981, problem-plagued New York City Municipal Assistance Corporation issued 9¾% bonds due in 1992. Their market price fell to 92 ($920). But the terms called for a portion of the bonds to be callable each January and July, at premiums: in 1983: 101.5 and 101, respectively. Smart investors were guaranteed a profit. Similar situations could occur elsewhere because many municipalities are faced with financial pressures that can be met only by liberal terms on new financing.

And some borrowings have what the professionals refer to as an "accreted call" provision. Kissimmee, Fla. floated 30-year electric revenue bonds at $680 per $1,000 bond: a current yield of 8.82%. Beginning in 1990, the bonds can be called at redemption values, rising annually, from $800 to

$1,000. If interest rates fall, the bond price will probably move over 100 but there will always be the chance that some of the debt will be subject to the lower redemption price.

With all tax-exempt bond issues, read the small print in the prospectus. When the debt is of a smaller community/agency, read it twice.

• **Yield disparities.** If you make a substantial purchase of tax-exempts, shop around. There are surprising disparities in yields, even of those with comparable ratings. The table shows that a shrewd investor could have locked in higher yields of over 1% with the right selection: for bonds due in 1985, 10.5% with Metropolitan Sanitary District of Chicago compared to only 9% for those of the State of Florida. With small investments, it's usually not worth spending the extra time so make your choice from your broker/dealer's inventory.

YIELD DISPARITIES IN TAX-EXEMPTS

ISSUE	YIELDS FOR BONDS DUE IN			
	1987	1992	1997	2002
State of Florida	9.0%	10.2%	10.9%	11.4%
Met. Sanitary/Chicago	10.5	11.5	12.4	12.7
General Obligation	9.25	10.25	11.0	11.25

SOURCE: Heuglin & Cashman

• **Price disparities.** Basically, this refers to discount bonds: those with low coupons whose prices have fallen as interest rates have risen. It's the old story: a competitive yield plus appreciation to maturity.

Examples: Not so long ago, a friend asked about a choice between two tax-exempt bonds of the Port of New York Authority: either (1) 10¼, 2017 at 101 with a 10.15% yield. They were callable at 103 in 1987 so the yield to call was only about 8%; or (2) 6¾, 2014 at 71 for a 9.75% yield. That means that there would have to be a 29+ point rise before any call. For a slightly lower yield and a much lower price, (2) was a better buy because of its appreciation and protection. Plus the fact that, if interest rates declined, the low coupon debt would rise more than the higher-yield one.

Jim Rogers, who expects to retire in 10 years, has $50,000 to invest. He pays federal taxes at the 50% tax rate. If he buys $50,000 of A-rated municipals, he'll get an 8.4% tax-free return: $4,200 a year or $42,000 over the next decade, plus the return of the $50,000—a total of $92,000.

With the same $50,000, he can buy a package of discounted tax-exempts with par value of $70,000 and a current yield averaging 7%. He will receive less income— $3,500 a year for a 10-year total of $35,000—but at maturity, the bonds will be worth $70,000. After paying a capital gains tax of $4,000 (20% of the $20,000 appreciation), his total will be $101,000: $12,000 more than from the bonds purchased at par.

Swapping Tax-Exempts

Generally, tax-exempts should be held to maturity but there are times when it pays to swap. Be sure to do your homework and obey the rules. At year-end, you may get a hard sales pitch from your broker. Just be sure that the benefits come to you, not just to him/her. The idea is to set up a tax loss and, hopefully, increase income.

Example: A couple of years ago, Bob Allen bought 25 New York Housing Finance Authority 7% bonds due in 1992 for $25,000. With the rise in interest rates, their value fell to 82.94 or $20,735. The income, $1,750, was an 8.44% yield.

Having made a few extra bucks during the year, Bob was looking for a tax loss, so he sold the bonds for a long-term loss of $4,265.

He waited 61 days to avoid the possibility of a wash sale (his funds drew interest in a municipal money market fund), then bought 25 New York State Housing Finance Mental Hygiene bonds for $21,120: a 7.3% coupon, maturity in 1994. Now the annual income was $1,825 for a current yield of 8.63%. On his tax return, Bob used the loss to offset a slightly larger profit from the sale of some IBM stock he'd bought 18 months before.

For more information on wash sales, see Chapter 20. You cannot declare a loss on a security if, within 61 days, you acquire substantially identical securities (as Bob eventually did).

Tax note: With municipals bought above par, watch the tax consequences. IRS requires that the premium be amortized over the life of the bond on a straight-line basis, so the cost basis is reduced each year.

Example: In 1982, hospital bonds are issued at $1,000 each with maturity in 2002. When interest rates dropped, their price rose to 120 ($1,200). Ruth bought 10 bonds for $12,000. The $200 per bond premium must be amortized over 20 years: $10 each year. If Ruth sells out in 1992, her cost basis will be $1,100 ($10 per year for 10 years). At a sale price of $1,050, her loss will be $50 per bond, not $150.

Tax Write-Offs

The biggest shock to hit the tax-exempt bond market came in the summer of 1983 when the court declared some bonds of the Washington Power Supply System (WHOOPS) to be in default. The debt of nuclear plants #4 and #5 is, in effect, worthless, but the losses cannot be written off until IRS is convinced that there's no chance of a payback. When this decision is confirmed, the loss will be considered a nonbusiness bad debt. Regardless of how long the bonds were held, the loss will be short-term and can be used to offset ordinary income on a $ for $ basis up to $3,000 a year.

DOs and DON'Ts for Tax-Exempts

DO keep *bearer* bonds in a safe place. They are fully negotiable. Title passes with possession. This makes it imperative that such bonds be kept in a safe deposit box or with your broker. These will be *old* bonds as, starting July 1983, all new issues will be *registered:* no coupons, no problems if lost or stolen and interest checks mailed directly to you.

DO check whether you need a tax shelter. This applies especially to professional men and women such as physicians, lawyers, etc. They can create their own retirement funds, where the income earned by the plan is free of all current income taxes. Not until they draw down benefits after retirement is there any tax on the basic contributions. Municipal bonds are tax-exempt so should not be held in pension plan portfolios.

DON'T report ownership or income on your income tax return. . . . except when calculating a possible tax on Social Security where a tax will be due when the base amount is $25,000 for an individual or $32,000 for a married couple filing jointly. The adjusted gross income includes wages/salary, dividends, interest, capital gains, etc., plus interest from tax-exempt obligations plus 50% of Social Security benefits. Everyone must pay taxes on capital gains with municipals but can use a loss to reduce other income.

DO deal only with a reputable brokerage firm. Bond selling, by an unscrupulous operator, can be very profitable— for the promoter. The growing popularity of tax-exempts with individual investors has spawned a modern version of the bucket-shop technique. Glib salesmen telephone prospects to offer bargains in "tax-free municipals." They lie about the bond's quality, issuer, return, yield, maturity date and true market price. Even if they tell the truth, the buyer has almost no way to check the quotations because they concentrate on secondary securities. These "fast-buck" operators prey on ignorance by selling bonds from their inventory (which was probably acquired at bargain prices). You can take a terrible beating if you end up with a mess of different bonds of little-known government agencies.

If you get a hard sell on tax-exempts, especially by phone, be *very* cautious. You will always be safer with your regular broker.

DO take advantage of serial maturities. Unlike most corporate bonds, which usually have the same redemption date, municipals mature serially: a portion of the debt comes due each year until the final redemption.

Example: State of Maryland $125 million State and Local Facilities Loan of 1983 has $5,640,000 due in 1985; $6,120,000 in 1986 and so on until $14,945,000 in 1997. The coupon interest rates rose from 8.20% to 8.40%. The bonds were priced so that the yields to maturity started at 5.75% for the two-year bonds and, each year, rose so that the 1997s carried a high 8.75%.

You can buy maturities to fit future needs: for college tuition, retirement, etc.

DO buy in December. This is bargain month for the municipal bond market. Many investors swap bonds at this time to set up tax losses. This selling pressure tends to lower prices so, temporarily, yields are higher.

DON'T borrow to invest in tax-exempts. It's illegal and you lose the tax benefits. This caveat applies to loans made to *either* husband or wife. With large, diversified portfolios, segregate the tax-exempts, set up a separate account, and keep full records of the source of funds invested. Then, make certain that if you do buy other securities in other accounts on margin, you space your transactions so that you don't borrow a bundle on Monday and, on Tuesday, invest about the same amount in municipals.

Tax-Exempt Bond Funds

Investors who want diversification, the benefits of compounding by reinvestment of interest, professional management, and, after retirement, monthly checks, should consider tax-exempt bond funds. As a rule of thumb, funds will be more rewarding for investments of less than $10,000. You can make small additions periodically and, for a modest fee, switch all or part of these savings to another fund under the same management when market conditions or needs change. There are municipal money market funds for short-term holdings but, for investors, there are two choices:

Unit trusts: closed-end funds that, usually, are sold with loads of 2.5% to 5%, charge annual fees of 0.15% (factored into the yield quoted by the broker) and redeem shares without cost.

Unit trusts invest all receipts from the sale of shares in a fixed portfolio. No new bonds are added. The funds themselves do not have a final maturity date but as a fund's holdings mature (or as the bonds are paid off through sinking funds), the proceeds are distributed on a pro-rata basis to fundholders. These funds are self-liquidating so that when assets drop below about 20% of the original investment, the fund goes out of business and you will get back only the current price of the portfolio.

Unit trusts are safe and assure regular income based on the yield at the time of the issue: about 7% for funds started in 1976; 8% for those floated in 1979; over 9% for those offered in 1980; and, since then, 8% or lower.

These unit trusts are safe and assure regular income based on the yield at the original offering: about 7% for those started in 1976; 8% for those floated in 1979; 10% for those sold in 1980; over 12% for some in 1981–82 and down in 1983. Since the base yields are fixed, the market value of the shares moves with interest rates and, a $10,000 holding, bought in 1972, was worth only $7,000 in 1981 but, since then, has recaptured about half its paper loss.

For those who have to pay state or local income taxes, there are state bond trusts. They invest only in tax-exempt issues in one state. And if you're safety conscious, find out about funds that are fully guaranteed by private insurers: their yields will be reduced, typically from 10.4% to 10%, but that's little to pay for peace of mind.

Managed tax-exempt funds: open-end, no-load funds where the management fees and charges average from 0.5% to 0.75% of the net asset value per share. Same benefits: prompt reinvestment, diversification, monthly checks, switching, etc. These are managed portfolios where the professionals buy and sell according to their *guesses* as to the future trend of interest rates. In theory, such "management" is supposed to produce capital gains to supplement the interest income. In practice, the results have been spotty. In the early days (mid '70s), the pros were slow to recognize the awesome impact of inflation and so sustained frequent losses (but gained in income on new commitments). By the early '80s, some of the managers seemed to have learned a few tricks and, with the pressure of high yields, scored high. And a few of the more daring even tried to hedge with financial futures to protect favorable positions. Once again, the choice is between safety and potential appreciation!

SOME UNIT TRUST BOND FUNDS

NAME	AVE. MATURITIES	MINI- MUM*	LOAD	SPONSOR
Tax-Exempt Trust Series 219	30 yrs.	$5,318	4.5%	John Nuveen
Muni. Invest. Trust Series 237	28 yrs.	1,017	3.9	Merrill Lynch
Tax-Exempt Trust Series 66	30 yrs.	1,038	4.2	Smith Barney
Muni. Bond Trust Series 123	30 yrs.	1,018	4.2	Paine Webber

* Plus accrued interest.

Discount bond trusts. This is the latest package to attract those who want tax-free income and are willing to pay taxes on realized appreciation. Recently, a $10,000 invest-ment in below-par bonds provided a current tax-free yield of 10.76% and, in 32 years, a $10,000 capital gain as the bonds would be redeemed at $20,000. The capital gains tax is paid when the shares are sold/redeemed. *Comment:* good deal for a swap of old bonds that are selling below par. You can take the tax loss now and pay capital gains after you retire.

N.B. One of the best features of all funds is the detailed, accurate reporting: (1) of the income that may be taxed under the new Social Security provisions; (2) of the date and cost of purchases so that, when sales are made, you can select shares that will assure the best tax breaks.

A managed fund is a better investment for those who expect to sell in less than 10 years. The shares react quickly to fluctuating interest rates. But you could pick a period when values were down.

Unit trusts are best for long-term holdings, especially when the initial yield is fairly high. Share prices will fluctuate but you bought income, not preservation of capital!

And, of course, as with all fixed income investments, inflation will erode the purchasing power of the principal and income! With tax-exempt holdings, you get current tax benefits but, after retirement, if your tax rate is much lower, these municipals may not be as rewarding as taxable securities!

15

Speculations: More for Excitement Than Profit

Speculations are not investments. This sounds simple but most people fail to make the distinction. Investments are made on the basis of fundamentals: the quality of the corporation and the value of the security. If you set strict standards, do your homework and buy at a fair price, you will *always* attain your investment goal of income or total returns.

Speculations involve risks and are profitable primarily from market fluctuations. *They should be entered into only when you understand what you are doing (or trying to do) and with money that you can afford to lose.* Usually, the profits will come quickly as the result of shrewd timing but there are speculations where success depends on an understanding of special securities/situations and patience. Speculative securities should *never* be included in fiduciary portfolios but they can be valuable with personal holdings to build capital and, perhaps most important, to add ex-citement to making your money make more money. Your spouse may remember the losses but you will probably be proud, and boastful, of the not-so-frequent gains.

Before getting into details about speculations:

• Recognize that there is, usually, a sound reason why a security is selling at a low price or a high yield. Investors are not interested so you better be darn sure that there are facts to justify higher future values.

• Be realistic with new issues because their market values depend largely on unsubstantiated optimism and hard selling by the sponsoring brokers.

• In making projections, cut in half the anticipated up-move and double the potential downswing. These "values" are seldom based on facts and usually reflect conditions over which you have no control. Once any industry or company becomes unpopular, the prices of its shares can fall rapidly. Conversely, the price rises are likely to be slower than projected by research—your own and that of your broker.

• Speculate only in a rising market unless you are selling short. Worthwhile gains will come when more people buy more shares . . . not likely in a down market.

• Be willing to take quick, small losses and never hold on with hope for a recovery unless there are little known/understood reasons for optimism.

• When you pick a winner, sell half of your shares (or set a protective stop-loss order) when you have doubled your money.

• Speculate only when you have time to continue research and watch developments, preferably daily and certainly, weekly.

• *And, most important, buy a rabbit's foot.*

Speculation is foolish for the novice, dangerous for the self-styled sophisticate and usually profitable only for those who are knowledgeable and experienced. Under all situations, start slowly, limit your dollars after a big winning streak and never risk more than 20% of your savings.

Leverage

Leverage involves the use of borrowed funds to enhance profits. With securities, it means buying on margin: using cash, stocks, convertibles, bonds, etc. as collateral for a loan from your broker or banker. When the borrowing is kept to a reasonable level and the interest costs are modest, buying on margin can be used effectively with investments and can be even more worthwhile with speculations.

With securities, the margin regulations are set by the Federal Reserve Board but your broker may set higher limits. Under current Fed rules, you can borrow only when you have at least $2,000 in cash or securities. The margin requirements are 50% initially and 25% for maintenance: i.e., with $10,000, you can borrow $5,000 and must maintain $2,500 in equity—the difference between the market value of your portfolio and the amount owed the lender.

Example: With $10,000 you buy 200 shares of a stock at $50 each. By using margin, you will have $15,000 so you can acquire 300 shares.

As with most stock market ploys, leverage works best when stock prices rise. If the stock moves up to 55, you will have a $1,000 (10%) profit in your cash account or $1,500 (15%) gain if you use a margin account. At this point, your cash account assets will be $11,000 so the margin account will be worth $16,500. The equity will be $11,500 ($16,500 minus $5,000). This will be above the maintenance minimum of $3,750 so you can increase your loan.

But leverage works both ways. If your stock starts to slide, you will lose money that much faster. With a 5-point drop in the value of the stock the cash account loss will be $1,000; that of the margin account, $1,500. If the decline continues so that your equity falls below 25%, your broker will issue a margin call and you will have to come up with more cash/collateral or be sold out.

Here are the current purchases that can be made with a $10,000 margin account:

$20,000 worth of marginable stocks

$20,000 worth of listed convertible bonds
$40,000 worth of nonlisted convertible bonds
$66,666 face value of municipal bonds
$200,000 face value of government bonds.

When the value of the portfolio drops too far, more collateral will be required. And there can be problems with low priced stocks. In margin evaluation, when the price of a stock falls below a full dollar figure, the next lower round-dollar value is used: i.e., when a stock drops from 100 to 99½, its new margin value is 99, a loss of less than 1% of its worth. But a stock trading at 10 that falls to 9⅞ is valued at 9, a 10% loss.

Use a margin account cautiously and always keep ample reserves. With bonds, margin can set up an excellent short-term speculation. The cost of the loan will be partially offset by the interest, which, in turn, is tax deductible and, when the bonds are bought at a discount with a short maturity, there can be sure appreciation.

Example (from A. G. Becker, Inc., a national brokerage firm): Dr. Pershing, in the 50% tax bracket, buys a discounted $1 million, 7.875% coupon Treasury bond maturing in 15½ months. Cost: $931,250 with commissions. He pays $50,000 cash and borrows $881,250 at a fluctuating interest rate that rides 2 or more points below the regular margin rate—an average cost of 13.5%.

In a little over one year, Dr. Pershing redeems the bond for $1 million for a long-term capital gain of $68,750. From this he deducts the interest of $59,445 to get a pretax profit of $9,305. That's an 18.6% return in 15 months.

The real benefits are still to come. After payment of the 20% tax, the $68,750 gain nets to $55,000. From this Dr. Pershing deducts the net interest cost of $29,722 ($59,445 minus the 50% tax credit). This leaves an after-tax profit of $25,278—a return of 50.6%! On an annualized basis, that's 39.2%.

That's the sales pitch, but there are risks if the interest rate on the loan rises. If it should go up to an average of 17%, Dr. Pershing would show a pre-tax *loss* of 39% but his after-tax gain would be a welcome 19.8%.

Typically, the broker will charge interest on a margin account at about 1% above the current call money rate at which he borrows from banks. When the spread between the cost of the loan and income from dividends/interest is small, margin can be attractive, especially for those in high tax brackets.

Examples; Jack Gotrocks, in the 50% tax bracket, borrows $5,000 on margin and pays interest at 12%: $600 a year. With that extra $5,000, he buys utility stocks that pay annual dividends of $500. His pre-tax cost is $100, easily offset by a small rise in the value of the shares. Jack will pay $250 income tax on the $500 dividends (net $250), but he can deduct $300 for the interest, so comes out ahead by $50.

Jill Worker, in the 33% tax bracket, won't make out so well. She will have to pay the same $600 interest which, after tax, means an outlay of $400. On the $500 dividends, she will pay $165 in taxes to net $335. Using margin will cost her $65 that year—justified if she can look for a small rise in the value of her investment. As with all phases of speculating or investing, check all costs and remember that there can be losses!

Extra Leverage

Many professionals purchase a company's convertible securities on margin rather than the common stock. With convertibles (assuming a purchase price reasonably close to investment and conversion value), risk is substantially reduced on the downside due to the price resistance encountered as the CV nears the floor provided by its investment value. On the upside, there's no such resistance and the full benefits of leverage are enjoyed. With a margined position in CVs, the risk may be no greater (and can be less) than would be incurred by nonleveraged ownership of the common stock of the same company, while the appreciation potential may be substantially greater.

Here's an example, based on an actual situation that took place a few years ago when interest rates were lower. It compares a leveraged investment in Toonerville Trolley 6½% convertible bonds with a $10,000 investment in the common stock of the same company. The CV was at par; the common stock at 8.

To buy 20 CVs, the investor put up $10,000 and margined the balance. At the same time he bought 1,250 common shares for $10,000 cash. The stock declined to 6 (down 25%). The CV, reflecting the downside support due to its inherent investment value and adequate interest, dipped 7% to $930 per bond (a 14% loss on the $10,000 investment).

In a few months, both securities were back to their original level. In the next 18 months, the bonds rose 80%, so their value was $36,000—a net profit of $16,000. The stock went up 50% to 12, or $15,000—a gain of $5,000. The leveraged position in the CVs produced both superior protection on the downside and superior capital appreciation on the upside.

Furthermore, over a year, the bond interest of $1,300 would have covered the $1,200 cost of carrying the margin account at 12%.

Note: If you had margined the stock, your risk would have been greater and your offsetting income less, but you would have done well. But if the prime interest rate had risen sharply during that period, the price of the CVs would have dropped farther.

Undermargined Accounts

If the value of your margin account falls below minimum maintenance requirements, it becomes undermargined and, even if the deficit is only $4, there will be a margin call. To check when you're approaching this 25% level, divide the amount of your debit balance by three and add the result to your net loan. Thus, one-third of $5,000 is $1,666, plus $5,000 equals $6,666. If the portfolio value is less, your account becomes restricted.

This limits the withdrawals. Here, the base is what is called the Special Miscellaneous Account, representing the funds in excess of margin requirements which come from price appreciation, dividends, proceeds of sale and cash deposits made to meet a margin call. At this point, you can withdraw funds above the maintenance minimum but you must deposit assets equal to the lesser of 70% of the market value of the securities taken out or the amount needed to bring the remaining equity back to 50%.

There is one way to get around these rules: *Buy and sell, on the same day, stocks of equal value.* But the 70% retention rule applies if the transactions are made on different days.

The Fed's rules are specific. On same-day deals, if the cost of the stock you buy is greater than the value of the one sold, you deposit 50% of the difference between the two prices. If the new stock is worth less than the old, only 30% of the difference is credited to the SMA.

If the equity drops below 30%, your account becomes *super-restricted.* All purchase and sales, even on the same day, are treated separately with each purchase requiring 50% margin and each sale releasing only 30% of the proceeds.

Advice: If you use margin, don't let your equity fall below 50%. In a volatile market, you can get in trouble mighty fast.

Margin Rules

FRB rules apply to stocks listed on registered U.S. exchanges, to stocks listed with NASDAQ and to unlisted securities whenever they are purchased "for the purpose of carrying listed stocks." Brokers cannot margin other stocks.

You can, however, use unlisted stocks, including Canadian issues, to borrow from your bank. On some high-quality, actively traded OTC stocks, banks often lend substantially more than permitted for listed stocks when purchases are *not* "for the purpose of carrying listed stocks."

While shares of most mutual funds are unlisted, their portfolios contain stocks and bonds listed on major exchanges. Therefore, mutual fund shares are subject to FRB margin requirements at banks.

The NYSE sets special margin requirements on individual issues which show a combination of volume, price variation or turnover of unusual dimensions. These requirements are intended to discourage the use of credit in certain issues because of undue speculation.

In addition, customers whose accounts show a pattern of "day-trading" (purchasing and selling the same marginable issue on the same day) are required to have the appropriate margin in their accounts before transactions in securities subject to the special margin requirements can be effected.

How to Figure Your Yield When Buying on Margin

To determine exactly what yield you get by buying on margin, you have to ascertain the return on your actual investment: the *margin equivalent yield.* You can calculate this from the accompanying formula or from the accompanying table.

The *cash yield* % is the return on securities bought outright. The same formulas can be used for both pre-tax and after-tax yields.

$$MEY = \left(\frac{100}{\%M} \times CY\%\right) - \left(\frac{100}{\%M} - 1\right) \times DI\%$$

MEY = Margin Equivalent Yield
%M = % Margin
CY% = Cash Yield %
DI% = Debit Interest %

Example: You are on a 50% margin base, receive 12% cash yield from dividends and pay 20% in your debit balance.

$$MEY = \frac{100}{50} \times 12 - \frac{100}{50} - 1 \times 20$$

$$MEY = 2 \times 12 = 24\% - 2-1 \times 20 = 20\%$$

$$MEY = 24\% - 20\% = 4\%$$

Thus, the 12% return, with margin, dwindles to 4%.

Special Types of Financing

When you have assets that are not working full time, some smart operator will come up with a proposal that will enable you to use them for collateral for what amounts to a loan that can be used for investments/speculations. As usual, the sales pitch is that the profits from the "investments" will be great enough to more than offset the costs of the loan.

One of the most popular variations was to combine the sale of life insurance policies with mutual fund shares. This approach was set back by the scandal of Equity Funding (which reinsured nonexistent life policies) but, with the booming stock market, appears to be making a comeback. Here's what is supposed to happen:

1. *Invest:* buy shares of a mutual fund.
2. *Insure:* select a life insurance program.
3. *Borrow:* using your mutual fund shares as collateral, get a loan (from the friendly insurance-mutual fund company) to pay each annual insurance premium.
4. *Repay loan:* at the end of 10 years you pay the principal and interest on the loan: either in cash, from insurance cash values or by redeeming shares.

Result: Any appreciation from your investment in excess of the amount owed is your profit. If you die, your heirs get full value because the loan will be paid by the insurance.

In effect you bought securities on margin to acquire life insurance rather than extra shares of stock. *Objective:* double mileage from invested dollars.

This concept has considerable validity in periods of rising stock prices and low interest rates. Presumably, the value of the mutual fund shares will reflect the long-term rise in the stock prices! And the dividends will help pay the interest on the loan.

Before you become entranced with the "logic" of this dual approach, consult a competent, impartial insurance adviser and make your calculations on the basis of a decline in the value of the stocks you buy.

Warrants for Swingers

The number of warrants traded publicly has declined recently because of the broad markets in options and the dismal prospects for most common stocks. Still, when properly selected and carefully managed, they can offer high leverage because of their low cost and fast market movements.

A warrant is an option to buy a stated number of shares of a related security (usually common stock) at a stipulated price during a specified period (5, 10, 20 years or, occasionally, perpetually). The price at which the warrant can be exercised is fixed above the current market price of the stock at the time the warrant is issued. Thus, when the common stock is at 10, the warrant might entitle the holder to buy one share at 15.

Since the two securities tend to move somewhat parallel to each other, an advance in the price creates a higher percentage gain for the warrant than for the stock.

Example: Let's say that the warrant to buy one share at 15 sells at 1 when the stock is at 10. If the stock soars to 20 (100% gain), the price of the warrant will go up to at least 5 (400% gain).

But the downside risk of the warrant can be greater than that of the stock. If the stock drops to 5, that's a 50% loss. The warrant, depending on its life span, might fall to ⅛: an 88% decline.

SOME POPULAR WARRANTS

COMPANY	EXERCISE TERMS	EXPIRATION Date	RECENT PRICE Common	RECENT PRICE Warrant
Alleghany Corp.	$ 3.75	Perpetual	56	52
Atlas Corp.	31.25	Perpetual	21 1/8	6 5/8
Charter Corp.	10.00	1988	12 1/8	5 1/2
Chrysler Corp.	13.00	1985	15 1/2	8
Eastern Airlines	10.00	1987	9 1/2	4 7/8
Grant Industries	11.36	1986	11 3/4	3 7/8
Mattel, Inc.	4.00	1986	13 1/4	9 5/8
Southmark (REIT)	7.50	1987	6 3/8	2 7/8
Towner Petroleum	14.75	1986	5 7/8	2 1/8
Trans World	31.00	1986	31 5/8	12 3/8
US Air, Inc.	17.31	1987	33 1/2	18 3/4
Warner Commun.	55.00	1986	28 1/2	10 3/4

SOURCE: Standard & Poor's STOCK GUIDE; Wall Street Journal

Profits with Warrants

Warrants are pure speculations. They have no voting rights, pay no dividends and have no claim on the assets of the corporation. They are not registered with the company and are generally issued in bearer form. If they are lost or stolen, there's almost no way for brokers or an exchange to "flag" them.

Warrants represent *hope.* When the price of the common stock with a related warrant is *below* the exercise price, the warrant has only speculative value. Thus, a warrant to buy a stock at 20 is theoretically worthless when the stock is at 19.

In practice, however, the warrant has a value reflecting

the prospects for the company, the life of the warrant, stock-market conditions, etc. Not so long ago, the common stock of a major utility was trading at 44 and the warrants to buy the stock at 52 were selling at over 7. *That's hope!*

When the price of the stock rises above the specified exercise price, the warrants acquire a tangible value that is usually inflated by speculation. Thus, when that utility stock rose to 52, the price of the warrant soared to 11½. *Now do you see why warrants are 100% speculations?*

The closer a warrant gets to its expiration date, the smaller the premium it commands. After expiration, the warrant is worthless. Conversely, the longer the life of the warrant, the higher the premium if there is real hope that the price of the stock will rise.

In recent years, one of the most profitable warrants has been that of Chrysler Corp.: rising from as low as ⅛ to 10½. And Mattel warrants rose 59% while its stock went up 41%. But the losses with warrants can be greater than those of the stock: with Action Corp., the stock fell 53% but the warrants were down 71%!

Dual Purpose Warrant

The combination of the flexibility of warrants and the packaging ability of Wall Street has led to a new hybrid: the dual option warrant (Du-Op). They were first issued by Trans World Corp. in mid 1982 and were a sellout despite a quarterly loss of $103 million.

For $22.50, the "investor" received one share of common stock plus one warrant to buy that stock at $25.50 through 1987 plus the provision that, between May 1983 and June 1984, each unit could be swapped for one share of TWC preferred paying 14%. This was an expensive way to raise money but made everybody happy: the investor could count on a floor for the stock because of the conversion to the high-yielding preferred; the speculator could hope for an ample profit. But there were still risks: that the price of the stock would fail to move over 25½ and that interest rates would rise, thus forcing a decline in the value of the preferred.

Calculating the Value of a Warrant

The speculative value of a warrant is greatest when the warrant price is below the exercise price. If the stock moves up, the price of the warrant can jump fast. Here are guidelines set by warrant expert S. L. Pendergast for the maximum premium to pay: when the stock price is at the exercise price (100%), this is 41% of the exercise price. Thus, with a stock at the exercise price of 30, the maximum price to pay for a warrant (on one-for-one basis) would be about 12. In most cases, better profits will come when the warrant is bought at a lower price.

Stock Price as % of Exercise Price	Warrant Price as % of Exercise Price
80%	28%
90	34
100	41
110	46

Keeping in mind that the market value of any warrants is hard to predict, there's a formula to determine the EV (Exercise Value):

$$EV = N(P - S)$$

N = number of shares of stock that one warrant entitles you to buy
P = current price of stock
S = per share price of stock at which warrant can be exercised

Example: ABC Corporation common stock is at 12; the warrant exercise price, on a one-for-one basis, is $3.75. The EV for the warrant is $8.25:

$$1(\$12 - 3.75) = \$8.25.$$

Warrants for Capital Gains

Generally, warrants are best in bull markets, especially periods of great enthusiasm. Their low prices attract speculators who trade for quick gains. At all times, however, use these checkpoints:

Buy only warrants of a common stock that you would buy anyway. If the common stock does not go up, there's little chance that the warrant's price will advance.

The best profits come from warrants associated with companies that have potential for strong upward swings due to sharp earnings improvement, a prospective takeover, newsmaking products or services, etc. It also helps if they are temporarily popular.

In most cases, the warrants for fast-riding stocks, even at a high premium, will outperform seemingly cheap warrants for issues that are falling.

At the outset, stick with warrants of fair-to-good corporations whose stocks are listed on major exchanges. They have broad markets.

When you feel more confident, seek out special situations, especially warrants of small, growing firms. Many of these "new" companies rely on warrants in their financing. Their actual or anticipated growth can boost the price of their warrants rapidly.

But be wary of warrants where the related stock is limited or closely controlled. If someone decides to dump a block of stock, the values can fall fast.

Buy warrants when they are selling at low prices. The percentages are with you when there's an upmove, and, with minimal costs, the downside risks are small. But watch out for "superbargains" because commissions will eat up most of the gains.

But watch their values and be cautious when their prices move to more than 20% of their exercise figure.

Watch the expiration/change date. After expiration, the warrant has no value. Generally, stay away from warrants with a life span of less than four years. When you know what you are doing, short-life warrants can bring quick profits if you are smart and lucky. But be careful. You could end up with worthless paper.

Avoid dilution. If there's a stock split or stock dividend, the market price of the stock will drop but the conversion price of the warrant may not be changed. The same caveat goes for warrants subject to call. Generally, warrants of listed companies will be protected against such changes, but take nothing for granted.

Once in a while, warrants will be reorganized out of their option value. This occurs with troubled corporations taken over by tough-minded operators who are unwilling to pay for past excesses or to provide profits for speculators.

Spread your risks. If you have sufficient capital, buy warrants in five different companies. The odds are that you may hit big on one, break even on two and lose on the others. Your total gains may be less than if you had gambled on one warrant that proved a winner, but your losses will probably be less if you're wrong.

Look for special opportunities such as "usable" bonds with warrants attached. With such a package, the speculator can acquire the stock either: (1) with the warrants at an exercise price of, say 20; (2) with the bond on a face value basis: at $1,000, 50 shares at 20.

Three years after the offering, the stock sold down to 15 with the bond at 60 ($600). The warrants were nearly worthless but the bonds could be turned into a nifty profit because each could be swapped for 50 shares worth $750!

Except in unusual situations, all warrants should be bought to trade/sell, not to exercise. With no income, usually a long wait for appreciation and rapid price changes, warrants are almost always profitable only for quick gains for speculators who have adequate capital and time to watch the market.

Selling Warrants Short

In bear markets, the leverage of warrants can be profitable with short sales. Basically, it's the opposite of buying long. You assume that the same relationship between the stock and warrants continues when their prices fall.

But short selling is always tricky and with warrants there can be other problems: (*a*) limited markets because of lack of speculator interest; (*b*) exchange regulations—e.g., the American Stock Exchange prohibits short selling of its listed warrants several months before expiration date; (*c*) the possibility of a "short squeeze": the inability to buy warrants to cover your short sales as the expiration date approaches; (*d*) the life of the warrants may be extended beyond the stated expiration date. This advances the date when the warrants become worthless, so a short seller may not be able to cover his position at as low a price as anticipated.

Warrants with Options

Swingers use warrants to speculate in options. The costs are low, the risks modest and the profit potential high, especially in erratic but uptrending markets.

Example: In October, TP Industries stock was at $14.50, and the warrants, exercisable until August the next year, were at $4.50. Trader Tom bought 1,000 warrants for $4,500 and sold 10 January options with a striking price of 15 for 1⅜, to net about $1,250 after commissions. If TPI stock stayed the same or went down by January, Tom would let the options expire and sell another 10 calls with an April expiration. If these also expire, he will sell 10 more options with an August closeout date.

If the stock went up, he would buy back the January options and sell 10 April calls at a higher premium, etc. He hoped to sell three sets of options, at an average return of $1,250 each, to net $3,750.

In August, if the stock was at $16.50, the warrants would be worth $2.75. He would sell them for $2,750 and deduct the $1,750 loss from the $3,750 profit on the options for a pleasant $2,000 profit on a net investment of $3,250.

If the warrants expired worthless, he would still be ahead of the game. That's what hedging is all about.

Special Situations

One of the most intriguing speculations involves special situations: mergers, acquisitions, recapitalization or reorganization, "sleepers" where securities are selling well below their historic multiples or their present book values; companies with a small number of shares; corporations loaded with cash; and firms whose shares are traded OTC and are ready and eligible for listing on a major stock exchange. Usually, these will be discovered by an alert researcher but, sometimes, they will be featured in news or feature articles. Since they involve significant changes, they must be considered speculations at the outset, but, on occasion, may become investments.

Worthwhile special situations are hard come by but there are some clues that may lead to profits:

Market activity: when there's unusual volume, and rising prices, in the stock of a little-known or pedestrian corporation. Something is happening or, at least, quite a few people think there are changes ahead: a new product, acquisition, merger, etc. Unless you are a trader willing to settle for a few points quick gain, take your time, get the facts and wait until there is a confirmed uptrend. You may lose the first 10% of the action, but with a target of 100% total return, this will not be important.

Stocks selling below book value: what the shareholders own after paying all debts. In one way, this means that the corporation may be worth more dead than alive: if there was a liquidation, shareholders would receive more for the sale of assets than they paid for the stock.

SOME STOCKS SELLING BELOW BOOK VALUE

COMPANY	BOOK VALUE	STOCK PRICE	PRICE AS % BOOK VALUE
Chi. Pheumatic Tool	$27.69	15 3/4	56%
Cone Mills	60.95	39	63
Dresser Industries	25.19	19 1/8	75
Gulf Oil	57.27	34 7/8	60
Ingersoll-Rand	58.87	47 1/4	80
Reynolds Metals	66.23	32 3/8	48
Smith International	29.36	24 1/8	82
Sperry Corp.	52.36	38 1/4	73
Texaco, Inc.	55.11	35 3/8	64
Vulcan, Inc.	16.17	10 1/4	63

SOURCE: Standard & Poor's OUTLOOK

Heed the type of corporation. Steel firms and manufacturers of heavy machinery have huge investments in plants and equipment so they have a high book value. But they rarely make much money. On the other hand, a drug manufacturer or retailer will have a low book value but will turn in excellent profits. The trick is to locate a company that has a low stock price compared to book value and is making a comeback that has not yet been recognized in the market place.

In such a situation, you will get a double plus: buying assets at a discount and a higher stock price due to the better earnings. Just make sure that the assets are real and that profits are the result of management's skill, not accounting legerdemain.

Takeover candidates. These make the headlines but, for most amateurs, are better for conversation than profits. Real success requires substantial capital, sharp timing, up-to-the-minute information, and concentrated attention— all characteristic of professionals. But amateurs can make out well if they already own the stock of the acquired company. This can happen when a company loses its quality rating because of industry problems or management decisions.

Example: Petrolane, a diversified firm with major interests in gas/oil distribution and drilling, sold off its supermarket and health care divisions. This left ample cash and a strong position in a temporarily depressed industry. The company no longer met quality standards but became a potential candidate for a takeover.

Commented one investor, "Petrolane stock is down but my original 100 shares, bought for less than $1,000, has grown to 400 shares worth $5,000 so I'll hold in hopes of a takeover that might quintuple my money again."

Speculating in takeovers, however, seldom permits delay. You must act quickly on the basis of answers to questions like these:

• Is this a friendly or hostile takeover? If it's hostile, there's likely to be a battle and higher offers. This can be profitable but will be nervewracking and there's always a chance that the deal will be called off and you'll be left with little or no gain. *Many takeovers fail: in 1982, of 52 tender offers, only 38 were completed.*

• Is the offer for cash, securities or both? For most people, cash is best because it's sure. But if you are in a high tax bracket (as you should be to be involved in such maneuvers), acceptance of cash for shares held for less than one year will result in a big tax bill.

• What is the *real* value of the offer—as calculated in the financial press or, better, by your broker's research department? If the stock price of the target company keeps moving up, insiders expect another bidder will move in.

• Who owns large blocks of stock? When the officers/directors of the acquiring company are major shareholders, they will probably stay the course. When a substantial portion of the shares of the target company are closely held, these insiders will call the shots.

• Does the tender offer apply to all or part of the shares? When Sunbeam was acquired by Allegheny International, the winning bid was $41 per share for 50% of the common stock. The rest was swapped for convertibles worth $29 each.

When you own shares of the acquiring company, it's usually wise to sell. Management is using your money for what it believes is a more profitable future but let 'em

prove it first! DuPont spent billions to take over Conoco and, three years later, had yet to report a nickel profit.

When you own shares of the target company, the odds are in your favor but can be improved by watchful waiting. Once a tender offer has been announced:

• *Sit tight.* Wait until all offers are in before you make any decision. Most offers are originally viewed as unfavorable by management. There's an irate outcry that the price is too low and a scurry to find another potential partner (white knight) to boost the proposed purchase price. Usually these maneuvers will boost the bid.

• *If the deal involves exchanging securities,* consider whether you want to own shares of the acquiring company. Usually, as with DuPont, the stock price will fall.

• *After the bidding has stopped and there's a firm offer,* sell on the open market rather than waiting for full details. This eliminates risks that: *(a)* the tender will be withdrawn (which can be done without legal penalties); *(b)* only part of your shares will be acquired and you will end up with a mix of securities you don't want; *(c)* poor timing will cost you money.

N.B. There's no explanation here of arbitrage because this is NOT for amateurs. Success requires a lot of money (at least $50,000), access to immediate information (difficult for busy people) and strong nerves (a wrong guess can blow half your capital). Basically, arbitrage involves buying the stock of one prospective merger partner (usually the one being acquired) and, at the same time, selling short the stock of the other firm (whose name will survive). If the merger is completed, you trade in the stock of the acquired company and receive shares of the surviving firm which are sold to pay back the loan on the short shares. The risks are high because you can guess wrong and the deal can fall through. It's possible to make a pile of money with arbitrage but even the professionals can be wrong and lose hundreds of thousands of dollars. You'll have more fun— and lose less—at Atlantic City.

Candidates for Stock Splits

For those who don't want to be involved in controversy, another area of profitable speculation (and often investment) is the corporation which may split its stock: i.e., issue one, two or three or more shares for each share outstanding. It is psychologically easier to buy 100 shares of a stock priced at 40 than 50 shares at 80. And, of course, commissions on round lots are less than those on odd lots.

Splits usually occur when the stock price moves to a historically high level and management becomes fearful that the high price will discourage individual investors.

Such bonuses can be welcome and profitable. The *speculator* who owned 100 shares of Tandy Corp. in 1970 ended 1982 with an *investment* of 3,200 shares plus stock in Tandy Crafts and Tandy Brands . . . and prospects of a further split by the parent company as the stock was trading in the mid 50s.

And the *investor* who discovered Josten's in 1974 and bought 100 shares started 1983 with 387 shares as the result of one stock dividend and four stock splits.

Stocks that are candidates for stock splits may not always be speculations but the ultimate results are just as profitable and much safer.

The NYSE encourages stock splits as part of its efforts to broaden public ownership of listed stocks. When more shares are available at lower prices, more investors become interested. This helps to assure both an adequate supply for daily trading and a more orderly market.

On the Big Board, the most popular price range has been 15 to 29. About 60% of all NYSE orders (in number, not in volume orders) to buy and sell stocks involved $4,000 or less, that is, an average per share price of $40 or less.

The possibility of a stock split is of primary interest to traders because it provides an opportunity for extra short-term profits. Serious investors buying for long-term capital gains should focus their attention on basic financial considerations. If a stock is not a good value at 100, it is no better at 50 after a two-for-one split.

The greatest immediate profits from stock splits often occur in the last six to three months before the directors take positive action. During this period, especially when there are earnings and dividend increases, anticipation can push up the price of the stock.

With stock splits, the Wall Street adage *buy on the rumor, sell on the news* is applicable most of the time. The typical pattern is as follows:

1. The price of the stock rises fairly rapidly before the public announcement: on the average, about 20%. This is due to the pressure of insiders, information leaks or shrewd guesses.

2. The price reaches a peak from 2 to 24 weeks before the announcement of the split. On the rare occasions when the secret has been kept, the peak comes just after the announcement.

3. For two days after the news, the price remains high. Five days later, a study shows, half the split stocks have declined in price.

4. Just before the actual split takes place, there is likely to be another rally, especially if the overall market is bullish.

Stock Split Ahead?

1. Is it to the corporation's benefit to attract more stockholders? This is a primary consideration in companies which deal with goods and services which stockholders can buy. The best candidates are companies involved with consumers: retail stores, manufacturers of food and drugs, oil companies and franchise firms. But there are also opportunities in fast-growing fields such as electronics.

Stock splits help a company to expand markets, make acquisitions and attract additional financing. When the stock is more widely held and more favorably known, the company can move ahead more rapidly.

SOME COMPANIES THAT HAVE SPLIT THEIR STOCK OR PAID STOCK DIVIDENDS FREQUENTLY OVER THE PAST 10 YEARS

Abbott Laboratories	Cubic Corp.	Keystone International	Revco D.S.
Advanced Micro Devices	Daniel Industries	Kinder Care Centers	Rochester Gas & Electric
Allen Group	Dome Mines	Kollmorgen Corp.	Rowan Companies
Amerada Hess Corp.	Dover Corp.	LaQuinta Inns	Ryder System, Inc.
American International Group	E-Systems, Inc.	Lifemark Corp.	Schlumberger, Ltd.
American Shipbuilding, Inc.	E.G. & G., Inc.	Litton Industries	Scientific-Atlanta
Anacomp, Inc.	Esmark, Inc.	Louisiana-Pacific Corp.	SCOA Industries
Analog Devices, Inc.	Esquire, Inc.	Macy (R.H.)	Sedco, Inc.
Anthony Industries	Federal Signal	Malone & Hyde	Sonat, Inc.
Archer-Daniels-Midland	Flight Safety International	Manor Care	Southdown, Inc.
Arkla, Inc.	Fluke (John) Co.	Mark Controls	Southland Corp.
Augat, Inc.	Freeport-McMoran	Mary Kay Cosmetics, Inc.	Southwest Airlines
Baker International	Frontier Holdings	Masco Corp.	SPS Technologies
Bangor Punta	Gates Learjet	Materials Research	Standard Oil (Ohio)
Belco Petroleum	GCA Corp.	Matsushita Electric	Stop & Shop Cos.
Bergen Brunswick	General American Oil	MCA, Inc.	Super Valu Stores
Big Three Industries	General Instruments	Mesa Petroleum	Syntex Corp.
Bob Evans Farms	General RE	Miller (Herman)	Sysco Corp.
Boeing Co.	General Tire	Mitchell Energy & Development	Tandy Corp.
Bowne & Co., Inc.	Goulds Pumps	Moore McCormack	Teledyne, Inc.
Brown-Forman	Grow Group	National Medical Enterprises	Texas Industries, Inc.
Brush-Wellman	Guardian Industries	Noble Affiliates	Texas Oil & Gas Co.
Burndy Corp.	Harland (John)	NVF Company	Tokheim Corp.
Butler International	Heileman Brewing	Overseas Shipbuilding	Toys "R" Us
Campbell Red Lake	Hecks, Inc.	Papercraft, Inc.	Tracor, Inc.
Carlisle Corp.	Hospital Corp. of America	Parker Drilling Co.	U.S. Bancorp.
Castle & Cook	Hughes Tool Co.	Parker-Hannifin	Wackenhut Corp.
Cincinnati Milacron, Inc.	Humana, Inc.	Parker Pen Co.	Wal-Mart Stores
Cole National	Hutton (E.F.) Group	Pay Less Drug, N.W.	Warner Communications, Inc.
Collins Food	Insilco Corp.	Petrie Stores	Wendy's International
Community Psychiatric Centers	Interfirst Corp.	Petrolane, Inc.	Western Co. of North America
Computervision Corp.	James River	Pioneer Corp.	Willamette Industries, Inc.
Condec Corp.	Jerrico, Inc.	Pioneer Hi-Bred	Wometco Enterprises
Cook United	Joslyn Mfg.	Quanex Corp.	Zapata Corp.
Cox Communications	Josten's, Inc.	Raytheon Co.	Zero Corp.
Crane Co.	Key Pharmaceutical	Reading & Bates	

SOURCE: Securities Research Company

2. Does management hold a small percentage of the outstanding stock? When there is a threat of an outside raid, companies often split their stock, thus making more shares available. Management, which retains its shares, hopes the lower price will attract more shareholders.

Conversely, if a few people own a substantial block of the shares, there will be little benefit for them in a split, unless there are future problems because of taxes, acquisitions or estate diversification.

3. Is the stock price above $75? The most attractive range for investors is $35 to $50 a share, so a stock almost has to be selling at a fairly high price to justify a split.

4. Has the corporation split its stock before? This is not always a reliable indicator, but it does provide a clue to management's thinking. Some companies have a policy of frequent, almost annual stock splits. Since 1977, Lifemark Corp., health care operator, has split its stock four times and declared a 50% stock dividend; Litton Industries, despite fluctuating earnings, has paid a stock dividend in 12 of the last 13 years; and Raytheon Corp., not exactly a swinger, has had two splits in the last six years and may be ready for another as its stock price moves above 50.

5. Are the earnings likely to continue to grow substantially? There will be little benefit from a stock split when the prospects for future earnings are dim. When the stock of a strong, continually growing company gets into a relatively high price range, there are good reasons to look for a split. Higher profits enable the corporation to increase dividends at the time of the split.

6. Is an OTC company progressing so well that management may be considering listing the stock on a major stock exchange? The NYSE requires 2,000 stockholders with 100 shares or more; at least 1 million shares of common stock publicly held and with a market value of $16 million; and corporate earnings, in the latest year, of $2.5 million before federal income taxes and $2 million pre-tax in each of the two preceding years.

Companies with a Small Number of Shares

In theory, corporations with a relatively small capitalization—say, fewer than 500,000 shares, should be excellent speculations. They are closely held, their shares seldom actively traded, their price/earnings ratios are low and their dividends relatively high. They are excellent prospects for mergers, stock splits and takeovers—all actions that should boost the values of their shares.

In practice, however, most small firms prefer to stay single. Over the past decade, about one-third of the same companies have stayed on this small share list; another one-third have issued more shares; and the balance have been acquired/merged or gone out of business. *Unless you know, and are impressed with, an officer or director of a*

Stock Dividends

Stock dividends are extra shares issued to current shareholders, usually on a percentage basis: i.e., a 5% stock dividend means that five new shares are issued for every 100 old shares. Such a policy can be habit forming and most companies continue the extra distributions year after year because it conserves cash, keeps shareholders happy, and provides an easy, inexpensive way to expand the number of publicly owned shares and, usually, stockholders.

For investors, stock dividends are tax shelters. Instead of paying the maximum tax on cash dividends, they pay the lower capital gains tax when the stock is sold. Be sure to keep accurate records of costs as the capital gain will represent the difference between the dollar cost and the dollar sale proceeds. If only a portion of the shares is sold, the cost must be calculated on a proportionate basis.

It's pleasant to receive such a bonus but be sure that such a payout is justified. The actual dollar profits of the corporation should keep rising. If they stay about the same or decline, stock dividends may be better for show than growth. To evaluate a stock dividend in terms of a company's earning power and the stock's current price:

1. Find the future earnings yield on the current stock price. Use anticipated earnings per share for the current year. If the projected profits are $3 per share and the current price of the stock is 50, the earnings yield is 6%: $3 divided by 50 = .06.

2. Add the stock dividend percentage declared for the current year to the annual cash dividend yield. If the stock dividend is 5% and the cash dividend is 2%, the figure is 7% . . . the total dividend yield.

If the #2 figure (7%) exceeds #1 (6%), a shareholder faces earnings dilution and probable price weakness *unless* the corporate prospects are strong.

But if the profits are $5 per share, the earnings yield is 10%. Since this is more than the total dividend yield (7%), the stock dividend is not excessive.

COMPANIES WITH SMALL CAPITALIZATION
(Under 600,000 shares of common stock)

AFA Protective	Hiller Aviation
AGM Industries	Holly Corp.
Alamo Savings	HS Group
Alaska NW Properties	Humphrey, Inc.
Allen Organ	Kahler Corp.
American Underwriters	Kenwin Shops
Andrea Radio	Key Co.
ANRET, Inc.	Kiddie Products
Berkshire Gas	Kleer-Vu Industries
Braun Engineering	Mangood Corp.
Care Corp.	Miller Bros. Industries
Chesapeake Utilities	Miller (H) & Sons
Clarostat Mfg.	Norwesco, Inc.
Conchemco, Inc.	Nutrition World
Consolidated Accessories	Park Electrochem
Cramer, Inc.	Penn Yan Express
Crowley, Milner & Co.	Pneumatic Scale
Danners, Inc.	Realex Corp.
Drewry Photocolor	Realist, Inc.
Driver-Harris	Ripley Co.
Edwards Industries	Sage Labs
Espey Mfg. & Electronic	Southwestern Electric
Esquire Radio & Electronics	Summer & Co.
Evans, Inc.	Tensor Corp.
Exolon, Inc.	Tinsley Labs
Fabric Wholesalers	TRC Cos.
Florida Capital	United McGill
Florida Public Utilities	Valley Resources
General Real Estate	Viatech, Inc.
Gray Communications	Weatherford (R.V.)
Grey Advertising	Wellco Enterprises
Gyrodyne Corp.	Weyenberg Shoe
	Wisconsin Southern Gas

SOURCE: Standard & Poor's

small company, be cautious about committing a large sum in its shares.

New Issues

All new issues, by definition, are speculations (except in the rare case where an established, closely controlled firm decides to go public). The key factor in speculating with shares of a little-known company is the underwriter: the financial firm that sponsors the new issue. When this is a reputable organization and other members of the syndicate are also familiar, the shares can be worthwhile for patient investors and for market-oriented speculators who are ready to take quick, after-issue profits. When the sponsor is recognized as a "new issue" firm, you may be lucky—at least for a while—but over the long-term of an investment, the odds are against you. And when the "great opportunity" is a penny stock, it's almost always a 100% gamble.

Before getting into details of new issues, let's look at the record. Of 500 issues floated in the hot market of 1961–62: 12% vanished, 41% went bankrupt, 25% are operating at a loss or minimal profit; 20% are making money but only 2.4% can be considered profitable holdings. To make money with most new issues, you must be nimble. Yet the sales pitch always envisions another Xerox or Polaroid whose shares will skyrocket and make you rich!

Building a profitable business today is a tough job. A new technique, concept or product may start off like gangbusters but the more successful a company becomes, the more difficult is the task of maintaining momentum. Competition, management problems, market saturation, new products and unanticipated events can cause strain and, usually, failure. And don't be impressed with the pontifications of professionals. According to David Dreman, one of the most astute market observers, the stocks that were the favorites of Wall Street—pundits and promoters—underperformed the overall stock market 80% of the time in the year after issue!

Broadly speaking, there are three types of new issues (in order of risk):

Penny stocks. Most of these have been, and still are, offered in Denver. If you are lucky or related to one of the promoters, you may make a lot of money. But most of these "opportunities" are better for their sponsors than for outside speculators. The markets for these shares are more or less controlled; their initial price is "negotiated" by the company, the selling shareholders and the underwriter and rarely have much relation to value. Most important, once the shares have been distributed there's seldom any sustained interest.

Most of these penny stocks are brought out by underwriters on a "best efforts" basis which puts such issues on shaky ground from the beginning. The promoters seldom pledge a nickel of their own funds to guarantee the selling out of the offering.

There is, however, one saving grace: full disclosure as required by the SEC. Few people bother to read the prospectus to discover that "The offering price . . . bears no relationship to assets, earnings, book value or other criteria of value. . . . There is no trading market for the securities . . . no assurance that such a market will develop."

The lure is the low price and huge number of shares. For $1,000, speculators can own thousands of shares and profit from a slight price rise (usually initiated by the promoters). But, over a period of time (as short as three months), the losses can be just as sensational because very few of the companies ever report significant earnings and, once the initial enthusiasm is withdrawn, no one is interested. With all penny stocks, you are shooting dice and the house sets the odds . . . against you.

High-technology stocks. These are typified by the glaring headline on the outside of an impressive-looking, red-sealed envelope THE CLOSEST THING TO A SURE THING WALL STREET HAS TO OFFER. Inside, the copy (which must have been written by an ex-circus barker) extolled the once-in-a-lifetime opportunity to buy shares of a new fund that would invest in "future" stocks of companies that will soar in value because of the expansion of a revolutionary industry, etc. In 10 years, you'll be rich!

To those on sucker mailing lists, this is familiar. A couple of years ago, the "bonanza" was real estate, then oil, and finally gold. The promoters were right about the price rises (for a while) but never mentioned the inevitable declines. *No business/industry surpasses "Wall Street" in the ability to fleece the public and do so more or less legally and with the enthusiastic cooperation of the victims.*

Most new hi-tech issues are floated by brokerage firms whose analysts have become proficient in the special language of chips, microprocessors, computer systems, etc. They paint a glowing picture of the potential of a product/service/process, project a future (in soaring sales and profits) as sensational as they make the past appear, and, as a clincher, just happen to mention the participation of a fancy-named venture capital firm to suggest success by association. And, of course, in other literature or comments, there are examples of past successes.

If you can afford to gamble, take a crack at some hi-tech stocks but temper your enthusiasm by diversifying with shares of at least three companies. With one winner, you may break even; with two, you should make a little IF you unload the losers promptly.

With hi-tech stocks, profits are made by trading, not investing. This is the opposite of what you are led to believe: that you are getting in on the ground floor and, with patience, will be a big winner. Even with such a sensation as Xerox, it took 10 years before the shares were worthwhile investments!

Alternative: buy shares of a venture capital fund. The first major offering, by Sequoia Fund, was a super-sellout so there will be many more similar opportunities in the future. The diversification, and so-called professional management, will be helpful but as one old-timer, commented: "The first successful venture capital fund, American Research & Development, was around for many years and had excellent management but most of its profits came from one investment: Digital Equipment."

In considering speculations in hi-tech stocks:

Concentrate on legitimate new issues: underwritings by established brokerage firms that seek to provide capital for expansion of proven-profitable companies rather than for promotion. The best deals use the new money to expand the business, not to bail out major shareholders. It's OK when a modest portion of the funds is used to pay off high-interest debt but the majority of proceeds should be reinvested for the future. That's what new issues are all about. Regardless of how enthusiastic your broker is, take time to do your homework.

Check the type of business. New ventures have the best chances for success in established growth areas such as electronics, retailing and special services. The risks are greatest with companies in exciting but only partially proven fields such as solar energy, thermal power and fish culture. Some concepts can be tempting but, in most cases, will not pay off without vastly more capital and research/development.

Look for a reputable sponsor: a well-known, established brokerage firm that will maintain interest in the stock by making a market (standing ready to buy and sell shares in the future).

Avoid issues underwritten by small, local organizations who work on a "best efforts" basis. They do not have to pledge one cent of their own funds to guarantee the sellout of a new issue. They merely promise to do their best.

Check the auditor. Skip any offering where the statements are certified by an unknown local firm. There's too much chance for favorable interpretations or even collusion.

Read the prospectus. This must spell out the history of the corporation and the background of its officers and directors, detail its financial record and, believe it or not, list the risks of ownership of its stock.

Look for *executives* who have held key positions with successful corporations, are willing to work for small salaries and hold large equity positions that will be valuable only if the company succeeds; *directors* associated with major organizations or, better yet, with successful venture-capital firms. At least you will know that someone has made a thorough investigation.

Avoid companies run by lawyers. By training, they are conservative and that's not what builds profitable growth.

With all new companies, the skill and competency of management are more important than the products or services offered.

Premium products that are already leaders in their field. With so much competition, there must be profit margins ample enough to provide funds for expansion of markets, to develop broader uses and to withstand price cutting.

Competent management that has had successful experience in this and other organizations, preferably those whose names you recognize. And the directors should include operating as well as financial executives who are willing to back their personal involvement with their own savings.

Financial strength based on the current balance sheet and past performance:

• *Debit less than 40% of total capital:* i.e., with $25 million assets, the debt should be no more than $10 million.

• *Sales of at least $50 million* to be sure that there is a market for the products/services.

• *Consistent growth of 25% a year compounded* for at least three years and with the probability of similar progress in the future.

• *High profitability:* at least 15% and, preferably 20% return on equity annually for three years. This will provide adequate financing for future expansion. Look for performance, not promises.

• *Conservative accounting:* no inflated property values nor trick allocations of costs to boost earnings.

Chances are that your broker will be pushing so hard that you won't have time to do this research but almost all of this information can be found in the prospectus (which MUST be provided) so if you take a chance, spend the next Sunday afternoon getting the answers to these questions. You may want to sell on Monday.

Set Targets for Profits

New issues require more care than those of established companies. In most cases, there will be spurts of expansion, in revenues and profits, then periods of struggle to continue growth. That means that the prospects and performance must be viewed in a broad context with greater flexibility than would apply to regular investments. Regardless of what some "experts" may pronounce, very few "new" organizations deserve a quality rating in less than 10 years and thus continue to be speculations.

That's why it's essential to have a clearly defined game plan and to set targets:

• *For investing:* to hold the stock for at least three years but be ready to sell if the price: (*a*) rises sharply as the result of market interest or a takeover offer; (*b*) falls because of declining profits or managerial changes.

• *For speculating:* to sell by formula of time or profit: (*a*) on the nineteenth day after issue (about the time when the underwriters ease or withdraw their support so that the stock will start to trade on its own merits); (*b*) when you have a 50% gain. This is a high return anytime. If you are still enthusiastic, sell half of your stock to back your capital for another new venture.

With both investments and speculations, set a stop-loss

Tax Saver

To help small corporations attract investment capital, Congress OK'd a special tax arrangement that allows "investors" to claim an ordinary loss deduction when the shares of a new/small company are sold at a loss or the business fails. The deal most involves a Small Business Investment Corporation with these limitations:

• The shares must be common stock of a U.S. corporation (no convertibles or bonds) issued for money or property, not for other securities.

• The total money or assets received by the corporation, for the stock, must be less than $1 million and used in a business, not for investments.

• The shares must be issued to you or a partnership in which you are a member.

The deduction must reflect a business loss and cannot be used to recover taxes already paid. The limit to the annual loss: $50,000 for a single taxpayer; $100,000 for a joint filer. Above these figures, there are no special tax benefits.

Example: Dr. R., married, invests $200,000 in Qhix-Tech which goes bottoms up after a couple of years. He bails out for $20,000. If he sells half of the shares in 1983 and the balance in 1984, he can write off $100,000 each year.

order about 10% below cost or recent high price. If the stock continues to move up, raise that figure proportionately. But do not lower that protection price. The first loss is almost always the smallest. If you hang on in hope, you will be bucking the odds. *Remember:* Two of every three new issues sell below their offering price within the next 12 months!

Speculating with Volatile Stocks

Both cyclical and leveraged common stocks in *all* price ranges can be highly volatile. Speculators take advantage of such situations by buying the most volatile stocks in rising markets or selling such stocks short in falling markets. Both approaches can be risky and profitable. *They are definitely special situations.*

Here's how the arithmetic of volatility works: suppose the DJIA moves from 800 to 1000 in a given period of time, say 16 months. This is a gain of 25%. In the same period, the stock in which you are interested moves from 10 to 14: up 40%. Divide .40 by .25 to get 1.6, which (because you are dealing in percentages) becomes 160%. That means your stock is far more volatile than the stock market average during this period of time.

Before you speculate in any stock, you should be aware of its relative volatility. A chart is also valuable. You can make your own or check *The Financial Weekly* (if it is a listed stock) or buy one from a professional service. Then compare the movements of your stock with that of the stock market as a whole. In combination with your own research, this information can give you a valid estimate of the volatility of any stock. Here's a scale for reference:

Use broad ranges. The volatility of a particular stock varies. On one market move, it may be 140%, on the next 110%.

Also check the action in different markets. Some stocks move up faster than they move down; others move down faster than they move up. If a stock tends to lose more rapidly than it gains, it is a candidate for short selling, but it probably is not suitable to the average investor. Conversely, true growth stocks will normally retain some of their previous market gains even in market dips—and so they are usually not considered special situations.

Relative Degree of Volatility	Percent Range vs. DJIA as 100%
Very high	140 and over
High	115–140
Average	85–115
Low	60–85
Very low	Less than 60

If you want to make this distinction, add a + to the stock that is more volatile on the upside; a − to indicate the reverse; and an = to show comparable volatility on both rises and declines.

Speculative Bargains

Here are two formulas that will help you find speculative bargains.

"Magic Sixes": stocks priced at less than 6 times earnings, yielding 6% and trading at less than 60% of book value. An improvement in any category can be profitable.

Square Root (SR) rule used by Yale Hirsch, publisher of *Smart Money*. The key is the Bull Market Increment (BMI), which varies according to the duration and slope of the market rise. When the upturn is modest, the factor is 1; when it's sustained, it's 3.

Take the SR of the stock's present price, add the BMI, then square the sum to predict the area the stock will reach. Thus, the SR of a stock at 4 is 2, to which 1 is added (to be conservative), and the answer is 3. Square this to get a goal of 9, a 125% gain. On the same basis, a $25 stock will rise only 44%!

When you try this formula, start with about $5,000; add $2,500 every few months—in the same stocks until their prices rise 25%; otherwise, in other opportunities.

With all types of speculations: (1) Use funds you can afford to lose. (2) Take risks only if you are lion-hearted enough to forget failure. (3) Set aside time to investigate first—and frequently. The odds are that 40% of speculative investments will be worthwhile and that only 10% will become really profitable!

And for those who look for bargains, ask your broker for names of smaller corporations that have ample liquid assets. These will not qualify as quality stocks, but if you are willing to take a chance, you can be sure that there are solid reasons for anticipating progress soon. That cash can be effectively used by smart management.

SOME SPECULATIVE, CASH-RICH COMPANIES

COMPANY	S&P RATING	CASH PER SHARE	RECENT PRICE	CASH AS % PRICE
Am. Shipbuilding	B	$6.73	12 1/2	53.8%
Drewry Photo	B	5.33	4 3/4	112.2
Eastmet Corp.	B−	5.27	4 7/8	108.1
Fisher Foods	B	8.37	8 1/8	103.0
Jaclyn, Inc.	B+	4.36	8	54.5
Meenan Oil	B	2.73	5 3/8	50.8
Michigan General	B−	1.54	3	51.4
Rockwood National	B−	0.73	1 3/8	53.1
Russell-Bird-Ward	NR	1.09	2 1/8	51.3
Simplicity Pattern	B	6.69	8 5/8	77.6
Thorofare Corp.	C	10.21	9 7/8	103.4
Viatech	B−	4.84	9 1/4	52.3

SOURCE: Financial World

16

Special Industries/Securities: Banks, Utilities, Foreign

This chapter is a mix of special types of investments that require somewhat different analyses or involve different types of securities. Data on Mexican savings account is omitted as the result of last year's warning by Eugene C. Latham, editor of Mexletter. For reader convenience, the text includes some explanations that, previously, were covered in other chapters.

Banks

Financial institutions are busting out all over. Their traditional image of conservatism, safety, high dividends, slow growth and stodgy management is changing rapidly. Banks and thrift institutions are "selling" money with hard-hitting promotional campaigns for special products, packaged plans and customer services; federal and state agencies are loosening regulations to permit expansion and acquisitions; and, in many cases, "you can't tell 'em without a scorecard."

These changes will accelerate in the year ahead: more financial supermarkets with insurance companies and retailers, control brokers or banks; more stores with banking centers and automatic tellers, and so forth.

It's exciting to learn that Big Bucks Corp. has bought a small bank or taken control of a faltering savings and loan association but, in most cases, such expansion is more likely to dent rather than swell future profits . . . at least for several years. The major financial institutions, whose stocks are listed on the NYSE, still derive the majority of their income and earnings from traditional loans to traditional customers.

Basically, all financial institutions try to borrow cheap—through deposits—and lend dear. In the past few years with superhigh interest rates, this process was reversed: institutions were locked in with low interest mortgages and forced to pay high yields on CDs. But, with help from federal agencies and special accounting, most institutions survived, and, generally speaking, are back to their old methods of operation with tighter controls, better credit checks, and, in many cases, more competent management.

Investments in stocks of banks and thrift institutions can be rewarding but, more than ever before, it is important to check the quality of the corporation and the ability of management to make money from operations rather than from financial juggling. The key criterion is Profit Rate or, as commonly used in the financial field, Return on Equity (ROE): the rate of return earned annually on stockholders' investments (see Chapter 4).

There are, however, other factors that should be analyzed. Space does not permit a full explanation but the table spotlights some handy checkpoints:

Assets: the bigger they are, the more difficult future growth. That's why so many bank holding companies are moving into peripheral, service areas.

Long-term debt as a percentage of capital. This speaks for itself. High debt does mean greater leverage in good times but when there are hefty, annual interest charges, there may not be sufficient money left over for growth and dividends. The quality limit of debt no more than 40% of capital is still a sound guideline.

Growth: four-year average representing what happened in the past difficult period: (a) of assets reflecting the money

MAJOR BANKS/HOLDING COMPANIES

COMPANY	TOTAL ASSETS $MILS.	LONG-TERM DEBT: % OF CAPITAL	GROWTH: 4 YEAR AVE. ASSETS	EQUITY	RETURN ON EQUITY 4 YEAR AVE.
Citicorp	$129,997	68.4%	11.4%	9.8%	15.0%
BankAmerica	122,221	32.3	10.1	8.6	14.8
Mfg. Hanover	64,041	41.8	14.1	8.4	14.0
1st Nat. Boston	18,267	31.7	12.0	11.1	10.8
Texas Commerce	18,217	10.7	19.3	16.8	21.5
NCNB	11,560	33.8	13.0	12.3	16.0
Republic (N.Y.)	9,280	38.9	35.4	19.2	23.8
Barnett Banks	6,932	24.1	20.5	12.1	16.6
Trust Co. Georgia	4,511	13.8	13.1	15.9	22.4
State St. Boston	3,915	22.0	15.8	16.9	19.3

SOURCE: Forbes Magazine; Business Week

available for loans and expansion (a 10% rate is good; over 15% is a mark of excellence); (*b*) of equity per share. This is similar to the **Earned Growth Rate,** indicating profitable progress. Here again, 10% is acceptable; 15% is best for new investments.

Return on Equity (ROE): for a top quality institution, an average rate of 15% a year, fairly consistently over good and bad times. As the table indicates, there are institutions that meet this standard IF you are willing to do a little research.

Once you have narrowed your choice of bank stocks, check further details with your broker's research department: loan losses, in dollars and as a percent of total loans; federal funds borrowed; size and status of foreign loans, for example. And when you deal with large sums, get comments from a firm, advisory service or broker that provides detailed comparisons. Continuing studies can catch trends early and help you to boost profits or minimize losses.

Bank Accounting

While the financial reports of banks are similar to those of corporations, there are special factors and methods of accounting such as:

• The tax rate is about half that paid by other corporations: about 20% vs. 46%.

• The ability to use investment losses to create substantial tax benefits. Normally, a bank will report financial results from operations and from investments. But, recently, there has been pressure to consolidate these statements. To avoid being forced to take future losses, from investments and foreign currency exchange, some banks took advantage of good profits in 1982 to write off their investment losses. This created tax credits and tidied up the portfolio.

Example: Chemical Bank had operating earnings of $270 million, up 25% from 1981. To reduce taxes, management threw in security losses, primarily from low coupon bonds, of $28.5 million. This also shortened maturities to 5.2 years from 7.2 years and assured greater liquidity and less exposure to shifts in interest rates.

• Starting in 1983, there is a new indirect tax on the bank's municipal bond portfolio: only 85% of the interest (vs. 100% previously) cost to carry these assets can be deducted from the bank's federal tax return.

Utilities

Traditionally, utility stocks have been favored investments of conservatives: ever-higher dividends and slow, steady growth in the value of the stock. That's still true in some cases but, for the immediate future, the best total returns will come from a handful of companies: those serving growth areas where the regulatory authorities recognize the need for a fair rate of return; the earnings are the result of operations, not accounting; and future capital costs will be largely paid from profits.

With stocks of quality utilities, the wise investor can count on total returns of from 15% to 20%, almost half from dividends and the rest from appreciation. At some

point, of course, the shares will become fully valued and, probably, should be sold. To build such profits, you must be *very* selective and start with information such as summarized on the *Checkpoints for Utilities.* These apply primarily to electric power companies but can be useful with gas and multienergy firms.

Regulatory rank. This rating, by Salomon Brothers, indicates how one firm views the attitude of state authorities toward permitting the utility to earn an adequate return: B+ in Indiana and Texas; a dismal E in Missouri. Ask your broker for his views.

Internal cash generation as estimated for 1983–85. This shows the ability of the firm to meet its capital needs for these three years. Northwest Public Service is likely to generate $1.50 for every construction dollar it will have to spend through 1985. But Public Service of Indiana will have to borrow heavily, possibly 96% of its capital expenditures.

Bond rating . . . as determined by Standard & Poor's. This is discussed in detail in Chapter 13. Just one caveat: NEVER INVEST in any debt issue rated below BBB.

Allowance for Funds During Construction (AFDC). Under this form of accounting, new construction and equipment expenses are shifted off the income statement (where they reduce earnings) on to the balance sheet (where they become part of the base used to ask for higher rates). This is legal, logical and generally approved by regulatory commissions, but it's a danger signal for investments.

AFDC is a noncash, bookkeeping transaction that lowers the quality of corporate earnings. Note that the *lower* the AFDC, the higher the bond rating: AA for Baltimore G&E with AFDC of 26% of earnings; BBB− for Union Electric where the figure is 121%.

On the other hand, a high AFDC ratio means that a substantial portion of the utility's dividend is a return of capital and thus tax-deferred so is not immediately subject to federal income tax (see Chapter 19).

EXTRA CHECKPOINTS FOR UTILITIES

COMPANY	Regulatory Rank	Internal Cash Generation	Bond Rating	AFDC/ Earnings	Oil as %Fuel
Baltimore G&E	C	65%	AA	26%	5%
Boston Edison	C	50	BBB	26	58
Cleveland Elec.	C	50	A	60	0
Common. Edison	B−	50	BBB+	86	6
Consol. Edison	B−	92	AA	4	41
Duke Power	C+	87	A+	68	0
Florida P&L	B	50	A+	40	40
Iowa-Illinois G&E	C	119	AA	62	0
Kansas G&E	C	33	BBB	122	0
Long Island	B−	63	BBB	111	68
Louisville G&E	C+	55	AA	0	0
Northwestern P.S.	D	150	*	5	0
Ohio Edison	C	26	BBB−	89	0
Pacific P&L	C+	63	BBB	32	0
Phila. Electric	C−	50	BBB−	76	8
P.S. Indiana	B+	4	BBB+	91	0
Southern Co.	D	55	*	34	0
Texas Utilities	B+	60	*	30	1
Union Electric	E	13	BBB−	121	1
Virginia E&P	C	48	A	40	6

* Holding company. Internal Cash Generation is estimated for 1983-85; Oil as % Total Fuel-1983.

SOURCE: Salomon Brothers

Oil as percentage of fuel: With lower costs for oil, earnings of some utilities have already started to improve. But this can encourage commissions to deny or limit rate increases. With coal, costs have edged up; with nuclear power, there are already problems and more to come so Long Island Lighting should be avoided.

Checkpoints for All Utility Stocks

• Favor utilities that use *normalized* tax accounting (setting up deferred tax reserves that increase operating expenses on which rates are based). This means higher rates to customers but gives management extra cash for operations/investments.

• Avoid those that use *flow-through* tax accounting (skipping deferred tax reserves and flowing tax savings through to consumers by reduced operating expenses). Customers pay for higher debt, equity requirements and the costs of inflation.

• Beware of depreciation of less than 3% a year. In effect, this waters the stock.

• Check the base on which rate of return is calculated. A 7% return on a plant carried at fair value or reproduction cost can be higher than 8% on the original cost.

• Beware of a low effective tax rate. It may mean too liberal accounting or deferred earnings.

• Watch special rate structures such as "lifeline" rates to smaller users through discounts keyed to time of day, season or age of the customer. These are, in effect, public subsidies at the expense of private profits. They denigrate the traditional sliding scales that have been so important in maintaining the viability of utility earnings.

• Look for diversification: where the core business is set up as a separate, wholly owned entity and new divisions/subsidiaries are created for exploration, development, production and sales of oil/gas/coal.

Arkla, Inc. still derives most of its revenues from gas distribution but also manufactures air conditioning products and chemicals; Enserch Corporation now gets about 55% of its revenues from gas distribution with the balance split between petroleum exploration and drilling, oil field services and engineering and construction.

Such diversification provides extra, less-limited sources of income but stock prices tend to be more erratic when the price of oil fluctuates: up higher, down lower than values of straight utilities.

Repeat: *Good* utilities can be profitable investments in the near future; *mediocre* companies will continue to provide high yields but their appreciation will probably be small; *poor* utilities (those in consumer-oriented states and/or with pedestrian management) will be lucky to maintain their payouts.

Foreign Investments

With the expansion of world trade, foreign business and investments are becoming more important and will be more so in the years ahead. When you buy shares of a major American corporation, chances are that at least 25% of its revenues and profits will be the result of business outside the USA. In some cases, the good re produced here and shipped abroad, but, increasingly e operations in foreign countries are joint ventures with ionals. And, of course, there are also foreign firms that nd/or manufacture in the USA.

With all companies that have substantia reign interests, there are extra risks resulting from ac nting practices, especially reporting gains or loses fro foreign exchange. Since the earnings are in local curren es, they can lose a portion of their value when transferred actually on the books, back into dollars. The stronger th dollar, the lower the net earnings reported by the parent company.

The impact, under new accounting rules, is not as unpredictable as in previous years but can reduce profits by as much as 10%. Some firms try to hedge against these currency swings but this can be expensive and not always effective.

The currency fluctuations also affect the value of non-monetary assets (plant, equipment, inventories). When the dollar's value rises, that of the foreign currency declines. But the assets are shown at the exchange rates that were in effect when the items were purchased.

Investing in foreign firms, consider the three Cs:

Country: political trends, inflation rate, government policies and economic growth within the home country. Without a strong base, the corporation cannot prosper.

Currency: the fluctuations of the local currency against the dollar. When the value of the dollar rises (as it has done lately), the worth of the foreign money declines. There will not be any accounting problems, as with American multinationals, but there can be real losses all the same.

Company: compared to American corporations, foreign firms provide less information about operations and finances, and the accounting and auditing practices are usually inadequate to say the least.

For information: read *The Economist* and *Investor's Chronicle* (London); *Far East Economic Review* (Hong Kong); and *Japan Economic Journal* (Tokyo). It's also wise to deal with an American broker with a department set up for foreign trading and research or with a foreign broker with offices in the U.S.: for instance, Daiwa Securities or Nomura Securities for Japanese securities.

Usually, there will also be extra commissions and charges for services and currency conversion. These can add 10% to 15% to your costs, so you will have to set your profit sights higher than you do with American shares.

Finally, there will probably be withholding taxes on dividends and interest. *Small solace:* these can be used to offset U.S. income taxes.

American Depositary Receipts

Fortunately, you don't have to go to such bother to invest in foreign corporations. You can buy shares that are traded on American stock exchanges as American Depositary Receipts (ADRs). These are issued by an American bank acting as depositary for shares of the foreign corporation held abroad. Each ADR is a contract between the holder and the bank. It certifies that a stated number of shares of the overseas-based company has been deposited with the bank's foreign office or custodian and will be kept there as long as the ADR remains outstanding. The U.S. purchaser pays for his stock in dollars and receives dividends in dollars. The bank, acting for the seller, notifies its foreign office, which provides the equivalent number of shares in London or Paris or Tokyo. When the foreign corporation has a large capitalization so that its shares sell for the equivalent of a few dollars, each ADR may represent more than one share: 10, 50 or even 100 shares in the case of some Japanese companies where there are tens of millions of shares of common stock.

N.B. The most popular ADR group is South African gold mining stocks.

Financially speaking, ADRs bridge the gap between foreign and American concepts of publicly owned securities. Outside of the U.S., Canada and, to some extent, Japan, stock ownership usually has been confined to a small group of insiders, often a family. Managements have tended to view investors, especially Americans, with suspicion. They prefer to deal with familiar institutions, such as their bank, which may be a correspondent for, or a branch of, a U.S. bank.

ADRs enable foreign companies to tap American capital and Americans to seek profits abroad. ADRs are easily transferable and are traded the same as other securities: a few on the NYSE, many on the AMEX, and an increasing number OTC.

American international banks, such as Morgan Guaranty and Citicorp, handle all mechanical transactions at normal cost. Almost all major brokers have specialists in ADRs, and many firms make markets in the U.S. and gain extra profits for themselves by arbitrage, that is, by the small, temporary differences between the prices of stocks on foreign exchanges and of ADRs in the U.S.

ADRs present no security problems because they are registered like regular stock. Most foreign securities are in bearer form. If they are lost or stolen, they can be sold by anyone who presents them to a broker.

ADRs also eliminate routine headaches. In some countries there's a stamp tax, and when the investor sells his securities abroad, he has to send in the shares and wait for his money.

The bank handles all mechanical details of dividends, receiving and reporting stockholder voting, etc. But there are often restrictions: ADR owners may not exercise rights issued by foreign corporations unless the new stock is registered with the SEC (a rare situation). Such rights are automatically sold by the depositary bank.

Foreign investments do have additional political and economic risks not possessed by U.S. stocks. But most of the corporations which have ADRs are large, international organizations which are not likely to be severely affected by shifts in their home country. For the average investor who does not have access to extensive research facilities, ADRs are a handy way to buy a position in the expanding world economy.

What it comes down to is that the investor anxious to benefit from foreign investments should concentrate on established corporations whose managements are able to set up policies and procedure that will assure the highest profitable growth and the lowest bookkeeping losses. At times, this can be extremely difficult. Even the top quality firms, IBM and Merck, continue to report foreign exchange losses. Fortunately, they have such strong market positions that they can achieve profits high enough to accept such erosion. But very few smaller companies are so fortunate . . . or smart.

SOME FOREIGN CORPORATIONS WHOSE SHARES ARE TRADED IN U.S. VIA AMERICAN DEPOSITARY RECEIPTS

Anglo-Amer. So. African	Kubota, Ltd.
Beecham Group	Makita Electronics
Blyvooruitzicht Gold	Matsushita Electric
Bowater Corp.	Minerals & Resources
Broken Hill	Mitsui & Co.
Buffelsfontein Gold	Nippon Electric
Canon, Inc.	Novo Industries
G.J. Coles & Co.	Pelsart
Courtlands, Ltd.	Pioneer Electronics
DeBeers Consolidated	Plessey Co.
Driefontein Consolidated	President Brand Gold
Dresdner Bank	President Steyn Gold
Fisons, Ltd.	Rank Organisation
Free State Geduld	St. Helena Gold
Fuji Photo Film	Sony Corp.
Hitachi, Ltd.	Tokio Marine-Fire
Honda Motor	Tubos Acero De Mexico
IDB Banking	Vaal Reefs Mining
Imperial Chemicals	Welkom Gold
Imperial Group	Western Deep Levels
Ito Yokada	Western Holdings

Foreign Investments

One way to avoid most of the currency problems is to buy foreign stocks—those listed in the British, French, German, Tokyo or Hong Kong Exchange. Many of these stocks soared in the late 1970s but, in the last couple of years, faltered and, with a few exceptions, have failed to zoom up with the American stock markets.

If you are wealthy and knowledgeable, diversify your holdings by companies, by industries and by areas; limit your commitments to 10% of your total assets; deal with an experienced broker whose firm has offices in the headquarter countries; and stay flexible.

Investment Companies

If you are willing to let someone else make the selections of foreign securities, there are several mutual funds that invest primarily in foreign securities. Generally, their performances were good in the '70s (but not all funds were operating at that time) but, since then, have faltered with the recession in many countries. Still, you are buying diversification and professional management. Here are some of the leaders:

Alliance International Fund
Canadian Fund
G T Pacific Fund
International Investors
Kemper International Fund
Keystone International
Merrill Lynch Pacific
Price International Fund

Putnam International
Scudder International
Templeton Growth
Templeton Global Funds
Templeton World
Transatlantic Fund

Special Foreign Securities

There are also foreign debt securities that provide high yields, short maturities and, generally, low risk. They include:

Yankee bonds. These are debt issues of foreign governments and corporations funded in U.S. dollars and registered with the SEC. Their yields have been as much as 1% higher than equivalent domestic debt; their maturities are relatively short (6 to 15 years); and many have mandatory requirements for the whole issue in equal annual amounts, usually after a grace period of five years. Thus, a 15-year issue would be retired in 10 equal payments between the sixth and the fifteenth year.

Common market debt. These are bonds of government/ industry groups such as the European Investment Bank and the European Community. The combine borrows in dollars, then lends the proceeds to individual companies for expansion and modernization. They are safe and carry yields 1% more than those of comparable U.S. issues but have limited marketability. They are best for major investors.

Convertible debt. To raise capital, some foreign companies offer special convertible bonds. Inco, Ltd., the huge nickel company, shares foreign exchange risks with investors by means of a 25-year bond with a 15¾% coupon. The plus is that the payment, at maturity, can be either in dollars or in sterling at the set rate of $1.98 per pound.

Canadian Securities

In earlier editions of *Your Investments,* Canadian securities were features in a separate chapter. But, increasingly, these stocks and bonds, and the exchanges on which they are traded, have become insular and, for most American investors, isolated.

In a push for nationalization, the Canadian government has discouraged outside capital by restrictions and by withholding taxes on dividends and interest. Add the declining value of the Canadian dollar, and profits have been hard to come by.

Furthermore, with few exceptions, publicly owned Canadian corporations do not meet quality standards: their capital is limited, their profits erratic and, relatively, meagre, and their management's ability is influenced by a small group of dominant financial institutions and individuals.

Even the biggest and best-known Canadian corporations have not been worthwhile holdings in recent years: Dome Petroleum, Massey-Ferguson and MacMillan-Bloedel were actually or technically bankrupt; Walker (Hiram) Resources has barely been in the black; and Alcan Aluminium and Inco Ltd. were hard hit by the recession.

Today, most Canadian stocks are better speculations than investments, so if you do go north of the border, heed these suggestions:

DO invest, not gamble. Look for companies that will benefit from the long-term growth of the country. Forget about "penny" oil/gas/mining stocks. There is almost no way you can be sure of the integrity of the promoter or the authenticity of the salesman's claims.

DO deal with a broker with good research facilities. Information on many Canadian issues is limited in the United States. Look for a major American brokerage firm with offices north of the border.

DO subscribe to a factual investment advisory service such as Canadian Business Service, 133 Richmond Street, West Toronto, M5H 3M8 Canada.

DON'T deal in shares of Canadian companies listed only on Canadian stock exchanges until you are familiar with the corporation. There are plenty of Canadian firms listed on American exchanges.

DON'T buy any security over the telephone. Despite attempts of authorities to control bucket shop operations, they still exist and continue to lure naive speculators.

DO make all investments in U.S. currency (unless you own property or travel frequently in Canada). Often, the Canadian dollar is worth less than the U.S. dollar.

CANADIAN STOCKS FOR INVESTORS

COMPANY	RECENT PRICE	RECENT YIELD	P/E RATIO
Very Conservative			
* Bank Montreal	31	6.3%	7.2
* Nova Scotia	44	4.4	6.9
* Royal Bank	35	5.7	7.8
* Royal Trustco	27	4.1	9.9
* Can, Pacific Ent.	24	3.3	12.6
* Can. Pac. Ltd.	46	3.0	17.7
* Dofasco A	49	4.1	13.4
* Moore Corp.	61	4.0	13.6
* Seagram Corp.	39	2.1	9.2
Simpson-Sears A	11	1.8	17.5
Conservative			
* Abiti Price	25	3.2	9.8
Labatt A	43	3.7	8.1
* Molson A	44	3.5	9.9
* Newf'd. L&P	27	6.7	7.6
* Union Gas A	10	8.0	8.3
Westcoast Trans.	15	6.9	8.3
Averages			
CHUM B	20	1.8	10.0
* Cons. Bathurst	23	3.5	6.9
* Imasco A	33	2.4	9.7
Standard Broad. A	12	4.2	10.9
Steinberg A	29	4.8	6.2
* Torstar B	13	3.1	13.0
Higher Risk			
DRG A	8	5.8	20.5
Electrohome X	7	1.4	17.5
* Gendis Inc.	22	2.9	11.3
Great Lakes Forest	85	1.4	20.0
* Ivaco	16	3.0	21.3
Shaw Industries	10	3.0	7.7
Westburne Inter	18	2.2	16.4

* Companies offer automatic dividend reinvestment plans or a choice of stock or cash dividends.

SOURCE: Canadian Business Service

17

Investment Companies for Almost Every Purpose

Not to be outdone by Wall Street's frenetic packaging, the investment company industry continues to proliferate with broader services, lower costs and special funds: for pension assets, for gold, for zero coupon bonds, for oil/gas exploration or development, for tax deferral and so on. You name your goal and it's available or will be soon.

But, in many cases, these new offerings are getting away from the basic concepts that made investment companies valuable: diversification, compounding, and professional management. More than ever before, it is important to choose carefully and be ready to shift your savings for the most rewarding returns.

Investment companies are best for those with limited money and who prefer to let someone else manage their assets. They are convenient but, if you are willing to do your homework, you can achieve better results on your own.

In Wall Street, investment companies are called "mutual funds" although, by definition, this appellation applies only to open-end funds that offer and redeem their shares at net asset value.

All investment companies operate pretty much the same way. They pool the money received from the sale of shares to buy and sell different types of securities for different investment goals: income, growth or various combinations. For this service, there's a fee, sometimes clearly stated but more likely included in the operational costs.

The two most significant features of all investment companies are diversification and liquidity. The investments are made in at least 50, and usually closer to 100, corporations/governments, and you can always get your money quickly: by redemption on demand or by sale through regular stock-trading channels.

Investment companies can be divided into two types in two ways: by structure and by sales acquisition costs.

Open-end funds stand ready to sell new shares or redeem old ones at net asset value: the current worth of the underlying securities.

Closed-end funds are similar to corporations. They have a fixed number of shares, often listed on major stock exchanges, that are bought and sold like regular stocks with standard commissions.

All funds can be categorized as:

Load funds that are *sold,* primarily by registered representatives of brokerage firms, but also by qualified-by-law individuals who work full- or part-time.

A sales charge, typically about 7.5%, is deducted from the amount of the investment. Thus, if the load is 7.5% (which represents 8.11% of your investment), your $10,000 investment is reduced to $9,250. The broker handles all details.

On large purchases, made directly or under an installment plan, the commissions are lower, usually on a sliding scale: down to about 4% on a single $100,000 purchase or commitment.

N.B. For estate and gift-tax purposes, shares of load mutual funds are valued at the *bid* price (without commissions) not the *asked* price (which includes the sales cost).

No-load funds are *bought* directly from the sponsoring company with no sales charge. You handle everything.

With both load and no-load funds, there is no cost for redeeming the shares, and management fees run from ½% to 1% of the value of the invested money. This seems small but can eat up a good chunk of your investment income. With $100,000 invested, an $8,000 annual return could be reduced by $750 every year.

Example: You have $10,000 to invest, and shares of

SOME CLOSED-END FUNDS

FUND	NET ASSET VALUE	PRICE	% DIFFERENCE
Stocks			
Adams Express	$17.67	15 3/4	−10.9
Baker Fentress	120.23	91	−24.3
Gen. American	19.10	18 5/8	− 2.5
Lehman	16.27	15 7/8	− 2.4
Madison	23.54	20 3/4	−11.9
Niagara Share	17.25	17	− 1.4
Overseas Sec.	6.25	8	+28.0
Source	31.48	27 7/8	−11.5
Tri-Continental	29.78	26 3/8	−11.4
US & Foreign	25.61	23 1/2	− 8.2
Bonds/Convertibles			
Am. Gen. CV	30.04	30	− 0.1
ASA	62.61	69 1/8	+10.4
Bancroft CV	24.20	23	− 5.0
Castle CV	35.78	34 3/4	− 2.9
Central Sec.	13.61	11	−19.2
Claremont	30.71	25 5/8	−16.5
Japan Fund	10.64	9 7/8	− 7.2
Nautilus	34.48	33 3/4	− 2.1
New American	36.17	29 1/4	−19.1
Petrol. & Resources	26.11	26	− .04
Precious Metals	20.32	19 3/8	− 4.6

SOURCE: Barron's

both types of funds, with comparable records, are quoted at $10 each. Your money will buy 1,000 shares of a no-load fund but only 920 shares of a load fund with an 8% sales commission. At the end of 20 years, the load fund must earn an average of ¾ of 1% more than the no-load fund to provide the same return.

Distribution of Income

To qualify for exemption from corporate income tax, a fund must meet these tests:
- At least 90% of its gross income in any taxable year must consist of dividends, interest and capital gains from securities.
- Not more than 30% of gross income in any taxable year may be from sales of securities held under three months.
- The fund must distribute to its shareholders as taxable dividends at least 90% of its *net* income for any taxable year, excluding long-term capital gains (which may be distributed or retained, in whole or in part). When distributed, they are taxable to the shareholder.

Closed-End Funds

With closed-end funds, the proceeds of the original sale of shares are invested and managed for specific goals: income or total returns. Some funds concentrate on specific types of securities: Bancroft and Castle on CVs; ASA on gold stocks.

Usually, shares of closed-end funds sell at a discount from Net Asset Value, apparently because investors feel that the fixed capitalization limits management's ability to take advantage of profitable opportunities. It would have to sell current holdings, possibly at a loss.

The discounts widen in poor markets, narrow in good ones and thus create extra gains, from the rise in the value of the investments plus a smaller spread. To take advantage of such a situation, buy shares of funds trading at higher-than-normal discounts, say 30% versus an average of 20%. Thus, for shares worth $10 each, you would pay $7. When the market rises 10% (to $11 per share), the discount might drop to 10%, so the shares would be trading at $9.90. After commissions, you would net 2⅝ points on your $7 investment: a 75% return on that 10% upmove.

With income-oriented funds, you can count on a better return, since the yield is based on the lower market value of the portfolio: i.e., with dividends averaging 10%, shares of a fund trading at a 20% discount (NAV of 10 vs. price of 10), the $1 per share dividend represents a 12.5% rate of return.

This opportunity can be useful in planning retirement. Dr. M. has a $100,000 portfolio of growth stocks that pay a low $3,300 in dividends. After selling out and paying the capital gains taxes, he has $80,000 which he used to buy shares of a closed-end fund selling at a 20% discount. He buys 4,000 shares at 20, pays the commission costs from other savings and now has holdings worth $100,000 with an annual income of $10,000. If the discount narrows, he'll have a pleasant profit.

According to Thomas J. Herzfeld, who specializes in closed-end investment funds, the best time to buy is when the discount is over 20% and the market is turning up. But, he admits, the rise doesn't always come as quickly as anticipated. So buy closed-end funds only for the long term and be ready to sell when you have a substantial gain.

Variety of Fund Objectives

Investment companies come in all sizes, shapes, and combinations. Fund managers have become merchandisers, just like food and drug manufacturers. They find an area of public interest (or create one) and develop a fund to meet this "need." They are, in effect, selling the sizzle, not the steak.

The broad objectives can be summarized as follows:

Income—concentrating on preferred stocks, common stocks that pay high dividends, the bonds with high yields. These funds are not adverse to capital gains, but it's a secondary consideration.

Conservative balance—primary goal: preservation of capital; secondary objective: moderate growth and income. Typically, portfolios contain a large percentage of bonds and preferred stocks plus quality common stocks.

Aggressive balance—aiming for capital gains from a diversified list of leading stocks plus, in some cases, a varying proportion of bonds. Companies which are fully invested in common stocks, except for a small cash balance, are known as *all-common-stock funds*.

Growth—investing for long-term capital appreciation and future income. In early years, dividends are small because the focus is largely on "stocks with a future."

Performance—these companies seek maximum capital gains by any and every means: fast turnover, use of "letter" stock and warrants, and concentration on limited-stock new issues which can be whipsawed, with the help of cooperating brokers and funds, to unreasonably high levels.

Special situations—these funds are, usually, venture capital sources which provide money to new companies. They combine their equity investments with senior securities such as convertible debentures and/or rights and warrants. Hopefully, these "kickers" *may* become valuable.

Specific types of special funds include:

Letter stock funds. These are strictly for the venturesome. They aim at capital growth and operate on the theory that gain comes first and risk second. They put most of their assets in "letter stock" (that is, in securities which have not yet been registered with the SEC for public sale and which must be held in the fund portfolio for a specific period of time or until registration).

Funds purchase these unissued shares at discounts of 25% to 30% below the price of the same, or comparable, securities which are traded on the open market. With few exceptions, the issuing companies are new firms, long on hope and prospects but short on cash and experience.

By every standard, letter stock is a gamble. The fund manager is hoping that the company will do so well that his shares can be sold, in a year or two or three, at a handsome profit. So far, there have been few successful letter stock funds, but hope—and the lure of a big killing—springs eternal.

High-yielding funds. These are another sales gimmick. They are designed for speculators who are willing to have their money invested in unrated, or low-rated, bonds that pay high interest and have prospects of capital appreciation.

Nicknamed "Super Income," they are popular with swingers and with registered representatives because they carry a hefty sales commission. Never buy them with money you will need in a hurry. Their prices can swing 30% a year, not exactly the mark of investment quality.

Index funds. These are composed of securities that make up a stock-market average such as Standard & Poor's Composite 500 Stock Index and are selected on a proportional basis. The idea is that by owning the average you will do as well as the overall market.

Since Wall Street seldom settles for mediocrity (at least not in the sales pitch), some funds try to beat the market by indexing only 200 of the most profitable S&P corporations.

There's no research, commissions are few because of the small turnover and the management fee is a low $2/10$ of 1% of share value. Usually, however, there's a sales load of 8.5% and a quarterly maintenance fee of $6 no matter how many shares you own. These have become less popular now that the overall market—and many stocks—is moving up so rapidly.

Equity and bond funds. This type of investment company invests 75% in discount bonds and 25% in equities that are indexed to the S&P 500 stock average. The Merrill Lynch offering will self-destruct on December 31, 1990. By that time, the investor will get back his money from the matured bonds (barring defaults) and will still own common stock that, hopefully, will be worth much more.

These are long-term holdings because: *(a)* the sales load is 4%; *(b)* the redemption fee is ½ of 1%; *(c)* there's no assurance that the bond discount will close much before the liquidation date; *(d)* the early returns of 4.5%, adjusted for operating expenses, won't move over 8% for some time; *(e)* the possibility of capital gains is better over the years.

Capital gains funds, where the holdings are always retained for more than 21 months so that the appreciation (if any) will be taxed at the lowest rate. E. F. Hutton's Directions Unit Trust invests in stocks of only 30 companies that meet strict standards of quality and growth. The selections are made from the most undervalued companies with the best prospects. This is a closed-end fund with a 3% load.

Speculative funds which, by charter, permit short sales (seldom possible with standard growth funds):

• Prudential-Bache Option Growth Fund. "To make money in any market environment," the fund uses: *(a)* short sales with stock options to limit risks; *(b)* futures contracts on stock market indexes.

• Permanent Portfolio Fund where the managers sell short, use options and similar techniques with "investments" in gold, silver, Swiss francs, etc.

• Massachusetts Financial Services bond fund that uses futures trading to hedge positions. There are some restrictions but, overall, this approach is highly speculative so do not be lured by the traditional "safety" of debt securities.

Socially conscious funds. With these, investments are not made in stocks of industries involved in areas that some people consider immoral, unethical or questionable.

TOP PERFORMING FUNDS: 1982

FUND	TYPE	YEAR GAIN
Oppenheimer Target	SL	+81.32%
Loomis-Sayles Capital	SNL	+78.92
NEL Growth	SL	+78.65
United Services Gold	SNL	+72.44
Strategic Investments	SL	+71.27
IDS Progressive	SL	+67.05
Fidelity Technology	SNL	+56.32
Putnam Vista	SL	+55.46
Mass. Finan. Emerging Growth	SL	+54.27
Fidelity Precious Metals	L	+54.14
International Investors	I	+51.92
Fund of America	SL	+51.79
Seligman Capital	SL	+51.60
American General Pace	SL	+50.37
American General Venture	SL	+48.96
Fidelity Magellan	SL	+48.06
Research Capital	SL	+46.84
Investors Research	SL	+46.68
Columbia Growth	SL	+46.56
Paramount Mutual	SL	+46.20

SOURCE: Lipper Analytical Services

Provident Fund for Income won't buy shares of companies in liquor or tobacco. Dreyfus Third Century buys only shares of corporations producing products for safety, purity, health, education, housing, environment, minority hiring, civil rights or consumer protection. With such investments, you have to sacrifice performance for ideals. That's not exactly a profitable financial criterion.

Fund funds. These are mutual funds that invest in other mutual funds. The idea is to keep moving out of poor-performing funds into those with the best current record. As usual, this is a better sales concept than investment vehicle. And you have to pay two management fees and hope that the "professional" managers are shrewd enough to time their investments profitably.

Commodities funds. These offer shares in professionally managed portfolios of commodities futures contracts. The commissions/charges are high, but similarly managed private portfolios, with broad diversification and computerized controls for signaling buy and sell points, have produced good results. (See the chapter on commodities.)

Tax-managed funds. These reinvest all income and make no distributions. They are an excellent way to save on taxes but their performance has been rather mediocre. Basically, they convert currently taxable dividends into long-term capital gains. This was fine when the top tax rate was 70% but is not so important now that it's down to 50%.

These special funds:

1. Reinvest all income/appreciation for compounding.
Example: ABC Corp. buys $1,000 worth of Exxon with a 10% yield: $100 annual dividends. The maximum tax for the corporation is 46%, and since $85 of the income is tax-free, the $15 is subject to a tax of only $6.90.

2. Avoid paying taxes by taking the 85% dividend exclusion available to corporations by investing primarily in preferred stocks and by setting up short-term losses and ample management expenses to minimize taxes.

3. Provide payouts to shareholders who need money by selling shares. Since this is a return of capital, it's not taxable.

One of the most successful of these special funds is American Birthright Trust, 247 Royal Palm Way, Palm Beach, Fla. 33480. It offers funds for both regular preferreds and those of utilities.

For another example of such tax savings, see the QDP portfolios in the chapter on preferred stocks.

Bond funds (taxable and tax-exempt). As explained elsewhere, there are two broad types of these fixed-assets funds: *unit trusts,* which buy bonds and seldom make changes, and *managed funds,* where the money managers try to gain extra profits by guessing the shifts in interest rates.

Option funds. These specialize in selling calls and puts for extra income. When conservatively managed, this approach can add 10% or more to the fund's normal return and can also limit losses. But, in an effort to beat competition, some fund managers speculate: buying and selling options without owning the related stocks. If they guess right, they can make a lot of money for shareholders. Even when they are wrong, the losses are (or should be) small.

Example: XYZ Fund buys 1,000 shares of ABC, paying a $3 per share dividend, at 50 and sells two consecutive six-month calls for 4 ($400) each. This reduces the effective cost basis to 46, so the amount at risk is $42,000. If the stock stays under 50, the fund keeps the stock plus $11,000 ($3,000 dividends and $8,000 premiums)—a +26.2% return. But if ABC takes off, the profits will be reduced.

Royalty trust funds. Here, the trustee deposits a defined package of income generating assets of oil and gas wells. The royalties are paid on the output. They are recognized by tax authorities as real assets and so are not the same as royalties that inhere in land ownership.

The royalties come off the top from gross income and are subject to operating expenses or a fraction of the net profit of the wells. They are not subject to corporate income tax so, typically, provide a steady 12% return as long as the wells produce.

Caution: Many funds offer shares at $2,000 each for pension funds. But IRS could call the payments unrelated business income which, by law, is taxable. It's difficult to determine which portion of a return is capital and which is tax-sheltered.

Income partnership funds. The income derives from producing oil and gas properties that have been in production for 5–15 years with reserves of 10 years or more. The partnership does no drilling. If the general partner is honest and capable and does not take too much off the top, these can work out well. See the chapter on tax shelters for checkpoints and buy shares only with money that you will not need until the wells run dry.

Bank-sponsored funds. These are small mutual funds offered by banks and thrift institutions. Usually, they have several funds with different objectives with the privilege of switching. When managed by a competent professional firm, they can be rewarding, convenient and time-saving because of the detailed reports. One of the best: funds managed by Wright Investors' Service.

Money market funds. These are a special breed covered in Chapter 12—excellent parking places for idle cash.

TOP PERFORMERS IN 1982

FUND	TYPE	% GAIN NET ASSET VALUE
Oppenheimer Target	SL	+60.92%
Fund for US Gov'ts	BNL	47.85
IDS Progressive	BL	44.66
Investors Selective	BL	43.15
Loomis-Sayles Capital	SNL	41.00
GE Long Term Interest	BL	40.95
Kemper High Yield	BL	40.81
Vanguard GNMA	BNL	40.75
NEL Growth	SL	40.29
Putnam Growth	BL	39.76

BL = Bond Load; BNL = Bond No-load;
SL = Stock Load; SNL = Stock No-load.

SOURCE: Lipper Analytical Services

Advantages of Mutual Funds

1. Diversification. Unless you have $50,000, it is almost impossible to have a properly diversified portfolio. It's costly to buy in odd lots, and if you buy round-lot shares of quality corporations, your average per share cost will be about $40, so you can own only about 12 different stocks at maximum. That's about a minimum for diversification in industries and types of investment objectives.

To buy just 10 shares of each of the 30 stocks which make up the DJIA would cost about $12,000. With a small investment (preferably supplemented by regular savings), you can buy wide diversification in professionally selected securities with mutual funds.

2. Systematic supervision. Investment companies have the personnel, research, facilities and experience to handle efficiently all details of stock transactions, dividends, war-

HIGH INCOME FUNDS: 1982

FUND	YIELD	CHANGE NET ASSET VALUE
Ace High	12.3%	+10.4%
Amer. General High Yield	12.4	+12.4
American Investors	12.6	− 1.6
Chancellor High Yield	12.8	+ 9.9
Colonial High Yield	12.7	+ 6.9
Federated High Income	12.2	+14.5
Fidelity High Income	13.5	+16.6
Fidelity Thrift	12.2	+ 9.1
First Investors Income	13.2	+ 3.0
High Income	12.8	+ 7.3
IDS Bond	12.3	+18.5
INA High Yield	13.0	+12.7
Intercapital High Yield	12.2	+16.3
Mass. Financial High Income	12.4	+16.5
Merrill Lynch Bond: High	12.9	+ 6.6
Merrill Lynch; High Quality	12.4	+12.0
Merrill Lynch Bond Inter.	12.3	+10.4
National Bond	14.0	+11.3
Northeast Investors	12.1	+19.6
Oppenheimer High Yield	13.1	+10.3
Phoenix Chase High Yield	12.5	+10.9
Price New Income	12.6	+ 8.6
Security Bond	12.2	+11.0
Shearson High Yield	12.2	+15.3
United High Income	12.2	+14.3
Vanguard High Yield	14.3	+ 9.1

SOURCE: Wiesenberger Services

rants, rights, proxy statements and other details of stock ownership. Well-run funds mail dividend checks promptly, provide accurate year-end summaries for income tax purposes and are ever ready to answer questions.

3. Professional management. While the records of a few funds look as if their money had been managed by astrology or advice from an African witch doctor, the great majority of investment companies reflect the time, experience and knowledge of skilled money managers. Most of the top executives are professionals. Even when they make mistakes, they do so after what they considered thorough research, study and analysis.

With better understanding of the informational-recording/reporting capabilities of computers, more fund managers are doing a better job. Unfortunately, there are still some individuals who set rigid formulas which trigger unwise and unwarranted selling of good stocks which experience temporary setbacks. Overall, however, the professional competence of many managers is improving, as has been shown by their better than average performance recently.

Unless you have ready access to current statistical information and can devote many hours to studying the economy, the stock market, industries and specific stocks, investment companies will get you results that are as good as, and usually better than, you can achieve on your own.

The true professional money manager establishes strict standards for the stocks he wants to buy and hold, acts primarily on the basis of facts and makes decisions which are keyed to the investment goals of the fund for which he is responsible.

4. Awareness. This includes direct and comparative knowledge of the conditions which affect the stock market: (*a*) money supply, interest rate, gross national product, industrial capacity, productivity, tax laws, etc.; (*b*) new developments in industrial technology and techniques which will influence the future of many corporations; (*c*) technical data on price and volume movements as best displayed on charts; (*d*) stock market activity such as insider purchases or sales, unusual transactions, etc.; (*e*) news reports of the Dow Jones News Wire. By the time the amateur gets the word or understands the significance, a stock may have moved a couple of points.

5. Lower costs. When you buy stock directly, you pay the full costs of commissions and taxes. When you buy shares of a mutual fund, these expenses are lower (because of the volume involved) and are spread over a broader base.

It is unfair to compare the cost of buying 100 shares of stock at, say, $40 with the cost of buying $4,000 of mutual fund shares. Your broker will charge up to $116 for a round-trip transaction. The load fund sale will cost about $34.

The proper comparison should be with the cost of investing $4,000 in the shares of a large number of securities. The total expense would be far more than that of acquiring the fund shares.

You can reduce the cost of buying load shares by larger commitments, either directly or through a letter of intention. This is a written statement that you plan to invest a stipulated amount over a given period of time.

6. Better performance. As the tables show, many funds have performed better than the overall market: higher total returns in bull markets and lower-than- average losses in bear markets. Over the years of a sound investment program, few individuals have achieved better results than those of consistently high-ranking funds (unless, of course, the investor followed the counsel of this guide.)

See for yourself. Pit your average annual returns (dividends and interest and capital gains) for the past 10 years against those of the funds you are now considering. All funds provide detailed information, and while you may have to dig below the fancy charts and chest-beating, the facts are there. Look for consistency rather than erratically brilliant performance—unless you are willing to spend the time and money to make frequent switches.

7. Switching privileges. When a management company sponsors more than one type of fund, all shareholders have the privilege of swapping on a dollar-for-dollar basis as the market or personal needs change. Usually, this involves a small fee of $5 per transaction.

Example: In 1976, Dr. Kneecap buys 1,000 shares of Super-Duper Growth Fund and arranges for reinvestment of all income and realized capital gains. The fund performance is fair with total returns averaging over 6%.

By 1978, Dr. K., taking a look at the 9% yield of a bond

HOW SOME LEADING FUNDS PERFORMED OVER THE YEARS

FUND	1982	1981	1980	1979	1978	1977	1976	1975	1974
Market	+19.6%	−9.2%	+14.9%	+ 4.28	+ 2%	−12%	+18%	+18%	−30%
Price New Horizon	+18.2	−10.2	+53.7	+33.4	+20.5	+12.6	+11.0	+38.9	−38.3
Istel Fund	− 3.7	−13.4	+35.5	+27.0	+15.1	− 1.8	+ 3.6	+21.4	−10.4
Investors Research	+41.2	−18.9	+70.9	+15.7	+14.2	+ 5.8	+11.7	+22.7	−12.8
Security Equity	+23.7	−18.0	+44.1	+29.9	+11.3	− 0.2	+33.1	+29.8	−23.8
OTC Fund	+ 8.7	+ 2.4	+18.9	+51.2	+30.1	+21.5	+33.0	+23.0	− 7.9
Axe-Houghton Stock	+25.4	− 6.3	+34.1	+20.2	+10.0	−11.2	+21.1	+17.5	−10.8
Financial Income (Bond)	+15.6	−12.4	+13.0	+21.7	+ 1.6	+ 3.9	+40.6	+34.3	−12.5
Am. General Harbor*	+34.2	−10.6	+26.0	+16.5	+ 8.8	+ 2.7	+26.5	+24.6	−11.3
Am. General Enterprise**	+16	−13.8	+72.1	+47.9	+21.0	− 6.8	+14.8	+33.6	−30.5
Pioneer Fund	+ 7.9	− 7.1	+25.8	+23.1	+11.5	+ 3.4	+36.3	+38.1	−17.2
Provident Fund	+32.4	+ 2.4	+ 3.0	+ 1.7	+ 7.3	+ 3.6	+26.8	+22.7	− 9.9
Chemical Fund	+17.6	− 7.4	+26.8	+21.0	+ 1.3	− 8.1	+ 8.6	+21.0	−24.0

* = Formerly Harbor Fund   ** = Formerly Enterprise Fund

SOURCE: Wiesenberger Services

Tax Considerations

With fund shares, there are opportunities to set up tax benefits but, if you are not careful, there can be unnecessary levies. You can reduce taxes by:

Buying after the dividend record date. Since the net asset value of the shares will be reduced by the amount of the payout, you'll pay less for the shares. You will miss the dividend but that's taxable.

Example: On April 22, Pretzel Fund pays a dividend of $3.28 per share. This was 17% of its net asset value. On April 21, the shares traded at $18.23 each; on April 23, they were selling at $14.91.

Buying before the end of the tax year. Under IRS rules, the capital gains tax paid by an investment company on retained gains is, in effect, credited to the tax account of each shareholder in proportion to the number of shares held on the last day of the tax year. Most funds pay out all their capital gain income so pay no tax on this distribution. *Advice:* A week or so before the last day of the tax year, buy the shares and, when you fill out Schedule D of Form 1040 the next year, list the amount of the retained profits, as reported by the fund, as a long-term capital gain . . . just as the fund does.

Usually (but not always), the fund will pay at a high rate, so if your bracket is lower, the excess payment by the fund can be used as a credit. With substantial sums, you might even get a refund if the credit exceeds your tax liability. In addition, the per share tax-cost base of your shares is increased by the undistributed gain per share remaining after the tax paid by the fund.

Selling short shares of closed-end funds before the record date for the dividend and closing out your position right after (when the price of the stock will decline by about the value of the payout). The dividends must be paid to the lender of the shares (unless you sell short against shares you own) but can be deducted on your tax return as an expense incurred in the production of income. But you can short only after an uptick in the price of the shares! If you make the short sale too early, you run the risk that the price of the shares will run up.

If you do sell short, advise fund management that you want the distribution to be paid in cash rather than in new shares.

Converting gains from short- to long-term. This is another trick with shares of a closed-end fund and is effective because when shares are held for more than 31 days, a capital gains dividend is considered to be long term.

Example: Dr. F., in the 50% tax bracket, has $20,000 in short-term gains. Normally, the tax bite would be $10,000. If he can shift them to long term, the tax will be $4,000.

The good doctor learns that ABC Closed-End Fund has declared a capital gains dividend of $2 per share, payable on December 30 to shareholders of record on December 15.

On November 26, Dr. F. buys 10,000 shares of ABC at $10 each. On December 29 (more than 31 days), he sells the shares at $8 (reflecting the $2 per share distribution). This sets up a $20,000 short-term loss to offset that $20,000 gain.

Dr. F. will have to pay the 20% capital gains tax on the $20,000 distribution ($4,000) but that's a lot less than the $10,000 he would have had to pay if he had done nothing.

N.B. *The long-term capital gain applies to profits of sales of stock held by the fund for more than 12 months. The investor must hold them only for 31 days.*

But this advantage does not always apply with state income taxes. Such a distribution is treated as ordinary income in Alabama, Arkansas, California, Delaware, Illinois, Mississippi, North Carolina, Pennsylvania and Wisconsin. The rest of the states follow the federal practice except Florida, Nevada, New Hampshire, South Dakota, Texas, Washington and Wyoming where there is no significant tax anyway.

With pension plans and small savings, there are no tax problems with investments in mutual funds, but when your personal portfolio includes $10,000 or more of these shares, be sure to check all the tax angles.

You may increase taxes if you switch shares from one fund to another at a profit. IRS treats each transaction as a sale and new purchase. If the old shares were worth more than their cost, the difference is taxable as a capital gain: short-term when held for less than 12 months; long-term when held longer. Similarly, capital losses on a swap are deductible.

Undistributed capital gains are taxable (unless attained in a pension fund) but you get a credit for a portion of the taxes paid by the fund . . . usually shown on the confirmation slip.

Be sure to keep full and accurate records (readily available from the management company) because there will also be taxes on the ultimate sale which, when dividends have been reinvested, can be hard to figure.

Example (from William E. Donoghue, mutual fund savant): "You invested $10,000 some years ago in shares of a mutual fund. All dividends and capital gains were reinvested so you now have $26,872: dividends of $3,048 that bought shares now worth $5,720; capital gains of $4,052 used to buy shares now worth $5,100. Thus, the total value of your present holdings is $37,692.

"Each year you paid taxes on dividends and capital gains distributions. Now your total taxes are due on $20,592: $37,692 minus your $10,000 investment plus $3,048 dividends and $4,052 in capital gains. The full $20,592 is taxed as long-term capital gains when you sell."

N.B. To make record-keeping easier . . . for yourself and your heirs . . . keep a log as shown in the table. For possible use, with IRS or by your executor, keep this on file for six years after the sale of the fund shares.

---

fund under the same sponsorship, arranges to switch from growth to income.

In late 1979, when interest rates soar, Dr. K. switches to a money market fund to get a 13% yield. In the summer of 1980, as interest rates decline, he moves part of his savings back to the growth fund.

In early 1981, when interest rates move up again, he shifts part of his portfolio back into the money market

fund and the balance to a unit trust bond fund where he's buying bargains.

And when yields drop below 12%, he starts to reinvest in stock funds and, soon, enjoys hefty gains.

Most brokers offer similar alternatives through a money market fund that can be used as an investment bank: drawing out to pay for new purchases; putting in proceeds of sales, dividends and interest; and, within limits, drawing

KEEPING TRACK OF YOUR MUTUAL FUNDS FOR TAX PURPOSES

INVESTMENTS

	Date	No. Shares	Cost per Share	Total Cost
Purchase	1/81	200	$12	$2,400
	12/81	50	7	350
	2/82	200	5	1,000
Reinvest.	12/82	50	9	450

REDEMPTIONS

Date	No. Shares	Price per Share	Proceeds	Shares Left
12/83	100	$8	$800	100
12/83	100	8	800	100

Redemption Tax Record

No. Shares	Date Purchase	Date Redeemed	Cost	Sales Price	Capital gain (loss)
100	1/81	2/83	$1,200	$800	($400)
100	2/82	2/83	500	800	300

checks for other expenses. You won't have the leverage of a margin account but you'll be getting, instead of paying, interest.

Be cautious, but not too cautious, about fund hopping. It makes sense to switch from growth to income when there's a strong downtrend and yields are high (vice versa in bull markets). But in many cases, quick switches are not worthwhile. This is especially true with money market funds, where an amazing number of "investors" jump monthly when the reports of yields are published. It might pay to switch for an extra 2% but it seldom is wise for 1% or less. Don't forget those costs of postage and phone calls (unless you use the 800 number).

Judging Investment Companies

Just as with all types of investments, the #1 factor is the competency of management as judged by the ability to meet or surpass stated goals fairly consistently over a fairly long period of time. Over the years, performance will vary but the "good" funds will prosper and the poor (usually promotional) ones will be liquidated or merged.

Be wary of highly publicized, aggressively promoted funds, especially those with a "gimmick." They may be attractive and profitable for a while, but over the long term of a personal or fiduciary investment program, quality will pay off!

If you are a speculator, you should realize that the risks do not vanish just because there's so-called professional management. They are gambling and may be lucky, but more likely will make costly mistakes.

With load funds, you have less money working for you but you have less work to do because the salesman/broker is supposed to handle all details. With no-load funds, you have the responsibility of sending in money regularly, switching funds when justified, keeping records, etc. But all of your money will go to work and should compound rapidly to make your personal involvement worthwhile.

Here are some key checkpoints:

Performance record. This is the key. New management may make improvements, but the only way any investor can judge the future is on the basis of past performance.

When you look at the record, keep in mind the objective of the fund: income, growth, balance, speculation, or whatever it may be. What you want to know is how and if the goal has been attained, preferably over 10 years.

Unless you are willing to settle for safety and income alone, the fund should have attained average annual total returns (realized gains, reinvested income, and unrealized appreciation) 2% greater than the yield of a quality corporate bond: historically from 8% to 15%, but higher in strong up markets.

Pay attention to that *average.* Several major funds have never been first in performance in any one year, but they do better than the market in good years and not as poorly in bear markets. Look for the fund's *total record*—in both *up* and *down* markets. In *up* years, the fund should beat the market. In *down* years, the losses, if any, should not be greater than that of a stock-market average such as the DJIA.

One of the best guides is the annual *Forbes* magazine mutual fund report (late August issue). This rates funds on the basis of performance in both rising and falling markets. To get a high score, a fund must perform consistently well

GOOD PERFORMERS IN UP AND DOWN MARKETS
1970-1982

FUND	TYPE	RATINGS IN MARKETS UP	DOWN	AVERAGE ANNUAL TOTAL RETURNS
20th Century Growth	NL	A+	C	21.5%
Fidelity Magellan	L	A+	B	19.0
Inter. Investors	L	A	A	19.0
Mutual Shares	NL	B	B	18.6
Pioneer II	L	B	A	18.5
Janus Fund	NL	A	A	18.4
Charter Fund	L	A+	B	18.0
20th Century Select	NL	A+	B	17.9
ASA Limited	CE	B	A	17.6
Templeton Growth	L	B	B	17.3
Am. General Pace	L	A+	A	17.0
Nicholas	NL	A	B	15.4
Am. General Comstock	L	B	A	15.4
Vance Sanders	L	A	C	15.2
Petroleum & Resources	CE	A+	B	15.2
St. Paul Growth	L	A	B	15.0
Putnam Voyager	L	A	C	14.7
AMCAP	L	A	B	14.3
Sigma Venture	L	A+	C	14.0

L = Load; NL = No Load; CE = Closed End

SOURCE: Forbes Magazine, August 30, 1982

in all three up and down periods. Adjustments are made to prevent exceptional performance (good or bad) in any one period from having undue influence on the fund's average performance—calculated separately for both up and down markets. Data include reinvestment of realized capital gains but not of income. The complete tables also show annual expenses, for fees and operations, as a percentage of average net assets. Recently *MONEY* magazine started publishing similar, but less detailed, summaries.

Investment portfolio. In their reports, always annual and usually quarterly, the management companies provide information on the securities bought and sold, the percentage of assets in cash or equivalents, in bonds, in preferred stocks, etc., and a list of the 10 best and worst performers during the reporting period. Only rarely do they show when the securities were acquired—so the popular holdings may have been bought just before the end of the quarter, not in the first month when their prices were lower.

These data can be revealing. A fund that:

• Holds a lot of cash after the start of a confirmed bull market is not making the best use of your funds.

• Has a high percentage of big-name favorites (Exxon, DuPont, Eastman Kodak, IBM, Schumberger). Except when these stocks are severely undervalued (as most were in late 1982), they represent security and reputation. You can do as well yourself, especially if you heed the Most Active List.

• Concentrates on unfamiliar companies whose shares are traded on the AMEX or OTC. That's OK if the prospectus states that the goal is speculative profits but these are not *investment* companies. And, as the record will show, these types of stocks are extremely volatile so that a fund that scores well this year may be way down the next.

If you're really research minded, ask for copies of the last three annual reports. Then check the portfolios to discover when major holdings were bought, how long held, and when and why sold. This will give you a good idea of management's skill in selection, objectivity, timing and patience . . . the marks of true professionals.

Zero in on big winners (IBM and GE) or big losers (Computer Vision and Storage Technology): were they added when their prices were low or high? Were they reduced or eliminated at peaks or valleys? And be wary if any fund continues to hold a large number of shares which have risen to record peaks. Who will buy them?

Just as with individuals, most funds make their biggest gains in a few stocks. They concentrate about 40% of their holdings in some 25 stocks. Check this emphasis. In the long run, proper selections can pay off. For the short term, this strategy can be devastating if a few of the stocks decline.

Finally, relate the results to the goals. A fund which opts for income may have most of its money in high-dividend-paying utility stocks or bonds. In periods of rising interest rates, changes are hard to make and will reduce real returns. The income will be offset by paper losses.

Size. The larger the assets of a mutual fund, the smaller the amount each investor pays for administration. If you choose funds with assets over $50 million, this should not be important. The management fee of $250,000 to $275,000 operational charges should be adequate to pay for able management and staff.

Stay away from funds whose assets have been under $50 million for over 10 years. If the fund hasn't grown, its performance must have been so poor that new shares could not be widely sold. If it's a new fund, there's no track record.

Conversely, when a fund becomes huge (over $500 million), there's a tendency for the managers to confine their investments to the relatively few major corporations that have millions of shares outstanding. In order not to offset the market, large holdings must be purchased and sold over a period of time and so may not always be traded at the most advantageous price.

This lack of agility makes it difficult for major funds to beat the averages. In a sense, they are the market. By contrast, smaller funds can score welcome gains if they pick three or four winners. But large funds are likely to be more consistent in their returns.

Turnover. This shows the dollar amount of stocks sold in relation to total assets. Thus, if a fund had assets of $100 million and sold $75 million in stocks in one year, the turnover would be 75%. This is high and may indicate that the fund managers either are speculating for short-term profits or are anxious to generate big commissions to reward a related brokerage firm or registered representative who pushes the sale of fund shares.

According to *Forbes,* the best performing funds are slow on the draw: They buy slower, sell slower and hold longer than the funds as a group. Frequent buying and selling means that the managers made wrong decisions at the start and repeated their errors over and over again.

Fund Services

Not all funds offer all services, but here are some of the most frequently available extras:

1. Automatic reinvestment. This means that all dividend and capital gains disbursements will be automatically and systematically reinvested to compound your earnings. This can be beneficial because there's magic in compound interest. With a total average annual return of 12%, your money will double every six years.

Note: This automatic reinvestment is a form of dollar cost averaging, but it may not always be in your best interests. Mutual funds pay their largest dividends in capital gains when the stock market is relatively high. Instead of reinvesting at the high level, you may do better to take the cash and wait for the market to decline. Your cash will buy more shares.

2. Beneficiary designation. With both single-payment and contractual plans, you can name your beneficiary by means of a trust agreement. This will assure that the investment will go directly to your designated heir when you die. There will be none of the delays and expenses of probate. Consult your lawyer because some states prohibit this transfer.

3. Life insurance—available, as term life, with long-term contractual plans. The insurance guarantees that your survivors will receive the full amount of your investment commitment. Or, for convenience, you can buy the coverage with your savings via regular deductions. Usually, there's no medical exam, the age limit to start is 55 and the total investment is $18,000.

4. Open account. This enables you to invest whenever you have extra funds or receive regular payments (Social Security or pension). The money buys shares immediately in fractional units. This arrangement is excellent for IRAs and Keoghs.

It's also possible to set up withdrawals, directly or through special checks. The minimum payout is usually $500.

N.B. Most no-load funds require that your signature be guaranteed by a commercial bank or brokerage firm. They want to be sure that the person redeeming shares is the lawful owner. If you deal primarily with a thrift institution, send your signature with a letter of explanation from the institution.

5. Regular income checks. These are available (by the month, quarter or other specified period) in several ways: (a) by buying shares in several funds, each with different dividend months; (b) by arranging for regular quarterly dividends to be paid in monthly installments; (c) by opting for a fixed income each month by permitting the sale of some shares to supplement the dividends. In addition, most funds will ease your tax reporting—and taxes—by providing printouts to show that the redeemed shares were those with a loss or with the least capital gains.

This is an ideal setup for retirement. Suppose you have $100,000—from savings and the sale of your home. You want a steady income of $12,000 a year or about $1,000 per month. That's a 12% yield, easily available from a well-managed fund without invading your capital. If you do need extra money for a new car or home repairs, you can withdraw more in a lump sum. If the fund managers earn more than 12%, you'll pick this up with compounding; if they invest only for income, you'll leave less to the children.

6. Loan program. Some funds permit shareholders to use their investments as collateral for loans at interest rates tied to the broker's call money rate. The minimum loan is $5,000 on a 50% margin. There are no set repayment terms and you can arrange for the interest to be paid from income or capital of your holdings.

Buying/Selling Fund Shares

Most redemptions of fund shares are done by mail but you can arrange for transactions to be made by phone—with proper identification.

If you have substantial assets, you can save (or make) a few extra dollars by:

• Buying near the 4 P.M. close of the NYSE. This is the time when the funds calculate the net asset values of their portfolios.

• Selling at the opening when, statistically, the market will be at its day's high—especially when the market was up at the close of the previous day.

Late News: *For load funds:* Keystone Custodian Funds have instituted a program for its 10 load funds in which the investor pays no commission when he buys new shares. But there's a redemption fee that declines on a graduated scale from 4% to 1% over four years. Thereafter, no fee for selling.

For no-loads: a new "contingent deferred sales charge" to discourage market-timing traders who shoot for quick profits by moving in and out of shares and thus force extra accounting costs.

Annualized Rate of Return

To determine what your annualized rate of return would be if you sold your fund shares, here's a formula courtesy of Donoghue's informative *MONEYLETTER:*

P = present selling price   G = capital gains
O = purchase price   N = number of shares owned
D = dividends receives   W = weeks you've owned shares

ARR = Annual Rate of Return

$$\frac{(P - O) + \dfrac{D + G}{N}}{O} \times \frac{52}{W} = ARR$$

Example: You own 100 shares of ABC Fund purchased 18 months ago for $11.01 each. The current market price is $13.59. You have received distributions of $77 in dividends and $85 in capital gains. What is the ARR for the 78 weeks?

$$\frac{(\$13.59 - \$11.01) + \dfrac{(\$77 + \$85)}{100}}{\$11.01} \times \frac{52}{78} = 25.4\%$$

HOW INVESTMENT COMPANY SHARES ARE QUOTED

FUND	52 WEEKS		Close	Week's Change	Income	Cap. Gains
Price Funds	High	Low				
Growth n	14.72	9.97	14.64	+ .19	.50	
Gr./Income n	11.29	10.64	11.29	+ .13		
Income n	8.57	7.66	8.55	+ .03	1.0708	
Inter. n	11.72	9.03	11.25	+ .01	.29	
New Era n	16.53	11.38	15.85	+ .04	.81	.072
New Horizon n	17.03	10.11	17.00	+ .12	.20	.758
Tax Free n	8.84	7.20	8.84	+ .11	.7987	
St. Paul Invest						
Capital	13.60	8.76	13.34	+ .20	.45	4.06
Growth	15.02	9.39	13.74	+ .16	.32	1.441
Special n	22.97	14.66	21.37	+ .25	.45	1.91

n = No load

SOURCE: Barron's

18

Options: Busting Out All Over

In the past few years, the options market has changed more than almost any other area of the financial/investment world. Now you can buy or sell options on hundreds of stocks, commodities, bonds, bills, currency and indexes. There's something for everyone: investors can use options to earn extra income on securities they own, to hedge positions, and to set up tax losses; speculators can use leverage to trade for quick profits, directly, through short sales, or with complex combinations. As you'll soon learn, the only *sure* winner is your broker. Still, everyone who manages his/her own money should understand the options market and should consider using these special securities to achieve financial goals.

But be careful and do not believe those tales of instant riches told in the locker room or touted by "advisory" services. Making money in the options market, over the long term, is hard work!

In Wall Street, nothing succeeds like success. First, in 1974, options on major stocks were listed on special exchanges. When volume soared, the professionals added financial futures (to attract the "monied" crowd). And when these proved profitable, they combined the two concepts with options on futures contracts. Each new "opportunity" has become more esoteric and more speculative. Don't let anyone kid you that these are "new" concepts. All that Wall Street has done is to merchandise a successful concept in a more complex package. "All options are like firecrackers with short, damp fuses. They may fizzle, expiring valueless in a few weeks' time. Or they may explode providing manifold profits before their demise." (Robert Metz, *New York Times*).

The options market is dominated by professionals. In the early years, the prices of most options moved with those of their related securities/commodities but, these days, with the erratic, fluctuating market, many options trade on their own—or, in some cases, on the dictates of the market makers whose success depends on their ability to guess option prices.

Still, there are opportunities for individuals to use options as part of their overall strategy. With careful selections and constant monitoring, *selling* options can boost annual income by 15% or more; *buying* options can bring quick gains; and both techniques can be used for tax benefits. With options, you have the power of leverage (a small sum can control a large investment); low costs (commissions are small compared to those of stocks); and a variety of choice (in types of underlying assets, strike prices and time frames).

Now, let's take a look at the most widely used options: those on stocks of over 300 corporations as traded on four option exchanges: Chicago Board of Options Exchange (CBOE); AMEX Options Exchange; Philadelphia Stock Exchange; and Pacific Stock Exchange. Later, we'll discuss more exotic variations that have been added recently.

Options are a cross between trading stocks and trading in commodities. They permit holders to control, for a specified period of time, a relatively large amount of stock with a relatively small amount of capital. They are rights to buy or sell a specified number of shares (usually 100) of a specified stock at a specified price (the striking price) before a specified date (the expiration date).

In effect, options are limited-life warrants. They pay no dividends and, by definition, are diminishing assets. The closer the expiration date, the less time there is for the value of the option to rise or fall as the buyer anticipates.

Buying options is speculation. Selling options can be investing.

The most popular and widely used option is a *call*—the right to buy the underlying stock. A *put* is the opposite—the right to sell the stock. For sophisticated traders, there are complex combinations: spreads, strips, straps and straddles.

The cost of the option is called the premium. It varies with the duration of the contract, the type of stock, corporate prospects and the general activity of the stock market. Premiums run as high as 15% of the value of the underlying stock: i.e., for a volatile stock selling at 50 ($5,000 for 100 shares), the premium for a call to be exercised nine months from now might be 7½ ($750) when the exercise price is also 50. Shorter term options on more stable stocks carry smaller premiums: from 2% for those expiring in a month or so to 5% for those with longer maturities. Commissions will cut those returns.

Definitions with Options

Striking price: the price per 100 shares at which the holder of the option may buy (with a call) or sell (with a put) the related stock.

For stocks selling under $100 per share, the quotations are at intervals of five points: 45, 50, 55, etc.

For stocks trading at over $100 per share, the quotations are every 10 points: 110, 120, etc.

New listings are added when the stock reaches the high or low strike price: i.e., at 40, when the stock hits 35 and 25 when the stock falls to 30. When you see a long list of strike prices, the stock has moved over a wide range.

Expiration date: Saturday following the third Friday of the month in which the option can be exercised.

Premium: the cost of the option, quoted in multiples of $\frac{1}{16}$ for options priced below $3, $\frac{1}{8}$ for those priced higher. To determine the percentage of premium, divide the current value of the stock into the quoted price of the option. When there's a difference between the exercise price of the option and the quoted price of the stock, add or subtract the spread.

HOW OPTIONS ARE QUOTED

OPTIONS/ PRICE	SALES 100s	OPEN INTEREST	HIGH	LOW	LAST	NET CHANGE
Harris May 40	128	886	11 3/4	9 5/8	10 1/4	−3/4
Harris May 40 p	59	344	5/8	1/2	1/2	−1/4
Harris May 45	128	540	8 1/4	6 1/2	6 1/4	−1/2
Harris May 50	267	376	5	3 1/2	4	−1/4
Harris May 55	104	59	3 1/8	1 7/8	2 3/16	....
Harris Aug 45	69	217	9	7	7 1/2	+ 1/2
Harris Aug 50	115	93	6	4 3/4	5	−1

p = put

STOCK PRICE: 49 1/2

SOURCE: Barron's

Here's how calls are quoted in the financial pages:

Explanation: On this day in April, when Harris Corp. (HRS) stock was at 49½ (bottom), the May 40 call (due in a few weeks) had sales of 128 contracts of 100 shares each with an open interest of 886 contracts. The high trade was 11¾ ($1,175), the low at 9⅝ ($962.50) and the last transaction at 10¼ ($1,025). The net change, from the close of the previous trading day, was minus 1⅛ ($112.50).

The second line lists the action with puts (p): sales of 59 contracts, open interest of 344 contracts, a high price of ⅝, a low of ½ which was also the price of the last trade. The net change was minus ¼. Note that investors were optimistic because this was the only put traded.

The major action was with the May 50 calls: 267 contracts with an open interest of 376 contracts. The high was 5 ($500), the low 3½ ($350) and the last transaction at 4 ($400) for a net change of minus ¼ ($25).

Note that the August quotations, at the 45 and 50 strike prices, were at higher premiums because of the time factor. Investors were optimistic and anticipated that the price of the stock would rise by that time.

The prices of the options, of course, reflect temporary hopes and fears, but over a month or two, they will tend to move with the underlying stock. But do not rely on this type of projection. The professionals create their own markets and, especially near the expiration date, will move the prices of options sharply in hopes of profiting from their personal positions.

The experts have their own systems, such as the one developed by Richard Brealey that: "the dispersion of the stock price changes increase roughly in proportion to the square root of the period of the option. A stock will fluctuate 2 or 1.41 times as widely over a six-month period as over three months." But even this approach may fail in an ebullient market.

One key factor to keep in mind is that the premium, at the outset, factors in the time factor. This will fall rapidly as the expiration date nears. In the last three months of a call, the premium, because of the dwindling time, can be cut in half.

Dividends and rights: As long as you own the stock, you continue to receive the dividends. That's why calls for stocks with high yields sell at lower premiums than those of companies with small payouts.

A stock dividend or stock split automatically increases the number of shares covered by the option in an exact proportion. If a right is involved, its value will be set by the first sale of rights on the day the stock sells exrights.

Commissions. These vary with the number of contracts traded: for a single call: a maximum of $25: for 10 calls, about $4 each. As a guideline, make your calculations, in multiple units, at $14 per contract . . . less if you use a discount broker.

When you are writing options and income is paramount, it's a good idea to try to work with a base unit of 300 shares of owned stock. For each side of the transaction the commission per call is about half that of a single option (about $14 versus $25).

RELATIVE PREMIUMS

As % of price of underlying common stock when common at exercise price

Months to Expiration	Low	Average	High
1	1.8– 2.6	3.5– 4.4	5.2– 6.1
2	2.6– 3.9	5.2– 6.6	7.8– 9.2
3	3.3– 5.0	6.7– 8.3	10.0–11.7
4	3.9– 5.9	7.9– 9.8	11.8–13.8
5	4.5– 6.8	9.0–11.2	13.5–15.8
6	5.0– 7.5	10.0–12.5	15.0–17.5
7	5.5– 8.2	10.9–13.7	16.4–19.2
8	5.9– 8.9	11.8–14.8	17.7–20.6
9	6.4– 9.5	12.7–15.9	19.0–22.2
10	6.8–10.1	13.5–16.9	20.2–23.6
11	7.2–10.7	14.3–17.9	21.4–25.0
12	7.5–11.2	15.0–18.8	22.5–26.2

You can save commissions when you write calls for a premium of less than 1 ($100). A call, traded at ¹⁵⁄₁₆ ($93.75) will cost $8.39 compared to $25 for one priced at 1 or higher.

Restricted option. This occurs when the previous day's price closed at less than 50¢ per share and the underlying stock price closed at more than 5 points *below* its strike price, for calls, or more than 5 points *above* its strike price for puts. Opening transactions (buying or writing) calls are prohibited unless they are covered. Closing transactions (liquidations) are permitted. There are exceptions so check your broker.

Writing Calls

When you write (sell) calls, you start off with an immediate, sure, limited profit rather than an uncertain, potentially greater gain. The most you can make is the premium you receive even if the price of the stock soars. If you write calls on stock you own, any loss on the price of the stock will be reduced by the amount of the premium. Writing calls is a conservative use of options. You have these choices:

On-the-money calls. These are written at an exercise price that is at or close to the current price of the stock.

Example: In December, Mr. Horwitz buys 100 shares of Almost Always (AA) at 40 and sells a July call at the striking price of 40 for 4 ($400). The buyer acquires the right to buy this stock at 40 any time before the expiration date at the end of July. Obviously, he anticipates that the price of AA stock will go up above 44.

Mr. Horwitz will not sustain a dollar loss until the price of AA goes below 36. He will probably keep the stock until its price goes above 44. At this price, the profit meter starts ticking for the buyer, so let's see how the speculator fares. By July, AA is at 50. The buyer can exercise his option, pay $4,000 and acquire the shares now worth $5,000. After deducting about $500 in costs (the $400 premium plus commissions), he will have a net profit of $500, thus doubling his risk capital.

But if the price of AA stock moves up to only 42, the buyer will let the call expire and take the loss. Mr. Horwitz will keep about $470: the $400 premium plus two quarterly dividends of, say, $50 each, minus the $30 commission paid for the sale of the call.

If the price of AA stock soars, Mr. Horwitz can still come out ahead if he is willing to come up with cash to keep the stock with its paper profit.

When AA stock hits 50, the July call will be quoted at about 11⅝. New corporate developments make Mr. Horwitz enthusiastic about further gains, so he buys back the call for $1,162.50. He takes a cash loss of about $787 (the $762.50 deficit from the $1,162.50 purchase price minus the $400 premium plus the commissions). But he has a $1,000 paper profit on AA stock.

Now, Mr. Horwitz can write a new call, at 50 with an October expiration date, for 3 ($300). This will cut his out-of-pocket loss. If the stock is called, in October, at 50, he is still ahead of the game.

With all calls, there's flexibility and, often, several alternative strategies.

In-the-money calls. This is a more aggressive technique that requires close attention but can result in fine profits and tax benefits for those in high income-tax brackets. The calls are written below the current stock price.

Example: You buy Glamour Electronics Co. (GEC) at 209 and sell two in-the-money calls, at a striking price of 200, for 25 ($2,500 each). If GEC goes to 250, you buy back the calls at 50 ($5,000 each), chalk up an ordinary loss of $5,000, then sell the shares for a $4,100 gain. In a 50% tax bracket, the loss saves $2,500 in taxes, and the after-tax gain is $3,280.

If GEC declines, there are no ordinary losses for tax purposes. But you can still make money if the stock ends its option period between 209 and 185. Between 209 and 201, everything is a capital gain. At 201, if the call is exercised, there's an initial $5,000 capital gain. You must deliver the shares for an $800 loss and can buy another 100 shares at market for another $100 loss. But the net is a welcome $4,100—all taxable at the low long-term rate.

At 200 or lower, the calls are worthless, so you pocket $2,500, after taxes, as ordinary income. From this, deduct the $900 loss on the stock for a net gain of $1,600.

Deep-in-the-money calls. These are calls that are sold at striking prices *below* the current quotation of the stock. Writing them is best when the investor is dealing in large blocks of stock because of the almost certain commissions which have to be paid when the underlying stock is called. With this approach, the best selection is a stable, high-dividend stock. Your returns may be limited but they are likely to be sure. Here are techniques used by professionals:

• *Using leverage:* when the exercise price of the call is below that of the current value of the stock, both securities tend to move in unison. Since the options involve a smaller investment, there's a higher percentage of return and, in a down market, more protection against loss.

Example: Pistol Whip, Inc. (PWI) is selling at 97⅝. The call price at 70 two months hence is 28, so the equivalent price is 98. If PWI goes to 105, the call should keep pace and be worth 35.

If you bought 100 shares of the stock, the total cost would be about $9,800. Your ultimate profit would be about $550, close to a 5.5% return. If you bought 10 options, the dollar profit would be a 22.4% return on the smaller $2,900 investment. If the stock does not move, you can let it go or buy back the calls at a small loss. If PWI declines, your maximum loss is $2,900, probably much less than that of the stock.

N.B.: All too often, this is more theory than practice. When an option is popular, it may trade on its own and not move up or down with the price of the stock. This separate value will shift only when the expiration date is near.

When one volatile stock was at 41 in March, the November 45 call was trading at 2¹⁄₁₆. Three weeks later, when the stock fell to 35½ (−16%), the call edged down to 2: a −3% decline. The professionals had moved in and set their own terms.

• *Creating cost:* basing your return on the total income received from the premium plus dividends.

Example: In January, one professional money manager seeking extra income for his fund bought 1,000 shares of Wellknown Chemical at 39½. He then sold April 35 options for 6⅞ each, thereby reducing the price per share to 32⅝. He could count on a 45¢ per share dividend before the exercise date.

If the call is exercised, the total per share return will be $7.21 on a 32.62 investment: a 22% gross profit in four months. Even after commission, the annual rate of return will be excellent. The stock will have to drop below 33 before there's any loss.

Out-of-the-money calls. These are the best deals for those who want to build extra income, raise target prices and set up tax benefits. They work best in a buoyant market with quality stocks that are bought when undervalued and when there are far-out calls with ample premiums. In effect, you ratchet up your potential profits.

If the value of the options fluctuates, you can buy back to set up a tax loss (because the cost of the call will be more than the original premium) and, hopefully, write a new call, at a higher exercise price for a premium that will be great enough to offset the loss and add 5 or 10 more points to your goal.

This strategy requires frequent checking and careful calculations but can provide excellent returns over several

SELLING AND BUYING BACK CALLS

Year I:	March: Bought 300 shares at 57¼ for net cost of $5,800	
	September: Sold 3 calls, 70 April @ 3¼	+928.78
	October: Bought back 3 calls @ 1¹⁄₁₆	−355.88
	Net Profit	+572.90
Year II:	March: Sold 3 calls, 70 October @ 2¼	+632.92
	March: Bought back 3 calls @ 1	−226.87
	Net Profit	+406.05
	April: Sold 3 calls, 60 July @ 1⅛	+288.44
	May: Bought back 3 calls @ ³⁄₁₆	−123.82
	Net Profit	+164.62
Year III:	October: Sold 3 calls, 70 April @ 4¾	+1,372.58
	January: Bought back 3 calls @ 2⅛	−697.03
	Net Profit	+603.55
	February: Sold 3 calls, 70 July @ 1½	+406.71
	March: Bought back 3 calls @ ⅝	−206.52
	Net Profit	+200.19

years. Your profits come from the dividends plus appreciation, and, often, plus the net premiums.

In the example: in March, Gentleman Jim bought 300 shares of Nifty Ninety at 57¼ for a net cost of $5,800. In September, when the stock price had moved up into the 60s, he sold three April 70 calls for 3¼: $928.78 net.

In October, the market dipped so he was able to buy back the calls at 1¹⁄₁₆—$355.88, leaving a net profit of $572.90. Later, he repeated these types of swaps and, in the third year, pocketed premiums of $1,947.31—about 33% extra income on his original investment.

The other table shows how Jim set up tax losses with another stock which he had held for some time. When the stock was in the mid 70s, in August, he sold three January 80 calls at 2 for a net of $558.97. In November, when he realized he could use a short-term tax loss, he bought the calls back at 4 for a cost of $1,249.28. This meant a tax loss of $690.31.

A week later, when the market turned up again, he sold three April 85 calls at 4: +$1,150.68. In March, after a pleasant short-term capital gain on another holding, he set up a small tax loss of $136.62 by buying back those calls at

SETTING UP TAX LOSSES

Base:	Long-term ownership of 300 shares of stock	
August:	Sold 3 January 80 calls @ 2	+558.97
November:	When he realized he could use a short-term tax loss, he bought back 3 calls at 4	−1,249.28
	to set up a short-term tax loss of	−690.31
November:	Sold 3 April 85 calls @ 4	+1,150.68
March:	After a hefty short-term capital gain on another holding, he bought back 3 April calls at 4⅛:	−1,287.30
	to set up a short-term tax loss of	−136.62
April:	Sold 3 October 95 calls at 4	+1,150.66
	Now he had raised his target price from 80 to 95, received $2,860.31 in premiums (plus dividends) and set up tax losses of $826.93	

$1,287.30. When the price of the stock jumped, he sold three October 95 calls at 4—net of $1,150.66 so, in effect, canceled out his earlier loss. Now his target price was 95. And so forth . . . if the price of the stock kept rising. If not, he could cash in at 95 for a worthwhile long-term capital gain.

Writing Naked Calls

If you maintain a substantial margin account, have considerable experience and feel confident that the price of a stock will stay flat or decline, you can write (sell) "naked" calls . . . without owning the stock. This is risky because, if the stock hits the strike price before or at the exercise date, you are obligated to deliver the shares which you do not own.

You can, of course, cover your position by buying calls but if the stock price soars, the loss can be substantial. At best, your premium income will be reduced.

One technique that works well is to write two out-of-the-money calls for every 100 shares you own. This gives you double premiums. Do not go too far out because a lot can happen in a few months.

Example: You own 300 shares of Pumpernickel at 32. The 35 call, due in four months, is 3 but you are not persuaded that the market, or the stock, will rise soon. You sell six calls, pocket $1,800 (less commissions), and hope the stock stays under 35. If it moves to 36, you can buy back three calls for, say, 1½ ($450) and let the stock go. But if the stock jumps to 40, you're in trouble!

Rules for Writing Options

When you write an option, you are betting that the stock will not fluctuate greatly: (*a*) that it will not go up by more than the amount of the premium (if the exercise price is below the present market price), or (*b*) that it will not go up beyond the exercise price plus the amount of the premium (if the exercise price is above the present market price).

Here's a digest of rules for a successful approach to writing options:

1. Work on a programmed basis. Have a minimum of $30,000 in securities on which calls can be written and plan to sell options every month or so but only when the premiums are worthwhile. Diversify your holdings and try to space the dates at which the options can be exercised so you won't get caught in a strong market and have to sell the shares.

2. Define your goals. If you want safety plus income, concentrate on stable stocks that pay sizable dividends and modest premiums for the options and write close-to-the-money calls.

If you want greater total returns, look for rising stocks, write out-of-the-money calls and hope for about 4% dividends, 10% premium and potential appreciation of 10% or so.

If you are aggressive, watch for volatile stocks where the dividends are low and both the premium and potential-to-strike price are high. And be prepared to lose the stock or accept a paper loss.

3. Set a target rate of return. To get a 15% annual return, you will have to get premiums of over 10% for six-month contracts or 6% for three-month expiration dates. The dividends and turnover can bring such income . . . most of the time. This target should be net after commissions and fees.

Set a target on the downside, too: at about one-half of the premium you received: i.e., if you sold a call for 3 and its value drops to 1½, consider selling. In a down market, you might hold a little longer to cover the costs of commissions but, unless the exercise date is near, take your profit and get ready to write new calls.

4. Concentrate on stocks that you would like to own on their own merits. Quality stocks are best for selling calls. Their potential can be projected with considerable accuracy and, in most cases, their price swings will be modest and relatively slow. Your goal should be income first.

5. Write long-term calls until you become experienced and can recognize shifting trends. The longer the option period, the greater the percentage of premium. With most stocks, profitable changes require at least four months—except in strong up markets.

6. Keep your capital fully employed. Well before the expiration date of your option, be ready to buy another stock or start over again. You are dealing in percentages so keep those premiums rolling in. With wise selections of option prices and dates, the odds are that you will retain the stock.

Best bet: Keep a list of 10 stocks: five in your portfolio, five others for replacement. Generally, the premiums move with the price of the stock but there will often be unusual opportunities with high premiums and/or appreciation.

7. Buy the stock first. When you become an expert, you can take the extra risk of writing the call and then buying the stock on a dip. But remember that this is a professional's market and amateurs can get caught short.

8. Calculate your net return. Add the premium, dividends and appreciation, then subtract the commission and fees—both when you sell the call and the stock. With 100 shares of stock bought at 30 and a call, at 35, with a premium of 3, the total commissions will be about $145. From the $880 income (including dividends), that's a net of $735 . . . about a 28% return in six months. That's a high, but possible, target.

9. Don't average down. Gamblers on a losing streak double up. If they bought an option at 4 and it drops to 2, they double up to get an average cost of 3. Now the option price need only move up one point to get out even. If it zooms, they make more money.

Like most theories, this sounds better than it is. A trend in motion is more likely to continue (in this case, down) than to reverse over the short life of an option.

10. Keep a separate bookkeeping system. Options are a special breed. Separate accounts make it easier for your accountant to prepare your annual tax return and to provide corroboration if the IRS makes an audit.

11. Be persistent. Once you have decided that you will write options as part of your investment plan, keep on doing so regularly regardless of what the stock market does. With the premium check in the bank (or your margin account), you are off to a good start. If you pick the right stocks, you will be able to maintain, and enhance, your capital.

12. Watch your timing. It's best to write a call when the stock has risen to a price which you think is too high. If you bought the stock at 45 and it has moved to 57, look for a setback. Then write an out-of-the-money call at an exercise price of 60. If you can get a 4-point ($400) premium, you gain downside protection to 53. If the stock is called at 60, you still do well: a 15-point profit in the stock plus 4 points on the call for a total $1,900 return plus dividends.

Timing is also a major factor in the value of the option premium. The closer the expiration date, the lower the premium. In July, premiums on January calls will be one-half a point or more less than premiums on comparable February options. *The reason:* the demand dwindles because investors looking for gains are beginning to move out of the market. This leaves fewer buyers, primarily short-term speculators, to make the market.

13. Protect your capital. When the price of your stock has dipped below your net-after-premium price: (*a*) sell the stock and simultaneously buy a call with the same striking price and expiration date as the one originally sold (this maintains most of your capital for reinvestment); (*b*) buy a call to close out your position and write a new call for a more distant expiration date. (See the example of Mr. Horwitz earlier.)

This is the kind of information that can be discovered by an alert broker or through special options advisory services.

14. Use margin. Leverage boosts profits. Under present regulations, stocks can be purchased on 50% margin. Since your premium should be 15%, margin can make your money go farther. If the stock price is unchanged or declines by expiration time, that 15% premium becomes a 30% return on your investment (minus interest costs). If you lose the stock, you'll still do better with margin than cash. But when interest rates are high, do your homework first.

15. Watch the record dates of high-dividend stocks. If you can pick a stock that will pay three quarterly dividends in the six months of the option, you'll have an extra profit even if the stock is called.

Buying Calls

This is speculating but with the right selections, can be rewarding in an up market and very profitable in a strong market IF you are smart and lucky.

All options are wasting assets in that, at expiration date, their values can decline to zero if the stock price falls or, at times, stays about the same.

Example: In May Hyde has $2,800 in extra savings and, from research, believes that oil stocks are due for a rise. He's willing to take some risks and since his capital is not enough to buy many shares, he speculates by buying options: 10 December 20 calls of Zip Oil at 2½. At the time, Zip stock is trading at 19⅝ so, to break even, after commissions, the stock will have to be selling at over 23 in the next seven months . . . quite possible.

By July, the stock inches up to 21 and, in September, spurts to 25 with the calls trading, somewhat enthusiastically, at 7½. Dr. H sells out and pockets some $4,700—taxable at his highest rate.

But if the stock price fell, Dr. H would lose, probably about $1,000 or the whole bundle if he hung on with hope.

Buying options can create false optimism and make you believe you're smart. Take the case of Neighbor Ned who started buying a few single options in early 1982. With the up market, he soon doubled his money. Entranced with the profit prospects, he subscribed to options advisory services and set up charts. By Fall, he had nearly $20,000 in positions: 3 to 10 long-term calls on a dozen good-to-quality stocks. When the market kept soaring, he moved into strips and straddles and while he had a few losses, most of his gambles were profitable. But, as usually happens, he began to believe his own publicity and took greater risks: bigger commitments with more volatile stocks. In April 1983 when the market dropped, he had a whopping paper loss and because most of his calls were due to expire that month, there was little time for a comeback. At last report, his 1983 record was in the red!

To make money buying calls, do so only in an up market with up stocks and then choose between:

1. Buying long-term, out-of-the-money options at a low premium (usually 1 or less). By diversifying with three or four promising situations, you may be lucky to hit it big with one and make enough to offset losses on the others.

2. Buying short- or intermediate-term in-the-money or close-to-the-money options of popular, volatile stocks (e.g., a call with two months to expiration date, a stock within 5% of striking price and a low time premium). If the stock moves up sharply and pushes the premium to double your cost, sell. If you have three or more options, sell when you have a 50% gross profit. Advice from one expert: "Never pay a premium of more than 3 for a call on a stock selling under 50 nor more than 5 for one trading over 60. Both prices should include commission costs."

Rule of thumb: The striking price of the option and the market price of the stock should change by about one half as many points as the change in the stock price: for example, if a 30 option is worth 5 when the stock is at 30, it should be worth 2½ when the stock falls to 25, and worth 8 when the stock moves up to 36.

And remember that all profits with buying calls are short term and taxable at your highest rate.

Trading Options

The new options market has opened new vistas for speculators. Trading is for cash, so there are no margin calls. The investments are relatively small, the potentials large, and there are always opportunities to hedge. Instead of risking their money in junky, low-priced stocks, speculators can get action with the same outlay for options on top-quality equities.

There are scores of speculative situations, so the examples have to be limited. Once you get the swing of trading options, find a skillful broker, do your homework and play the odds. Success in options is a matter of percentages. Because calls are traded daily, there's instant information, and gains or losses can be taken any time during the life of the contract.

You can dabble with one or two calls but to really play the options market, you should work with $8,000 a month, spend time enough to make frequent checks and have a fast, reliable source of information: daily from your broker or weekly from specialists in options information.

If you have time to watch developments closely, you can let your profits run, but, for most amateurs, the best rule is to set target prices for gains of 15% to 25%—after deducting commissions and depending on the size of your investment, the prospect of the stock market, and the volatility of the stock.

The sale of multiple options against a single stock position can assure extra protection in a decline, added income if the stock stands still and bigger returns when there's a modest advance. This works best following a strong market advance, when there's likely to be a temporary lull or fallback.

Example: You own 300 shares of So Long, Inc. (SLI), trading at 25. You believe the market is topping out, so you sell six calls at premiums of 2½ each: $1,500. Here's what could happen:

Price SLI	Gain/Loss	Price Call	Gain/Loss	Net
20	−1,500	0	+1,500	0
25	0	0	+1,500	+1,500
30	+1,500	5	−1,500	0
35	+3,000	10	−4,500	−1,500

You will profit as long as the stock stays between 20 and 30, but you'd better be ready to cover your position if the stock zooms over 30. Some shrewd buyers may exercise the calls before the expiration date.

Caveat: Don't try this multiple writing with volatile stocks. Their rapid price swings can narrow that profit zone in a short time.

In trading, it's important to have a frame of reference for the value of the option, follow the market trend, concentrate on volatile, low-dividend-paying stocks and watch the time factor.

The action of the stock will be the determining factor in profits and losses, but gains are easier to come by when you:

1. Check these points.

Time before expiration. The longer the period before the exercise date, the greater the chance for appreciation. Unless you are sharp, observant, and lucky, it seldom pays to trade in calls with less than two months to run. Profits can be made only with volatile stocks in an erratic market and that's no spot for the amateur.

Volatility. The best bets are options on stocks which swing over 25% a year. This criterion rules out slow movers such as utilities, steels, and financial institutions. It highlights swingers such as Pennzoil, Tandy and Williams Cos.

Price of the stock. The greatest percentage gains can be made with low-priced stocks; the lowest percentage gains, with costly equities such as Superior Oil. But each has its day of glory.

Striking price of the option. This selection depends on your experience and trading goals. Buying deep-in-the-money calls offers the best leverage because their premiums are relatively small.

Yield of the stock. The higher the dividend rate of the stock, the lower the premium of the option—usually. For quick-profit trading, stick with low or no-dividend payers.

2. Follow these rules suggested by Peter deHaas of Lehman Brothers:

Buy the option when the market is going down but when you **anticipate a turnaround soon.** This will give you the benefit of both the temporary and long-term price rises.

Buy options where the underlying stock is trading below, but close to, its striking price. The premium will be smaller and will rise when the stock moves above the exercise price.

Pick options with small premiums and the stocks appear to have prospects of fast, upward action.

Stick with high-quality stocks until you are experienced. With options, the risks are enough without adding the danger of poor investments.

Don't enter market orders. Give your broker a specific price or, if you are anxious, a price range at which to buy. In fluctuating markets, an active option can move more than ½ point and can cut deeply into your potential profits.

Spreads for Profit and Protection

Hedges can be profitable with calls when the spread is narrow, usually no more than ½ point between the cost of calls exercisable at different dates and/or different prices.

A hedge involves buying one option and selling another short, both for the same stock. *Your goal:* to capture at least the difference in premiums. Dollarwise, these are inexpensive because, under current margin rules, your long option is adequate to cover the short option. Thus your cash outlay is small: $50 for that ½-point spread. And if you deal with five or more calls, the commission per call will run around $25.

Here's an example involving POP stock priced at 50 in April. The premiums for 50 calls are: for July, 3½; for October, 4.

Sell July 50 for 3½	+ $350
Buy October 50 for 4	− 400
Cash outlay	− 50
Commission	− 25
Total cost	− 75

If POP is below 50 in July, you keep $350 and still own an option worth $250 to $300.

If POP goes up by October, the option will be worth $500 or more so you have a profit of $850.

If POP is at 60 at the end of July, that month's option will be worth 10, so you have to buy it back at a loss of about $650 plus in-and-out costs. But the October call might be at 14, so you could sell that for a gross profit of $1,000 to offset the July loss.

If the stock falls below 46½, you will lose money unless there's a recovery by October. But with such a stable stock

in a rising market, this is not likely. The key factor is the small spread which keeps the maximum loss low.

Perpendicular spread. This is based on buying and selling options with the same exercise date but different striking prices.

Example: Easy Rider (ER) is at 101¾. The market is moving up and you are bullish. Sell ten ER October 100s at 12¼ and buy October 90s at 16⅞. This requires an outlay of $4,625. Your maximum loss will occur if ER plunges below 90.

If it goes to 95, you will still make $375. At 100 or higher, your profit will be a welcome $5,375, a 120% return on your investment.

If the market is declining, set up a bearish spread. Psychologically, the risk is greater, so it is best to deal with lower-priced stocks, selling at, say, 24⅝.

Buy 10 October 25s at 2⅛ and sell 10 October 20s at 5⅜. This brings in $3,250 cash. Since the October 20 calls are naked, you'll need $5,000 margin (but the premiums cut this to $1,750) to control nearly $50,000 worth of stock.

If the stock goes to 22, you will make $1,250. At 20 or below, your profit is $3,250 for a 180% return. With perpendicular spreads, you know results at any one time. With horizontal spreads, there's the added risk of time.

Butterfly, or sandwich, spread. In this case you are multihedging. Here's what to do: In the spring, when your stock, hypothetical Busty Bertha, is at 96¼, with July 80 calls at 17⅛, July 90s at 12⅛ and July 100s at 7⅛, *buy* one July 100 and one July 80 and *sell* two July 90s. This provides $2,425 in cash, but it requires at least $1,000 margin.

If you can set up such a combination, *you cannot lose money.* If the stock ends July at 80 or below, or at 100 or above, the buy and sell sides offset each other.

You make money if BB stock is between 81 and 99 (that profit zone again). At 94, you will lose $800 on the sell side but make $1,400 on the buy side for a $600 gross profit.

At 90, you get the best profit. The July 80 call is worth 10 (a loss of $712.50), and the July 100 expires worthless for a loss of another $712.50. But the two July 90s also expire at zero, so the investor pockets $2,245 on the sell side for a net gain of $1,000, or 100% on the money he put up.

There are dangers in such complex combinations:

1. With one call each, the commissions will eat you up.

2. Such spreads are difficult to execute at the same time.

3. Early exercise by the buyer can destroy the hedge and create a new ball game.

4. Lifting a leg of the spread can: (*a*) increase the risk from temporary market fluctuations, (*b*) create an unprofitable tax situation. The potential profit on the short side could be larger than the loss on the long side. If both are closed out or expire, the taxes could take all the gains.

Advice: Set up butterfly spreads *only* if you have a shrewd, knowledgeable broker, time enough to watch changes and money enough to make such speculations worthwhile. Otherwise, your broker will be the winner.

Mistakes with Options

These comments are based on counsel from veteran Max G. Ansbacher, vice president of Bear, Stearns & Co., New York City.

Failing to include all costs in calculating profits. Since the profit from writing calls is always limited, be sure to deduct—mentally and actually—the costs of commissions.

Example: Mr. Flack buys 100 shares of stock at 22 and writes a call, at 20, for $3. That's a gross spread of $1 per share. This appears to provide reasonable returns:

• when bought for cash, of 5.2% ($1 divided by the net cost of $19).

• when 50% margined, of 12.5% ($11 cash minus $3 premium equals $8, which is divided into $1).

With four months to run before expiration, the annualized rates of return would appear to be 15.6% and 37.5% respectively.

But with 200 shares and two options, the per share commissions total $1.01: to buy the stock, 43.7¢ ($87.40); to sell the options, $15.90 per option; and, if the call is exercised, 41.6¢ ($83.20). So Mr. Flack really lost money!

Being too bullish. No matter what your long-term forecast for the stock market, it will have little effect during the short life of most options.

Over the short term, it is just as likely that the market will go down as well as up. This applies especially to buying options. *Advice:* If you trade, never put all your money in options on one side of the market.

OPTION STRATEGIES

(In order of benefits)

VERY OPTIMISTIC
  Buy call with strike price above market
  Buy call with strike price at market
  Buy call with strike price below market
  Buy stock on margin
  For speculations, combine one of these:
  Sell put with strike price above market
  Sell put with strike price at market
  Sell put with strike price below market

MODERATELY OPTIMISTIC
  Buy stock, sell put
  Buy stock, sell call with strike price above market
  Buy stock, sell call with strike price at market
  Buy stock, sell call and put, both at market
  Buy stock, sell call and put, both with strike prices away from market

NEUTRAL
  Buy stock, sell one call with strike price above market, one at market
  Buy stock, sell two or more calls with strike price above market
  Sell put and call both with strike prices at market (straddle)
  Sell call with strike price at market, put with strike price below (combination)
  Buy stock and one put with strike price at market (call)

MODERATELY PESSIMISTIC
  Buy stock and two puts
  Sell call with strike price at market or lower, buy call at higher strike price (bear spread)
  Sell naked call with strike price above market
  Sell stock short, buy two calls
  Sell stock short, buy one call at market (synthetic put)
  Sell naked call with strike price at market
  Buy one call and two puts, all with strike price at market

VERY PESSIMISTIC
  Buy put with strike price at market
  Sell naked call with strike price below market
  Sell stock short, buy call with strike price above market price (partial put)
  Buy put with strike price below market
  Sell stock short

SOURCE: Max G. Ansbacher, THE NEW OPTIONS MARKET

Forgetting loss potential. When selling calls, your profit is limited but your potential loss is almost unlimited if the stock goes down. Use a stop-loss order to sell the stock when it has declined to a predetermined price. At that point, the call can be continued naked or bought back.

Overplaying leverage. In theory, $2,000 invested in options should do 10 to 20 times the work as the same sum invested in the stock. But leverage can work against you even more than for you. If you use $2,000 to buy calls, you can lose everything.

The proper way to look at leverage with options is this: for $200 in an option, you can buy the same profit potential as $2,000 in the stock. The other $1,800 can stay in the bank or be used to diversify your risks.

Puts for Protection and Profit

Most of this chapter has concentrated on calls because they are the most widely used form of options. The same strategies/techniques/counsel applies to puts but, generally, puts are best suited for down markets.

In the broad sense, a put is the opposite of a call. But there are significant differences, partly because their volume—and thus price changes—is less than that of calls and partly because it's easier and more enjoyable to look for price increases rather than declines. But, over the years, the stock market will decline about one-third of the time, so, in such periods, puts can be more profitable than calls. (See table.)

A put gives the option owner the right to *sell* a specified number of shares (usually 100) of a specified stock at a specified price before a specified date. Puts have the same expiration months and price intervals as do listed calls.

In theory, the price of a put moves counter to that of the related stock: up when the value of the stock falls; down when it rises. You buy a put when you are bearish and anticipate the market/stock will decline. Vice versa. But, as with all options, its value is a wasting asset and will diminish with the approach of the expiration date as the time factor dwindles.

As with calls, the attraction of puts is leverage. For a few hundred dollars you can control stock worth thousands. Generally the premiums will be smaller than those of calls because of lesser demand. In the stock market few people are pessimistic.

The best candidates for stocks involving puts are:

• *Stocks paying small or no dividends.* You are hoping for the value to decrease. Dividends tend to set a floor for stocks as, even in bear markets, yields are important.

• *Stocks with high price/earnings ratios.* These are more susceptible to downswings than stocks with lower multiples. A stock with a P/E of 20 has a lot more leeway for a drop than one with a P/E of 10.

• *Volatile stocks.* These are issues with a history of sharp, wide swings. Stable stocks move slowly, even in active markets.

Selling puts. In writing (selling) puts, you receive an instant profit but must be ready, with cash or collateral, to buy the stock if it is selling at or below the exercise price.

Example: The stock is at 53. You think it will go higher

but would like extra income. You write an in-the-money put at 50 for 2 ($200).

As long as the stock stays above 50, the put will not be exercised. But once it falls below 50, you must be ready to buy the stock or buy back the put . . . cutting or eliminating your profit.

For safety, it's best to diversify with at least three different puts. The prices of most stocks can swing widely in the six to nine months before the expiration date.

Buying puts. This is speculating and even more risky than buying calls . . . except in a confirmed down market. The same caveats apply: do your homework, diversify, consider taking profits when you have doubled your money and always keep in mind that you can lose part, or all, of your money.

If you are experienced, keep close tabs on developments, and deal with volatile stocks—whose prices can drop fast and far—you can make money, sometimes in flat periods and always in down markets. Besides, puts are not subject to such wide swings as calls because fewer professionals are involved.

Hybrid Options: For Experts Only

Once you understand options, you can take a fling at combinations. In most cases, these are too complex for amateurs but if you like to use a calculator and hedge your positions, these hybrids can reduce your risks and, on occasion, boost your profits. For most folks, the rewards of the excitement are greater than the returns. But your broker will be happy with the extra commissions. Here are examples of what can be set up:

Straddle—a double option, combining a call and a put on the same stock, both at the same price and for the same length of time. Either or both sides of a straddle may be exercised at any time during the life of the option—for a high premium. These are profitable when you are convinced that a stock will make a dramatic move but are uncertain whether the trend will be up or down.

Traditionally, most speculators use straddles in a bull market against a long position. If the stock moves up, the call side will be exercised and the put will expire unexercised. This is more profitable than writing calls because the straddle premiums are substantially higher than those of straight calls.

But this can be costly in a down market. If the underlying stock goes down, there's a double loss: in the call and in the put. Therefore, when a straddle is sold against a long position, the straddle premium received must, in effect, protect 200 shares.

In a bear market, it is often wise to sell straddles against a short position. The odds are better.

Here's how one self-styled trader did it:

"In January, QRS stock was at 100. This was close to the last year's high and since the stock had bounced as low as 65, I felt the best straddle was short term so I picked a February expiration date. Simultaneously, I bought a call and a put, both at 100: 5 ($500) for the call and 4 ($400) for the put. With commissions (for buying and selling) of about $100, my exposure was $1,000.

"To make money, QRS had to rise above 110 or fall below 90. I guessed right. The stock's uptrend continued to 112. I sold the call for $1,300 and was lucky to get rid of the put at $50: profit—$350 in one month!

"I would do OK if the stock fell to 88. Then, the call would be worth ½ but the put would bring at least $1,200, so I end up with about $250.

"The risk was that the stock's price would hold around 100. This would mean an almost total loss. But, from experience, I know that I'll lose on about 25% of my straddles so I have to shoot for a high return on the other deals."

Spread—a variation of a straddle in which the call will be at a price above the current market and the put at a price below the current market. Essentially, this is a cheaper form of straddle, carrying a lower premium because of the lower risk to the seller.

Strip—a triple option: two puts and one call on the same stock with a single option period and striking price. A strip writer expects the stock to fall in the short term and rise over the long term. He offers to sell 100 shares he owns above the market price or take 200 shares below the market. The premium is higher than for a straddle.

Strap—also a triple option: two calls and one put on the same stock. The writer gets top premium. He's bullish over the long term, but more negative than the strip seller on short-term prospects.

Insurance. To protect a profit, buy a put on stock you own. *Example:* Your stock has soared from 30 to 60, so you expect a setback. You buy a short-term put, at 60, for $400. If the stock dips to 50, the put will be worth 10 ($1,000) so you sell for a profit of $600 and still own the stock.

If the stock keeps moving up to 70, the put expires worthless. You lose $400 but you have a paper profit of $1,000 on the stock, so are $600 ahead.

Lock in capital gains. The same technique can be used to lock in a capital gain. By buying the put at 60 for $400, you reduce the stock value to 56. If it falls to 50, you sell the stock at the exercise price of 60 for $6,000. Deduct the $400 premium from the $3,000 profit (from cost of 30) and you still have $2,600. That's $600 more than if you had held the stock until its price fell to 50.

Option Funds

For those who want the profits of options but don't want to be bothered with management, there are mutual funds

---

SOME OPTIONS—INCOME FUNDS

NAME	ADDRESS	PHONE NO.
1st Investors Option	120 Wall Street New York, N.Y. 10005	800 223-6300
Gateway Option Income	1120 Carew Tower Cincinnati, Ohio 45202	513 621-7774
Kemper Option Income	120 S. LaSalle Chicago, Ill. 60603	800 621-1048
Oppenheimer Option	2 Broadway New York, N.Y. 10004	800 221-9839
Putnam Option Income	1 Post Office Sq. Boston, Mass. 02109	800 225-1581

whose managers seek extra income by writing calls. The costs are, relatively, high but you can count on complete records and can add or withdraw money easily.

In the early years, their projections were greater than their performance but in the recent surge, their yields have risen handsomely, some to over a 20% annual rate. Here are some of the leaders:

Wash Sale

With this, you take a loss on the stock and buy a call on the same stock. Or you can sell the shares and write a naked in-the-money put on the same stock. This is a wash sale when the time spread is less than 31 days.

Example: Silent Sam owns XYZ Oil at 67½ and sells at a loss. He buys a February 70 put for 3½. As long as the put is exercised at more than 31 days after the stock sale, the loss can be taken in that year. The adjusted cost is computing by subtracting the premium (3½) from the strike price (70) to get 66½ (plus commission).

If the shares are over 70 in 31 days after the stock loss sale, Sam can buy back the put and the stock to reestablish his position. But if the stock is sold at 71, that $1 per share profit is taxable.

Tax Treatment of Options

All profits and losses from all listed options are short term. That means the highest tax bite for gains and, for losses, deductions on a dollar-for-dollar basis up to $3,000 a year.

But when you write calls, there can be tax benefits in that when the option on owned stock is exercised, the tax holding period is determined by how long you have held the stock. The date of the purchase of the option is irrelevant except, of course, with naked options.

If the ownership of the stock, with or without the option, is less than 12 months, the gain/loss will be short-term. But if the total time span of ownership is more than 12 months, the sale proceeds of the stock are long term so only 40% of the profits are taxed and any loss is deductible. The premium becomes part of the purchase or sales price of the stock so, in effect, reduces the tax base.

• *With calls,* the premium increases the amount realized by the writer on the sale of the stock: i.e., when a stock is bought in January at 30 and, in February, the investor writes a July 30 call at 35 at a premium of 3, the cost basis is 33. If the call is exercised in July, there's a 2-point short-term gain. But if the stock does not reach 35 and the call expires, the 3 premium is a short-term loss.

Now let's assume that the investor keeps the stock and, in August, writes a January 35 call at 2½. If the stock is called away in January, the tax base is 32½: 30 cost plus 2½ premium. The 2½-point profit is long term. (None of the examples include commissions.)

• *With puts,* when the option is exercised, the writer subtracts the premium from the price paid for the stock: i.e., when the stock is acquired at 30 and the put was sold at 3, the tax base is 27.

With both calls and puts, when sold at a price below cost, that difference is a short-term capital loss.

At year-end if the value of options has increased, you can set up a rollover by buying back the call or put, taking a loss on this year's tax return and selling a similar option with an exercise date in the next year. This profit, if any, will be taxable on that year's return.

If you wrote a naked call, you can extend the holding period by buying the underlying stock before the expiration date. If the price of the stock moves up and you face the possibility that the option will be exercised and you will have to sell the stock before holding it 12 months, consider buying another 100 shares and deliver the "new" stock for a short-term loss and hold the "old" stock for a long-term capital gain.

If you deal in puts, there's an exception: when you buy a put on the same day that you buy the stock and notify your broker that you intend to use the stock to satisfy an exercise of the put, you are then said to have "married" the stock to the put.

Now, the holding period of the stock starts on the day you acquired it. If the price of the stock declines and you sell the put but keep the stock, the holding period, for the stock, starts on the day that you sold the put, not when you originally bought the stock. If the price of the stock goes up, you add the cost of the put to the tax basis of the stock.

For tax planning, read the American Stock Exchange booklet "Tax Planning for Listed Options." A typical example:

In September, you buy 100 shares of XYZ at 97¾ and write a January 90 call for 13¾. In mid-January, the stock is at 94¼ and the call at 4¾. You must decide whether to close out the call or wait for exercise.

If the stock went below 90, the call would expire and you would have a short-term gain of $1,375 plus an unrealized loss in the stock.

Closing Purchase	
Premium income	$1,375.00
Cost of buy-back	−475.00
Short-term gain	$900.00
Unrealized loss on stock	($287.50)
Exercise	
Exercise price	$ 9,000.00
Premium received	1,375.00
Total proceeds	$10,375.00
. . . or Gain	
Proceeds of exercise	$10,375.00
Tax basis of stock	−9,737.50
Short-term gain	$ 637.50
No commissions, cost included.	

Your decision should be made in consideration of your total tax picture, especially when you have short-term losses to offset.

A similar situation develops with profits from writing puts. If the price of the related stock rises, you have a short-term capital gain from the lapse of the put. If the trend is down, you have a short-term loss but may be able to acquire the stock at a more favorable price. Again, the tax decision should *never* be the key determinant.

Special combinations. To split tax liabilities or benefits, you can close out legs of a spread in different taxable years. And you can set up a spread that involves writing a call that is likely to be exercised on a long-term, profitable stock. With careful timing, you may be able to realize a long-term capital gain on one side and a short-term loss on the other.

But these trick deals can spark tax problems. If you purchase and sell options with identical maturity dates and striking prices, the IRS could consider these as a single transaction and thus eliminate the tax advantages.

With straddles, the taxes apply to the components. All premium income or loss to writers from a closing purchase or lapse of an option is considered a short-term capital gain or loss.

With all types of options, operate on the premise that profits or losses will be short-term. Once in a while, it may be possible to set up a capital gain, but in most cases, this will be due more to luck than to skill.

One final comment: Options are best for personal portfolios, but when you are experienced and have adequate assets in your pension fund, writing calls can add to your incomes . . . without tax consequences.

19

Tax Savings/Tax Shelters

With more people moving into higher tax brackets, there are greater benefits from tax savings and tax shelters. In most cases, the savings come from taking advantage of securities with tax breaks peculiar to that industry/company: the tax shelters come from special benefits legislated by Congress that, basically, mismatch income and deductions. In the early years, the deductions (to compensate for the presumed extra risks) predominate so the investor gets a tax loss or, at least, taxable income that is less than actual income. Eventually, however, these deductions are used up and taxable income predominates and, in many cases, the early deductions are fully or partially recaptured. With all types of tax shelters, there can be excellent tax benefits but, as the result of recent legislation, there's no free lunch. More and more, legitimate tax shelters are becoming investments more than speculations.

Saving taxes is intriguing but it's easy to go overboard and get into situations that sound better than they really are. Just because you move into a higher tax bracket is not an automatic signal that you should start looking for a tax shelter, as you will be urged by mail, phone and personal solicitations. Even in the highest federal tax bracket (currently 50%, but soon to drop to 49%), a tax shelter may not always be worthwhile and for those who pay at or below the 35% rate (33% in 1984), the tax benefits will seldom be meaningful but the investment itself may be worthwhile. Always DO YOUR HOMEWORK AND CONSULT YOUR TAX ADVISER, NOT YOUR BROKER.

Some people feel there's something shady about tax shelters: "They may be legal but not entirely ethical." *This is not true.* The benefits of tax shelters were legislated by Congress to encourage investment in areas that otherwise might not attract sufficient capital. With real estate, the deductions for interest and depreciation make it possible to build and own apartments and office buildings at a lower cost than would otherwise be possible. With oil and gas deals, the write-offs of intangible costs for exploration and drilling and the depletion allowance help to offset the high risks. Properly structured tax shelters are a vital force in our economy. They not only are legal but also can be rewarding for investors.

Unfortunately, tax shelters, by nature, are subject to exploitation and misrepresentation. It's amazing how stupid some people can be in their efforts to avoid or minimize taxes. How can any intelligent individual even consider putting his savings into a research project to develop fish fertilizer for catfish farming? And even honest deals can fail when circumstances change, i.e., those "can't miss" leases for railroad cars, computers and coal reserves were "ideal for the wealthy conservative" until the bottom fell out of the businesses. If the shelters don't generate income, all you buy is a tax loss and most folks can acquire those without the aid of a promoter.

Three of the most useful tax shelters—tax-exempt bonds, personal pension plans, and real estate—are discussed elsewhere. This chapter concentrates on tax-saving investments in securities, and tax shelters such as oil and gas deals, cattle and equipment leasing, and adds a few suggestions useful in estate planning.

The primary objective of investing is to make money, not to avoid taxes. Yet, tax savings are important in that they can provide good-to-excellent net returns. The profits do not always have to be shared with Uncle Sam as do cost savings and higher earnings. In the 50% tax bracket, each tax dollar saved is worth twice as much as an increase in taxable income of the same amount.

Tax Savings Through Investments

Tax savings are available through safe securities by: (*a*) holding for more than 12 months to benefit from the lower tax rate on capital gains: (*b*) investing for growth rather than for income: (*c*) buying shares of companies whose dividends are fully or partially tax-free.

Hold for over 12 months. The easiest, most logical and most effective way to reduce taxes is to choose long-term capital gains over dividends or interest. The federal income tax applies to only 40% of the profit on property held over one year: For most people, this means a tax rate below 20%—e.g., in the 40% tax bracket, the levy is 16% (40% × 40%).

The holding period is actually 12 months and one day; for securities, the starting date is the settlement day, and the eligibility date is the settlement day for gains, the trading day for losses. This information appears on your broker's confirmation slip.

If the purchase was made on the last day of any month, the long-term gain does not take effect until the last day of the twelfth following month regardless of the number of days in each month.

When you buy a stock that is moving up, check the calendar: (1) on the anniversary of the day you made the purchase; (2) for the date when the chart first showed a confirmed uptrend with rising volume. One year later, if there are gains, major investors will often start to take their profits, so the price may decline temporarily. By careful monitoring, you may be able to sell at or near this interim peak.

Profitable companies that pay no dividends. Their management believes in reinvesting all earnings. Such stocks can be excellent for those in high tax brackets.

Stingy dividend payers. Most true growth companies build their capital value (and, eventually, the market price of their stocks) by reinvesting a large percentage of their earnings rather than paying them out as dividends. As long as the corporation prospers, the investor wins. If a company earns 20% on shareholders' equity, pays out 5% in dividends and reinvests 15%, everything will double in about five years.

The growth can be even greater when the dividends are stingy—roughly, less than 25% of profits. *Example:* Masco Corporation earned an average of 20.9% on each invested dollar in the 1973–82 decade. On an adjusted basis, the dividends still rose from 6¢ to 42¢ per share; book value from $2.06 to $11.10 (beginning of 1983); and earnings increased from 45¢ to $1.78 with prospects of $2.00 in 1983. Over the years, MAS reinvested 81¢ of every earned dollar for growth. The price of its stock, despite some problems in 1981–82, rose from 9 to 34½. In 10 years, an original investment of $900 would have grown to $3,659: $2,550 appreciation plus $1,109 in dividends which, after a 50% tax, would be worth $3,155. And a smart trader who moved in and out with market swings would have done far better.

Aggressive corporations that continue to reinvest a large

SOME MAJOR CORPORATIONS THAT PAY NO CASH DIVIDENDS

COMPANY	S&P RATING
Advanced Micro	B
Aydin Corp.	B
Caesar's World	B
CCI Corp	B
Computervision	B
Crown Cork & Seal	B+
Data General	B+
Datapoint Corp.	NR
Digital Equipment	A—
Dome Petroleum	NR
Electronic Mem	C
Federal Express	B
Floating Point System	NR
Flow General	B
General Data Comm.	B—
ICN Pharmaceuticals	C
Jewelcor	B—
MCI Communications	NR
Modular Computer	B—
National Semiconductor	B
Prime Computer	B
Rollins Environ.	NR
Spectra-Physics	B
Tacoma Boat	NR
Teradyne, Inc.	B
Thermo Electron	B
Tymshare, Inc.	B+
U.S. Surgical	B+
Whitehall Corp.	B+
World Airways	C

SOURCE: Standard & Poor's

share of profits in research, development, new plants, new facilities and new markets; Automatic Data Processing, Digital Equipment, Hewlett-Packard and Schlumberger, for example.

As long as the growth is real (based on substantial gains in stockholders' equity) and consistent (lasting for at least five years), the company will prove to be a profitable investment. Sometimes that superior performance will not be immediately recognized in the market price of the stock, but eventually quality and value will pay off.

The careless stockholder who fails to do his homework will take a beating when the company promises more than it can produce. Litton Industries, Boise Cascade, L.T.V., Whittaker and other one-time wonder stocks soared but failed to stand the test of consistent performance. Eventually, some of these come back and become worthwhile investments but it usually takes many years.

New, small companies that need every nickel to hold and improve their competitive position. Some of these are marginal investments but good speculations. There is almost no way to be sure that any new company, no matter how exciting its prospects or how glowing its promise, will become successful.

The odds are 10–1 against skipped dividends ever coming back but the gamble lessens with time. After five years, the odds may be down to 5–1, so your risks are still high. But if the company does make it, the rewards can be substantial. You must decide how long you are willing to wait.

Check historical stock dividend pattern. Buy stocks of companies that have a history of declaring stock dividends. Such a policy keeps increasing the number of shares and, until you sell, there's no tax to pay. When you do take a profit, you will have a lower tax base because the cost declines each time there's a bonus.

To find the tax base, divide the original cash investment by the total number of shares sold. With Archer-Daniels-Midland, which, since 1971, has paid one 10% stock dividend and six 5% ones plus two 2–1 splits and two 3–2 splits, the original 100 shares have grown to 1,326 and the value from $900 to $34,476. The cost basis is 68¢ per share. If sold at the recent price of 34½, the maximum tax would be $6,715.20 . . . plus annual taxes on the small cash payouts.

Children on Payroll

If you own a business, consider putting your youngster on your payroll for work after school and during vacations. Be sure he/she has specific assignments, reports to work and that full records are maintained.

Anyone qualified to work can earn $5,300 a year without paying federal income taxes: $1,000 personal exemption; $2,300 zero bracket (standard deduction); $2,000 (fully deductible) investments in IRA. With a corporation, however, there will be taxes for Social Security, unemployment, etc. Still, this tactic can be a big tax saver and you might get some excellent service!

Utilities with Tax Advantages

The specific tax benefits of reinvestment of dividends of qualified utilities is discussed in Chapter 25, but, if you are willing to settle for less-than-top quality, buy shares of utilities that pay dividends that are partially or fully tax-free. Because of the intricacies of utility accounting and the huge structure of depreciation, many utilities (usually lower rated ones) pay a dividend bigger than either current or

SOME UTILITITES WITH TAX ADVANTAGES

COMPANY	% DIVIDENDS RETURN CAPITAL	DIVIDEND
Boston Edison	0-10	$2.80
Consumers Power	50-60	2.44
Dayton P&L	0-30	1.90
Detroit Edison	25-50	1.68
Eastern Utilities	0-10	1.70
Kansas G&E	80-90	2.12
Niagara Mohawk	30	1.80
Ohio Edison	75-100	1.76
Pub. Service N.H.	100	2.12
Puget Sound P&L	50	1.76
Toledo Edison	40	2.36
Union Electric	50	1.52

N.B. These figures refer to 1982 and may not be available in later years. The tax-free portion of the dividends reflects accounting methods that provide different reports for IRS and shareholders. By and large, these benefits are the results of losses, not profits.

SOURCE: Standard & Poor's OUTLOOK

retained earnings would appear to warrant. The dividend—or part of it—is financed out of depreciation cash flow.

But any portion not justified by current or retained earnings is considered, by tax authorities, as a return of capital to shareholders and thus not taxable on a current basis.

BUT the tax-free portion: (1) reduces the cost basis of the shares so more tax has to be paid when the shareholder sells his stock; (2) does not qualify for dividend reinvestment exclusion since it is already tax deferred.

Tax Shelters

Tax shelters usually sound better than they really are (especially when described by an eager, not-so-knowledgeable broker). They do make it possible for the investor to retain more of his earnings as he moves into a higher tax bracket but with the maximum 49% tax rate, this advantage may not always be as rewarding as projected. Before you shell out your savings for any type of tax shelter, make sure that it is a sound investment. Tax benefits should always be secondary.

With tighter restrictions, due to TEFRA, and more involvement by major brokerage firms, tax shelters are shifting more to income plus tax benefits rather than tax savings alone. But the basic problem continues: too many people are so intent on avoiding taxes that they fail to check the assumptions, let alone the facts. An accountant can verify the figures, but he seldom looks behind them. And the optimistic salesman is reluctant to explain what could happen if the projections fail or if the deal is so successful that, after the write-offs have been used up, the entity is still producing taxable income. With all types of all tax shelters, it's easy to get in but hard to get out!

Almost all tax shelter deals are complex and require substantial commitments for a fairly long period of time. Until you become experienced or work with partners whom you *really* trust, use only money that you can afford to lose; be willing to come up with more if necessary and be patient . . . usually for at least three years.

The term *tax shelter* refers to an "expense"—a payout of cash or a charge representing the using up of capital that can be deducted from gross income in arriving at the amount of an investor's income subject to tax.

Among typical tax deductible expenses are: depreciation, interest, the cost of feed in fattening livestock, the intangible drilling costs connected with oil and gas exploration, etc.

Most of the "expense" items are noncash charges. You subtract depletion and depreciation from taxable income, but you do not actually pay the cash to anyone. Thus, it is possible to have *losses* for tax purposes while having *income* in a cash sense.

Example: You are in the 50% tax bracket and make a $10,000 investment in a tax shelter that will, you hope, generate $10,000 in deductions. As income, that $10,000 would be cut to $5,000 after taxes. If the investment can generate a $10,000 deduction, you have "saved" $5,000 in taxes.

The most common tax shelter is built around a limited partnership. This involves a *general partner* who has expertise in the operations of oil, cattle, crops, etc., and *limited partners* who are the investors seeking specific profit opportunities and tax benefits.

The general partner assumes management responsibilities and makes all decisions. Under recent IRS rules he must have a minimum 1% interest in partnership losses as well as gains. Generally, he is a knowledgeable individual who puts up a little money, receives a sizable share of the profits, is assured of income while the project operates and accepts liabilities for losses in excess of partnership capital.

Private offerings, involving about 35 partners, start with an investment of $25,000. Public offerings, with more than 100 participants, must file a prospectus with the SEC and meet certain financial standards. In an oil-gas deal, the manager must have substantial net worth, not less than 15% of the money raised or $250,000.

Several states set minimal requirements for investors: in California, you must be in the 50% tax bracket and have $200,000 in assets; in Illinois and Texas, the minimums are $5,000 for investments and $200,000 for net worth.

Increasingly, investors are getting greater protection. Members of the NASD must exercise "due diligence": discovering whether the general partner is competent and honest; comparing the proposal with similar deals; evaluating the likelihood of the proposed tax benefits; and determining the fairness of the proposed method of sharing profits and expenses.

In all tax shelters, be wary and use common sense. Many are wasting assets: you get tax benefits and/or excellent income for a limited time but, at the end, there's nothing left: with a lease, a completed contract; with an oil well, the equivalent of a dry hole; with R&D packages and movies, cans of film or foreign rights that involve higher expenditures than income.

Most troubles result from slick salesmen who quote tax opinions prepared by "captive" lawyers as part of the offering proposal. The SEC requires only full disclosure. There can be no legal action unless there is proof of violation involving "misstatements or omission of material facts that may be considered fraudulent even if not made for the specific purpose of cheating."

As the head of a major syndicating firm put it: "Tax shelters are like fire. They can be valuable tools if intelligently selected and managed. But they can be dangerous unless you are in a high tax bracket, deal with reputable sponsors and realize that, in most cases, if they won't work as investments, they won't work at all. They are seldom worthwhile for investors who need ordinary income and cannot fully benefit from tax deductions."

N.B. The negatives have been stressed so frequently that it's time to be positive and see how oil and gas tax shelters can be rewarding speculations and, sometimes, investments.

Oil/Gas Partnerships

To give you an idea of how tax shelters work, here are excerpts from an article in *Physician's Management*. The description covers a public fund where units are available at $5,000 each. Private funds operate the same but involve a relatively small group of individuals who are able to put up at least $150,000 each.

The interview was with Robert J. Bernstein, president of RBA Group NA, an Atlanta-based, international firm that acts as consultant, adviser and manager for oil/gas limited partnerships and joint ventures. It took place in June 1983.

Q. Can you describe the current situation with oil/gas deals and explain how they can be wisely and profitably used?

A. In the U.S.A., most oil is discovered and produced by independent operators. With minimal capital, they rely on financial help from outsiders, usually through limited partnerships (LPs) where shares are sold to individuals and groups.

The general partner (GP) does all the work; *in a drilling deal,* he finds and leases acreage, drills the wells and, if successful, produces the oil or gas and sells it to refiners or pipeline companies; *in an income partnership,* the GP locates and screens producing properties, purchases the future cash stream at a discount and sells the output. In both cases, the revenues, after expenses, are shared between the GP and LPs on a predetermined basis.

To encourage exploration and production, Congress provides tax incentives through write-offs against ordinary income: (1) intangible costs for fuel, labor, supplies, rig rental; (2) depreciation and investment tax credits on tangible costs; (3) depletion allowance for the wasting assets.

There were some revisions under TEFRA but, for most folks, oil and gas partnerships can create substantial first-year write-offs, reduce their effective tax rate by one-third and, if the investment works out, provide annual income of 15% to 18% for 10 or more years.

Q. How does this work?

A. Table A details a drilling/exploratory deal. The original investment, for easy illustration, is $20,000. Of this, 90% ($18,000) is deductible in Year I for intangible drilling costs. For the investor in the 50% tax bracket, this means tax savings of $9,000 on other income, so the net, after-tax investment, for accounting purposes, is $11,000.

With a moderately successful venture, the gross revenues, over the life of the well, can be expected to be $50,000, operating expenses of $10,000 so the net income is $40,000 before depletion allowance.

This depletion allowance is 15% of the $50,000 gross so

How to Read a Prospectus Fast

By law, every major tax shelter/limited partnership must submit a prospectus to shareholders. These may appear to be formidable and dull but it will pay you to spend a few minutes in reviewing the facts, figures and statements. For those who are in a hurry:

• Read the summary at the opening word by word.
• Check the accounting projections and footnotes.
• Find out the use of proceeds: how much will go for fees; how much will go to work for your interests?
• What is the compensation to the General Partner?
• Review, line by line, the track record of the sponsors/participants/employees.
• Read, with help from your tax adviser, the discussion of tax consequences. This can be tough going but never invest in anything that you do not understand.

totals $7,500. But it is deducted from the net of $40,000 so the taxable income is $32,500. At the 50% tax rate, half ($16,250) goes to the investor and half to Uncle Sam.

TABLE A

AFTER-TAX CASH RETURN ON OIL/GAS DRILLING INVESTMENT

Assumptions: investor in 50% tax bracket; recovers $40,000 over life of investment (2:1 return); expenses are 20% of revenues; depletion is 15% of gross revenues; both investor and property qualify for percentage depletion. Sale price of oil/gas: $30 per barrel.

Investment	$20,000
90% deduction for intangibles: $18,000	
Tax savings @ 50%	9,000
After-tax net investment	11,000
(net for accounting purposes)	
Gross revenue from wells	50,000
Expenses from operating	(10,000)
Net income before depletion	40,000
Assumed allowable depletion: 15% X gross revenue	(7,500)
Taxable net income after depletion	32,500
Tax @ 50%	(16,250)
Net after-tax income	16,250
Add back depletion	7,500
Total after-tax cash flow	23,750
After-tax return on net investment	
(23,750 minus 11,000)	12,750
Return on investment ratio	216%

SOURCE: RBA Group, NA, Atlanta, Ga.

TABLE B

OIL/GAS INCOME DEAL

Assumptions: investor in 50% tax bracket; price of oil remains constant at $30 per barrel (no adjustment for inflation); expenses of 20% of revenues; depletion and depreciation equal to cost of investment.

Investment	$10,000
15% front-end expenses: commissions, fees	(1,500)
Available for purchasing properties	8,500
% $8.50 per barrel purchase 1,000 BBLs	
10 year gross revenus @ average wellhead price of $30 per BBL	30,000
Expenses from operating @ 20%	(6,000)
Net income before depreciation/depletion	24,000
Depreciation/depletion	(10,000)
Taxable income	14,000
Tax @ 50%	(7,000)
Net after-tax incdme	7,000
Add back depletion	10,000
Total after-tax cash flow	17,000
After-tax return on net investment	
17,000 minue 10,000	7,000
Return on investment ratio	170%

SOURCE: RBA Group NA, Atlanta, Ga.

Now comes the big benefit: The $7,500 depletion is added back to the net after-tax income to set up a cash flow of $23,750. Since the original, net investment was $11,000, this means an after-tax return on investment of $12,750, a 216% ratio of return.

As a rule of thumb, it will take 10 to 15 years for this income stream to flow to the investor. At the end, the wells will be economically dry so the partnership will be terminated and, assuming there's no salvage value for the equipment, the shares will be worthless.

Even if prices never increase, this type of deal should provide an after-tax, annual rate of return of approximately 15%.

With drilling deals, there are extra risks such as dry holes, but, with the maximum deductions, the most you can lose is half your money. That's why they are best for those in high tax brackets with enough personal savings to withstand real losses if the venture fails.

Q. What about income deals?

A. Here, the investments are made in proven, producing wells. The risks are less and the deductions smaller but the income is relatively secure, with average annual returns of 12% to 15%. These are excellent for pension fund holdings.

As shown in Table B, the original per share investment is $10,000. From this, deduct 15% ($1,500) for commissions and fees, so there's $8,500 to invest in oil in the

ground. This should sell for about $8.50 per barrel so the investor acquires 1,000 barrels. At a well-head price of $30, this means gross revenues of $30,000 over about 10 years.

Operating expenses will run some 20% ($6,000), so the net income is $24,000. From this, deduct depletion/depreciation of $10,000 (equaling the original investment) to get taxable income of $14,000. In the 50% tax bracket, this leaves $7,000.

Again, add *back* the depletion of $10,000 to reach a total, after-tax cash flow of $17,000. Finally, deduct the original $10,000 investment to get a $7,000 after-tax return: 70% on your money.

Q. What are the different types of partnerships?

A. The general structures are similar but the details vary:

• **Functional allocation:** where the costs are shares on the basis of their classification for tax purposes. The investors assume the deductible costs—typically 75% to 85% of the total project costs while the sponsor bears the tangible costs that are capitalized for the tax benefits: pumps, pipes, storage tanks, etc. The ultimate revenue split runs from 40% to 50% for the GP with the balance for the LPs. This is the riskiest type because the LPs put up all the risk capital before the GP is obligated to spend any money: i.e., there's no reason to buy pumps and pipes if they're all dry holes!

• **Reversionary interest:** where the investor bears all, or most, of the costs but the GP does not get any money until after the LPs have received a "paycheck." This sounds attractive but the GP tends to charge higher, front-end costs to make up for the delay in receipt of his profit.

• **Carried interest:** where the LPs pay all, or most, of the costs and receive a diluted percentage of the ultimate revenues: i.e., the LPs pay 99% of the costs for 80% of revenues. The GP gets his share after the first barrel produced.

With such deals, the investors assume all the risks and GP has "no real skin in the game" in the event of a bust. This is the type promoted by GPs with minimal capital.

• **Promoted interest:** where the sponsor bears a portion of costs in return for a larger share of the revenues: say, when the GP puts up 10%, he gets 25% of the revenues. This is the best deal because the GP has a commonality of interest with the LPs.

Q. What happens when you want to get out of the partnership?

A. This should always be considered *before* any commitment. The choices are:

1. To sell the shares, hopefully for a capital gain. The amount subject to tax will be the proceeds minus the tax base so will probably be a combination of capital gains and ordinary income representing the recapture of intangible drilling costs and depletion.

2. To make a gift: (*a*) To a relative in a lower tax bracket. If the total value is under $20,000 for a couple filing jointly, there will be no gift tax. IRS sets formulas but, usually, the transfer value will be less than 30 cents on the real dollar value.

But these discounts can be used by holding the shares for two years to take advantage of the write-offs and then transferring the shares to children, via a Clifford Trust, for their college education. (*b*) To a charity IF the recipient is willing to accept. Most institutions are leery because they may have to pay taxes on future income and profits from a sale.

3. To make an exchange by incorporating and transferring the units of the partnership to the corporation. Be cautious because there may be taxes if the shelter interest is subject to liabilities greater than the tax base.

Q. What's the bottom line with oil/gas deals now?

A. As the result of lower prices, drilling for oil and gas is down 60% from 1981. The cost of acquiring reserves, either by drilling or buying production, has dropped almost 40% compared to a price decline of about 20%. At this time, oil/gas deals are bargains that can produce tax benefits plus income and/or appreciation. What matters is what the price of oil/gas will be three to 10 years from now. Whether you drill for, or buy, reserves, you're investing in assets that are bound to be worth more over the years.

Checkpoints for Oil/Gas Deals

1. Do business only with reputable, established firms that perform "due diligence" or hire qualified consultants to do so, on the GP's financial statement, track record, experience and technical expertise.

2. Determine the value of what you're buying. Every tax shelter should be an investment first and a tax-saver second. If the enterprise cannot be expected to be profitable, the tax breaks can be meaningless.

3. Doublecheck the fairness of the deal itself with information from such services as:

Limited Partners Letter, P.O. Box 1146, Menlo Park, CA 94025

Investment Search, Annapolis, MD 21404

The Stanger Report, 623 River Road, Fair Haven, NJ 07701

Brennan Reports, P.O. Box 882, Valley Forge, PA 19482

4. Watch out for conflicts of interest: whether the partnership is "self-dealing": buying properties adjacent to those of the GP or in which he has an interest or contracting with drilling companies and suppliers that are affiliates.

5. At least 85% of the investment should be devoted to the objective of the partnership: drilling or acquiring wells. Guideline: 5% to 7% for the sponsoring management organization; 8% to 10% for commissions to brokers.

6. Assessments should be spelled out in detail. Preferably, the amount of these extra funds should be limited but if the well is successful, few people will object to adding money.

7. Review all revenue assumptions to learn whether they are exaggerated by future appreciation or escalation of production.

8. Check the exit ability. Terms should be spelled out in the prospectus.

9. For drilling funds, invest early in the year so you can take full advantage of the write-off. If you get in after July, the benefits will be spread over two years and you'll have two small deductions rather than one big one.

10. Beware of high-multiple, first-year write-offs. These will involve loans through the partnership. It's always risky to use borrowed funds because if there are losses, the debts must be paid. In some cases, you could incur "phantom" income where all the cash flow is being used to repay the bank but your share of this profit creates a significant tax liability.

11. Tailor your investment to your funds. With drilling deals, use only personal money, part of which you can afford to lose; with income deals, use either personal savings or a portion of pension fund assets.

12. Review every deal every three months and compare the results with the projections.

13. Make certain that all commitments are fulfilled promptly: accounting and tax returns; promised cash distributions, etc.

14. Watch the financial press for news of financial problems, governmental intervention/investigation, etc. Ask the GP to inform you of any legal action against the partnership.

Cattle Breeding/Feeding Shelters

These programs are best for the wealthy and patient but can be worthwhile for those who have special knowledge or enjoy special situations. They require expertise and capital.

As outlined by Garrett P. Cole, vice president of Oppenheimer Industries, Kansas City, Mo., an experienced, professional management firm, there are two major types of cattle investment partnerships: breeding and feeding. With both, there are special tax benefits: cash basis accounting, rapid depreciation, investment tax credits, etc. The provisions are complex so make no commitment without careful review with a tax adviser experienced in this area. Basically, the taxes can be deferred and profits can be paid at the low capital gains rate. Here are summaries of what you can expect:

Breeding cattle: herds of cows, calves and bulls retained for breeding purposes. Markets exist in thousands of rural centers; prices are quoted in the daily press; and cattle ranchers are experienced businessmen. If you live in or near a farm/ranch area, you can set up your own herd or work with neighbors. Otherwise, hire a professional manager. The minimum investment should be about $25,000 plus about half that amount each year thereafter if you wish to build the herd with tax-deductible dollars.

Table A shows a typical situation. You buy 100 cows at $550 each: $55,000, 10% cash and the balance by a promissory note. You prepay some interest and advance money for breeding fees and a portion of the herd maintenance expense. The total cash outlay comes to $23,000: $5,500 down; $2,500 for prepaid interest; $1,800 for breeding; and $13,200 for feed and management. Since these are *business* expenses, most of the investment can be deducted in the year of payment.

TABLE A
CATTLE BREEDING TAX SHELTER

Current year

Buy 100 cows @ $550 each		$55,000
90% loan @ 12%	$49,500	
10% cash down payment		5,500
Expenses paid to 12/31		17,500
Total cash outlay		23,000
Depreciation/net expenses/year		25,750
Percentage deductible from income		112%
Investment tax credit		5,500

Five years later

Proceeds from sale of herd	$108,000	
Ordinary and capital gains tax	(26,000)	
Investment tax credit recapture	–0–	
Net sales proceeds		82,000
Total cash investment	103,000	
Tax savings: 50% tax bracket	59,000	
After-tax cost		44,000
After-tax profit		$38,000

SOURCE: Oppenheimer Industries, Kansas City, Mo.

There are three tax advantages. (1) Depreciation on an accelerated basis over five years, with 15% of the purchase price of the cattle deductible in the year of acquisition regardless of the purchase date. (2) Investment tax credit: calculated at 10% of the purchase price, for cattle already "in service," the maximum base of $12,500. (3) Capital gain tax rate when "qualified" animals are sold at a profit.

Since cattle breeding is a continuing tax shelter, there will be new outlays to maintain the expanding herd: from $10,000 to $20,000 annually and fully tax deductible... great for those in high tax brackets.

There will be a death loss but many ranchers provide indemnity when this is above 3% annually. There's periodic income from the sale of steer calves and unfit animals and, of course, the herd keeps increasing as the retained heifer calves become cows.

With cash-basis accounting, all cattle born to the herd have a zero cost basis. When sold after the 24-month holding period, the proceeds are long-term capital gains with a

maximum tax of 20%. In about five years, a sale of the herd should net about $108,000, depending on the market at the time.

This is the point at which you need that savvy tax adviser. Assuming you're in the 50% tax bracket, the taxes will be $26,000. This drops the $108,000 sale proceeds to $82,000. Thus, in five years, the total cash investment of $103,000 has created $59,000 in tax savings, so the after-tax cost is $44,000 and the net profit is $38,000... on a basic *cash* outlay of $23,000 with its tax benefits.

Feeding Cattle: where the partnership buys steers, feeds them until they are sold and rolls the proceeds over into a new deal, so deferring taxes as long as desired.

This involves *greater*: (*a*) leverage (through borrowing more); (*b*) risks (because of the fluctuations of market prices); (*c*) investment ($100,000 or more). In many cases, there are more advantages for individuals than partnerships. Again, check the expert FIRST (Table B).

Bill Bush buys 500 steers at $450 each: $220,000 with $11,250 down and a hefty 95% loan of $213,750 at 12% interest.

Bill must also advance $140,000 for the purchase of feed and the payment of fees and operating expenses. This can be deducted immediately so, in the 50% tax bracket, he saves $70,000.

Bill makes his money by selling the cattle at the end of the feeding period, hopefully when prices are high. Usually, he rolls over his profits into a new deal and so defers taxes until he is in a lower tax bracket.

TABLE B
CATTLE FEEDING TAX SHELTER

First year

Buy 500 steers @ $450 each		$225,000
95% loan @ 12%	$213,750	
5% down payment		11,250
Purchase feed, fees, etc.		140,000
Total cash outlay		151,250
Deductions for operating costs		140,000
Percentage deductible from income		93%
Tax savings in 50% tax bracket		70,000

Second year

Cash flow		
Gross proceeds from sale of steers		375,000
Less repayment of loan		213,750
Cash received		161,250
Taxable income		
Sale price cattle	$375,000	
Cost basis cattle	225,000	
Ordinary gain		150,000
Tax due in 50% bracket		75,000

SOURCE: Oppenheimer Industries, Kansas City, Mo.

Under IRS rules, feeder cattle are business inventory so do not qualify for capital gains tax treatment. The profit is always fully taxable income. But there are ample tax benefits.

In Year I, Bill gets a tax write-off of $140,000: 93% of his cash input of $151,250; $11,250 cash down plus $140,000 for purchase of feed, fees, etc. If he sells the cattle in Year II for $375,000, he must repay the $213,750 loan so nets $161,250 in cash: a $10,000 cash-on-cash profit on his short-term investment. From the $375,000 gross receipts, he deducts the $225,000 cost basis to get a profit of $150,000, which, when taxed as ordinary income, leaves $75,000. But he can defer taxes by rolling over his money into a new deal.

Other Popular Tax Shelters

In an effort to spur investments, Congress has expanded or accelerated tax benefits so that almost every type of major financial commitment can be structured to avoid, defer or minimize taxes. Basically, they involve financing equipment/projects so that the investor gets early-in-the-game deductions for investment tax credit, prepaid interest and fast depreciation and, from lease/rental, gets a tax sheltered cash flow which, hopefully, can be turned into a profit when the property is sold or a new contract negotiated.

On paper, these tax shelters can look mighty attractive . . . for the well-to-do . . . but there are risks and costs that are usually mentioned only in the small print and that seldom take into account changes in legislation. A couple of years ago, the "hot" deal was leasing railroad cars. For $30,000, largely borrowed, the "shrewd investor" could own a hopper car that would provide annual tax benefits of up to $5,000 and, in five years or so, would reap a $10,000 per car profit because of higher replacement value. But, with the depressed economy, most cars were idle and worth less and less so that when renewal time came, many of these deals ended in losses in real dollars far greater than tax deductions.

There are some "good" deals because some airlines, computer manufacturers, etc., lack capital and are willing to pay well for the use of expensive equipment but most of these are for wealthy specialists who can afford to tie up their money.

Movies. One of the most aggressively promoted (so far, only on the West Coast but going national soon) new types of tax shelter involves movies for TV. The promotion is all Hollywood: glittering sales meetings complete with video sales presentation, glossy prospectus and alluring "stars of the future." All you have to have is $5,000.

The pitch: opening the golden world of show biz to the little guy . . . full or partial guarantee of your money back and prospects/hopes of huge profits when the show becomes a worldwide hit . . . like *Tootsie*. (But what they don't tell you is that, with Delphi I, a loss of 70% seemed almost certain until the sudden success of *Tootsie*.)

These movie deals are limited partnerships (similar to those of oil/gas deals). What the promoters have done is to develop a quick, cheap way to raise millions of dollars. You put up the dough and become partner in the production, distribution and promotion of films for TV. You get no interest/income until everything (and I mean, *everything*) is paid for and the film becomes profitable: as only 1 in 6 do.

DELPHI II offers tax benefits because the partnership gives investors only a partial guarantee of return of their money. The first-year deduction is about 70% of the origi-

nal investment; thereafter, the cash flow is sheltered, but, warns the prospectus, IRS may audit and, in varying degrees, some of the benefits will be subject to recapture.

SILVER SCREEN PARTNERS does not reduce taxes because the sponsors guarantee investors a return of 100% of their money (on a present-value basis) five or six years hence even if one or more of the films is a flop. With the $100 million from the public, SSP will produce 10 to 12 films which are already the exclusive property of Home Box Office TV for English language pay cable and syndication, domestic and foreign.

With both "opportunities," if any of the productions is a hit, the income flow will start in about 18 months with quarterly cash distributions. The LPs get 99% of the proceeds of each film until they get back their investment plus 10% return, on a film-by-film basis. After that, the LPs get 85% of the revenues and the GPs, 15%. Sounds great? Well, get out your calculator and do some projecting: no income for at least a year and a half, continuing off-the-top expenses, only a 16% chance of a real success, no compounding, etc.

The prospect is a gem of skillful presentation that makes it appear that you're bound to be a millionaire. The hard facts are not so optimistic. You're shooting craps in one of the most unpredictable, speculative businesses in the world. The producers get cheap money and the partners buy glamour, tax benefits and dreams of jackpots. But for the same money, most folks could probably win more at Atlantic City and enjoy the entertainment!

Research and development shelters. These are the latest "surefire path to financial success." They are limited partnerships that receive special tax benefits under recent congressional action aimed to encourage American ingenuity. But, so far, most of the deals have involved minimum investments of $150,000.

Most of the shelters involve companies doing research in computer technology or genetic engineering. The general terms are similar to those outlined earlier: risks limited to the amount of investment (including bank loans); off-the-top loads of about 15%; and a predetermined split of receipts between the LPs and GP (the syndicator). The profits come from a successful product/technique that can be licensed, manufactured or used by others.

Theoretically, the partnership will receive about 10% of royalties on sales and, in a relatively short time, get back two to six times the investment. The key words are *partnership profits and losses*. The contracts spell out allocation of costs but these expenses are very difficult for the amateur to judge: What is a fair fee for the actual R&D? Is there a built-in profit for the company doing the research? What provisions are made for prompt marketing/production of the discovery/development?

Example: Storage Technology raised $50 million in an R&D partnership. Projection: on each $150,000 unit, a net cash return of $589,921, *possible only if ST sells $6.6 billion* worth of mainframe computers by 1991 as well as raising working capital to finance production and sales. As Edward J. Gaudino, writing in *Barron's* on the broad subject, commented: "The only way to invest in any R&D program and still sleep at night is to assume you will lose every penny you put in. You must have steady nerves and money to burn."

Royalty trusts. These are shares in the income from oil/gas wells. The trust controls oil rights for large areas. If oil or gas is discovered, the drillers (usually major oil firms) pay a percentage of the revenue to the trust. These royalties are "off the top"; i.e. if the oil company drills a dry hole, there will be no royalties but neither will there be any costs to the trust.

All earnings are paid out, so the trust pays no taxes and the shareholder gets the full revenue from the royalty. The IRS recognizes that shareholders have a personal stake in the assets that provide income to the trust, so part of the cash payout is regarded as a return of capital and not taxable. For example, you buy a trust share at $40. Its assets are depleted at 8% in Year 1, so $3.20 of the total yield is tax sheltered. If the payout is less, there's no tax. If it's more, the tax applies to the excess: at $4.00 per share, 80¢ is income. You must pay a capital gains tax on this money. Each year, your cost figure is reduced, for tax purposes, by the amount of the depletion. When you sell for more than the adjusted cost, you pay a capital gains tax on the excess.

Units in some trusts, similar to shares of corporations, are traded on the NYSE. The yields, representing earnings based on royalty payments, have been small lately. Since they are before-tax benefits, you can guesstimate the equivalent return of a taxable investment by multiplying the royalty rate of return by 1.5: thus, when Blowout Royalty yield is 8%, this is equal to a taxable 12%.

Deferred Annuities

Under TEFRA, some of the short-term benefits of tax-deferred annuities were eliminated but most of the long-term advantages are still available. You can count on relatively high rates of return, no taxes on investment income until withdrawal, and, at death, the assets will go directly to your beneficiaries without the bother and expense of probate.

Deferred annuities can be an alternative to tax-exempt bonds. They are contracts that can be bought from most insurance companies by almost any adult. Usually, the payment is a lump sum, but it can be made in installments. At age 65—or later, if so desired—the purchaser is assured income as long as he, and when he so designates, his spouse, lives.

The tax break comes because all income—from dividends, interest or realized capital short-term gains—accumulates tax-free until withdrawn. At that time, part of the monthly income is tax-free as a return of capital. The rate of accumulation depends on the return from investments made with the money. Currently, some companies offer yields of over 10% but these are guaranteed only for a limited time. The terms of the contracts vary by states due to insurance regulations. If the investments return more than projected, the investor wins; if the returns are less, he is still sure of the predetermined amount.

There are also special single premium life policies that combine tax benefits, death protection, low-interest loans and, eventually, lifetime guaranteed income. Keystone Provident Life, for example, offers a single premium policy that works like this:

Dr. Louis, age 40, invests $100,000 which immediately provides $151,600 worth of whole life insurance under Keystone's three-year guaranteed plan. In the first year, the cash value totals some $9,000. Dr. L. can then borrow this at 8% and does not have to report it as taxable income.

The next year, Keystone applies an offsetting credit so there's an actual out-of-pocket payment for the interest on the loan. This credit comes in the form of an increase in the policy's cash value. If the insured should die, the borrowed amount will be deducted from the payment to the beneficiary.

Keystone builds in a "floor" rate: currently, if the yield drops below 8% in the first nine years, the policy can be cashed in for an increased surrender value. And, because this is a life insurance policy, the income is tax-deferred

TAX SHELTERS

TYPE	TAX BRACKET	MINIMUM INVESTMENT	SHELTERED INCOME	CASH FLOW	LIQUIDITY	APPRECIATION POTENTIAL	1st YEAR DEDUCTIONS	RISKS
REAL ESTATE								
Residential	35%	$2,500	Yes	Fair	Low	Fair/Good	Limited	Moderate
Commercial	35	2,500	Partial	Fair/Good	Low	Fair/Good	Limited	Low
New Bldg.	49	10,000	Yes	Low/Good	Low	Fair/Good	Limited	Fair/High
OIL/GAS								
Drilling	49	5,000	Partial	Low/Fair	Low	Low/Fair	Yes	Fair/High
Producing	35	5,000	Partial	Low/Fair	Fair	Low/Fair	Low	Low
CATTLE								
Feeding	49	100,000	No	0	Good	Uncertain	Yes	High
Breeding	49	25,000	Yes	Low	Low	Uncertain	Yes	High
Farming	49	10,000	Varies	Fair	Low	Fair/Low	Fair	High
Movies	49	10,000	Yes*	?	Low	Uncertain	Fair	High
Equipment Leasing	49	5,000	Yes*	?	Low	Limited	Varies	Varies
R & D	49	5,000	Capital Gains	?	Low	Good	High	High

* Yes, until crossover

SOURCE: Physician's Management

until withdrawn and there will be no federal income tax on the death benefit. The insured or beneficiary may utilize a number of alternative payout options.

Checkpoints for Deferred Annuities

How long is the interest rate guaranteed? More than one year is probably a good deal.

Bailout. This allows you to get out without a penalty when interest rates drop: i.e., if the guaranteed yield is 10%, for eight years, the bailout point might be 9.5%.

Load charge. Most deferred annuities are no-load but some carry up-front commissions of 5.5% to 8.5%. That's a good chunk of money that won't work for you.

Withdrawal charge. Some companies allow you to pull out up to 6% of your principal yearly (tax-free as a return of capital). Others allow more: up to 10% a year.

If you take out more than the allowed amount, there's usually a penalty that disappears with time. A typical charge is 6, 5, 4, 3, 2, 1, 0. That means a 6% charge the first year, 5% the second, etc., and no charge in the seventh year.

Other companies have a nondisappearing charge: a constant 7% levy on withdrawals unless you select an annuity for your payments.

Types of investment. You can choose between fixed returns, where your money is invested in debt issues such as mortgages or bonds, or variable, where the money is invested in a diversified portfolio of stocks and bonds. With the latter, you may get more if the market goes up but will get less if it declines.

And remember that an annuity is a safety blanket where there will be nothing left at the final death. As Jonas Blake put it, "You need an annuity only if you have no dependents, no charity to take your money, nobody to leave it to and you want to be sure that you will have money as long as you and your spouse live."

Tax Saver with Discount Bonds

If you are persuaded that interest rates will not go up much soon and have a strong relationship with your local bank, here's a way to use leverage to get tax benefits and make some money.

Dr. Pill, in the 50% tax bracket, buys $100,000 worth of utility bonds due to mature in one year, for $93,000: $3,000 cash and a $90,000 loan from his bank.

In a year (and a couple of days to qualify for long-term capital gains), he redeems the bonds for $7,000 profit. After paying the 20% tax of $1,400, he has $5,600 plus interest income of $2,230 net ($4,460 gross minus 50% tax) for a total of $7,830.

He pays out $11,000 in interest, which, fully deductible, nets to $5,500, so he ends up with $2,330 on a $3,000 cash outlay.

But if his loan had carried a flexible interest rate and the cost of money rose during the year, his gains would be far less. And, of course, the bonds must be at a bargain price.

20

Taxes Are Not THAT Important with Investments

With taxes, there are three things for the investor to consider: (1) all income from interest and dividends is taxed at the highest rate; (2) profits on property held for more than 12 months are subject to the low, long-term capital gains tax rate; (3) realized losses can be used to offset other taxable income.

How these affect your investment tactics depends primarily on your income tax bracket: the higher your rate, the greater the tax benefits—to limits set by law. With long-term capital gains, the tax applies to 40% of the realized profits: thus, for the wealthy individual in the 50% tax bracket, the tax rate is 20%: 40 × 50. For one in the 40% tax bracket, 16%: 40 × 40.

With losses, there can be deductions to a maximum of $3,000 a year: for *short-term* (for property held for less than 12 months), dollar for dollar; for *long-term* (held over one year), $1 deduction for every $2 loss. Losses in excess of $3,000 can be carried over to the next year.

When you have, or plan to have, tax losses, separate them into short- and long-term and then offset them for the greatest tax benefit.

• **Avoid offsetting long-term gains with short-term**

losses. Each dollar you offset that way saves only 40¢ worth of taxable income.

• **Apply long-term losses against short-term capital gains.** This saves a full dollar of taxable income.

When you have a capital gain, try to hold the stock for 12 months so that the tax will be lower. When you have a capital loss and there are little prospects for a price advance soon, sell before the holding period reaches one year.

Example: In December, you buy $20,000 worth of Super-Swing, Inc. Earnings fail to meet projections and, by October, the shares are down to $18,000. Unless there are strong reasons for optimism soon, sell, take the $2,000 loss and use the full $2,000 to offset other income. If you wait a few more weeks, the dollar loss will be the same but the tax benefit will be only $1,000.

Conversely, the potential gain can be considered the cost of eliminating the market risk in holding on to the security for more than one year. If you take your short-term gain, you are sure of a profit. But your taxes will be greater. If you have a week or two to wait for the 12-month limit, hang on unless it's an erratic market and a volatile stock. But be cautious when the wait is longer. A lot can happen quickly, especially in the swinging markets that have been frequent recently. Just be sure the potential tax savings are worth the added risk.

Don't Wait for Year-End

Tax selling and switching should *not* be solely a year-end affair. Action should be taken whenever advantageous and should *always* be secondary to investment considerations. Unfortunately, most people delay thinking about taxes until near the end of the year because they are not sure of their net capital position or whether their gains, or losses, are long- or short-term. It is wiser, easier and more rewarding to keep running records that will enable you to approximate your tax position.

When you review your portfolio quarterly, make marginal notes on the taxes due on gains or credits possible with losses. If you are planning to upgrade your holdings, weigh the desirability of taking some short-term gains and losses simultaneously so that you can realize some of the gains without taxes.

As year-end nears, watch the timing. In a bear market, do not sell losers in December. Everyone else is doing the same thing so the price you get will probably be below your projection.

Check with your broker as to deadlines: to establish a gain, you must have the proceeds in hand on the last business day of the year: in 1984, Monday, December 31. Since it takes five days for the transaction to clear and the 25th is Christmas, the trading deadline is Monday, December 24.

To establish a loss, you can trade on the last day, Monday, December 31.

But, with the help of your broker, you can get extra time: for a gain, Friday, December 28 with a "next day" sale that will be settled on Monday, the 31st. Or a "cash" sale on the 31st because settlement will be made the same day.

It is also important to be aware of state laws and how they affect your tax status. In several states, the capital gains tax does not allow for carry-forward losses; in others, retirees get extra credits.

Watch Out for Wash Sales

A *wash sale* is a sale for a capital loss where you buy the "same or substantially identical" securities within 30 days *before* or *after* the loss sale. That means a time span of 61 days. Losses from wash sales are *not* deductible on your federal income tax. Gains are taxable. These rules do not apply to securities acquired through gift, inheritance or tax-free exchange.

"Substantially identical" means just that: a common stock, option or voting certificate representing that stock are considered the same. Voting stock and nonvoting stock paying the same dividend and selling at about the same price are *not* the same. Nor are two or more series of bonds of the same corporation with different coupon rates or maturity dates, nor a stock and a related warrant nor a call on a security.

These are the tax consequences of a *wash sale:*

1. The disallowed loss is *added* to your purchase price for the new securities to establish the base for determining a gain or loss on the future sale of these securities.

2. The holding period (over 12 months for long-term tax benefits) for the repurchased securities is extended to include that for the original securities.

Example: You buy 100 shares of International Eye Chart (IEC) at 40 on July 1. By October 15, the stock has dropped to 30, so you sell for what you believe is a tax loss of $1,000, as an offset against realized capital gains.

By November 1 (less than 30 days after the October sale), the price of IEC is down to 25. You feel that the stock is a good buy and likely to move up again soon. If you buy, your anticipated tax loss of $1,000 will be disallowed.

Warning: The wash-sale rule applies to call options, too. You cannot take a tax loss in a security and maintain your position in the stock by buying calls. The IRS will clamp down and disallow the tax loss if an option on that stock is bought within 30 days before or after the date of the stock sale.

To avoid wash-sale penalties: (*1*) Buy the stock of an equally good company in the same industry. (*2*) Buy an equivalent number of shares of the same security, then hold both blocks for 31 days to establish a loss on your original holdings. This requires additional capital and there's no way to know whether the future price will mean an even greater loss.

Special Considerations

Once in a while, it pays to accept penalties of a disallowed wash sale. This happens when a security drops sharply in price between the date of the sale and the date of repurchase and then moves up again.

If IEC bounced up to 40 after you bought it at 25, your $1,500 paper profit would more than outweigh the loss of the $1,000 tax benefit.

Similarly, the longer holding period for the new purchase (including the original holding period) could also be favorable. It might enable your profit to qualify for the lower long-term capital gains tax rate. In the previous example, had you delayed your repurchase until November 16 (31 days after your sale on October 15), your new purchase would not become long term until mid May the next year. But by making a wash-sale repurchase on November 1, you throw back the start of the holding period to July 1, so you can take your long-term profit (if any) in January.

No hanky-panky. IRS: (1) wants no trick deals such as the husband making the sale and the wife buying the same stock within 30 days; (2) frowns on losses between related parties: member of the same family, controlled corporations, trusts, etc.

In both situations, there is modest balm: that, when the securities/property are sold, for a capital gain, only that portion of the gain in excess of the disallowed loss will be taxable.

Example: if you sold stock that cost $10,000 to your brother for $7,600, the $2,400 loss is not deductible. But if your brother sold the stock for $10,500, the taxable gain is only $500 because the $2,400 loss offsets the $2,900 gain. If your brother sold the stock at a further loss, he could deduct only his loss.

Selling to Increase Yield

If you need extra income and decide to sell a low-dividend payer to buy a high-yielding utility, factor in the tax consequences with this formula:

SY = Switch Yield (new security)

HY = Hold Yield (present security)

TP = Tax-bite Percentage

$$SY = \frac{HY}{100 - TP}$$

Example: You purchased 100 shares of ZZZ at 20 because of the 10% dividend: $200 annual income. With new corporate management, the stock takes off and soars to 50 but the dividend stays at $200, so the yield is now 4%.

On the $30 per share profit, the tax, at the long-term capital gains rate, for your 50% tax bracket is 20% or $600. With commissions for both buying and selling, you now have $4,200. To come out seven, the new yield must be 5%.

$$SY = \frac{4}{100 - 20} \quad \frac{4}{80} = 5\%$$

But to get the original 10% return, the new investment must pay $420 a year—possibly with some utility stocks and bonds.

How to Calculate Commissions/Costs

The commissions paid your broker and the fees and taxes on securities transactions can be used to cut your taxes. IRS considers the buying commission a part of your original cost and the selling expenses a deduction from the next proceeds.

Example: You bought 100 shares of a stock at 20 and sold them at 19¼: a dollar loss of $75. But, for income tax purposes, the loss would be considerably greater.

Assuming a buying commission of $45.14 and 80¢ in fees, your cost would be $2,045.94, not $2,000. Your selling proceeds would not be $1,925 but $1,876.42 because of the deductions for $43.99 in commissions, state tax of $3.75 and transfer fee of 84¢. Thus, on your tax return you could deduct $169.52, not just $75.

Tax Savers

For most investors, tax saving maneuvers will be more bother than worth. But there's never any reason to pay Uncle Sam more than justified. Here are some convenient tax savers:

To convert capital gains from short to long term (and thus take advantage of the lower tax rate), find out about these opportunities:

• *Check the professionals at your mutual fund* to learn about year-end distributions of capital gains. If you own shares even *one* day before the payout date, the money qualifies as long term. And if you hold for 31 days and then sell for a capital loss (possible because the value of the fund shares will drop because of the distribution), it's short term and provides extra tax advantages.

Example: Shrewd Sam has a $50,000 short-term gain and wants to avoid paying half to Uncle Sam. He buys enough shares of XYZ Fund to get a capital gains distribution of $50,000. He has exchanged a $50,000 short-term profit, taxed for $25,000, for a $50,000 long-term capital gain taxed at 20% or $10,000. So he saves $15,000.

After 32 days, if he's lucky, he can sell some shares at a loss for an offset to other taxable income. Usually, it takes time for the shares to bounce back after the payout.

• *Buy T-bills in the fall to defer income to next year.* Since these are sold at a discount, there are no taxes due on the interest until maturity.

Example: Author Al gets an unexpectedly large royalty check in November. Since he anticipates lower income next year, he buys a $10,000, one-year T bill, paying 8.6% interest, for $9.140. Next November he will get $10,000 and add $860 to his income. This 8.6% discount is equivalent to an annual yield of 9.4% and, in states where there are income taxes, the interest is not taxed.

To set a choice for allocation of profits, sell shares in the last four trading days of the year. Since it takes five days to receive payment, you can report the gains to your best advantage: this year or next.

To set up a short-term gain to benefit from a short-term loss on other investments: sell T-bills before maturity. Part of the appreciation is taxable as capital gains, not as interest.

Example: In January, Mr. Goldberg pays $34,000 for $40,000 worth of T-bills due in 12 months. If he holds to maturity, he will have a $6,000 profit, which, as interest, will be taxed as ordinary income at his 50% tax rate: $3,000. But in April, he incurs a short-term loss of $1,000. In June (six months), he sells the bills for $38,000: a $4,000 profit. The IRS permits this to be prorated from its discounted basis: $3,000 interest and $1,000 short-term capital gain. He pays the full tax on the $3,000 ($1,500) but uses the $1,000 gain against his short-term loss.

To eliminate immediate tax consequences: use an installment sale agreement to sell securities to your son/daughter who repays, as a loan, the interest that starts at the date of transfer. There will be no taxes, except on the interest income, but any appreciation profits will accrue to the child, not you.

To turn gains from short- to long-term with options.

Example: In January Year I, Frank buys stock for $10 a share. By December that year, it is at 25. To protect his position, he buys a January Year II put at a strike price of 25 for 1 ($100 per 100 shares). If the stock price drops to 20 by the end of January, he can exercise the option for a $14 per share gain: $15 profit minus $1 cost for the put. The gain will be taxable in Year II.

In December Year I, Rose buys a stock at 40. By November Year II, it has zoomed to 68. If she sells, she will net $14 per share because, in her 50% tax bracket, she will have to give half to Uncle Sam. To avoid this, she sells a January Year III call at 60 for 9. If the stock stays at 68, the option will be exercised and she will get $29 per share: $20 from the stock and $9 from the call. The total profit is regarded as a capital gain so the tax will be 20% and the net return $23.30 per share. But there is a danger: that the call will be exercised in December and the tax advantage lost.

In much the same way, calls can be used to set up tax losses, almost short-term, so used for maximum tax benefits. This tactic makes sense with a moving-up stock.

Example: In August, I bought 300 shares of NoNag Drugs for 73 and sold three January calls, at 80, for 2 for a net-after-commissions of $558.97.

In November, I realized I could use a short-term tax loss so bought back the calls, which had risen to 4, for a net cost of $1,249.28 to set up a fully deductible tax loss of $690.31.

Immediately thereafter, I sold three April 85 calls (5 points higher than before) for 4 to bank $1,150,68—almost what I had lost on the buy-back.

In March, after I had sold another holding for a welcome short-term gain, I bought back the NND April calls for a net cost of $1,287.30. This set up a small short-term tax loss of $136.62 (I made the mistake of buying at market rather than at a specific price so paid the penalty of being impatient). I recouped quickly by selling three October 95 calls for $1,150.66.

In eight months, I raised the target price from 80 to 95, received $2,860.31 in premiums (plus dividends) and set up tax losses of $826.93.

Tax Factors in Deciding When, Whether and What to Sell

The two big questions on tax selling are always:

Am I using my investment funds to maximum advantage today?

Will my plans bring maximum returns from my investments tomorrow?

The price you pay for the security has little to do with the answers to these questions. The important thing in successful investing is TOMORROW.

It is discouraging when you have a severe loss in the price of a stock, but this gloom can be dispelled if the stock

---

SETTING UP TAX LOSSES

Base: long-term ownership of 300 shares of stock

August:	Sold 3 January 80 calls @ 2	+558.97
November:	When he realized he could use a short-term tax loss, he bought back 3 calls at 4	−1,249.28
	to set up a short-term tax loss of	− 690.31
November:	Sold 3 April 85 calls @ 4	+1,150.68
March:	After a hefty short-term capital gain on another holding, he bought back 3 April calls at 4 1/8:	−1,287.30
	to set up a short-term tax loss of	− 136.62
April:	Sold 3 October 95 calls at 4	+1,150.66

Now he had raised his target price from 80 to 95, received $2,860.31 in premiums (plus dividends) and set up tax losses of $826.93.

---

has the ability to recover its previous value and, even better, move up even more. If there is no realistic probability for a worthwhile advance, stop dreaming and *sell.*

Suppose you paid $1,000 for 100 shares of Sexy Electronics. It is now quoted at 5, might possibly get up to 7 in a bull market, but has little hope of hitting 10 for a long time. You will be better off to take your $500 loss as a tax offset and reinvest the balance (with some added savings) in a stock that has higher quality and greater promise.

Always take losses promptly when the prospects of the company are not good. As is stressed throughout this guide, the first loss is almost always the cheapest. More investors lose more money more often by holding stocks in an effort to justify their original judgment than in any other way. Forget about pride. Sell and put the proceeds into more rewarding situations.

Don't hold too long. Some folks avoid decisions by buying growth stocks and never selling. This will prove profitable if you live long enough but wise selling and, often, rebuying will be far more rewarding. The market fluctuates and so does the value of individual stocks.

The basic theory is to buy low and sell high and to do so when the tax benefits are greatest. But taxes alone should rarely be the primary factor in any investment decision. You can never escape a capital gains tax on a profit unless you hold an appreciated asset to death or give it to an approved charitable, educational or other nonprofit organization. Holding a profitable security only defers the ultimate tax and, of course, carries the risk of a price decline.

Periodic selling takes advantage of market swings and new buying opportunities. Over the years, market averages swing, up and down, as much as 50% and, in normal years, the price of a typical stock will rise or fall 25%. By wise selling, you can profit from these actions: selling at a temporary high and buying back at a temporary low. This applies primarily to trading but, with top quality stocks, with investments, too. IBM moved from the 70s to 55, back into the 70s, down to below 50, up to 66, down to below 58 and then way up above 100. The investor should not have sold at every peak or valley but judicious trading would have been wise and the tax bite relatively small.

Furthermore, at all times, some stocks will be relatively

undervalued and some groups will be performing better than the average. By justified changes in your portfolio—especially low-taxed ones—you can be in a position to catch some winners.

Once a stock reaches a target range, its advance is likely to slow. Postponing capital gains taxes at this point may cost you more than you could save because your profits on other investments could be greater. When any stock becomes overpriced, get ready to sell. This may be a tough decision when a stock runs up fast and you're in a high tax bracket.

Example: Steve, in the 50% tax bracket, buys 100 shares of Tiddly-Winks at 28. In nine months, its price is 42—the target price that represents a 50% gain. If Steve sells, he will have to pay Uncle Sam $700 of his $1,400 profit. But if he can hang on for three more months, that tax will drop to $280 for a saving of $420—roughly 4¼ points in the price of the stock . . . or 37¾.

Steve sets a stop-loss order at 39 ½ and waits because the overall market is strong and the last quarter report of TW was excellent. In the fourteenth month after purchase, TW hit 48 so Steve sold, had a gross profit of $2,000 minus $400 tax for a net-before-costs of $1,600.

But his neighbor, Rose, in the 25% tax bracket, made different calculations under the same conditions. Her potential $1,400 profit would be cut by $350 tax to $1,050. Her long-term gain of $2,000 would be reduced by only $200 to $1,800.

What it comes down to is that, with a profitable, growing portfolio, it's usually wise to plan to switch 20% of the securities each year. This will spread out the tax bite and will eliminate the weak holdings. If you sell only the winners, your taxes will be greater and your wealth less.

Suggestion: If you have a stock with a hefty short-term capital gain, sell it to one of your minor children. The sale can be made at your cost and the guardian/trustee can then sell the shares and take the short-term profit and pay no or little tax.

Deductible Investment Expenses

On your federal income tax return, you can deduct legitimate expenses incurred in managing your money such as:

Subscriptions to investment advisory services, financial publications and statistical services

Cost of books on investments (such as *Your Investments)*

Stock transfer taxes

Custodian fees to banks, mutual funds and investment manager of income-producing property/savings (including IRAs)

Accounting and auditing expenses

Investment counsel and management fees

Legal fees in connection with investments

Fees for preparing tax returns

Interest on margin accounts/loans

Office expenses related to investments: clerical salaries, portion of home office used for money management

With short sales: dividends paid to buyers and premiums for borrowed stock

Trustee fees

Rental of safe-deposit box used for investment assets/records

Commissions to brokers on sale of property

Postage/telephone expenses in connection with investing

21

Commodities and Collectibles: Only for Speculations

This chapter tries to explain two speculative areas: (1) trading futures contracts of commodities, metals and foreign currencies; (2) acquiring collectibles such as gold/silver, coins, stamps, diamonds, etc. Because of their special characteristics, financial futures are discussed separately.

Commodities are almost always 100% speculations in active, volatile markets, but, under certain conditions, can be used to hedge and sell short to protect positions; collectibles are somewhat more stable, require special expertise

and, occasionally, can become investments over the long term. Everyone should understand trading in commodities but few amateurs should become involved. And collections are usually more worthwhile for personal pleasure than financial gain.

As with all speculations, there are special risks that, often, are beyond the individual's ken or control and should be undertaken only with spare cash, preferably money that you can afford to lose. But there's always the hope of a big, quick profit. In reality, of course, the odds are always against the amateur: 85% of all commodities speculators lose money. And their aggregate losses tend to be six times as great as their gains. You win only with a few supersuccessful deals!

Commodities trading is for speculators who are tough-skinned, strong-minded, willing to take risks and have adequate capital. The techniques can be grasped and utilized when you take time to learn the ground rules, study the pertinent factors and forces and do your homework. You must be able to spot situations where the possible rewards are greater than the sure risks. With the odds in your favor and the use of leverage, you can achieve excellent profits if you guess right. But success is hard to come by and, often, fleeting.

Example: A few years ago, I interviewed a trader for a feature article. The key transaction was a soybean deal where, on a $1,500 investment when contracts were at $4.54 per bushel, the price soared to $12.90: a $28,300 short-term profit in less than eight months. But two years later when I called the same individual for another interview, his phone was disconnected!

With commodities, the cash requirements are low: 5% to 10% per contract, depending on the commodity and the broker's standards. Unlike margin for securities which is an interest-bearing cost, margin for commodities is a security deposit. There are no interest payments on the balance but, when the price dips, more money/collateral must be deposited or the position will be closed out.

The lures of fast action, minimal capital and high potential profits are enticing—but before you start trading contracts for corn, wheat, soybeans, silver or any other commodity, heed these warnings from professionals:

• **Be emotionally stable.** You have to be able to control your sense of fear and greed and train yourself to accept losses without too great a strain. Until a few years ago, some brokerage firms refused to accept female customers!

• **Be ready to risk at least $10,000:** $5,000 at once; the rest to back up margin calls.

• **Deal only with a knowledgeable commodities broker** who keeps you informed of new and potential developments.

How the Market Operates

Commodity trading is different from investing (or speculating) in stocks. When you buy a common stock, you own part of the corporation and share in its profits, if any. If you pick a profitable company, the price of your stock will eventually rise.

With commodities, there is no equity. You buy only hope. Once the futures contract has expired, there's no tomorrow. If your trade turned out badly, you must take the full loss.

The economic reason for a futures market is hedging (that is, reducing the risk of a commitment by taking an offsetting one). A farmer who borrows money to plant a 5,000-bushel soybean crop in the spring may be asked, by his banker, to sell a futures contract (5,000 bushels) for November delivery. The contract calls for a fixed price of $6.90 per bushel (quoted in the financial press at 690 cents

per bushel). If the price, in November, is down to $6.50, the farmer loses 40¢ per bushel on the sale but makes up this loss by buying back his contract for less than he received. He comes out even and earns his normal profit on the crop.

On the other hand, a food processor who sells his products throughout the year wants a predetermined cost price for his soybean purchase, let's say, $6.90 per bushel. He buys that November futures contract at $6.90 to lock in his cost. If the price, in November, is $6.50 per bushel, he sells the futures contract at a 40¢ per bushel loss but can acquire the soybeans at below his projected cost to complete a protective hedge.

In most cases, it's not that simple. The opposite side of each transaction is picked up by a speculator who believes he can make money by a favorable price change in the months before delivery. Speculator Sam might buy that November contract, in April, for $6.90 per bushel ($34,500 with a $1,500 margin). In July when the price rose to $7.10, he would sell for a gross profit of 20¢ per bushel or $1,000 to net, after commissions/costs, about $900 for a 60% return in four months.

But if Sam guessed wrong and soybean prices fell, he would have to put up more margin and, when he did sell, chalk up a sizable loss. In almost every case, Sam will act before the contract becomes due. That's the excitement and profit potential of trading in commodities!

Steps to Take

1. Read a good book about commodity trading. Your broker can provide you with a folder from his firm or the commodity exchanges. Or study the books listed in the Bibliography. Then decide if you have the stomach and the funds to start speculating.

2. Get current information. There is no inside information about commodities. All statistics are available in government reports, business and agricultural publications, newsletters and special service. Always check two or three for confirmation and then review your conclusions with your broker. It will help to become something of an expert in both the fundamental and technical aspects of a few major commodities. Later, when you become experienced, you can move into other areas where information is not so widely available.

3. Choose an experienced broker. Deal only with a reputable firm that (*a*) has extensive commodities trading services, and (*b*) includes a broker who knows speculation and can guide you.

4. Zero in on a few commodities, preferably those in the news. Staples such as corn, wheat and hogs always have strong markets, but the best speculative profits can be made in the active groups, recently natural resources such as metals and petroleum.

5. Avoid thin markets. You can score when such a commodity takes off but the swings can be too fast and may send prices soaring, or plummeting, so that the amateur can get caught with no chance of closing a position.

6. Look for a ratio of net profit to net loss of 2:1. Since the percentage of losses will always be greater than that of profits, choose commodities where the potential gains (based on confirmed trends) can be more than double the possible losses. When you make such projections, include commission costs as they can be a major factor when dealing in small units and small price shifts.

7. Prepare an operation plan. Before you risk any cash, test your hypotheses on paper until you feel confident that you understand what can happen. Do this for several weeks so you get the feel of different types of markets.

With one active commodity, "buy" contracts at several delivery dates and calculate the potential profits if the price rises moderately, say +3%: for the soybean contract, 21¢ per bushel, from $6.90 to $7.11. This would mean a gain of $3,555, minus $50 commissions, for a net profit of $3,505 on that $1,500 margin (that 2:1 profit ratio).

Next, assume that the price drops 3% to $6.69 per bushel. With every 5¢ decline, you must increase your margin by $150, so your invested capital (if you hang on), would be $2,100. The loss will be $1,150 plus commission.

8. Never meet a margin call. When your original margin is impaired by 25%, your broker will call for more money. Except in most unusual circumstances, do not put in more money. Liquidate your position and accept your loss. This is a form of stop-loss safeguard. When a declining trend has been established, further losses can be expected.

9. Be alert to special situations. Information is the key to profitable speculation. As you become more knowledgeable, you will pick up many points, such as:

• If there's heavy spring-summer rain in Maine, buy long on potatoes. They need ideal weather.

• If there's a bad tornado over large portions of the Great Plains, buy wheat contracts. Chances are the wheat crop will be damaged, thus changing the supply/demand.

There are, of course, many other factors to analyze before reaching any final decision. As with everything involving the profit potential of money, knowledge plus luck are important.

10. Through classes or books, learn how the markets work and why prices move as they do. No one really can be sure at all times but, since you will be working in retrospect, you can get a pretty good feel of background conditions. You'll find some fascinating lore: economic recovery in Europe usually means higher soybean prices in Chicago which, in turn, may boost the price of silver in New York.

11. Trade with the major trend, against the minor trend. With copper, for example, if you project a worldwide shortage of the metal and the market is in an uptrend, buy futures when the market suffers temporary weak spells. As long as prices keep moving up, you want to accumulate a meaningful position.

Corollary to this, never average down. Adding to your loss position increases the number of contracts that are returning a loss. By buying more, you put yourself in a stance where you can lose on more contracts if the price continues to drop.

Generally, if the trend is down, either sell short or stay out of the market. And never (well, hardly ever) buy a commodity after it has passed its seasonal high or sell a commodity after it has passed its seasonal low.

12. Watch the spreads between different delivery dates. In the strong summer market, the premium for January soybeans is 8¢ per bushel above the November contract. Buy November and sell January.

If the bull market persists, the premium should disappear and you will have a pleasant, limited profit. Carrying charges on soybeans run about 6½¢ per month, so it is not likely that the spread will widen to more than 13¢ per bushel. Thus, with that 8¢ spread, the real risk is not more than 5¢ per bushel.

13. Never spread a loss. Turning a long or short position into a spread by buying or selling another contract month will seldom help you and, in most cases, will guarantee a locked-in loss. When you make a mistake, get out.

14. Do not take a position until profit potential is 8 to 10 times commission. Newcomers are intrigued with the idea that, each day, they can make a profit that can be partly removed immediately. Just to cover the loss trades and commissions, they have to be right nearly half the time. Such day-trading can be exciting but it's too fast and volatile for the amateur. Look for trends, not interim movements.

15. Treat paper profits as though they are real money. This will give/teach you greater respect for the impact of losses.

16. Risk no more than 10% of your trading capital in any one position and no more than 30% of all capital in all positions at any one time . . . except when you have caught a strong upswing and can move with the trend. These limits will ease the effect of a bad decision. Few professionals count on being right more than half the time.

17. If you cannot afford to lose, you cannot afford to win. If you are not in a position to accept losses, either psychologically or financially, you have no business playing with commodities.

18. If you are not sure, don't. Never get carried away by the unreal world of paper. You may be watching tapes, reading reports or plotting charts, but you are doing business with *real money*. If there is *any* question in your mind about the future of the price of the commodity, do not buy or maintain a position. It is better to miss a few profit opportunities through caution than to throw away savings in reckless speculations. To be a successful commodity trader, *you gotta believe.*

Commodity Pools

For most amateurs, the easiest, safest and most profitable (or, at least, least costly) way to play the commodities market is through shares in managed funds. These are pools structured as limited partnerships with units sold for $1,000 each (but, usually, with a minimum purchase of five). The sales pitch is enticing: "for a few thousand dollars, you can buy participation in a diversified portfolio of commodities futures which, with professional management, will double or triple your assets in a few years. By using computers that catch trends, set signal points and adhere to proven profitable disciplines, the managers can minimize losses and maximize profits."

The harsh reality is that most of these professional funds have not been around long enough to have developed any real track records. In any one year, about half the funds will be big winners and the other half big losers. It all depends on whether the pros were smart, or lucky, enough to zero in on superachievers.

In 1983, Harvest I, started in 198, matured enough to be up +33.4% but Peavey II, a newcomer, was down −35.5%. *You pays your money and makes your choice.*

The computers do help to keep losses low but profits depend on catching fast up-movers. In January 1983, several funds made a bundle because of a sharp rise in the prices of precious metals. In February, those who failed to get (about half the publicly quoted funds) lost as much or more

HOW SOME COMMODITIES FUNDS PERFORMED

NAME/	UNIT VALUE			PERFORMANCE			Since
START-UP	Offer	12/81	2/83	1981	1982	1983	Start
Admiral 12/81	$1,000	$ 955	$1,076	(4.5%	33.6%	15.1%	43.9%
Boston I 1/80	957	1,065	682	18.9	(34.5)	22.0	(9.7)
Enterprise 11/81	1,000	997	1,086	(0.3)	8.9	8.8	18.2
Harvest I 6/78	1,000	2,987	3,784	(2.2)	33.4	35.1	456.4
Harvest II 2/89	970	491	661	(2.7)	34.6	40.4	(4.3)
Heinold III 1/78	1,000	2,584	2,878	75.6	0.8	(4.1)	175.9
Peavey II 4/81	847	892	575	25.3	(35.5)	23.0	(16.5)
Resource 8/78	1,000	3,411	4,248	38.8	24.5	8.6	361.3
Western I 11/81	1,000	922	423	(7.8)	(54.1)	(1.9)	(58.5)

SOURCE: Financial World

As with most technical approaches, the idea is to move with the trend. But, with commodities, so subject to world economic and political pressures, changes come so fast that these trends seldom develop and, if and when they do, are difficult to confirm. The computer signals lag so the manager has to guess the future . . . and that's often more luck than skill.

The terms of each pool vary but generally call for:
• Limitation of sales to individuals who have a net worth of: (*a*) $50,000, exclusive of home, furnishings and automobiles; or (*b*) $25,000 and an annual adjusted income of $25,000.
• Purchase or sale of participations at the end of each reporting period (monthly or quarterly). If you have to sell in a hurry, you'll probably have to take a loss.
• Front-end loads of 3% to 10% (so less of your money goes to work).
• Fixed management fees of 4% to 6% per year plus.
• Incentive fees, paid only when there are profits, from 17% to 20% of cumulative net realized and unrealized gains.
• Reporting and legal fees: 12% to 20% of total expenses.
• Brokerage commissions (usually below the rates charged individual traders) that, on an annual basis, run from 30% to 100% of net assets.
• Costs offset, in part, by interest income from Treasury bills that are used, in lieu of cash, as margin in about 80% of commodities positions.

Example: In one month when the fund value was about $5.9 million, the total expenses were $86,069 ($55,525 commissions plus $30,544 management and incentive fees). The net gain after expenses was $183,471: $108,703 realized and $74,768 unrealized.

Four months later, when the stated equity of the same fund was $5.3 million, the costs were up to $124,518 ($84,734 commission plus $39,794 fees). But the fund lost $306,162: $361,668 realized losses offset by unrealized gains of $55,506.

There are some major advantages for those with ample assets, in a high tax bracket and a willingness to stay the course . . . for several years:
• On the average, fund managers keep 60% of your money in Treasury bills 80% of the time. That means your assets are earning some income (though not exactly as fast nor as much as you anticipated).
• *Tax break:* Taxes are payable on unrealized as well as realized gains. At the end of each year, all open positions of the fund are valued at the market. Net realized totals (gains and losses) are adjusted by net unrealized totals (gains or losses).

These results flow through to the individual investor's tax return because of his position as a limited partner. At this point, losses can offset gains on other capital assets but the gains are taxed at a maximum of 32% because profits, realized or unrealized, are considered to be: 60% long-term. Since only 40% of such gains are taxed and the maximum tax rate (at this time) is 50%, that means a tax levy of 12%. 40% short-term! These are fully taxed but again, at the top 50% rate, this works out to 20% for Uncle Sam. *Commodities trading is the only investment area where some of your short-term profits are taxed at the low long-term rate.*

Fund Management

As professionals, the most experienced fund managers try to take small, quick losses and let their profits run. They know that they can lose money on a majority of positions but can generally count on big gains from a few successful holdings.

This strategy isn't easy. When there are net losses on 60% of the trades (not unusual in a swinging market), each profit must produce 1.5 times as much money as each loss took away—just to break even.

Each fund manager has his own style. One of the deans is Richard D. Donchian, who manages one public and one private fund for Shearson–American Express. Donchian relies on trends. He believes that "once a trend, in either direction, is established, it has a strong tendency to continue. The trick is to catch the trend early and ride it until it starts to shift."

One of the trend-determining tools Donchian uses is a moving average (MA). Each day he adds the previous day's closing price of each commodity and drops the earliest figure. With a 20-day MA, for example, he totals the closing prices for the past 20 trading days and divides by 20 to get the base data. On Day 21, he drops the Day 1 price and adds the Day 21 quotation.

Explains Donchian, "the value of an MA is that no commodity can stage an important uptrend without its price moving above the MA as the result of more buying than selling. Vice versa on the downside.

"When the closing price of a commodity crosses the MA by a present amount, we act: buying when the breakthrough is up; selling when it's down. The required amount of MA penetration is based on past patterns. Over the years, this indicator has produced good profits and avoided heavy losses."

Checklist

If you do decide to speculate . . . and that's the basic nature of all commodities trading . . . look for funds that have these safeguards:

• The right to withdraw at the end of a regular reporting period with no more than 15 days notice.

• A 50% dissolution clause, where the fund must be dissolved when equity falls below half of the original assets.

• Trading policy that limits fund investments to 20% of assets in any one commodity.

• Regular reports with understandable information on transaction costs and results.

• No payments to advisers on the basis of volume. Such a policy could lead to churning.

In making a choice, check the records of several funds over several years and, for each of the three last annual reports, note the three most profitable and the three most devastating positions. Winners are great but the lack of losers can make the difference.

After if you are nervous, sell half your holdings when you double your money. You'll have reserves for new opportunities with the same or new commodity funds.

Speculating in Foreign Currencies

For swingers—and those who have ready access to international financial information—trading in foreign currencies can be exciting, and, these days, profitable. And for superswingers, there are currency options.

Futures contracts on foreign currency are traded on the International Monetary Market Division (IMM) of the Chicago Mercantile Exchange. Basically, positions are taken by importers and exporters who want to protect their profits from sudden swings in relationship between the dollar and a specific foreign currency. A profit on the futures contract will be offset by a loss in the cash market. Or vice versa. Either way, the businessman/banker guarantees a set cost.

The speculation performs an essential function by taking opposite sides of contracts but, unlike other types of commodities trading, currency futures reflect reactions to what has already happened more than anticipation of what's ahead.

For small margins of 1.5% to 4.2%, roughly $1,500 to $2,500, you can control large sums of money: 100,000 Canadian dollars; 125,000 deutsche marks; 12.5 million Japanese yen, etc.

The attraction is leverage. You can speculate that at a fixed date in the future the value of your contract will be greater (if you buy long) or less (if you sell short).

The daily fluctuations of each currency futures contract are limited by IMM rules. A rise of $750 per day provides a 37.5% profit on a $2,000 investment. That's a net gain of $705 ($750 less $45 in commissions). If the value declines, you are faced with a wipe-out or, if you set a stop order, the

loss of part of your security deposit. Vice versa when you sell short.

One of the favorite deals is playing crosses: taking advantage of the spread between different currencies: buying francs and selling liras short, etc. The shifts in currency rates have been so explosive lately that, for illustration, let's go back a few months when, relative to the U.S. dollar, the West German mark was falling faster than the Swiss franc. Speculator Stan set up this spread:

April 15: Buys a June contract for 125,000 francs and sells short a June contract for 125,000 marks. The franc is valued at 50.64¢, the mark at 46.03¢. Cost, not including commissions, is the margin: $2,000.

May 27: The franc has fallen to 48.58¢, while the mark has dropped to 43.22. The speculator reverses his trades, selling the June contract for francs and buying the mark contract to cover his short position.

Result: The speculator loses 2.06¢ per franc, or $2,575, but he makes 2.81¢ per mark, or $3,512.50. The overall gain, before commissions, is $937.50, a return of 46.9% on the $2,000 investment . . . in about six weeks.

These days, commissions are negotiable and vary from $25 to $75 per contract. At worst, the speculator pays about $150, leaving $787.50 net profit. Now his return is 39.4%.

Warning: IMM is a thin market. The speculator may not be able to get out when he wants at the price he expects. On a one-day trade, the value of the currency can still fluctuate. All the speculator can do is to watch helplessly and hope that his projections work out.

For information on trading foreign currencies, send $15 for IMM's home-study course: International Monetary Market, 444 West Jackson Boulevard, Chicago, Ill. 60606.

Currency options. These are traded on the Philadelphia Exchange in five currencies: West German mark, British pound, Canadian dollar, Japanese yen and Swiss franc. The premiums range from $300 to $1,500 each depending on the price/terms. The most the option *buyer* can lose is the price of the premium. There's no expiration date so no need for additional margin. The investor can hold his option as long as he wants, no matter how steeply the currency moves in the wrong direction from the contracted price.

These options are still new but, so far, have been used primarily by American corporations seeking to assure a fixed price for goods/services rendered or purchased abroad.

Example: LMO Corp., a construction firm, bids 10 million marks (at the time, $4.2 million) to build a factory in West Germany. Management is worried about the currency fluctuations so buys options for 10 million marks for $48,000. If, before the work starts, the mark's value should drop from 42¢ to 39¢, the dollar loss would be $300,000. But with the options, the maximum loss would be $48,000. Some speculators would sell the contract.

Gold: For Speculation Only

To millions of people (very few of whom are investors), gold is the finest form of tangible wealth. It is a symbol of security that protects the individual against inflation, confiscation of income through taxes and worldwide threats of war and revolution. They enjoy the thrill and comfort of owning the precious metal as bullions or coins and boast of their profits from its ever-rising value. In the years since January 1975 when gold could first be bought by Americans, the price did rise from $197.50 to close to $900 an ounce, and then, fast and erratically, fell below $300! Since then, it's been yo-yoing but slowly and with smaller fluctuations. The people who have really made money with gold, in any form, are those who were willing and able to trade frequently: buying low and selling, or selling short, at an interim high; rebuying and hanging on when there's an uptrend; and repeating the process. As one shrewd broker told me: "The only way to profit with gold is to trade, at least once a year and, most of the time, every few months. Gold should be bought only by those who do not need income, have time to watch the markets and guts enough to let facts dominate emotions."

If you do succumb to gold fever, here are some choices:

1. Companies listed on major stock exchanges. Most of these are large, relatively stable U.S. and Canadian corporations with other mineral assets. They provide full, detailed reports to stockholders and their shares can be bought and sold easily. But their values fluctuate with the price of the metal: shares of Homestake Mining (adjusted for splits) soared from 22 to 45, fell to 8½, bounced up to 32—all in three years, 1980–early 1983.

2. South African gold mining companies whose shares are available as ADRs (Chapter 16). They pay high dividends—from 14% to 18%—but are extremely volatile, again with the price of gold.

3. Holding companies: A.S.A. Limited, a closed-end investment company with some 70% of its assets in South African gold mining shares; *Anglo-American Corporation,* the largest mining finance firm and the number one producer of both gold and diamonds; *Anglo-American Investment Company,* with holdings in a number of gold mines. With all of these, you are buying the equivalent of shares in a mutual fund.

4. Gold certificates. These are certificates which represent ownership of a specific portion of bullion stored in a Swiss bank. There's no U.S. bank account, no sales tax and no report to IRS.

The sales price includes fees for insurance and storage plus commissions, which run from 3% to 1% depending on quantity. The certificates are not negotiable nor assignable, so they must be sold back to the dealer—a difficult task when they are in an estate.

5. Gold future contracts. These give the speculator the biggest bang for the buck. They are similar to commodities futures, can be handled by most brokers and are actively traded on Comex and IMM.

You can buy and sell 100-ounce contracts with different future delivery dates on margin of 5% to 15%. Thus, with gold at $412 an ounce, $1,700 margin can control 100 ounces worth $41,200. If there's a $17 per ounce rise, you can double your money. But if the price falls, you will have to come up with more margin. Most brokers require a minimum balance of $10,000.

It's always wise to set target prices. You can let your profits run, but to protect your holdings, give the broker a stop-loss price: either at the point at which additional margin will be needed or at the average price of the last 30 trading days. Thus, if you bought a contract when gold was $400 an ounce and used a 10% margin, the sell price would be $360 if you are conservative. As the price of the metal moves up, boost the stop-loss accordingly.

Even stops may not protect you. Commodity traders try to knock off those stops late in the afternoon—e.g., when the price of gold drops below $365, the professionals, knowing that amateurs have set stops at $360, will go short. This will drop the price again so that the trader may be able to buy back his contracts at about $350. He makes a quick profit and you're out of luck . . . and money.

6. Gold coins (non-numismatic). These are special coins minted only to take advantage of the gold craze. They are best for display and pride of ownership. Comments one veteran trader: "These coins are like real estate: easy to get in but tough to get out of. I've sold them to hundreds of customers and have never known a single individual to make a respectable profit."

Krugerrands: South African coins in four sizes according to the gold content: 1 oz., ½ oz., ¼ oz. and 1/10 oz. The sales pitch is that you can check the daily value of your holdings in the press or from radio/TV reports.

Because of coinage and distribution costs, Krugerrands sell at a 5% to 8% premium over gold. Local sales taxes can add another 8%. Before you buy these "golden opportunities," do your homework and calculate how much you can lose. The loss will be tax deductible but as Barnum proved. . .

U.S. Medallions: in ½ and 1 oz. units. There's no sales tax and you can buy only three units of each kind per year. It takes five weeks for delivery; the weight and fineness are not marked; the cost is about 2% above the New York "spot" price; and there's no major market for resale.

7. Gold options. These give you the right to buy gold at a set price before a set date. They are great speculations because they can be highly leveraged. But they are volatile!

Example: In February, Curt was uncertain which way the price of gold might move so hedged: bought both a June 500 call (right to buy at $500 an ounce) for $4,100 and a June 500 put (right to sell at $500 an ounce) for $1,900. His total outlay was $6,000 (but Curt had just scored a big hit and was feeling flush).

In two weeks, the price of gold dropped so that the June contract was quoted at $430.50 per ounce. The call option zonked to $450 for a paper loss of $3,650. But the value of the put soared to $9,200 for a "profit" of $7,300. Elated, Curt called his broker to close out both positions for an overall, gross profit of $3,650: the $7,300 gain on the put minus the $2,650 loss on the call . . . all in two weeks. No wonder options are speculative!

8. Installment buying. These are billed as "sure-fire" systems. They require consistent investing with the goal of building substantial holdings. You buy bullion on the installment plan. It is stored abroad or in a state where there are no taxes.

New York's Citibank sets an initial minimum of $1,000 with additions in units of $100. There's a 3% load and a 1% fee on the sale.

Merrill Lynch's Sharebuilder Gold Plan requires a basic $100 with additions units of $50. The gold is purchased at $1 an ounce above the London price.

Usually, there are two types of contracts:

Unit price averaging: where the investor agrees to buy a fixed amount of gold regularly: paying less when the price is low; more when high.

Cost averaging: investing a fixed sum at periodic intervals: buying more when the price is low, less when high. Attractive packaging doesn't change the risks.

Lookback Options

To solve the problem of timing purchases of gold or silver, some specialists offer lookback options: a *call* to enable you to buy the metal at its lowest price during a specific period, usually nine months; a *put* to permit you to sell the metal at its highest price during the option period.

Each option covers one contract: 100 ounces of gold or 1000 ounces of silver. They are not cheap.

When gold was $500 an ounce, Gambling Gus bought a call for $18,445. A month later, the price was down to $400, so Gus exercised the option with $40,000. Now, to cover his costs, the price of the metal had to go up to $584.45 an ounce. Above that figure, Gus will earn $1,000 for each $10 price gain.

Rules for Trading Gold/Silver

Here are some caveats suggested by Paul Sarnoff, Director of Research, Rudolf Wolff Commodity Brokers:

• Never commit more than half your money at risk. If you have $50,000, use only $25,000. Put the balance in money market funds for quick retrieval.

• Limit the possible loss to 25% of the total account.

• In trading, stay flexible and alert.

• Paper trade for at least one month before you commit any dollars. Make decisions, calculate margins, set stop-loss prices, etc.

• Check three commodities firms and read all their bulletins and reports.

• Use charts to check price movements and trends.

• Never give discretionary powers to anyone.

• Check the broker/dealer via bank references and written recommendations by customers. According to a former SEC employee, "You would be amazed at how many firms with high-sounding names bounce checks, have low lines of credit and illegally commingle customer and company funds."

And for those whose hopes are greater than their wisdom, there are gold funds: United Services Gold Shares, P.O. Box 29467, San Antonio, TX 78229 or Select Portfolio-Precious Metals, 82 Devonshire Street, Boston, MA 02109.

Collectibles for Pleasure, Not Profit

Some folks, alarmed at inflation and dire predictions of professional doomsayers, prefer to own tangibles such as

TERMS FOR TRADING METALS

	EXCHANGE	CONTRACT SIZE	CONTRACT MONTHS	MINIMUM FLUCTUATION	MINIMUM INITIAL MARGIN
GOLD					
Futures	Comex	100 oz.	Current month, next two months & Jan/Mar/May/July/Sept/Dec.	10¢ oz = $10	$2,500
	IMM	100 oz.	Jan/Mar/Apr/July/Sept/Oct/Dec. plus spot month	10¢ oz = $10	3,500
	CBT	100 oz.	Feb/Mar/Apr/May/June/Aug/Oct/Dec.	10¢ oz = $10	2,500
	MidAm	33.2 oz.	Mar/June/Sept/Dec.	2.5¢ oz = 83¢	900
Options on futures					
	Comex	100 oz.	Closest 2 mos. plus next 2 mos. of Cycle 1; Cycle 1: Apr/Aug/Dec. Cycle 2: Feb/June/Oct.	10¢ oz = $10	Strike prices at each $10 per oz.
	MidAm	33.2 oz.	All months	2.5 oz = 83¢	Strike prices at $10 per oz.
SILVER					
Futures	Comex	5,000 oz.	Current month, next two months and Jan/Mar/May/July/Sept/Dec.	10/100¢ oz = $5	$4,000
	CBT	5,000 oz.	Feb/Mar/Apr/May/June/Aug/Oct/Dec.	10/100¢ oz = $5	2,500
	CBT	1,000 oz.	Feb/Mar/Apr/May/June/Aug/Oct/Dec.	10/100¢ oz = $1	500
	MidAm	1,000 oz. (NY contract)	Current month, next two months and Jan/Mar/May/July/Sept/Dec.	10/100¢ oz = $1	800
	MidAm	1,000 oz. (Chicago contract)	Feb/Mar/Apr/May/June/Aug/Oct/Dec.	10/100¢ oz = $1	800
	IMM (US Silver coins)	$5,000	Mar/June/Sept/Dec.	$2 per $1,000 bag = $10	$25,000

IMM: International Monetary Market; CBT: Chicago Board of Trade.

diamonds, art, antiques, stamps, coins, and so forth. If you enjoy them, great, but *never consider them as investments.* Their handling costs are high: at least 15% to buy and another 15% to sell. So, at best, any profit is reduced, with other costs, by about one-third: a hefty bite under any circumstances.

Worse yet, the values are volatile and are likely to soar for a few years and plummet later. With sharp timing, these fluctuations can be profitable IF you are smart, lucky and do your homework. Diamonds are a good example of the teeter-totter of almost all collectibles: a one carat, flawless, round-cut stone sold for about $1,000 in the late 1960s, as much as $60,000 in 1980 (an astounding gain) but, in early 1983, at about $13,000.

Still, if you are fascinated with the lure/romance/profit potential of rare stones, watch for financial news about partnerships such as Balance Gemstones, Inc. This group is trying to transform collectibles into securities and is seeking SEC approval for a "fund" to back gems with a certificate of authenticity from the Gemological Institute of America plus a repurchase agreement guaranteed by a major insurance company: to rebuy the stone at the original price for six years.

Collectibles should be for personal pleasure, not investments, especially pension funds where the assets should be reasonably liquid and with steady income. This was clearly spelled out by Congress that banned collectibles in IRAs and permitted them in Keoghs only when bought and managed by outside professionals. Their value will be considered as a premature distribution of fund assets and thus subject to penalties.

And if you are reluctant to follow my advice, just read aloud this comment from a professional appraiser/collector: "In the last couple of years, many investors have discovered that in their mad rush to avoid the ravages of inflation, they acquired collectibles that are now classified as junk. They are not necessarily fakes (although there are plenty of these) but the items have been doctored and thus are not saleable at a reasonable price, let alone a profit. This is especially true with coins and stamps but also applies to art and furniture. Well, if they had dealt with a reliable firm, they would not have bought 'em anyway!"

22

Guessing Games: Financial Futures and Stock Indexes

With the fast fluctuations in interest rates and the stock market, the two hottest games in Wall Street are speculating in financial futures and stock indexes. Both are promoted as "hedging vehicles to protect positions" and some professionals really do use them for such a conservative goal but, for most individuals, they are just another way to make . . . or lose . . . a fast buck. To be successful: all you have to do is to correctly predict the short/intermediate-term trend!

The major difference is that financial futures involve debt issues while the new indexes are tied to stock market averages or small groups of stocks. With tiny margins—as small as $800 for the financial futures—you can control up to $1 million of loans. If interest rates shift just ½ of 1%, you can double your money . . . or lose most of your investment.

The margins with the indexes are slightly higher but the swings can be faster and wider. These packaged pools can give you the greatest rollercoaster ride of all. On one Friday afternoon, the S&P Index futures dropped $325 per contract on news of an unexpected decline in the money

supply. Two minutes later, when the FRB cut the discount rate, their price zipped up $675 per contract.

Financial Futures

Basically, financial futures are a new form of commodities contracts widely used with wheat, corn, silver, etc. They are standardized packages of debt securities whose prices move with the cost of money: *up* when the interest rate falls; *down* when it rises. With stock index futures, the base is the stock market itself.

Major investors, such as banks, insurance companies and pension fund managers, use financial futures to hedge: buying one contract while simultaneously selling another. Or vice versa. As businessmen, they prefer static, predictable assets and rates of return. By hedging, they protect their positions because what they gain (or lose) in the cash market will be offset by the loss (profit) in the futures market.

As with commodities, someone has to take the opposite

side of the contract. This may be a speculator seeking a quick profit by buying or selling short, according to his view of the cost of money in the days or months ahead.

Financial futures is a professional's game. *Only 20% of the transactions are profitable.* True, the profits can be big and quick but the losses can be bigger and quicker. As one veteran trader warns, "You can make enough money in the morning to send your kids to college. But in the afternoon, you can lose enough to force you to think of mortgaging the house."

When you guess right (and don't let anyone kid you that success is based solely on skill), you can do well, but all futures are a zero-sum game: for every winner, there's a loser. In the stock market, you will usually be moving with the majority. If the market goes up, nearly everyone wins. If it goes down, nearly everyone loses. But not with futures! And while research is important and valuable, dealing in financial futures is a *guessing* game.

Price movements. So we'll all be on the same wavelength, here are some basic data on quotations and price movements of financial futures:

• Prices for contracts for T-bills and CDs are quoted in basis points: increments of $\frac{1}{100}$ of 1%. Thus, a rise or fall of one basis point is $100. Since these contracts are quoted on a 90-day basis, divide by 4 to get $25. Normal daily price limits: $\frac{25}{100}$ of 1% (25 basis points) or $625 per contract above or below the previous day's settlement price. Price limits do not apply to trading in contracts for delivery during a specific month or after the first notice day for deliveries during that month.

• Prices of Treasury bond and Ginnie Mae futures are quoted in $\frac{1}{32}$ point per 100 points: $31.25 per contract. Normal daily limits on price movement: $\frac{24}{32}$ of a point ($750 per contract) above or below the previous day's settlement price.

Examples: In June, Swinging Sal believes that interest rates will drop. She buys 10 futures contracts on five-year, 8% Treasury notes (traded in units of $100,000) at $95\frac{16}{32}$ each ($95,500) and puts up $9,000 margin ($900 per contract). This is more than the exchange required but what her broker demanded.

Sal's right. By September, the cost of money is down so the price of the notes is up to $99\frac{16}{32}$ ($99,500). She sells for a $40,000 profit ($4,000 per contract) minus commissions and fees.

In October Sal decides that interest rates will rise soon. At this time, those five-year, 8% Treasury note contracts are trading at $98\frac{8}{32}$ ($98,075). She sells 10 contracts short, again with $9,000 margin.

Her guess is good. By late November, interest rates edge up and the value of the futures contract falls to $93\frac{24}{32}$ ($93,075). Sal covers her position for a gross profit of $50,000, then takes off for Europe!

Obviously, these successes reflect both luck and skill. If Sal had been wrong and interest rates had moved opposite to her projection—because of unexpected world or domestic events—she would have had to come up with more margin and, eventually, sell at a whopping loss. But, by now, Sal was sharp enough to set up stop-loss orders and take quick losses. She knows that some 75% to 80% of all trades are losers!

Hedging

Keeping in mind that the basis market relies on professionals, here's an example cited by the Chicago Board of Trade in its promotional literature. The figures are a bit outdated but, these days, you never can tell about interest rates! As this is not a speculation, margin is not a factor. But someone has to be on the opposite side of every transaction.

CASH	FUTURES
Jan. 15	
Owns $5 million 14.5% T-notes due 5/5/89	SELL 71 June ten-year Treasury futures @ 75-21
Current Price: 107-08 (yield 13.13%)	
90-day T-bills (10.85%)	
April 15	
Sell $5 million T-notes @ 99-24 (yield 14.54%)	BUY 71 June ten-year Treasury futures @ 70-22
90-day T-bills (14.80%)	
RESULTS	
Holding T-notes for this three-month period cost the portfolio $375,000 (107-08 minus 99-24)	A gain in the futures position of $352,781 (75-21 minus 60-22 × 31.25) reduces the opportunity loss to $22,218.
The portfolio manager was able to pick up 395 basis points in the purchase of T-bills, for a gain, in interest income, of $49,375.	

Mr. Pension Manager holds a large portion of a fund's assets in 10-year Treasury notes. At this time, long-term interest rates exceed short-term ones, so he will get a higher return by holding to maturity. But Mr. PM looks for a relative rise in short-term returns. When this happens, the yields on T-bills will rise faster than those of the 10-year. And, he knows, the prices of both will fall. He has two choices: (1) Shift to shorter maturities as soon as rates begin to rise to avoid losses in the T-note portfolio. This will mean that he will have to accept lower yields on new purchases since the yield curve is positive (the indicator he uses to project a rise in short-term rates). Or (2) wait until yields on both bills and notes rise further as anticipated, at some future point, when the yield curve becomes negative. This would mean a loss on the sale of the 10-year notes.

Here's the strategy as explained by the Chicago Board of Trade: to protect the principal value and holding return on the long-terms while waiting for short-term rates to rise above long-terms, he sells 10-year Treasury futures. As interest rates rise, the loss on the cash Treasury note portfolio is offset by a profit in the futures position. The hedge enables him to sell his notes, later, at a higher effective price.

The hedge used 71 contracts based on a conversion factor of 1.4269 for a 14.50% coupon due in 9.5 years. If the hedge had been maintained for an extended period, it would have been necessary to reduce the amount of contracts used as the maturity of the T-note decreased.

In this case, the entire loss was not offset, due to a weakening basis, or negative move, in the difference between the cash and futures prices: here, the basis moved from 31–19 ($31^{19}/_{32}$) to 29–02 ($29^{3}/_{32}$).

Spreads

Usually, speculators trade financial futures by going long on one position and short on another with both contracts due in the same month. But you can also use spreads: buying one contract month and selling another. This technique is used when there's an abnormal relationship between the yields and, thus, the prices of two contracts with different maturities. These situations don't come often but when they do can be mighty rewarding because the gains will come from a restoration of the normal spread.

Example: Eagle-Eye notes that June T-bonds are selling at 80–11 (each $^{1}/_{32}$ of 1% equals $3.125 of a standard $100,000 contract) and that September's are at 81–05. The basis for quotations is an 8% coupon and 15-year maturity.

Having a keen memory, EE decides that this $^{26}/_{32}$ difference is out of line with normal pricing. He *sells* the September contract and *buys* the June one. In a couple of weeks, prices begin to normalize: the September contract edges up to 81–08 and the June one surges to 80–24. Now he starts to cash in: he loses $^{3}/_{32}$ ($93.75) on the September contract but gains $^{13}/_{32}$ ($406.25) on the June one: $312.50 profit minus commission. With his 10 contracts, EE pays for a Florida holiday.

Follow Strict Rules

If you have money you can afford to lose, time enough to keep abreast of developments in the financial world, strong nerves and a trustworthy, knowledgeable broker, trading in financial futures may be rewarding and, surely, will be exciting. Of course, if you're involved with substantial holdings, you probably are already familiar with hedging so can stick to protective contracts. Otherwise, follow these rules:

• *Make dry runs on paper for several months.* Interest rates change slowly. Pick different types of financial futures each week and keep practicing until you get a feel of the market and risks and, over at least one week, chalk up more winners than losers.

• *Buy long when you look for a drop in interest rates.* With lower yields, the prices of all contracts will rise.

• *Sell short when you expect a higher cost of money.* This will force down the value of the contracts and you can cover your position at a profit.

• *Set a strategy and stick to it.* Don't try to mix contracts until you are comfortable and making money.

• *Set stop and limit orders, not market orders.* A market order is executed immediately at the best possible price. A stop order, to buy or to sell at a given price, becomes a market order when that price is touched. A limit order is the maximum price at which to buy and the minimum at which to sell.

• *Buy two good-luck charms.* Even the best traders guess wrong now and then. They may have a long winning streak but there are too many unforeseeable factors that can force unexpected shifts. No matter how intense your research, there will be occasions when your timing will be wrong . . . and that's essential for successful trading.

Stock Index Futures

These are the latest "opportunities" served up by the Welcome Wagoneers of Wall Street. *Surprise:* at least one ma-

FINANCIAL FUTURES

CONTRACT	EXCHANGE	UNIT EXCHANGE	MARGIN PER CONTRACT Hedgers	Speculators
DEBT INSTRUMENTS				
Bank CDs	I.M.M.	$1 million	$1,500	$1,500
Eurodollars	I.M.M.	1 million	1,500	1,500
Ginnie Maes	C.B.T.	100,000	1,500	2,000
Treasury Bills	I.M.M.	1 million	1,500	1,500
Treasury Bonds	C.B.T.	100,000	1,500	2,000
Treasury Notes	C.B.T.	100,000	1,500	1,500
FOREIGN CURRENCY				
British Pounds	I.M.M.	25,000 pds.	1,500	1,500
Canadian Dollars	I.M.M.	100,000 (U.S.)	900	900
Japanese Yen	I.M.M.	12.5 mil. yen	1,500	1,500
Swiss Francs	I.M.M.	125,000 francs	2,000	2,000
German Marks	I.M.M.	125,000 marks	1,500	1,500
STOCK INDEXES				
NYSE Index	N.Y.F.E.	Index X $500	1,500	3,500
S&P 500 Index	C.M.E.	Index X $500	3,000	6,000
Value Line Index	K.C.B.T.	Index X $500	2,500	6,500

I.M.M. = International Monetary Market; C.B.T. = Chicago Board of Trade; N.Y.F.E. = New York Futures Exchange; C.M.E. = Chicago Mercantile Exchange; K.C.B.T. = Kansas City Board of Trade.

jor brokerage firm advises their registered representatives to limit trading in these futures to individuals with net worths of $100,000 exclusive of home and life insurance.

These are futures contracts based on standard stock market averages. In theory, these indexes are to be used to hedge large portfolios directly or through options; in practice, aided by the roaring bull market, they have become popular speculations because: (*a*) the margins are low, roughly 10%, so a 10% jump in an Index can double your money; (*b*) traders soon discovered that the prices of indexes do not always move parallel to the stock market.

Currently, these are the contracts available:

• **Standard & Poor's 500:** stocks of 400 industrials, 40 financial companies, 40 utilities and 20 transportations issues . . . all listed on the NYSE. They are weighted by market value. Contracts are valued at 500 times the index: at 160: $80,000. They are traded on the Chicago Mercantile Exchange. Generally, this is the Index favored by big hitters as contracts are extremely liquid and it's widely used to measure institutional performance.

• **New York Futures Exchange (NYFE):** an index of all common stocks (about 1,525 issues) traded on the Big Board, weighted by market value. Contracts are also valued at 500 times the index: at 95, $47,500. Contracts are traded on a unit of the NYSE. These are popular with retail traders because of the small size of the contracts, so that margin is less.

• **Value Line Futures:** an equally weighted geometric index of about 1,700 stocks, actively traded on NYSE, AMEX and OTC. Here again, the contracts are quoted at 500 times the Index: at 200: $100,000. This tends to be difficult to trade because it's a thin market on the small Kansas City Board of Trade. There are standard delivery months: March, June, September and December. A 1-point change is worth $500. Each "tick" or move is $5/100$ of a point or $25 up or down.

Margins run about 10% so the speculator can control $50,000 to $100,000 worth of stocks for about $5,000: in cash, collateral such as interest-bearing T-bills, or a letter of credit from a bank. There's no physical delivery. Nothing changes hands except cash.

Each account is marked to market at the end of each trading day, so after a down session, the trader must come up with more margin: i.e., if the contract value dips 1.15 points, he will have to add $575 before the next day's opening or be sold out and billed for the shortfall.

There are no daily limits for NYFE but, with both S&P and Value Line, position limits are 5,000 contracts and daily price limits 500 points ($2,500).

N.B. All contracts have major tax benefits: as commodities future, there's no holding period for capital gains and the tax rate is 32%!

Cutting the Risks

Here are digests of examples cited by *Business Week:*

Basic bull: In June, you are confident that market will be higher by year-end. *Buy* a December contract at 120.60 ($60,300 worth of stocks); $6,000 margin. By December expiration date, index is 129.58, so your profit is 8.98 points or $4,490.

Basic bear: In June, you look for a down market. Sell short one December contract at 120.60. If you're wrong and the market rises 10%, you're out $4,490 plus commission. But if you were right and the market fell 10%, your profit would be $4,490 less costs.

Anticipatory hedge. Again in June, you are optimistic, so you tell your broker you plan to buy some stocks in July with proceeds from a matured CD. Buy a September futures contract at 119.50 ($59,750 stock value). This qualifies as a hedge position so you put up $2,500. By July, the stocks you like are up $6,000 but the September index contract is up 13 points so you're in great shape.

Short hedge #1. You have a $60,000 portfolio selected for the long haul. But you're nervous so sell short one September index contract at 119.50 to provide insurance. By mid September, the index is up to 120 so you didn't need the protection. You accept the $250 loss and smile when you see the portfolio value is up $1,000.

Short hedge #2. You like Big Blue Chip but fear the market. Buy $60,000 worth of BBC and sell a September index contract short at 119.50. At expiration, the index is down to 106.02 so you cover with a profit of $6,740. But BBC stock is down only $3,000, so you're ahead by $3,740 (not counting commissions).

Other guidelines:

• *Follow the trend.* If the price of the index was higher than the day before which, in turn, was higher that the previous day, go long. If reverse, sell short.

• *Set stop-loss prices at 3 points below cost.* If they are too close, one erratic move can stop you out at a loss even though the market may resume its uptrend soon.

• *Recognize the role of the professionals.* To date, most contracts have been traded by brokerage houses active in arbitrage and spreads and in hedging large block positions. Only a handful of institutional managers have done more than experiment. So the amateur is competing with top professionals with plenty of capital, no commissions to pay

STOCK INDEX FUTURES

EXCHANGE	UNDERLYING INDEX	CONTRACT MONTHS	CONTRACT SIZE	MINIMUM FLUCTUATION	DAILY LIMIT	MINIMUM INITIAL MARGIN
Chicago Merc.	S&P 500	3-6-9-12	500 X S&P index	0.05 pts. = $25	5 pts. = $2500	6,000
NY Futures	NYSE Comp.	3-6-9-12	500 X NYSE index	0.05 pts. = $25	None	3,500
"	NYSE Financial	3-6-9-12	1,000 X index	0.01 pts. = $10	None	8,500

SOURCE: Commodities Magazine

and in positions to get the latest information and to make quick decisions.

• *Study the price spreads.* Contracts for distant months are more volatile. In a strong market, buy far-out contracts and short nearby months; in a weak market, buy the closer months and short the distant ones.

• *Be mindful that dividends can disort prices.* In heavy payout months, these discrepancies can be significant.

• *Use a hedge only when your portfolio* approximates that of the index: roughly a minimum of $250,000 (very rarely does a major investor buy only 100 shares of a stock). In most cases, any single portfolio has little resemblance to that of the index.

Example: Neighbor Ned, who owned about $500,000 in 20 stocks in 8 industries, felt that the market was due for a temporary tumble. Intrigued by the idea of hedging, he sold 8 S&P Index Futures at 100, putting down $48,000 in T-bills (reserve account). Ned was wrong. The market jumped over 10% so he lost $40,000: $5,000 per contract . . . in CASH.

Meantime, his narrow list of stocks edged up only 3%: a PAPER gain of $15,000 so his net loss was $25,000.

If his portfolio had been a mirror of S&P, it should have risen $50,000, more than enough to offset the $40,000 loss. *Hedges with stock indexes seldom make sense for individual investors.*

OPTIONS ON FUTURES: T-Bond Contract

Executed in February when June T-bond contract was quoted at 72-05 (72 5/8) with these quotations for options

| BOND PRICE | QUOTATION IN | |
	Points	Dollars
CALLS		
72	2-06	$2,093.75
74	1-20	1,312.50
76	0-46	718.75
PUTS		
68	0-30	$ 468.75
70	0-61	953.13
72	1-54	1,843.75

SOURCE: Stanley W. Angrist, Forbes Magazine

Options on Futures

There are also options on most financial futures contracts and stock indexes. These are for professionals and real swingers. If you ride a strong market trend, you can make a lot of money for a small outlay and rapid fluctuations; if you do your homework, you can use hedges successfully; but *use options only when you have plenty of time and money.* It's easy to con yourself into thinking you're a genius (in three months or sooner) but unless you bank half your profits, you will lose money over a period of time if only because of the commissions.

Options on debt issues. As with all types of securities/contracts, a *call* is the right to buy at a preset price, usually before a preset date; a *put* is the mandate to sell the same

item. The cost of the option is the premium and varies with the exercise price and time frame.

Since the values of debt issues move opposite to interest rates, you think backward with these options. Compared to futures contracts, they are more volatile but less expensive. The maximum loss is the premium. Here's how they are quoted/traded:

Options on T-bills/bonds reflect the discount yield. With an 8% yield, the T-bill price basis would be 92 ($9,200). The option might trade at 93, 100 basis points away from the strike price.

The premiums are quoted at intervals of $5 each in trade lingo, as follows: "6 to 10, 25 up, last 7" for calls offered at 10 basis points of $50 each. This means that someone is bidding 6 ($30); there are 25 calls available on either side; the last trade was 7 basis points ($35) an option. If interest rates fall the price of the call will rise. If they remain stable, the price of the call will dwindle to zero because all options, with set expiration dates, are wasting assets.

To get an idea of how options differ from futures contracts, study the box and remember that these illustrate profitable trading which, over the years, represents a minority of all transactions.

HOW OPTIONS FUTURES ARE QUOTED

BOND PRICE		CALLS
72	2-06	$2,093.75
74	1-20	1,312.50
76	0-46	718.75
		PUTS
68	0-30	468.75
70	0-61	953.13
72	1-54	1,843.75

Options in Action

Here's how futures and options compare as described in *Commodities* magazine: December 1982 T-bond futures at $72\frac{2}{32}$; options at strike price of 72.

October 1: Projection: lower interest rates so higher bond futures prices. Choices:

(1) Buy T-bond futures at $72\frac{2}{32}$: margin: $3,000.

(2) Buy call option at 2–03: $2,000 plus $\frac{3}{64}$ or $1,000: $2,046.88.

October 4: Futures down to $70\frac{16}{32}$ so need more margin. Call down to $1\frac{20}{64}$ ($1,312.50); no margin call.

October 13: Futures up to $78\frac{3}{32}$: + $6,000 profit. Call to $6\frac{15}{64}$ ($6,234.38): +$4,187.50 Less than futures but no margin call.

October 1: Projection: higher interest rates add lower futures prices. Choices:

(1) Sell futures at $72\frac{2}{32}$.

(2) Buy put option @ $1\frac{59}{64}$ ($1,921.88).

Futures: after early gain, loss of over $6,000 by October 13.

Put: value up to $2\frac{46}{64}$ ($2,718.75) at outset but calls to $\frac{10}{64}$ ($156.25) by 13th. Decline less than $6,000 for futures but need more margin and still in market.

Hedge Possibilities

Options provide excellent opportunities to set up hedges IF you carefully plan your strategy and understand the risks and rewards. Here's an example cited by Stanley Angrist in *Forbes* (see table):

In March, the June T-bond contract is selling at 52–05 (72⅝). Calls, at 72, 74 and 76 are quoted at premiums of 2–06, 1–20 and 0–46, respectively; puts, at 68, 70 and 72 are available at 0–30, 0–61 and 1–54. Wally thinks that the market will remain stable so makes these paper projections of hedges with a margin of $3,000.

Sell June 72 call	$2,093.75
Sell June 72 put	1,843.75
Total income	$3,937.50

If the T-bond is still worth 72 at June strike date, both options will expire worthless so Wally has an extra $3,937.50 minus commissions.

Sell June 74 call	$1,312.50
Sell June 70 put	953.13
Total income	$2,265.63

This is less risky, and less profitable, because both options will expire worthless if the last day price is between 70 and 74.

Sell June 76 call	$ 718.75
Sell June 68 call	468.75
Total income	$1,187.50

If final price is between 68 and 76, Wally will do OK. He swaps a lower income for a broader price range.

Stock Indexes. With these, options create a synthetic position in stocks at a fraction of the cash outlay that would be required to buy the stocks outright or with 50% margin. Again, if you're bullish, you buy calls and sell puts. Vice versa when bearish.

The hottest plays are on special stock indexes such as the CBOE consisting of 100 major industrials or AMEX Major Market Index based on 20 Blue Chips: American Express, A.T.&T., Coca-Cola, Dow Chemical, DuPont, Exxon, Eastman Kodak, General Electric, General Motors, IBM, Johnson & Johnson, Merck, MMM, Mobil, Philip Morris, P&G, Sears, Standard Oil of California and U.S. Steel.

This last is a simple, unweighted averaged calculated as follows: total the price of the 20 stocks, divide by 10 to get the index price; multiply by 100 to determine the value of the option. On opening day, the closing value of this index was $1,228.80 so the stated price was 122.88. This was up 1.57 ($157) for the day. Strike prices are above and below the nearest break-even price: 115, 120, 125, etc. Expiration dates in three of four months: January, April, July and October.

With all options on indexes, settlements are made in cash. When the option is exercised, the holder receives the difference between the exercise price and the closing index on the date the option is exercised. *Watch out:* this can be far from the price the day the assignment notice is received. A hedge can lose on both the long and short side!

Dangers with Financial Futures

At the risk of being boring, let me reemphasize some of the dangers of trading financial futures and indexes and/or options thereon. These markets lack many of the safeguards of stocks and bonds:

• **No ban on inside information.** With stocks, executives and brokers who use inside information to anticipate or cause stock movements are subject to severe penalties and even jail. Futures traders have no such restraints.

• **Limited public disclosure.** Investors who own 5% or

OPTIONS ON STOCK INDEXES

EXCHANGE INDEX	CONTRACT MONTHS	SIZE	STRIKE PRICE INCREMENTS	POSITION LIMIT	MINIMUM PREMIUM TICS	MARGIN (BUYER)
AMEX Index	3-6-9-12	100 X Index divisor	Below 100: 5 pts. Above 100: 10 pts.	$40,000 contracts	Under $3: 1/16; over $3: 1/8	Premium + 10%
CBOE 100	3-6-9-12	500 X Index	5 pts.	$300 million	Under $3: 1/16; over $3: 1/8	Premium + 10% of value
NYSE Index	3-6-9-12	100 X Index	5 pts.; utilities: 2 pts.	$300 million	Under $3: 1/16; over $3: 1/8	

OPTIONS ON STOCK INDEX FUTURES

EXCHANGE	UNDERLYING CONTRACT	STRIKE PRICE INCREMENTS	MINIMUM FLUCTUATION	EXPIRATION
Chicago Merc. Exchange	S&P 500	5 pts.	0.05 pts. = $25	
NY Futures Ex.	NYSE Composite	2 pts.	0.05 pts. = $25	2 days before futures expiration

Options have same dates, terms, size, limits, etc. as underlying futures contracts.

SOURCE: COMMODITIES Magazine

Commissions. You pay regular commission, taxes and fees on the initial short sale and subsequent purchase of the stock. If you deliver your own stock, you save the buying costs.

Interest. There are no interest charges on the margin account.

Premiums. Once in a while, if the shorted stock is in great demand, your broker may have to pay a premium for borrowing, usually $1 per 100 shares per business day.

Dividends. All dividends on shorted stock must be paid to the owner. That's why it's best to concentrate on warrants and stocks that pay low or no dividends.

Rights/stock dividends. Because you are borrowing the stock, you are not entitled to the use of rights or the receipt of stock dividends.

If you know or suspect that a company is going to pass or decrease its payout, you can get an extra bonus by selling short. The price of the stock is almost sure to drop. *But be careful.* The decline may be too small to offset the commissions.

Sales price. All short sales must be made on the uptick or zero tock: i.e., the last price of the stock must be higher than that of the previous sale. If the stock is at 80, you cannot sell short when it drops to 79⅞ but must wait for a higher price: 80⅛ or more. Or with a zero tick, the last two sales must have been at the same price.

Taxes. All gains or losses on all short sales are short-term and thus taxable at the highest personal income-tax rate. But the profit on owned stock against which the short sale is written can become long-term when the shares are held over 12 months.

Candidates for Short Sales

In choosing stocks for short selling, professionals use computers to analyze economic, industry and corporate factors. Amateurs must rely on simpler indicators such as insider transactions, volatility and relative strength as measured against the overall market or an industry group. Most of this basic information is available in financial publications but, usually, you'll do better when you make your own calculations.

As a rule of thumb, the best candidates for short selling are: (1) Stocks that led the bull market surge in volume and percentage gains. (2) Has-been glamour stocks that have reached their peaks and are being sold heavily by institutions. Once out of favor, such stocks can fall far and fast . . . which is just what the short seller wants. (3) Stocks that have already begun to decline. They've shown their weakness and have little or no sponsorship.

More specific criteria used by professionals include:

Insider transactions disclose the number of corporate officers, directors and major shareholders who bought or sold stock in the previous few months. The assumption is that when the number of insiders selling exceeds the number buying, the stock is at a high level and these knowledgeable people believe a decline is due.

It's best to wait for reports of at least two quarters to confirm the trend.

Volatility. The Zweig Security Screen, an investment advisory letter, measures volatility by *beta,* the historical relationship between the price movement of the stock and the overall market and interest rates.

Each stock has a beta number: 1.0 moves with the market; 1.5 is highly volatile (Holiday Inns, which swings 50% more than the market); 0.7 is relatively stable (General Motors, which is 30% less swinging than the stock market averages).

Relative strength with emphasis on poor performers is a calculation that takes into account the consistency and growth of earnings and whether the last quarterly earnings were lower or higher than anticipated by Wall Street. These data are available from statistical services such as *Value Line* and *Standard & Poor's Earnings Forecast,*

Selling Against the Box

This is a technique for freezing your paper profits or postponing taxes. Here's how it works:

On March 1, Dr. Mary buys 100 shares of Geewhiz Electronics at 40. By July, the stock is at 60 but the market is weakening and Dr. Mary gets nervous. She sells short 100 shares of GW with her own shares as collateral.

• If the price of GW stays around 60, she will lock in her gains minus commissions. She will sell the stock at 60 for a $20 per share profit: the 60 sale price minus the 40 cost.

• If the price of GW rises to 70, she'll still do OK. She delivers her own stock. She won't make that extra 10-point profit (from 60 to 70), but she will still have a $2,000 gain: the difference between her 40 cost and the 60 selling price.

• If the price of GW drops to 50, Dr. Mary has two choices:

1. To cover her short position by purchasing new shares. She will break even because her 10-point profit on the short sale will be offset by a 10-point loss on the value of the stock. Her net will be cut by the commissions.

2. To cover her short position with the shares she owns. She makes $1,000 profit on the short sale but has a smaller profit on the stocks she owns: $1,000 versus the $2,000 gain she had before.

Selling against the box is a favorite year-end tactic. The short sale brings in immediate cash, and the profit (or loss) is deferred until the short position is covered the following year or even two or three years hence.

But be careful:

• Commissions can eat up profits rapidly.

• Once the trend of the stock turns up, it is more likely to continue to rise than to fall. You may postpone some taxes, but you may also find that your year-end profit, from a lower-than-sold price, will be narrowed or eliminated.

• Under the wash sale rule (see chapter on tax rules), there will be no tax loss if the short sale is covered by buying the same or identical securities within 31 days after the date of the original short sale.

• With gains, the taxes can be long-term when the shares are held for more than 12 months. This can be tricky so check with your registered representative. The holding period for the owned stock stops when the short sale is made and begins again when the short sale is covered by a stock purchase. Thus, to qualify for long-term capital gains, a stock must be held for one year—i.e., nine months before the short sale is made plus 91 days after the short position is covered.

which report estimates of earnings made by analysts of major brokerage firms and advisory services.

When corporate earnings are lower than the estimates, the stock is a candidate for short selling. When they are higher than projected, the stock should not be sold short.

Avoid: (1) Thin issues where there is a small number of shares outstanding. A little buying can boost their price so you can be caught in a short squeeze and have to pay to borrow stock. (2) Stocks with big short interest. They have already been pressured downward. When the shorts are covered, their prices will rise. (3) Shares of low-debt, asset-rich companies. They can be takeover candidates, especially if they sell at substantial discounts from asset value and have hefty cash assets.

Case History

Here's an example of how a professional makes money with short selling, as reported by Andrew Kern of Avatar Associates. The transactions took place in the erratic market of mid-1982. Note that Kern reports losses as well as gains.

SELLING SHORT

SHARES/ STOCK	SOLD SHORT Date	Price	COVERED Date	Price	PROFIT/LOSS (before costs)
500 Frigitronics	8/9	12 7/8	8/24	13	(38)
300 Hilton Hotels	8/5	32	8/24	30	600
300 IC Industries	8/6	25 1/4	8/24	25 1/2	(170)
100 IC Industries	8/9	25 5/8			
300 Key Pharma.	8/6	28 1/2	8/24	29 1/4	(225)
400 Tony Lama	8/5	26 1/2	8/24	19 3/8	2,850
			Net before costs		+$3,017

SOURCE: Andrew Kern, Avatar Associates

DOs and DON'Ts for Short Selling

DON'T buck the trend. Avoid short sales unless both the major and the intermediate trends of the market are down. The idea is to make the market work for you.

You may be convinced that an individual stock is vastly overpriced, but unless you have great patience, do not sell short until there is clear evidence of a fall in the market and in your stock specifically.

DO short well-known stocks in unpopular industries. When institutional investors sour on any group, they get out at any price. This constant pressure sparks more selling and the decline accelerates. Within the groups, look for stocks of companies that historically, as shown on charts, have had sharp, long swings, down and up: *with oils,* Occidental Petroleum and Tesoro Petroleum; *with conglomerates:* Gulf & Western and Litton Industries; *with electronics:* National Semiconductor Corp. and Compugraphic Corp.; *with retailers:* Genesco, Inc. and Safeway Stores.

DO short warrants (if you can find 'em). They are low priced, volatile and pay no dividends.

DO be patient. Wait for the stock to top out and start to decline. You may have to hang in there for several months but when you are convinced that your drop-down analysis is correct, keep the faith. Forget about intermediate market rallies and use charts and trendlines to check past patterns. As long as the major trend . . . of the market or your stock—is down, hold your short position. At the outset, set a target price, or when you are experienced, get ready to cover when there's a reversal of the down trend that is confirmed by other indicators.

DO short a stock after it has rallied after an initial downswing. This is usually a last gasp. But remember that you can sell short on on an uptick so the stock price must go higher to permit the short sale.

DON'T short stocks with a large short interest (equal to three days of normal trading). Every short seller is a potential buyer. If there are too many short positions, the stock can rally sharply when the professionals start to cover their positions. But watch out when the stock is involved in a takeover as arbitrageurs can take over.

A high and rising short interest usually indicates that investor bearishness is being overdone and that the market is ready for a rise. When short sellers fear higher prices, they run for cover and buy heavily, thus boosting the market.

A low and shrinking short interest warns that investor bullishness is excessive, that there's little short selling and that a market top is approaching. Here again, there are many indications that the short sellers are almost always wrong. *Explanation:* Many traders have different objectives than investors.

Short-interest figures of the NYSE and AMEX stocks are published midmonthly in *The Wall Street Journal* and *Barron's.*

DON'T sell short at the market when the stock price is heading down. Place a limit order at the lowest price at which you are willing to sell short.

DO set protective prices. *On the upside,* 10% or more above the sale price—with flexibility for volatile stocks; with a stock bought at 50, at 55 or 57½. *On the downside,* below your sale price: 15% if you are conservative, 20% if you are aggressive (42½ and 40, respectively).

Be careful with stop orders. You may be picked off if the stock rises to the precise point of the stop order and then declines. To maximize your profits, move that stop price with the decline: to 40½ or 38 when the stock falls to 45.

DO rely on the odd-lot selling indicator. This is available from several technical advisory services or can be set up on your own. It is calculated by dividing the total odd-lot sales into the odd-lot short sales and charting a 10-day moving average. When the indicator stays below 1.0 for several months, it's time to consider selling short. When it's down to .50, start selling.

Conversely, when the indicator rises above 1.0, do not sell short and cover your positions. And if you hesitate, cover all shorts when a one-day reading bounces above 3.0.

DON'T short several stocks at once . . . until you are experienced. Start with one stock and if you make money, you'll have a base to cover future losses.

DO short when insiders, such as stock exchange members and specialists, are active. They usually sell short before major declines and buy ahead of big rallies. Member short selling should exceed 85% of total round-lot short sales. Cover when that figure is below 60%.

Similarly, go short when short sales, by specialists, exceed 65% of total round-lot short sales; cover when this is below 40%.

DO cover positions on weakness. And always cover when, as far as you can determine, all bearish news is out and the stocks are down to a level that affords a fair profit. And always cover at market. Once you make a decision, act.

DO concentrate on shorting stocks on which options can be written.

Hedging with Calls

When you sell short, there's always the danger that your calculations are wrong or that something unexpected will boost the price of the stock. To limit your liability, buy out-of-the money calls. Since the option permits you to cover your position, you will protect yourself in that your loss will be less than it might have been.

Example: Swinging Sam shorts 100 shares of HTH at 19 and buys a call exercisable at 20 for $200. If the stock falls to 15 and Sam covers, his $400 profit will be cut to $200 because the call will be worthless. But if the stock rises to

25 before the option exercise date, he covers for a loss of $600 but can sell the call for at least 5 ($500) so his loss is only $100—not counting commissions.

To show you how to calculate potential profits of a short sale with a CV preferred, follow this table. This technique is explained in greater detail in Chapter 10.

CALCULATING POTENTIAL PROFITS OF SHORT SALE

If common's price (now 15)		Goes up 50%	Stays Same	Goes down 50%
1.	Common stock	22½	15	7½
2.	Convertible preferred	26¾	19	14¼
3.	Common gain (loss)	(5,250)	0	5,250
4.	CV preferred gain (loss)	7,750	0	(4,750)
5.	Subtotal (Lines 3 + 4)	2,500	0	500
6.	Dividend on CV preferred	1,100	1,100	1,100
7.	Commissions	(500)	(500)	(500)
8.	Net gain (loss), lines 5,6,7,8	3,100	600	1,100
9	% return (line 9 divided by investment of $19,000	16.3%	3.2%	5.8%
10.	Margin interest on $9,500 @12%	(1,140)	(1,140)	(1,140)
11.	Net gain (loss) using margin (Line 8 minus 10)	1,960	(540)	40
12	% return when using margin (line 11 divided by $9,500)	20.6%	(negative)	4.2%

24

How to Profit from Forecasting and Patterns

To paraphrase the wisdom of J. P. Morgan, "The only sure thing about the stock market is that it will fluctuate." Over the short term, these changes in value reflect real or imagined fears or hopes triggered by temporary developments/news: international tensions, oil prices, rise/fall of the value of major currencies, quarterly earning of a major corporation and, most important, the interest rate. Short-term shifts can be accurately predicted. They are significant primarily to speculators. They are more annoying than meaningful to investors.

Long-term trends, however, usually follow established patterns. Some of these may not be clear until they are well under way but there are areas where actions can be forecast with reasonable accuracy and utilized to add profits and

reduce losses. For the long-term investor, they are most beneficial in timing both buying and selling. For the trader, they are useful in making or postponing decisions.

Patterns should never be taken as gospel, especially in the erratic type of markets that have been occurring lately. There have been major changes in the American economy so that forces that were powerful in the past may not be so important today. Still, in the stock market, past is prologue—most of the time.

Traditionally, December has been an *up* month but in 1979 and 1981, as the result of political and economic troubles, the market was down. Over the years, September has been down more often than up but in 1982, the market was roaring ahead. Before you make a major commitment,

MONTHLY ADVANCES AND DECLINES IN THE DJIA SINCE 1897

MONTH	NUMBER OF TIMES UP	DOWN
January	52	33
February	39	46
March	50	35
April	46	39
May	42	43
June	42	43
July	53	32
August *	57	27
September *	38	46
October *	44	40
November *	50	34
December	61	24

* Market closed in 1914

SOURCE: Dow Jones & Co.

take a look at the seasonal patterns and, if there's no rush, wait for a month where, historically, the odds for an up-move are with you.

From 1897 through 1982, the DJIA rose in 574 months and fell in 442. That's a favorable 56% on the upside. But monthly figures can be deceptive because one day can make a major difference in the month-end average.

Obviously, the same forces do not apply at all times but the shifts appear to be the result of: (1) in January, a heavy flow of year-end dividends and bonuses into the market; (2) the drain of income tax payments reflected in the frequent lows in May; (3) the summertime optimism often sparked by anticipation of a pickup of business in the fall; (4) the frequent tax selling and switching in November and December; (5) the relatively strong markets at the end of quarters (March, June, etc.), when institutional investors

buy stocks that have had a big move in the last two months. Since they seldom report when these winners were acquired, they "paper" their performance.

Monthly patterns. Based on advances, the best months to *buy* are February and September (if you can catch the low points); to *sell* are January, July, August and December.

Summer rally. Since World War II, the odds are 3–1 that the June opening prices will be lower than those in September and at year-end. And the declines during the summer are far less frequent than the advances. There were significant drops only in 1966, 1969, 1973, 1977 and 1981 and a modest decline in 1982.

The gains, while not always strong, have been more or less steady and, over the past decade, the May/June lows to the summer highs have averaged +7.5%—not bad considering this period included some dismal markets.

Year-end surge. December is almost always a good month for investors. Since 1897, the market has risen in 61 years and declined in only 24. In most years, the high has occurred around the middle of the month before year-end tax selling has started to depress prices.

January indicator. January is always a key month. Even fundamentalists place considerable faith in its forecasting ability: what happens in the first days, or better, in the full month, predicts the year's action.

Some technicians rely on market action on the first trading day but this indicator has limited value for most major investors. When there has been a disparity between the first and five day's action (about one-third of the time in the twentieth century), the five-day forecast has proved more accurate (56% vs. 44%), especially since World War II (77% vs. 23%).

If you're an eager beaver, watch that first five days in January. Its forecasting accuracy has been practically as

SUMMER RALLY

YEAR	% CHANGE: June-August
1960	− 0.3
1961	+ 4.9
1962	+ 8.0
1963	+ 4.6
1964	+ 1.3
1965	+ 3.7
1966	− 9.1
1967	+ 3.5
1968	− 0.6
1969	− 2.4
1970	+11.3
1971	+ 3.5
1972	+ 2.6
1973	− 4.7
1974	+ 0.1
1975	+ 0.1
1976	−17.4
1977	− 6.4
1978	+ 5.9
1979	+ 5.4
1980	+ 9.5
1981	−10.0
1982	+14.9

SOURCE: Dow Jones & Co.

THE JANUARY FORECAST

YEAR	S&P 500 STOCK COMPOSITE January	Year
1960	+ 0.4%	+ 8.5%
1961	+ 6.3	+23.1
1962	− 3.8	−11.8
1963	+ 4.9	+18.9
1964	+ 2.7	+13.0
1965	+ 3.3	+ 9.1
1966	+ 0.5	−13.1
1967	+ 7.8	+20.1
1968	− 4.4	+ 7.7
1969	− 0.8	−11.4
1970	− 7.6	+ 0.1
1971	+ 4.0	+10.8
1972	+ 1.8	+15.6
1973	− 1.7	−17.4
1974	− 1.0	−29.7
1975	+12.3	+31.5
1976	+11.8	+19.1
1977	− 5.1	−11.5
1978	− 6.2	+ 1.1
1979	+ 4.0	+12.0
1980	+ 7.0	+26.0
1981	− 4.6	− 9.2
1982	− 2.0	+15.0
1983	+ 3.0	

SOURCE: Wright Investors' Service

good as that of the full month. It has correctly indicated the direction of the stock market for the full year two-thirds of the time since 1900 and 80% of the time since 1945. But, in the last 10 years, its batting average has been only 60%.

The full-month January forecast has the best record: calling the shots about 70% of the time and, in comparison with the five-day forecast, has been right 75% of the years.

Note, however, that this indicator can be wrong: in 1982, the January market was down 2% but the year-end stock prices were up +15%. In 1983, the five-day forecast was a favorable +2.8% and the monthly indicator was even better: +3.0%.

But, to put this technical sense in perspective, a 3% gain for the DJIA at 1000 means a rise of only 30 points!

Special Indicators

There are scores of other signals that are used by professionals. Most of them have been reliable over a limited period of time and involve calculations too complex for amateurs. But there is one indicator that has had a 60-year perfect predictive record: the "two tumbles and a jump" concept developed by Norman G. Fosback, editor of *Market Logic*. Whenever the Federal Reserve Board (FRB) lowers one of its three policy variables—discount rate, bank reserve requirement, brokerage house margin—over any time period, stock prices will jump the next year. Two cuts signify a decisive shift toward easier credit and a bull market. According to this theory, the market will be higher in six, nine and 12 months with an average gain of +17.8%, 23% and +32%, respectively (with one exception in the Great Depression).

Fosback has recognized that the single most powerful force in the stock market is the interest rate as determined by the FRB. When the cost of money goes down, the price of securities—bonds and stocks—goes up. And vice versa when the interest rate rises. When you remember that the prime rate was 21½% in early 1981 and, recently, was down to 10½%, it's logical to look for a stronger market in the future.

Special Price Patterns

The heavy institutional activity has confused the daily market pattern, but you may be able to pick up a few extra dollars by timing your purchases or sales in line with these not-so-well documented interim market actions:

Within any month, the stock market is often a bit stronger just before the end of a month and just after the start of the new month. *Sell around the end of the month.* Institutional investors frequently place orders in anticipation of their inflow of funds on the first of the month. With increasing redemptions of mutual fund shares, this is not as regular an occurrence as in years past, but especially in active markets, this still appears to be a time to gain an extra ⅛ or ¼ of a point.

Within any week, you will do better to buy Monday morning and to sell Friday afternoon. Here again, there's been some change due to the heightened role of institu-

tions, but over a 42-year period, Merrill Analysis, Inc. found that the DJIA went up 63% of the time on the closing day of the trading week and went down 54% of the Mondays. In bear markets, there is often a long stream of blue Mondays.

One study shows that the average investment was 0.12% higher at the close on Friday than at the close on Thursday and about 0.22% lower at the close on Monday than at the close on Friday.

Within any day, the first and last hours are likely to be the most active. The opening hour volume is boosted by overnight decisions and, it appears, many investors review the market about 2 P.M. and make their moves before closing.

On the other hand, the 11 A.M. to noon, and 1 P.M. to 2 P.M. periods tend to show less price movement, regardless of which way the overall market is moving.

Another pattern that is repeated is a strong close followed by a strong opening the next day; then come buying opportunities.

And the studies show that stock prices decline in the last hour of trading as the professionals take their day's profits—or losses.

Before holidays, the market tends to rise. According to analyst Arthur A. Merrill, the DJIA rose almost two-thirds of the time before a one-day holiday and about three-quarters of the time before a three-day weekend.

Before the ex-dividend date, sell at the slightly higher price and buy back afterwards *if* you feel confident of the company's near-future prospects and want to shift profits from high-taxed dividends to low-taxed capital gains.

Bright Fridays. Over almost two decades, the market rose on 62.2% of Fridays.

Blue Mondays. Historically, the market has gone down more often than up on Mondays: 60.5% of the time, down; 39.5%, up.

Therefore, if you are in doubt about carrying a long position over the weekend, don't. Sell on Friday and consider buying on Monday.

The Best Day of the Month

The stock market rises more often (66.7%) on the second trading day of the month than on any other. A period of four consecutive trading days (the first, second, third and last) of each month outperforms all others in price rises.

According to Yale Hirsch, these "good" days occur because people operate on a monthly fiscal basis. The majority of systematic investment programs (mutual fund contractual plans, union pension funds, etc.) all tend to act at the same time.

Stock Market Forecasting

According to John C. Touhey, in his book *Stock Market Forecasting for Alert Investors,* the stock market can be forecast 80% of the time. His comments do not fully qualify as forecasts but they are close enough to be summarized here. Here are some of the checkpoints he recommends:

• **Brokers' cash accounts.** When these increase for two

consecutive months, *buy*. When they decline for the same period, *sell*.

• **Call loan interest rate.** When this declines by more than 3% in any one month, *buy*. When there are three consecutive monthly increases, *sell*.

• **Brokers' margin credit.** *Buy* when the monthly totals for the past 60 days are greater than those of the previous two months. *Sell* (or sell short) when they are less for two months.

• **Prime interest rate.** When this is lower than the yield of AAA corporate bonds, *buy*. When it is higher, be cautious and, generally, *sell* or do not buy.

William E. Donoghue, the ebullient editor and publisher of money market/mutual fund letters and books, recommends the *12 Percent Solution:* that when the yield of money market funds falls below 12%, the outlook for stocks is favorable and money should be shifted from fixed income securities/funds to equities. And when the money fund returns rise above 12%, it's time to ease savings back into money funds. Like most formulas, it works only when the investor exercises discipline!

GM Bellwether

Robert Stovall, Dean Witter Reynolds' stock market pundit and frequent guest on *Wall Street Week,* is once again enthusiastic about the General Motors Bellwether: that each new high for GM stock extends the "all clear" period four more months into the future.

Since the 1920s, Stovall avers, this signal has had an accuracy rate of about 80% and has been flawless since 1981.

The theory holds that when, in a market uptrend, if four months pass without GM shares touching a higher high, we may conclude that a reversing "early warning" or "sell" signal is being given. Conversely, in a downtrend, when four months pass without GM being sold down to a lower low, the general market is about to reverse direction and rally.

In May 1983, Stovall concluded: "GM has been in a buy mode since March 1982 . . . and now tells its fans that the entire stock market will experience no serious problems until late August."

25

How to Make the Most of Formula Plans

Formula plans are always better than the "lock-'em in the safe-deposit box" approach, usually superior to random, impulsive choices; and never as effective as thoughtful, well-planned, well-timed investing. They average out, missing maximum profits and skipping big losses. Carried out consistently (which rarely happens), most formula plans buy relatively cheap and sell relatively dear. They are safe and, if you are patient and persistent, can provide better-than-average profits. With small portfolios they usually cut losses, but with large holdings they are seldom worthwhile because the basic diversification tends to smooth out results. In all cases they remove the fun, thrill and pride of judgment-based investing.

These days when the stock market is so volatile—with the Dow moving up and down as much as 100 points in a few months—formula plans have extra appeal for long-term investors. There's no system that can guarantee that a fool cannot lose money but, when carried out, formula plans can avoid the two most common investment mistakes; buying too high and selling too low.

Some mechanical systems are worthless; others may

seem to have certain limited usefulness; and others show flashes of brilliant success at times, giving the illusion that they are the answers to the vagaries of the stock market. The difficulty comes when, flushed with success, the investor begins to believe he has found the magic formula and neglects to do his homework and use common sense.

Formula plans sound simple but, in practice, they can be difficult to maintain. Most investors cannot convince themselves to sell when things are going well and to buy when the market action is unfavorable. They will seldom achieve a big killing but they can stop you from being killed.

Types of Formula Plans

With investment by rote, there are two broad categories: (1) Ratio plans where action is taken on predetermined buy and sell signals. (2) Automatic plans where commitments are based on a specific number of dollars of predetermined time period; investing fixed dollars and/or in fixed time periods.

Ratio Plans

Ratio plans compel caution in bull markets and bravery in bear markets. They force purchases as prices rise and switches or sales as prices decline. They are best for cyclical stocks in cyclical markets because, broadly speaking, they require the investor to be cautious in bull markets and confident in bear markets. The goal—to buy low and sell high—can usually be achieved over several years but is difficult for the short term. Here are the methods most widely acclaimed by professionals:

Percentage of stocks. With this plan, you decide what percentage of your investment funds should be in stocks: 25%, 50%, 75%, etc., and how much in reserves. You then set intervals—months, quarters, years—at which you sell or buy to restore or maintain the set ratio. This must be taken regardless of the level of security prices.

Example: You start with $25,000 and plan to have 75% in quality common stocks and the remaining 25% in a money market fund (or if you have large savings, in bonds or a bond fund). You buy $18,750 in stocks and put $6,250 in a money market fund.

After six months, the market goes up so that your stocks are now worth $22,000 and the money market fund shares are up to $6,700. The total portfolio is now $28,700. To keep the set ratio, $21,525 (75% of $28,700) must be in stocks so you sell $475 worth of stocks and deposit the proceeds in the fund.

If the market goes down so that stocks are worth only $15,000 (but the money market shares are still up to $6,700), you take $1,275 from the fund and buy stocks so that the equity portion goes up to $16,275 (75% of $21,700). Now the reserve assets are down to $5,424.

You obey the formula no matter how scared you are that the market is going to drop more. With all formula plans, you must learn to regard falling prices as a chance to buy more stocks at lower prices to help make up for paper losses. That's not easy! Most investors cannot convince themselves to sell every time the portfolio is doing well and to buy each time the market is acting poorly.

An easy way to follow this system is to buy shares of a stock mutual fund. Because of its diversification, their value will bounce back faster than will a single stock (unless you pick a big winner). Conversely, the decline of the fund shares is likely to be slower than that of a single stock.

Percentage changes. With this type of formula plan, actions are taken when the value of the portfolio increases or decreases by a set percentage. The change can be the same each way or varied—e.g., sell when the value of the portfolio goes up 25%; buy when it drops 20%. You start with $2,000, equally divided between stocks and bonds. When you have a 25% gain, sell some stocks and buy bonds. Or when the value dips 20%, sell some bonds and buy stocks to get back to the original balance.

Compared to a buy-and-hold strategy, this plan provides a 5% gain. With wider swings, the profits can be greater.

For most folks, this is more interesting than practical. Most of us are not willing to accept such strictures because we believe that a rising stock (and market) will continue to go up and that a falling stock (or market) will somehow reverse its trend. But, statistically, over several market cycles, this will work out well.

A variation is the 10% approach. There are no value judgments or complicated calculations. Each week, you add up the worth of your portfolio based on the closing prices. Then, you set up a 30-day moving average (MA) (see Chapter 7). As long as the MA continues to rise or hold steady, you maintain a fully invested position.

When there's a dip of 10% or more below the previous high, sell out or, if you're cautious, sell the losers. Do not start buying again until the MA rises 10% above the monthly low point. Then go back to a fully invested position.

This sounds better for trading than for investing but, surprisingly, it doesn't work out that way. Most trends continue longer than anticipated, and with a diversified portfolio of quality stocks, that 10% decline will not come as quickly nor as often as you may think. Vice versa for that 10% upswing. But not with volatile holdings where you can be whipsawed and hurt by too many commissions.

Variable ratios. These apply primarily to mixed portfolios. The key is the percentage of stocks held; up as stock prices decline, down as they rise. It's a defensive plan that works best when the market moves within a fairly limited range. In a bull market, the percentage of stocks might drop from 75% to 50% or less. Toward the end of a bear market, the buying starts again. In each case, the shift is from stocks to fixed-income holdings.

The focal point is a central average that calls for investments half in stocks, half in bonds—e.g., when the DJIA is at 850. You buy more stocks at low prices and sell more at high prices.

The problem is to determine that central price average. If stock prices zoom up past your selected median, you'll be almost out of stocks and miss maximum appreciation. On the downside, however, you will always build protection, but you will not get back into stocks at the right time—unless you're lucky.

A compromise is to tie the central zone to some outside-the-market criterion such as (1) growth of Gross National Product (this is hard to follow, and you will miss sharp, temporary rallies; still, that's the idea of formula plans—you act on rote, not judgment) or (2) determinants of stock prices rather than the stock prices themselves. Thus, if the P/E ratio of the DJIA is between 13 and 15, the ratio might be 50% stocks, 50% bonds. When the multiple falls below 10, the percentage of stocks might rise to 60%—and so on. The difficulty is that there is no way of knowing how long the new base will continue. In the late 1960s, a P/E ratio of 12 was low; by 1979, it was high.

The formula for this variation is as follows: Divide the average cost per share by the current price per share and multiply by the amount invested periodically, say $100 per month. The average cost is $9 per share; the market price is $8 per share. Divide 9 by 8 to get 1.125. Multiply this by $100 to get the necessary investment: $112.50.

If the average cost per share is $9 and the market value $10, it's $\frac{9}{10} \times \$100$ or $90 investment.

How to Improve Formula Plan Results

The essence of all formula plans is to sell most stocks before bull market peaks and to buy most stocks before bear market bottoms. Since you are operating under a formula, you cannot use judgment in deciding whether a bull or bear market will continue. But there are some supplementary techniques which can help improve your profits.

1. Wait 30 to 60 days before buying or selling. Once the formula has given a signal, wait for confirmation of this trend. You will have to develop your own timing schedule, but a month is minimal and two months may be too long.

2. Act only at the midpoint of the zone. This is another delaying tactic. It shifts the action point up or down.

3. Use stop orders. When your formula stock-selling point is reached in a rising market, place stop orders to sell a few points below the current market level. If the uptrend continues, you will not sell your stocks too soon.

In the opposite direction, when your formula buying point is reached in a declining market, put in an order to buy at a few points above the current market. If the downtrend continues, you will not buy too soon.

4. Change ratios or zone. When you find that the formula plan is out of step with realities, you probably have been too conservative. Any change at or near the top of a bull market will not be effective. You will be almost out of stocks anyway. This is the wrong time to invest more heavily in stocks.

It is probably more effective to make a zoning change at the time when the market drops into the middle or lower ranges. You will hold more stocks, so your profits should increase as the prices rise.

With this type of formula plan, investments are made in fixed dollars and/or at fixed times. It's an installment plan and works best when all income, from interest and dividends, is promptly reinvested. Since the same dollars buy more shares are low prices than at high, this system must be maintained for years—as long as 20—to be truly worthwhile.

Dollar-Cost Average (DCA). This is the most widely used direct-investment formula plan. It eliminates the difficult problem of timing. You invest a fixed amount of dollars at specific time intervals: one month, three months or whatever time span meets your savings schedule. Your average cost will always be lower than the average market price during the accumulation period.

The table illustrates how DCA works: what happens when you invest $100 regularly, regardless of the price of the stock. The lower the market value, the more shares you buy. Thus, the per share average cost is $4.255 but the average price per share is $5.80. The profits come over the long term as the price of the stock rises.

With DCA, the type of stocks acquired is more important than with strict formula plans. You want quality stocks that have these general characteristics:

• **Volatility** . . . but not too much. Preferably, the 10-year high price should be 2½ times the low. These swings are more common with cyclical stocks such as motors, machinery and natural resources, but they can also be found with industries whose popularity shifts: drugs, electronics and food processors.

In bear markets, your dollars buy more shares but your paper losses on already held stock will be high so you will have to have a stout heart and confidence enough to maintain your commitment. That's where quality counts.

• **Long-term growth.** These are stocks of companies that can be expected to continue to boost revenues and earnings and outperform the overall stock market. If your stock fails to keep pace with the market comeback, you will lose the main advantage of DCA. Look for stocks that are more volatile on the upside than on the downside.

• **Steady, ample dividends.** It is true that dividends, as such, have little to do with formula plans but they can help to provide regular sums needed for periodic investments, especially when you find it difficult to scrape up spare cash.

With the right stocks and modest commitments, you may find that, in a few years, the dividends will be enough to meet those periodic payments. *Timing hint:* Start your program a week or two before the date you expect to receive a dividend check from the company whose stock you plan to buy.

If you use margin, your dividends should more than cover the cost of the interest.

• **Better-than-average profitability.** The average profit rate of the company over a decade should be at least 10%. It's fine to be able to buy more stock when the price is low, but there's little benefit if its value does not move up steadily over the years. Corporations able to show consistent profitable growth will always be worth more in the future. With DCA, you are striving to accumulate greater wealth. This can always be done best by buying stocks of companies that make better-than-average profits.

• **Good quality.** This means stocks of companies rated not less than B by Standard & Poor's. More conservative investors should stick with A-rated companies.

Avoid companies with high debt ratios. In recessionary times, they may find it difficult to meet their debt obligations, let alone show a profit.

Shares of mutual funds are excellent vehicles for DCA. They provide diversification, generally stay in step with the stock market as a whole and usually continue to pay dividends.

Note: A study by *Forbes* magazine raised doubts as to the true value of DCA. A survey of 12 NYSE stocks over a five-year period found that: (*a*) the average cost under DCA exceeded the median for all purchase prices; (*b*) with eight of the stocks, the investor would have beaten DCA by buying a single block on any randomly chosen date; (*c*) the gains of the four "successes" averaged only 7.9% a year; (*d*) the commissions of DCA cut the gains in half.

DOLLAR-COST AVERAGING

Price per share	$100 will buy
$10	10 shares
8	12.5
5	20
4	25
2	50
Total shares	117.5
Total investment	$500
Average cost per share	$4.255
Average price per share	$5.80

STOCKS FOR DOLLAR COST AVERAGING

Archer-Daniels-Midland	Melville Corp.
Beatrice Foods	Merck & Co.
Blue Bell	PepsiCo, Inc.
CBS, Inc.	Pillsbury Co.
Coca Cola	Pitney-Bowes
Delta Airlines	Procter & Gamble
Dow Chemical	Rollins, Inc.
Emhart Corp.	Rubbermaid, Inc.
General Foods	Sonat, Inc.
Goodyear Tire	Times-Mirror
Holiday Inns	Upjohn Co.
Houston Natural Gas	Winn-Dixie
Lilly (Eli)	Xerox Corp.
Long's Drug Stores	

SOME NON-UTILITY CORPORATIONS WITH 5% DISCOUNT DIVIDEND REINVESTMENT PLANS

ACF	Mercantile Texas
Allied Corp.	NCNB Corp.
American Express	Oneida, Ltd.
Bankers Trust	Panhandle Eastern
Carter Hawley Hale	Tenneco, Inc.
Chase Manhattan	Union Carbide
CSX Corp.	United Telecommunications
Equimark Corp.	Universal Foods
Fleming Cos.	Warner Communications
Inco, Ltd.	Wells, Fargo & Co.
Macy (R.H.)	

SOURCE: Standard & Poor's

Dividend Reinvestment

This is a variation of DCA that involves prompt reinvestment of dividends, often with a discount on new stock purchases. This service is offered by a number of corporations to strengthen stockholder relations and raise additional capital at low cost; for investors, it is a handy, inexpensive means for regular savings. It avoids the nuisance of small dividend checks and forces regular investments. It's good for growth but not for current income as you never see the dividend check. Many companies offer these new shares at a discount and some permit extra cash deposits, typically to a maximum of $3,000 each dividend time.

Under such a plan, all dividends are automatically reinvested in the company's stock. With the shareholder's OK, a bank or broker buys the required number of shares in the open market. The company then credits the full or fractional shares and pays dividends on the new total holdings. The commissions are pro-rated among participating shareholders and average about 1% of the value of the investment; there is also a service charge of about 5%, with a maximum of $2.50 per transaction. The savings are welcome: with $100 in dividends from a stock selling at $20 per share, the five new shares would carry a commission cost of $7.25 plus tax if they were bought directly. The bank charges only about $3.81. You get credit for fractional shares, and your dividend rate is adjusted accordingly. On closeouts, you receive the shares or cash. And under current IRS regulations, the service charge can be taken as a deduction in computing your federal income tax.

With A.T.&T., there are small commissions and the stock is available at a 5% discount. When the stock is sold, the base price, for tax purposes, is the actual cost, not the then current market price. In an up market, this can save a few dollars in taxes.

Through 1985 (under present legislation), there are extra tax benefits with shares of qualified-by-IRS utilities with dividend reinvestment plans. Investors can exclude from taxable income $750 for a single return; $1,500 for a couple filing jointly. (See Chapter 21.)

The dividends must be automatically reinvested to buy newly issued shares of the utilities' common stock. The new stock gets a zero-cost basis for tax purposes. If it is held for at least one year, any appreciation is taxed at capital gains rates.

Nearly all public power and light companies qualify for the exclusion. Telephone companies are not eligible. Clearly, the best investments are those of companies that offer a 5% discount.

Warning: There may be problems with shares of utilities that pay a dividend bigger than either current or retained earnings because part of the dividend is financed out of depreciation cash flow. In such a case, part of the dividend is considered a return of capital and thus is not taxable on a current basis. The cost of the shares is reduced when the shareholder sells the stock.

Example: An investor owns $12,000 worth of stock of a qualified utility. It yields 12.5%, or $1,500. A dividend of $1,000 is paid out of earnings but $500 is a return of capital. Under IRS rules, each dividend share is pro-rated so only the $1,000 is eligible for dividend-reinvestment treatment. To make sure that a shareholder does not sell other shares of the utility out of his portfolio, the IRS considers the sale of any shares of the stock during the minimum 12-month holding period to be a sale of dividend shares. Thus, if you sell shares early, you forfeit capital gains treatment of an equal number of shares issued, under the automatic reinvestment plan, during the previous year.

For information on companies that offer dividend reinvestment plans, write Standard & Poor's, 25 Broadway, New York, NY 10004.

26

Real Estate: Best for the Wealthy and Patient

Real estate has been, is now and will continue to be a rewarding investment. But long-term success takes hard work and patience and is most beneficial to those whose ample incomes make possible the greatest benefits for tax deductions.

The attractions of almost all real estate are:

1. Growth: 15% to 20% annually in the 1970s but, recently, less than half that rate even in expanding areas.

2. Leverage: small down payments (seldom more than 10%) and large, long-term mortgages.

3. Tax benefits: deductions for interest, real estate taxes, investment tax credit and fast, 15-year depreciation (although Uncle Sam will recapture some of the benefits when there's a profitable sale).

Real estate investments can be worthwhile but, from my experience (and that includes booming Florida), most individuals will make more real, spendable money with less risk and worry, by concentrating on securities of profitable, growing, quality corporations.

The majority of people who make money in real estate do so by doing their homework and using common sense, not by heeding magic formulas touted by self-styled experts. Unless you have nothing to do and cash to spare, do not bother to buy books/letters or attend seminars, of these miracle-workers who reveal *How to Be a Millionaire by Age 28* with "no money down" and "little more than part-time work."

Perhaps some of these get-rich quick formulas succeeded when interest rates were 8% and annual property appreciation was 15%, but when the cost of money is 15% (or more) and appreciation is 5% (or less), it's almost impossible to make extraordinary profits. Most of these "authorities" make their big money from royalties on their books and from fees for lectures rather than on real estate investments!

Not an Organized Business/Industry

In recent years, with soaring property prices, so many people have made so much money (more often on paper than in cash) in real estate (with their home, bought for $30,000 and now appraised at $100,000), that they forget to review the real estate market by business or investment standards. The situation is improving but investing in real estate still is:

1. Cumbersome, time-consuming and inefficient.

2. Based on sporadic trading and limited price information.

3. An incomplete, unstable market almost always with an imbalance of sellers and buyers.

4. Lacking in reliable information and meaningful research.

5. A complex area involving scores of investment options and requiring special legal counsel and tax analysis.

6. An area where the professional has a substantial edge over the amateur.

What a contrast to the regulated securities industry with its established markets, strict rules for accounting and reporting and standardized structures and flexible costs for transactions!

Need for Skillful Guidance

If you plan to become seriously involved in real estate, it is essential to work with knowledgeable real estate and tax advisers and, whenever possible, to be willing to do your own personal research. Unfortunately, the real estate business is not noted for integrity or skilled management. Too many real estate "experts" are promoters who operate with too little capital. When there's a bind, they cop out! *More than in any other form of investing, it is imperative to deal with only reputable, competent, experienced individuals and organizations.*

Finding the right adviser is difficult. In small communities you can do well with a local broker. When you move into broader areas, always get references and check reputations and results with banks and professional investors.

Success takes time, patience and research. You should have a thorough knowledge of the area, the growth pattern, transportation and highway plans, and present and potential competition. Always double the number of years for the payoff claimed by the promoter-developer. And never (well, hardly ever) invest money that you will need in the next five years. *The single greatest danger in real estate investing is the lack of liquidity.* If you have to sell in a hurry, you are almost sure to take a loss, or, at best, receive less than the real value. *Exception:* shares of REITs listed in major stock exchanges are liquid but not always profitable investments. If you buy low and hold, you will win if corporate management is honest, reasonably competent and involved with properties in growing or stable areas.

If you are making a sizable investment, inspect the property personally and retain competent local counsel to make sure that the location, price, yield and depreciation schedules and tax shelters of present and potential properties conform to expectations. Most real estate investments have *long-term* payouts. *Always project for at least 5, and preferably 10 or even 20, years.*

You don't have to be a millionaire to make money in real estate. There are many excellent local opportunities: housing, gas stations, small shopping centers, office buildings, apartments, etc. Check with a commercially oriented real estate firm or do your own research, first by car, then on foot.

Mortgage Investments

The safest income-producing type of real estate investment is a mortgage: a yield of 13% or more with a first mortgage with a maturity of 20 years or so; 18% for second mortgages, usually for less than 10 years and, often, with a balloon (full payment) at the end.

With any type of mortgage, when made to a reliable borrower, you are almost always sure of a competitive yield and of getting your money back at a fixed future date. But you must tie up your funds; the values of both the interest and principal will be reduced by inflation; and you will probably have to take a loss if you need money in a hurry.

These days, most mortgage investments are by necessity rather than by choice. To sell your new home . . . whether you are a rising young executive shifted to a new territory . . . or a retiree moving to a smaller house . . . you will probably have to take back a loan in some form. This can provide excellent income if the borrower keeps up payments and maintains the property but the income will be fully taxable and if there should be a foreclosure, this can be a difficult, irritating and costly procedure.

Try to avoid such a commitment if you can. Any loan that is subordinate to another mortgage, especially one made by an institution, involves risk so should provide a higher reward: a yield that is at least 3% above that of the base loan. To avoid legal hassles, always check with a lawyer and have a written contract that spells out such items as:

• **A penalty clause for late payments.** If the interest rates rise, the borrower has an incentive to pay on time. Without such an arrangement, you may have to foreclose. That's not easy if you are dealing with a local family.

• **An acceleration clause.** This gives you the option, in the event of a resale, of continuing the second mortgage with the new buyer or demanding that the note be paid off in full before the property can be sold.

• **A priority clause.** This provides that there can be no increase in the first mortgage without the second mortgage being paid off. Without such a clause, the borrower can refinance the first mortgage, get his down payment back, abandon the property and lose nothing. You would have to assume the first mortgage or lose your entire stake.

• **A notification clause.** This puts you on record that, in the event of a default on the first mortgage, you are willing to continue the payment on it. In return, you must be noti-fied in advance of any forthcoming foreclosure. If the borrower kept up his payment on the first mortgage and defaulted on the second, the property might have to be auctioned off to satisfy the primary lender. This would leave no funds for you to claim.

Be wary of pools of second mortgages where participations are sold for as little as $5,000 each. Many promoters who trumpeted yields of 25% or more have gone bankrupt. And even those who promised a "modest" 20% return have been slow with payments. Too often, the loans were based on the value of the property and not on the ability of the homebuyer to meet the high payments. Foreclosures are expensive and can tie up your money for years.

Be alert to the chance to sell the mortgage to Fannie Mae (Federal National Mortgage Association). Contact a local lender to get details. The purchase price will be at a discount but you'll get cash and lose a possible headache.

And if you feel forced to take over a mortgage—to help a member of your family buy a home, find out about the Shared Appreciation Mortgage (SAM). With this, the investor gets a share of the appreciation when the property is sold in return for providing part of the down payment or subsidy of the monthly payments. With some deals, the investor can get a portion—or all—of the tax deductions for interest and real estate taxes. Legally, the homeowner makes a "loan" to the investor who then takes the proceeds to "pay" part of the mortgage interest and taxes. Typically, no money changes hands and the "loan" may even be interest free. The investor gets 40% of the appreciation when the property is sold. There can be problems with the allocation of costs/profits of repairs, renovations and additions but some of these details are being standardized and some thrift institutions are offering these packages through limited partnerships. The idea makes sense IF it can be structured according to IRS rules and contains sufficient safeguards for all parties.

Investments in Raw Land

These are wise only for those who can afford to be patient, do not need current income and are interested in long-term capital gains. Again, it is more important to know how to get *out* than to get *in*. For the land to become more valuable, someone must be willing, able and ready to make use of it. Always think ahead three, five, or even 10 years to project the possible future for the property.

Typically, a raw land purchase is financed by a commercial bank. But you should always try to get the owner to carry the mortgage. Do not assume that the seller wants only cash; many older farmers prefer to have an assured lifetime income and may even settle for a specific monthly payment with little heed to the interest rate.

Be slow to improve the land in a way which will make it easier to sell or develop. The IRS may consider you a developer, and then the ultimate profit could be taxed as ordinary income.

Raw land, whether pasture, forest, field or farm, should:

• *Be in the path of progress:* near highways, not far from other housing or commercial developments or recreation areas.

• *Be available with considerable leverage:* not more than 30% down payment and, preferably, with a mortgage whereby only interest is due for a few years and there's no penalty for prepayment.

• *Have a potential of a minimum rise in value of 50% in three years, 100% in five years.* A somewhat lower target may be acceptable if there is assured income from rentals to a farmer, an outdoor group or a camping club.

• *Have annual carrying charges (taxes, interest and maintenance) of no more than 15% of your cost.* Inflation will help but you cannot wait too long as taxes will rise.

• *Be developable at a reasonable price.* It may sound exciting to join with friends in buying 100 acres of woodland with the idea of splitting the land into homesites, but unless you build your dream cabin, be cautious. You will tie up cash, can seldom get a bank loan, will have to pay a high commission when you sell and land values may not rise as rapidly as you anticipate.

Working farms are excellent investments if you do not pay too much and you have a competent tenant or manager. Be prepared to become personally involved if only to understand what must be done to operate profitably.

Unless you are experienced and have ample time and energy, do not try to run an investment farm yourself. Uncle Sam insists that, to permit tax deductions, there must be a profit in at least two of the first five years. Otherwise, the IRS may classify the operation as a hobby and thus eliminate tax benefits.

Handy hint: By using a trust to hold the land under an investment building, it's possible to deduct the cost of the land. Here's how a Florida lawyer set up his deal: Lou Legal buys a rental property for $100,000: $80,000 for the building; $20,000 for the land. He places the land in an irrevocable trust for his children. As owner, Lou pays a rental fee for the use of the land, so these payments become a deductible business expense. The rents, by the tenants, are sheltered by depreciation but when they start to become income, Lou makes a gift to the children who are in a lower tax bracket. Now do you see the wisdom of retaining a savvy real estate lawyer?

Other Real Estate Investments

With housing and commercial properties, it's best to split the deal into two parts: (1) the *underlying land* to be owned by an investor who wants income but cares little for tax deductions. That means a pension fund or trust. Usually, the lease calls for a percentage of gross rents with a minimum yield and a share of the profits at sale or refinancing; (2) the *buildings* to be held by an individual or group that wants maximum tax benefits and, eventually, modest income and capital appreciation. Keep this breakdown in mind when you discuss any joint deal. Developers always need money, so set up an arrangement that will meet the objectives of both parties.

Before getting into examples, let's discuss deductions that can be used against other income. They can be taken by an individual directly or through a partnership/syndicate. Thus, for those in the 50% tax bracket, every $100 tax benefit reduces taxes by $50.

The deductions related to investment dollars are for in-

terest on the mortgage, real estate taxes, a first-year Investment Tax Credit on the cost of equipment (furnace, air conditioner, etc.) and depreciation (wear and tear).

Under recent legislation, depreciation can be taken over 15 years with Accelerated Cost Recovery System (ACRS): 6⅔% of the cost is written off annually. (If you buy the property on July 1, however, you get only half the write-off: 3⅓%.) The write-off is against costs: cash plus mortgage.

Tables A, B and C show the alternatives for Dr. F, in the 50% tax bracket, who buys an office building for $500,000: $100,000 cash plus a $400,000 mortgage. The $100,000 value of the land is not depreciable. He buys the property on January 1 and the net income offsets the debt service so there's zero cash flow. Table A shows how this works with a five-year deal.

If Dr. F chooses a more rapid write-off, he works from Table B. On the surface, this is better than the Table A method: deductions of $184,000 vs. $133,333 with higher tax savings. But, as explained by Joseph Graf, "If he uses the accelerated method, all of his gain when he sells the property will be treated as ordinary income rather than capital gain to the extent that all prior cost-recovery deductions are taken. By using the accelerated method, he gives up the opportunity to transfer ordinary, fully taxed income into tax-favored capital gain. If he uses straight line ACRS, he deducts from fully taxed income but when he gets the money back on a sale, he's taxed on the capital gain—a maximum of 20% versus 50% on ordinary income." In other words, if you deduct $10,000 from a $100,000 prop-

TABLE A
HOW ACRS WORK

YEAR	STRAIGHT LINE DEDUCTION	TAX SAVING 50% BRACKET	RETURN ON $100,000 CASH INVESTMENT FROM TAX SAVING
1	$26,666	$13,333	13.3%
2	26,666	13,333	13.3
3	26,666	13,333	13.3
4	26,666	13,333	13.3
5	26,666	13,333	13.3
Total	$133,330	$66,665	66.5%

SOURCE: Physician's Management

TABLE B
RAPID WRITE—OFF

YEAR	ACRS DEDUCTION	TAX SAVING	RETURN ON $100,000 CASH INVESTMENT FROM TAX SAVING
1	$48,000	$24,000	24%
2	40,000	20,000	20
3	36,000	18,000	18
4	32,000	16,000	16
5	28,000	14,000	14
Total	$184,000	$92,000	92%

SOURCE: Physician's Management

TABLE C
ACCELERATED DEPRECIATION vs. STRAIGHT LINE

YEAR	ACCELERATED	TAX SAVING	STRAIGHT LINE	TAX SAVING	EXCESS
1	$48,000	$24,000	$26,666	$13,333	$10,687
2	40,000	20,000	26,666	13,333	6,667
3	36,000	18,000	26,666	13,333	4,667
4	32,000	16,000	26,666	13,333	2,667
5	28,000	14,000	26,666	13,333	667
Total	$184,000	$92,000	$133,330	$66,665	$26,335
Less tax on disposition	X .50 =	92,000	X .20 =	26,666	
Net		0		39,999	

SOURCE: Physician's Management

erty, and then sell for $100,000, Dr. F will have a $10,000 profit.

If he computes the $10,000 deduction on the straight-line basis, the profit is a capital gain. If he uses the accelerated method, the profit is ordinary income. But if he sold the property for $115,000, the additional $15,000 would be a capital gain in both cases.

To compare the alternatives, check Table C... assuming that Dr. F sells the property for $500,000 after five years. It shows that he should choose the straight-line method. He will have the use of extra money—$10,667 in Year I, etc., but the accelerated method saves $24,000 vs. $13,333 straight-line—more than he could expect to earn by investing the cash savings.

Unless you're sure you'll be holding the property for a fairly long time—at least 10 years—stay away from the fastest recovery method.

Bargains in multifamily units. These days, it's still possible to pick up bargains with income-producing real estate. Builders/developers need cash and lending institutions are not anxious to foreclose on major properties. For groups of local investors, with the aid of an honest, reasonably competent promoter/manager, there are excellent opportunities to save taxes, build tax benefits and, soon, achieve substantial capital gains.

Here's a case history in Palm Beach County, Florida. The purchase involved the last 10 of 48 condominiums, most of which had been sold, individually, for about $75,000 each. The builder needed cash to start a new project so the real estate agent negotiated a total price of $620,000: $62,000 each. The idea was to turn them into rental apartments for both full-time and seasonal residents. Since the vacancy rate in the area was about 2%, this appealed to the thrift institution that held the mortgage.

The land was valued at $100,000; the buildings at $600,000; the closing costs were $20,000. The deal required $70,000 cash with a $550,000 mortgage at 13.5% because it was payable, at a 20-year amortization rate, in five years. That meant a hefty balloon payment but chances were good that this could be handled by refinancing or a sale.

The buying group was a partnership of five investors, all in the 50% tax bracket, so the projected deductions were:
Depreciation: straight line over 15 years, 6.67% annually on the $500,000 value of the buildings (but not the land): $33,333 a year.
Interest on the mortgage: starting at $73,901 the first year and dropping to $63,788 in Year V.

Against these would be net income, increasing at a projected 12% annually: rental minus costs. This starts at $39,250 and rises to about $71,000 in the last year.

Since the deductions will be greater than the income, the investors get annual tax benefits (deductions from ordinary income) of $67,984 in Year I down to $41,360 in Year V. In the 50% tax bracket, they "save" a total of $139,611.

The optimistic agent predicted 12% annual appreciation so that, hopefully, at the end of five years, when the mortgage was due, the property could be sold for $1 million. When the balance of the loan ($521,373) is paid, there will be some $479,000 less commissions.

Under IRS rules, the tax savings must be recaptured. For every $5,000 in write-offs, the profit is increased, for

Swapping Saves Taxes

When you become really involved with real estate investments, swapping can be both a tax saver and money maker. This is a tax-free exchange of like-kind property. The mechanics are tedious and deals are hard to put together unless handled by an experienced real estate professional.

Example: Some 15 years ago, Ethel bought an office building for $100,000: $50,000 cash and a 10-year mortgage, which, by now, has been paid off. The building was depreciated by a low 3% a year ($3,000) so the cost basis is now $55,000: $100,000 cost minus $45,000 depreciation.

The property is now worth $200,000, so if Ethel sells, she would pay a capital gains tax on the $145,000 difference: in her tax rate, $29,000 for Uncle Sam.

Ethel needs more space for her growing business and finds one that's available for $300,000. The owner is willing to swap: $100,000 cash plus the old building. Now the $29,000 tax levy is deferred until the new property is sold or until death if no cash profit is realized. At Ethel's death, the building, at the stepped-up value goes into her estate. The executor can then sell with the tax base at the higher time-of-death value.

Thus, if the new property is depreciated to $125,000 but is actually worth $1 million, it can be sold for $1 million without capital gains tax liability. The $125,000 basis disappears.

In addition, there will be depreciation on the new building, probably at the same 3% rate. This is based on the $55,000 cost basis of the original property plus the $100,000 cash received: $4,650 annually. This is $16,500 more than was available with the old property.

When there is no cash involved in a swap, there are no extra taxes. But, in this example, the $100,000 received by the owner of the new building is taxable as a capital gain. When a deal involves a mortgage, IRS no longer regards this as a like-kind property exchange and there will be taxes.

Swapping can be great if you have a knowledgeable agent and attorney, do your research and can count on a little luck.

tax purposes, to $10,000. As this becomes a long-term capital gain, only 40% is taxable. At the 50% tax rate, this means a 20% tax bite. So, for each $5,000 deduction taken over five years, $3,000 is added to the after-tax profit. But since the investors have had use of the tax savings, they will have, in effect, a tax-free loan from Uncle Sam. (Yes, I realize that the maximum tax rate in five years is now scheduled to be 49%, but 50% is easier to work with.)

Special-purpose properties: service stations, fast-food restaurants, convenience stores, etc. The investor builds or renovates to standard designs, then leases to an operator on a net-net basis. When a major corporation such as Exxon, McDonald's or 7–11 is involved, its reputation will make it possible to secure a higher mortgage (especially if the parent company provides some sort of participation with the franchisee). This will reduce the cash investment and, probably, the return. But with regular rent and depreciation, there will be tax-free cash to pay the mortgage and, hopefully, assure extra profits with renewal of the lease or sale of the property. Most of these are packaged deals prepared by local promoters, so you won't have much leeway on terms.

With such net leases, the possibility of a profitable sale may disappear. If the tenant has unlimited options to renew the lease, the building may never be sold. The fixed rent cuts the value of the return on investment year by year. *Best bet:* include a clause that provides for rising rent and an option to sell the building at some future date.

Other excellent local opportunities are: small apartment houses in an accessible location; strip shopping centers with a cluster of small stores anchored by a banking office; and professional buildings for physicians and dentists.

As a rule of thumb, says one developer, "Try to keep the cash outlay to 20% of the first $1 million and 15% thereafter. To do this these days, you may have to give the lender a piece of the action: an equity position in warrants for the stock of the corporation, a percentage of profits, or a share of the proceeds of a profitable sale. Still, a well-designed unit in a good location can be profitable."

He might have added this caveat: "Be cautious with deals involving specialized businesses: bowling alleys, motels, marinas, etc. Their yields will be higher, but if there are problems, you'll find yourself having to take over operations. It takes expertise to manage such enterprises, not just money."

Rehabilitations. These involve fixing up older buildings. To encourage such deals, the new tax law provides credits on qualified improvements: 15% for nonresidential property at least 30 years old; 20% for nonresidential property 40 years old; and 25% for certified historic structures. These can be good deals when the costs are reasonable and the location suitable.

Example: In New York City, Lazard Realty turned a grimy factory with over one million square feet into a smart office building. By buying at a bargain price, face-lifting the exterior and breaking up the interior, the firm was able to rent at $20 a square foot compared to $60 in mid-Manhattan, a short subway ride away.

A similar deal requires that the building facade be donated to a qualified preservation organization through a "preservation easement." The tax benefit is the difference between the fair market value of the property (and land)

before and after the easement: deductible up to 50% of the adjusted gross income of investors in the year of donation with a five-year carryover of any value in excess of 50%. But once that donation has been made, no one can alter the facade or demolish the building. *Potential:* first-year pretax return of 55% and, if held for five years, the tax credit is not subject to recapture.

CALCULATING PRESENT VALUE

Discount Factor to Use as Multiplier

	INTEREST RATE							
YEAR	10%	11%	12%	13%	14%	15%	16%	17%
1	0.91	0.90	0.89	0.88	0.87	0.86	0.85	0.84
2	0.82	0.81	0.80	0.78	0.77	0.75	0.73	0.71
3	0.75	0.73	0.71	0.69	0.67	0.65	0.62	0.60
4	0.68	0.66	0.64	0.61	0.59	0.57	0.54	0.51
5	0.62	0.59	0.57	0.54	0.52	0.50	0.46	0.43
6	0.56	0.53	0.51	0.48	0.45	0.43	0.39	0.37
7	0.51	0.48	0.45	0.42	0.40	0.38	0.33	0.31
8	0.47	0.43	0.40	0.37	0.35	0.33	0.28	0.26
9	0.42	0.39	0.36	0.33	0.31	0.28	0.24	0.22
10	0.38	0.35	0.32	0.29	0.27	0.25	0.20	0.19

SOURCE: Research Institute of America, SET FOR LIFE

In making comparisons of properties, a handy tool is *Present Value:* future worth, cash flow and payments discounted over a set number of years. It's like calculating the purchasing power of the dollar under various rates of inflation.

Example: Mike has narrowed his investment choices to two identical homes:

A: cost $90,000; $20,000 down, 30-year 17% mortgage for $70,000.

B: cost $105,000; $35,000 down, 5-year zero mortgage for $70,000.

To find the PV, he multiplies each annual $14,000 payment by the 17% interest rate discount factor:

Thus, the $105,000 house is really being sold for $78,260: $35,000 down payment plus mortgage with a present value of $43,260. This is less than the $90,000 house before the down payment and tax factors.

Year I:	$14,000	X 0.84 =	$11,760
Year II:		X 0.71 =	9,940
Year III:		X 0.60 =	8,400
Year IV:		X 0.51 =	7,140
Year V:		X 0.43 =	6,020
	Total		$43,260

Syndicates and Partnerships

While it is possible to make money with real estate that you own alone or with a member of your family, most people do not have cash, credit or time to do it themselves. Major real estate investments are usually made through syndicates or partnerships.

Syndicates are limited partnerships that sell shares for as little as $5,000 each. They may be formed by local real estate agents or, more likely, by divisions of major broker- age firms. The offerings are for a specified sum, so once the purchase is made, you are locked in. With larger syndi- cates, there may be a secondary market for the shares, but generally resales can be made only to other participants. That's why it's a good idea to work with friends or business associates who are able, and willing, to bail you out. Or vice versa.

Public partnerships, with more than 35 participants, must be registered with the SEC. Typically, they require that the investor have $30,000 annual income plus $30,000 net worth for low-risk deals: $75,000 income plus $65,000 net worth for high-risk offers. That net worth does not in- clude the value of your home, furniture, and automobiles.

Private partnerships are designed for the wealthy: annu- al income of $100,000 and net worth of $750,000. Some states require more.

Broadly speaking, both syndicates and partnerships have two classes of investors: (1) general partners who put up a little money, assume full responsibility for operations (including liability for some debts), and take most of the profits; (2) limited partners who provide most of the mon- ey but who are liable only to the extent of agreed-upon contributions.

Under partnerships, all losses, depreciation, income and capital appreciation are passed through to the investors. These individuals pay taxes at regular income-tax rates on their returns and get the full benefit of any tax losses. This escapes the double taxation of corporations. The investors can use ordinary losses to offset ordinary income and carry them back or forward. Limited partners have the right to withdraw or assign interests, and death does not necessar- ily dissolve the partnership.

Multi-investor programs can be structured to meet spe- cific tax shelter needs of the investors as shown in the ta- ble. These are projections for a shopping center:

• A **moderate tax shelter** where the cash investment is low in the first year, peaks in the second year and requires substantial, but decreasing, sums through the next three years.

The cash distributions are modest and the tax loss, for accounting/tax purposes, is greater than the investment in the first year, about 72% in the second year, then slowing to 56% and 37% and so forth. There are no tax losses after Year VI but the cash flow should be enough to cover re- ported income. Over five years, the reported tax loss is $107,503, so in the 50% tax bracket, worth $215,060, more than the $208,127 cash investment. And there's a welcome $42,601 cash flow.

• A **maximum tax shelter** with the investment dollars less than half as great: $3,711 at the start and a maximum of $20,924 in the second year for a total of $97,666. The cash distribution is small: only $5,894 vs. $42,601 in the moderate deal, but the reported tax loss is more than dou- ble: rising from $835 in the first year to $47,748 in the second year and gradually diminishing to an ample $36,903 in Year VI. But when the tax losses stop, the cash flow will not be enough to cover the tax burden so smart operators will sell and use the profits to cover their tax liability.

These days, with ever-greater needs for capital, profes- sional real estate oriented firms are coming up with special

TAX SHELTER: MODERATE vs. MAXIMUM

YEAR	CASH INVESTMENT	CASH DISTRIBUTION	REPORTED TAX LOSS
Cash Flow & Moderate Tax Shelter			
1	$ 9,392	$ 1,204	$ 10,425
2	59,819	8,024	43,099
3	50,955	10,769	28,108
4	46,306	10,168	17,263
5	41,655	12,436	8,635
5 Yr. Total	$208,127	$42,601	$107,530
Maximum Tax Shelter			
1	$ 3,711	$ 0	$ 8,535
2	20,924	378	47,748
3	19,757	776	44,675
4	18,600	1,167	41,613
5	17,758	1,579	39,264
6	16,916	2,004	36,903
6 Yr. Total	$97,666	$ 5,894	$218,738

deals. Here are some of the more widely promoted:

To finance 11 new hotels for $365 million, Marriott Corp. sold the hotels to a limited partnership (LP) but re- tained all cash flow and a substantial portion of the poten- tial appreciation. Technically, the LPs owned 3,000 rooms, but, legally, according to the legal experts, they own the depreciation so can take tax write-offs for 15 years and get back nine times their investment! IRS may disagree be- cause Marriott retains most of the economic interest in the properties.

Southwest Realty, a limited partnership, dreamed up an- other "opportunity": to exchange interest in some 25 part- nerships for depositary receipts that are traded over the counter. Until the receipts are sold, the investors continue to get the tax benefits and cash distributions.

Koger Co., a southern builder/operator of office build- ings, splits into two separate corporations: Koger Proper- ties, Inc., the developer, and Koger Co., the owner of the buildings. The company pays out, in tax-free dividends, nearly 100% of its net cash flow from depreciation. These distributions appear to erase the reported equity so Koger floats more stock or sells/swaps one or two properties. They are carried on the corporate books at cost which is, usually, below market value.

And, typical of the imaginative approach, Koger fi- nances new construction with 9% appreciation notes, sold at 93¢ on the dollar. The accrued interest is equal to the projected rise in the value of the property and rental in- come. This interest will not be paid for six years after issue, but, for tax purposes, Koger deducts them currently and also takes a tax credit on the depreciation. That's cheap financing.

Guidelines for Real Estate Syndicates/Partnerships

1. Deal only with reliable, capable, reputable syndica- tors. Check bank references, standing with the local Cham- ber of Commerce, real estate board and past clients. Be- ware of anyone who tells you he's never had a loser. An average of 80% success is tops.

2. Review the agreement with an experienced real estate lawyer and/or accountant, not your faithful family retainer.

Many syndicates are headed by shrewd, aggressive operators who take advantage of every legal loophole and tax dodge. There may be clauses in the contract and related documents of which you are unaware or which you do not fully understand. In the end, these may cost you money or tie up your funds. Part ownership of a lease is worth much less than equivalent ownership in the leased property.

3. Never judge any syndication on its tax shelter potential. If there are no profits, you will be shelling out hard-earned dollars for little or no gain. You are making an investment. The tax benefits should be secondary.

4. Worry about what you will make, not how much the syndicator will take out. You are buying brains, so you will have to pay well for top results.

For your own profits, a rule of thumb is to try to make cash flow, tax shelter and equity buildup add up to 3% more than the current mortgage loan rate: 18% for residential and office properties and 20% for motels, bowling alleys, etc.

5. The more of his own money the syndicator puts up, the better the project. He is likely to work harder when he stands to gain.

6. The higher the percentage of the first mortgage, the better the operation. Some financial firm must have confidence in the project to put up so much money. Besides, the leverage is higher.

7. The longer the mortgage, the greater the leverage. You want a mortgage that runs well beyond the time you expect to put the property on the market—at least 10 years, with no earlier call.

8. Never invest cash you may need in the next five to 10 years. If you take out your money before that time, you may have to accept a loss and miss some tax benefits. Real estate is always a long-term proposition for investors.

9. Be skeptical of all appraisals. As one veteran SEC official comments, "Appraisers are independent only if they're not getting paid by those asking for the appraisal." If you are making the investment on your own, arrange for two separate appraisals.

On the average, a fair purchase price will be four times annual rent for office buildings, 10 times annual cash production for apartments and nine times rent for a shopping center. But these figures assume solid, regularly paying tenants, so always allow leeway for delinquency and for lower rentals if there's a chance of competition or overbuilding.

10. Be wary of projections of future value. If you buy at the right price and manage the property well, the ultimate value will be greater if there is no deterioration of the neighborhood or no unusual developments such as new highways, devastating fires, etc.

11. Check the track record of the promoter/builder with banks and mortgage lenders. If possible, get audited statements of operations of apartment houses and commercial buildings. Prospectuses may distort occupancy rates or fudge on gross profits.

12. Beware of promoters who call themselves investment advisers. These are the types who run a computerized analysis of your financial condition and then recommend that you "put some of your money in stocks, bonds and insurance and 50% in tax-sheltered holdings such as real estate"—and then casually mention some deal they happen to know of.

13. Have your accountant explain the financial statement, tax reports, etc. They can be obtuse and frustrating but, in time, you will learn how to interpret them and IRS regulations.

14. Do not rely on the opinion of outsiders such as bankers, attorneys and accountants as to the present and potential value of any property. Usually, it's the blind leading the blind. Unless they have personally inspected the property and market, they know as little as you do.

15. Keep reviewing every deal to discover why one was profitable and another a loser. In real estate, experience is almost as important as knowledge.

Watch Out—for

Deals that offer immense, quick depreciation: "wrap 'em and rip 'em" partnerships set up by fast-buck operators. As a starter, those promoters mark up the "value" of the property from $3.5 to $4.5 million. To finance the deal, which has an old 10% mortgage, the general partner offers to add a wraparound mortgage at 16% or more.

Soon, the debt service exceeds the cash flow from rents after operating expenses, so the friendly GP agrees to add the unpaid interest to the mortgage principal. In a few years the debt is unpayable, so your old friend, *sadly,* reluctantly forecloses and charges all costs against the property. The investor is doubly rooked because now there's no profit on the sale.

Possible changes in zoning, planning commission rules, environmental controls, easements, availability of utilities, potential assessments, etc. If you have to sell when any of these areas are under change, you may have to settle for a lot less than anticipated.

Offers to exchange shares of a public corporation for your interest in the limited partnership. The prospectus makes this "explanation": you will get: (1) a quick, easy, inexpensive tax-free exchange with no recapture of the depreciation already taken; (2) shares in a diversified real estate firm which owns and controls income-producing properties; (3) ability to sell your stock on the open market at any time.

But there's seldom mention of these factors: (1) the IRS has not yet approved the elimination of the recapture of depreciation; (2) you will probably lose tax on appreciation, because the new stock takes the same tax basis as that of the property you had; (3) you will lose cash flow because the previous income will probably cease and if there are cash dividends, they will be taxed at the highest rate; (4) there could be mortgage problems that might require refinancing the old property at a higher cost; (5) you will suffer an immediate dilution of your assets because: (*a*) the promoters get 15% of the stock; (*b*) added fees for appraisal, commissions, etc., will chip off another 10%. That 25% off-the-top will be more than the maximum 20% tax on long-term gains; (6) the true worth of corporate assets will be optimistic since it is probably based on the earnings record of the properties, not on the higher cash flow of your partnership; (7) the value of your new stock will probably drop when other swappers get out.

Sales/operating costs over which you have no control:

research fees, acquisition commissions, printing the prospectus, accounting/legal charges, amount of working capital and, often, special compensation for the current owner.

HOW SYNDICATE FEES MOUNT UP

$1.25 Million Apartment House

Spent for	Amount	Percentage
Cash closing costs	$500,000	44.5%
Consulting fees	150,000	13.3
Noncompetition fee	100,000	8.9
Selling commissions	88,000	7.8
Legal/accounting/printing/ administrative	62,000	5.5
Initial management fee	60,000	5.3
General partner's fee	40,000	3.6
Working capital	20,000	1.8
Mortgage interest*	45,000	4.0
Guarantee fee	60,000	5.3
	$1,125,000	100.0%

*comparatively low as the commitment was made before interest rates skyrocketed.
SOURCE: Executive Wealth Advisory

Here's an example of a $1.25 million apartment building. Note that only 44.5% of the investors' money went for the building. The majority of the proceeds were used by and for the promoters: $160,000 to the GP ($60,000 initial management fee, $40,000 general partner's fee and $60,000 to guarantee a letter of credit or to meet any negative partnership cash flow).

These costs are startling to the uninitiated but if the ultimate deal proves profitable, they are not significant. Still, they point up the extra risks of real estate investments, especially if the projections are inaccurate or fail to work out.

As with all third-party investments, the key is management. A properly structured deal, with the money invested in prime income-producing properties, can result in steady cash flow, excellent depreciation and, eventually, capital appreciation. But once that money is in the hands of the promoters, they tend to want to put it to work, and too often they will take unnecessary risks. *With all real estate, it is more important to know how to get out than how to get in.*

Added caveat: As always happens when some investment area becomes profitable, fast-buck operators move in. With one Florida real estate syndicate, investors put up 90% of the capital for 30% of the company—which has never declared a dividend, pays $1.5 million in salaries to its officers plus $60,000 to the promoter's father and never reveals the purchased properties until long after the sucker's check has cleared (and not always then).

Real Estate Investment Trusts (REITs)

These are similar to closed-end investment companies in that their shares are not redeemable upon request but are traded like regular stocks so that their prices reflect supply and demand. REITs sell shares to the public and invest the proceeds in real estate, usually in a diversified portfolio of commercial, industrial and residential properties. In the early 1970s, they were great for income, then became growth favorites but later bombed with mismanagement, fraud and recession. Many went out of business and even more were reorganized.

Most of the survivors are pretty well managed and offer opportunities for profits if only because their present properties are carried at below market value, managers have been tested by time and adversity and objectives have shifted to growth more than income. If you pick the right REIT, and are patient, you may make a lot of money as the real estate market comes back and expands.

Shares of leading REITs have bounced up a few points (after favorable press or broker reports) but generally have not been among market leaders. To spark investor interest, there are new packages/concepts such as:

• MCO Holdings, whose shares are traded on the AMEX. They will swap one share per $10 of appraised equity valuation of real estate holdings of $2.5 million or more. The transaction is tax-free and enables the locked-in partnership to gain greater liquidity. But the shrewd promoter kept 15% of the stock so there's an immediate dilution for the investor.

• Landsing Capitol Corp. offers a self-liquidating trust: a sell-out of all assets, presumably at a rewarding profit, after 10 years. If you can wait that long, this may prove worthwhile, but, meantime, the shares are trading at substantial discounts. That's OK when you're buying but not when you're selling.

And for those who want to know why some REITs prosper, here are guidelines used by Lomas & Nettleton Mortgage, a consistently profitable operation:

• Debt/equity ratio never above 2.5:1.

• Borrowing short-term so make only short-term loans.

• Always have commitment from third party to buy out interest.

• Use own architects/engineers to retain control.

• Maintain 40% of the portfolio in single-family homes.

Common Mistakes with Real Estate

Every successful investor in real estate will tell you that there are three basic criteria: *location—location—location.* This is a solid basic concept but once you understand what you're doing, study the market, line up a continuing source of mortgage money, be patient and try to avoid simple mistakes such as these outlined by George Bockl, who has never found a way to pyramid $1,000 into $1 million.

Don't buy any property for depreciation alone. If it's not a good investment, it's not a good tax shelter.

Don't look for sensational returns. Be willing to shoot for yields about 5% above that of the cost of money and settle for 3%—these days 16% to 18%. If you're patient, you'll do well with low-taxed appreciation.

Don't buy problems, such as buildings in need of repair or tenanted by eccentric or unreasonable people.

Don't get into any deal that you cannot control. You can get fleeced as a small partner in a big deal. Start with property that you can manage or monitor yourself.

Don't invest in commercial property at the outset. Apartments are safer and steadier. You can understand what's happening and will not have to contend with the volatility of business/professional tenants.

Don't pay all cash. Leverage is the key to successful real estate. Borrow judiciously and, when possible, for the long term.

Don't let ambition override common sense. When you listen to applause instead of costs, you get into trouble.

Don't overpay. Investing in real estate is a cautious game. Stop, look and listen and re-examine the facts, figures and projections. When you fall in love with a property, you may be buying luxury rather than profits.

Don't accept unreasonable terms. Make sure that every investment can show a profit, after expenses and taxes, of

at least 15% and can have reasonable expectations of annual appreciation of 10%.

Don't invest outside your community in the beginning. Chances of success decrease with distance.

Don't invest in downtown property unless it's cheap, you have an unusual idea or there is confirmed redevelopment. When property is run down, it can take years for a comeback—no matter what you may read in magazines or *How I Made $20 Million in Real Estate* books.

27

Pension Plans for a Financially Secure Retirement

Personal pension plans are the most rewarding vehicle for investments. To individuals, they provide tax deductions for the contributions, tax-deferral of all income and appreciation and, at withdrawal, regular payments while the balance of the assets continue to compound tax-free. Over 30 years, an annual contribution of $2,000, at a 15% yield, will compound to $869,000. The same $2,000 annual savings, without the shelter benefits, will grow to only $163,000: a huge difference of $706,000!

Every American who earns money can have his or her personal pension plan and, when started early enough and invested wisely, can build a million dollar nest egg over 40 years, with annual contributions of only $489 when the money earns 15% a year. Granted that the million dollars will not buy as much in 2024 as today, it's still a nice target and should provide more than enough income for a couple to enjoy a money-carefree retirement even if they both live to age 100.

If you are covered by a pension plan where you work (and nearly two-thirds of full-time employees are), you can set up an Individual Retirement Account (IRA) with earned income. You can contribute up to $2,000 a year ($2,250 with nonworking spouse). Invested at a modest 12%, these savings will grow to nearly $40,000 in 10 years; to over $160,000 in 20 years; and to more than $500,000 in 30 years. When withdrawn at 15% annually, these assets can provide after-work income of $6,000, $24,000 and $75,000 a year for as long as most people will live.

For the majority of people who buy this guide, the net cost of an IRA will be about $2.75 per day or $83 a month.

Example: George and Louise, in their early 30s, have a total income of $32,000 a year: George earns $20,000 as an engineer and Louise $12,000 as a nurse. On their federal

tax return, they can take a 5% credit on the lower salary: $600 (5% of $12,000). This reduces their taxable income to $31,400, which, in rough figures, will be taxed at about $5,800.

As George can add to his corporate pension plan contributions, Louise sets up her own IRA with $2,000 a year. This cuts their tax base to $29,400 and the tax to about $4,800: a savings of $1,000 a year. Thus, the "cost" of the IRA is about $83 a month or $2.75 per day . . . to build a half-million nest egg for after-work income.

WHAT IT TAKES TO BE A PENSION MILLIONAIRE			
Rate of Return	Annual contribution for		
	20 years	30 years	40 years
8%	$20,235	$8,174	$3,547
10	15,870	5,527	2,054
12	12,390	3,700	1,164
15	8,488	2,002	489

Personal Pension Plans

The two other types of personal pension plans are:
• **Keogh (HR-10):** for self-employed individuals and proprietors of small companies with few employees.
• **Professional Corporation (PC):** typically set up by a small group of well-paid professionals such as physicians, dentists, lawyers, etc., and their employees. The pension plan is only one of the benefits of this type of organization.

Under the Tax Equality and Fiscal Responsibility Act (TEFRA) of 1982, there were drastic changes for both

Keoghs and PCs but not for IRAs. The rules were tightened so that employer benefits are restricted and those of employees expanded; integration with Social Security is limited; and contribution maximums revised: *up* for Keoghs; *down* for corporate plans. But the key criteria continue: tax deductions at the time of the contributions; tax-deferral of all income on assets until withdrawn; and special benefits on payouts while living and after death. It's a brand new ball game, so check your legal/tax adviser.

Here are highlights:

Individual Retirement Account (IRA): for those who (*a*) do not earn enough to justify a Keogh or PC; (*b*) want to set up a supplement to their current pension plan.

Maximum annual contribution: $2,000 with $2,250 with nonworking spouse. Since you own all the assets, there are no problems of vesting or eligibility. No more contributions after age 70½ but you can make contributions to your spouse's IRA until she reaches that age.

A variation is the Simplified Employee Pension (SEP) that permits employers to make contributions to individual IRAs of eligible employees. The maximum allocation is 25% of compensation to a maximum of $30,000 a year. The annual amount can be increased or decreased. There can be no discrimination in the percentage applied and employees can make extra contributions on their own, to a limit of $2,000 a year.

Caveats: (1) In some states, contributions may not be deducted from state/local income taxes. (2) All participants are 100% vested immediately so employees can take all assets if they quit. (3) All employees must be included even if they resign before the end of the plan year. (4) The plan cannot excuse part-time workers who earn $200 a year in any of three of the five preceding years.

Keogh Plan: full coverage for all employees with 1,000 hours of service per year after three years or sooner if the plan permits. Vesting is immediate: once an employee is eligible for the pension plan, all contributions in his/her account belong to the employee.

Professional Corporation (PC): each plan sets its own terms. Typically, coverage starts at age 25 after one year of service. Vesting is mandated: 100% after three years of service or 20% in Year II with an additional 20% each year to 100% in Year VI (when using one year of eligibility).

Specific Plans

Within these frameworks, the basic types of plans with Keoghs and PCs are:

• **Defined Contribution (DC):** where the annual allocation is predetermined and the participant's retirement income is variable. The contributions are set forth in the plan document by formula, usually a percentage of earned income to a maximum of 25% of compensation or $30,000 a year. The percentage must be the same for all participants.

• **Defined Benefit (DB):** where the ultimate income is determined and the annual contributions, plus anticipated income, are made to accumulate the necessary assets. Retirement can be no earlier than age 62 and the benefit a maximum of 100% of compensation or $90,000 a year.

• **Profit sharing:** where contributions are based on the profits of the business or profession. When profits are up, the contributions can be raised to the maximums; when earnings are down, the set-asides will be less. There can be variations whereby there is a minimum profit level with all profits above this amount contributed to the pension plan.

• **Target benefit:** similar to DB except that, at retirement, the benefit will vary with the plan's actual earnings even though it was funded toward a standard benefit.

• **Combination plans:** for the DC portion, up to 10% of compensation fixed in advance; for the DB portion, the amount needed to fund the predetermined benefit. The calculations are complex but the totals must stay within the maximum limits: annual contribution of $30,000; annual retirement benefit of 100% of compensation to $90,000.

• **Voluntary contributions.** With Keoghs and PCs, each participant can make voluntary contributions up to 10% of annual compensation but only 6% when total contributions/forfeitures are over $30,000.

These are *not* tax deductible, but if you can add $2,000 a year for 10 years, the tax-deferral of income will mean that you should have some $40,000—less taxes—to pay for the children's college costs.

Withdrawals of Assets

With all three types of plans, payments made before age 59½ are subject to a nondeductible penalty of 10% of the amount disbursed. *Exception:* when there's financial hardship, illness or disability. At termination, of course, the participant is entitled to his/her vested assets. In corporate plans, nonvested assets are forfeited, usually to reduce future contributions.

After age 59½, withdrawals can be made at any time and must be started at age 70½. These disbursements are taxable because you got a tax break when the money was put in and Uncle Sam won't let you have it both ways.

If payouts are made in a lump sum, you can use either five- or 10-year averaging for the taxes, according to IRS formulas. The five-year calculations are based on total income for the past five years. To use 10-year averaging, you must have been enrolled in a Keogh or corporate plan for five years. The tax is paid on the basis of 10 years and is calculated as if you were single, with no exemptions or deductions, and taxable income equal to 10% of the total sum. This quotient is multiplied by 10.

Example: In 1983, Dr. Q received $100,000 from his pension plan. The tax base is $2,300 plus 12% of $100,000: $14,300. From Schedule X, Form 1040, he finds that the tax is $308: $1,385 plus 22% of $1,400 ($308, the amount over $12,900 in the tables); a total of $1,693. He multiplies this by 10 to get $16,930, his full tax payment, so he has $83,070 to invest.

Suggestion: If you have ample outside income at retirement, and thus will be in a high tax bracket, consider taking out half of the vested assets in a lump sum, using 10-year averaging and investing the after-tax proceeds in tax-exempt bonds.

BUT IT MAY BE MORE REWARDING TO KEEP THE

PENSION PLAN AND ARRANGE FOR PERIODIC WITHDRAWALS.

At 70½, Uncle Sam mandates invasion of capital of a pension plan. The withdrawals are based on the anticipated life span of an individual or a couple as set by IRS: i.e., for the 70-year-old male, 12.1 years; female, 15 years; for both age 70, 16.4 years.

The distribution must be made on an increasing percentage of assets: with a life expectancy of 16 years (for easy figuring): $\frac{1}{16}$ in Year I; $\frac{1}{15}$ in Year II, etc. until 3½ months before the end of the last year when the full balance must be taken out (and often, will be a *large* sum). You must pay a full tax on each payment but the remaining assets continue tax-free. In effect, you continue the pension plan . . . any type . . . for a preset number of years.

For projections, check with your actuary or pension department at your mutual fund. Typically, with a $100,000 pension plan rolled over into shares of a fund yielding 10% and liquidating over 16.4 years, the annual payment would rise from $6,356 in the first year to $10,416 in the sixth year; to $18,830 in the twelfth year, to $27,966 in the sixteenth year followed by a final check for $11,956: a total of $248,087, about two-thirds from income and the balance from principal. You can, of course, arrange a different schedule as long as the payments are above the IRS minimums.

Special IRA for Minors

A relative (grandparent, uncle, aunt but not parent) can make gifts to children/grandchildren's IRA if the youngster earns money on his/her own. Maximum: $2,000 a year.

Example: Stan Smith, age 16, earns $100 a month from odd jobs. He sets up an IRA to which his grandfather gives $1,200 annually. When Stan is on his own, he can take over and will have a solid base for his retirement.

IRA Rollover

This is a special form of IRA that can be used to continue to shelter money withdrawn early from a corporate pension or Keogh plan. The original payment must be in a lump sum and can be part or all of the individual's vested assets. In the IRA Rollover, the savings continue to accumulate tax-free until payouts start at age 70½ (or before if so desired when after age 59½). There can be no additional contributions; the transfer must be made within 60 days after the distribution and must go directly into the new IRA. *If any of the money is deposited in your personal account, the entire withdrawal will be taxable.*

Added plus: no tax on any capital gains attained during the waiting period: i.e., if Lonnie receives a lump sum payout of $75,000 cash and $75,000 stock. Within a month, the stock value rises to $85,000. Now, Lonnie can start the IRA Rollover with $160,000 and pay no tax on the $10,000 capital gain.

Examples: After 17 years of faithful service with a medical group, Dorothy moves to be closer to her daughter. From the corporate pension plan, she receives a lump sum distribution of $21,000. Because she expects to continue working and still is only in her 50s, Dorothy rolls her money over into an IRA. She does land a new job with a dental clinic and is soon enrolled in a Keogh plan. Now she can look forward to two-pension retirement.

BIG BENEFITS OF IRA ROLLOVER

	TAXABLE	IRA ROLLOVER
Lump-sum distribution	$100,000	$100,000
Tax on distribution	19,150	0
Amount invested (A)	80,850	100,000
Build-up: age 50-65		
Earnings before taxes	170,924	264,248
Taxes @ 32%	54,696	0
Net earnings (B)	116,228	264,248
Value @ age 65 (A+B)	197,078	364,248
25 Year Payout		
Income earned/paid	443,426	0
Income earned/compounded	0	980,905
Taxes @ 32%	141,896	0
Net earnings after taxes	301,530	980,905
Total distribution	0	1,345,153
Taxes @ 32%	0	430,449
Total after taxes	$498,608	$914,704

SOURCE: Rollover IRA, Gary J. Strum of Lord, Abbett & Co.

In 1981, at age 50, Gene decides to take his $100,000 pension fund assets and move into another area where he plans to work for 15 years, then have the account paid out over the joint life expectancy of 25 years (his wife is now age 45). Here are the calculations in "Rollover IRAs" by Gary J. Strum (table). Because of changes in the tax law, the current figures would be slightly different but the concept is sound.

Gene has made most of his money by stock options so he is in the 32% tax bracket and his actuary assumes a 9% return in investments. These are his options:

• **Lump sum payout with 10-year averaging:** after tax net, $80,850. When invested, this earns $7,277 in Year I. Since this is taxable, he pays Uncle Sam $2,329 that year. By age 65, the total after-tax earnings compound to $116,228, which, plus the base of $80,850, total $197,078. With a 25-year payout and the 9% annual yield, he and his spouse will receive $498,608 if both live.

• **IRA Rollover.** Since the full $100,000 is invested, the Year I earnings, again at 9%, are $9,000 tax-free. Gene cannot touch the money (nor does he need to), so, by age 65, the account will grow to $364,248. Over the next 25 years, withdrawals, after continuing earnings, will be $914,704—almost double those without the IRA.

N.B. If the distribution from a pension plan includes life insurance, you will probably owe a tax on the cash value. To avoid this, borrow against the cash value and roll that money over into an IRA and keep the policy for protection.

IRA Better than Money Fund

When savings in an IRA are withdrawn before age 59½, there's a nondeductible penalty of 10% of the payout but it still may pay you to set up such a personal pension plan rather than keep your money in a liquid assets/savings account/fund.

Reason: The IRA savings accumulate tax-free so that, for the individual in the 50% tax bracket, the IRA will be worth more in from four to seven years depending on the rate of return—even after the penalty. Here's how many years money must stay in an IRA for the contribution to be superior to a regular investment earning the same rate of return:

Tax Bracket	Rate of Return		
	8%	10%	15%
30%	7	6	4
40	7	5	4
50	6	5	4

You will have to pay a regular income tax on the withdrawal but the contributions, when made, are tax-deductible.

BENEFITS OF PENSION PLAN
$2,000 Annual Contribution to IRA

Start at age	In IRA	Not in IRA	IRA Advantage
10% Return			
25	$885,000	$185,000	+$700,000
35	329,000	95,000	234,000
45	115,000	44,000	71,000
55	32,000	16,000	16,000
15% Return			
25	$3,558,000	$405,000	+$3,153,000
35	869,000	163,000	706,000
45	205,000	61,000	144,000
55	41,000	18,000	23,000

SOURCE: Scudder, Stevens & Clark

Pension Plan Investments

Pension fund assets should be invested for: (1) safety; (2) income; (3) growth. You can shift those priorities when you have built ample assets or will not have to rely primarily on your pension for after-work income. Pension contributions are fiduciary funds: held in trust for you, your heirs and your employees. By law, the investments must be prudent; by common sense, they should be secure and rewarding. The key criterion is quality: securities of financially strong, profitable corporations and real estate that is well built, well located and well managed. That's why this book can be valuable!

These standards eliminate many of the specially designed packages of oil/gas deals, commodities funds, precious metal partnerships and other speculations that are aggressively promoted in the media and by mail. Before you fall for some of these sucker deals, consider the consequences if that "special opportunity" should fail and decimate your savings.

If you can afford to lose half of your assets (and those of co-workers), some speculations may be justified but it's always an unnecessary, and usually a foolish, risk.

With no taxes to pay, some hot-shots try trading for quick gains; buying options, commodities and financial futures; speculating in new issues; and even selling short. This may be acceptable if you, and your spouse, are the only participants, but it's stupid when other people are involved. Under the Employee Retirement and Income Security Act (ERISA), the employer is responsible for the prudent management of all retirement plan contributions. Unless you are an expert in a field and willing to defend your decisions before a governmental agency or court, concentrate pension plan money in assets that meet the prudent man rule.

In making investments, be realistic. If you start with $2,000 in an IRA, choose a thrift account or mutual fund. Commissions for buying stocks or bonds will reduce your investable assets. If your time and knowledge are limited, let someone else make the decisions. But if you are serious and anxious to make the best use of these savings, do it yourself by following the principles outlined in *Your Investments*. As shown by the results of the sample portfolios, you can outperform the market and most professionals.

Here are the most widely used investments for retirement funds:

Common stocks: only of quality corporations that have made lots of money and have logical prospects of continuing to do so in the near future. You can choose income (utilities, banks and a few out-of-favor companies) or total returns (modest dividends and substantial appreciation). It's best to look for some income because it's not taxed. You'll find lists and guidelines throughout this guide. As explained elsewhere, convertibles qualify as common stocks and can be excellent long-term holdings.

Debt issues: government bills, notes and bonds, corporate notes and bonds. Just be sure that their interest is taxable as the pension plan is a tax shelter. If you go this route, keep an eye on debt that will mature at a future date when cash will be needed for termination or retirement. For total returns, buy discount bonds that will assure good income plus sure appreciation.

Thrift accounts: available from your local bank and thrift institutions. These are *safe*—insured up to $100,000 by Uncle Sam, *reasonably rewarding*—currently 8% to 10% with, at times, compounding; *inexpensive*—from as little as $500 and no commissions and no, or small, administration fees: *convenient*—just walk down to the corner and set up your IRA or arrange for a Keogh or Corporate plan under terms developed with your tax adviser and actuary.

If you choose this route, diversify by maturities so that there will always be ample cash to make payments for the benefits of employees who leave, die or retire. Otherwise, an early withdrawal will require penalties, typically the loss of three months' interest. And *never* get locked into any holding that mandates the method of payout. You want to have a choice based on conditions when you quit work. But while these CDs may pay well today, they have not always been overly rewarding.

U.S. Government retirement bonds. These are sold by Federal Reserve Banks and the U.S. Treasury in denominations of $50, $100 and $500. They are eligible only for retirement plans. They yield 9% compounded annually. If they are redeemed prior to age 59½ (except for disability), the proceeds are taxed as income in the year they are cashed plus a penalty of 10% of the proceeds. After age 59½, they can be redeemed with taxation of the proceeds as income in the year of redemption.

These are poor investments but may have some use as a continuing tax shelter after retirement. They are safe but little more.

Mutual Funds. Your savings are pooled for investment according to your plan goal. You have a wide choice and, in most cases, can switch funds under the same management for a modest fee. You can choose money market funds for high income; bond funds for steady returns; growth funds for capital gains and low dividends; or diversified funds for those who cannot make up their minds.

As explained in the chapter on investment companies, there are numerous extras: the opportunity to borrow with the shares as collateral; computer readouts to keep track of purchase dates so that taxes, at withdrawal, can be kept low; low-cost life insurance (when you're not too old); and, of course, convenience in that all you have to do is send in checks.

In most cases, the total returns will be less than you can achieve yourself. Even with no-loads, your net will be cut by about 1% because of administration fees and other costs. And once in a while, the returns will be unusually high if the manager was smart and lucky.

Real estate. If you are knowledgeable, you can invest in real estate on your own. One of the better ways to do so with pension fund assets is to buy the land and let the promoter/builder own the building and take the tax deductions for depreciation, interest on the mortgage, investment tax credit, etc. Then, lease the land on a percentage of rent basis with an escalator clause so that your investment will benefit from higher rentals and, on sale, from a share of the capital gains. Builders always need cash so you can make a profitable deal. Just be sure that this is an arm's length transaction: that you do not have any personal money in the deal. Many professionals use their pension fund for the land, then work with colleagues who use personal money. On the next project, the colleagues put up their pension money and you use your savings in the ownership of the building.

Be cautious with all real estate. It is always easier to get in than to get out. A well-structured pension plan should be flexible and liquid enough to provide money quickly to pay for benefits due participants at severance, death or retirement. Do not invest fiduciary money in real estate until total assets are $100,000 and then, keep the percentage below 20%.

Guaranteed Income Contracts (GICs). These are sold by insurance companies and recently guaranteed yields of over 11% for three or more years. The minimum investment is usually substantial: $100,000 or more, with an agreement for regular future contributions.

GICs were popular a few years ago when interest rates were high but have not done so well of late because of better returns . . . with comparable safety . . . in other holdings. Still, they are safe and you get detailed reports.

Zero coupon bonds. These are the latest Wall Street package to attract managers of pension funds, both professionals and amateurs. These are debt issue offered at huge discounts: one-quarter to one-third of face value with redemption, at par, at the end of a pre-set number of years, eight, 10 and, sometimes, longer. No interest is paid. Thus, a bond, bought for $250, will be paid off at $1,000 10 years from now.

Under IRS rules, individual investors must pay taxes on the assumed interest but pension plans, with no taxes to pay, can benefit: a fixed, fairly high rate of return because of compounding plus call protection because the bonds are not likely to be redeemed early.

Zerialists do lock in a preset yield but there are risks that: (1) interest rates will soar and thus denigrate the value of the bonds; (2) the company may not be able to pay off at maturity; (3) the true value of the paid-up loan will be reduced by inflation.

For those who don't want to be bothered with problems of reinvestment, these zerialists can be welcome, especially when they are selected to mature at retirement time.

Offbeat "Investments" such as art, antiques, stamps, coins and so forth. In 1981 Congress banned these collectibles from self-directed personal pension plans: all IRAs and Keoghs and Corporate plans that give employers control over plan investments. *Exception:* portfolios directed by an outside trustee. Congress felt that these professionals will act with prudence either because of special skills or the necessity to adhere to legal and ethical standards. Anyway, most people are happy about such discrimination because, in the last couple of years, the values of almost all collectibles have fallen through the floor.

Managing Pension Investments

You can manage your own or plan money through your broker by placing the pension plan with a fiduciary such as a bank or trust company. Check on the details as some arrangements keep idle cash under $1,000 in a noninterest-bearing account. *Best bet:* a program where spare funds, from dividends/interest, are automatically swept into a money market fund.

For the trustee/custodian/reporting services, typical charges range from one-time opening of $25 to $100; administration, $40 to $75 a year; per transaction levy of $3; trustee cost of $\frac{1}{10}$ to $\frac{3}{4}$ of 1% of portfolio value. With almost all of these, you get a printout of all transactions, income, withdrawals, etc., to keep everyone informed and to aid in filing tax returns when required.

Beneficiary

Pension assets can be passed on to heirs with minimal taxes when the trust agreement is properly prepared. Normally, the beneficiary will be the spouse but the children can be named or, when substantial sums are involved, all or part can go into a trust.

Be sure to keep the designation of the beneficiary(ies) up to date. It will take precedence over the provisions of a will. If you fail to name a beneficiary in your pension plan, the assets will probably go into your estate with the result that they will be distributed according to your will or, if you are stupid enough not to have one, as the court mandates. There are no special terms for IRAs but, with Keoghs and PCs:

• The first $5,000 of a lump-sum distribution will be income tax-free.

• The first $100,000 will be excluded from the gross estate. Assets above that figure will be taxed at both federal and state level unless they are part of the marital deduction bequests—soon to be $600,000.

When the payouts are in the form of an annuity, partly paid for by voluntary contributions, the beneficiary must pay, within 36 months, taxes on the difference between the annuity payments and the after-tax dollars originally invested.

Example: Fred's pension plan includes an annuity that pays his widow $12,000 a year. He has made voluntary contributions of $20,000 to the plan. After his death, Mrs. F. reports no taxable income in Year I. But in the Year II, IRS sets a balance-of-cost basis: $8,000 taxable income, representing the $20,000 contribution minus the $12,000 benefits already paid. In Year III, the balance, $12,000, is taxed as ordinary income.

Loans from a Pension Plan

You *cannot* borrow from an IRA unless you own less than 10% of the business. Withdrawals made before age 59½ are subject to a penalty and cannot be replaced.

If a loan is made, the owner must pay a nondeductible 5% tax on the amount of the loan each year the loan is outstanding. If he fails to repay within 90 days after the IRS order, the tax climbs to 100%.

You *can* borrow from a Corporate pension plan when a loan is permitted under the trust agreement, bears a competitive rate of interest, carries a schedule of payments of interest and principal and is available on the same terms to other eligible employees.

Any participant can borrow a minimum of $10,000 and a maximum of $50,000 as long as the loan is less than 50% of the individual's vested accrued benefits: i.e., with $200,000 in vested assets, a physician can borrow $50,000; with a vested balance of $20,000, a nurse can borrow $10,000.

Each loan must be repaid in five years unless the money is used to acquire, construct or rehabilitate a dwelling used as a principal residence by the borrower or *a member of his/her family.* That covers your son or son-in-law!

Don't Save Too Much

With the substantial maximum contributions to Corporate plans before TEFRA (defined benefit of $136,425 and de-

fined contribution of $45,475) and the magic of compounding of investment income tax-free, the pension assets of many high earners, such as physicians, dentists and lawyers, are . . . or will be . . . well into six figures.

After retirement, their income, from their pension and investments, will put them in the highest tax bracket: after 1984, 49% with taxable income of under $162,400; 45% at $100,000. This raises the question, "Why am I still pouring money into my pension plan if the taxes, when I withdraw the money, will be as high as when I put it in?"

To provide a frame of reference, check with your actuary/investment adviser to estimate your after-work money-earning assets, then calculate the anticipated rate of return and assume a 15% annual rate of withdrawal. This may require invasion of principal (mandated by IRS) but with investments yielding 12%, you can take out that 15% annually for 14 years—longer than the actuarial life span of a 70-year old male and just about as long as a 70-year old female can expect to live.

As a rule of thumb it's wise to review your pension plan when your share of retirement savings is more than $600,000. This will assure annual income of $90,000 which, plus Social Security and other income, should be ample. At this point, it may pay you to curtail pension contributions, despite their tax deductions, and buy tax-free bonds.

Buy Retirement Benefits, Not Life Insurance

Life insurance is not a wise investment for pension and profit-sharing programs. It is not permitted in Individual Retirement Accounts, is of minimal value with Keogh Plans, and can be used effectively through professional corporations only under special circumstances.

The primary purpose of *life insurance* is protection against death: to build an instant estate and assure assets for your heirs in case you die early.

The primary purpose of a *pension fund* is to provide income after retirement.

Most important, the premiums for life insurance are not tax-deductible. The most effective use of life insurance in a pension plan is to guarantee the ultimate benefit to the beneficiary if the participant dies, especially with defined benefits plans.

There are ways for those who receive high compensation under Professional Corporations to utilize life insurance under a pension/profit sharing plan. The corporation can take tax deductions on the corporate contribution but the participant must pay taxes according to an IRS table. For details, see an experienced life insurance agent as these plans are complex and are worthwhile only for those in high income brackets.

N.B. This does not mean that you should not consider having an insurance company handle your pension plan. They can do an excellent job of setup and administration, arrange for a convenient payout and provide full reports. But such services are not inexpensive, so get quotations first.

Annuities in and After
Pension Plans

All types of annuities involve retirement because they guarantee income, usually for life, after a certain age. Straight annuities can be purchased within a pension plan while working or, after retirement, with withdrawals. Deferred annuities are special types of tax savers bought with after-tax dollars.

All annuities are contracts with insurance companies to make a monthly payment for: (*a*) as long as one or both partners live; (*b*) a period certain, say 10, 15, or 20 years; (*c*) for life with 10 years guaranteed with, at early death, the balance going to heirs.

When you buy any type of annuity, you choose *security* over *income*. Except with (*c*), there will be nothing left at the final death whether it comes two months or 30 years after the first payout. *With annuities, you win only if you and/or your spouse outlive actuarial life expectancies.*

You can specify how your savings will be invested: for *fixed-income,* where the holdings will be bonds and mortgages to provide a set sum each month or *variable-income,* where the investments are split between bonds and stocks and the returns will fluctuate but will never be below a guaranteed minimum.

Within pensions plans annuities can be bought with tax-deductible contributions. In most cases, this approach is more convenient than rewarding: the insurance company handles everything and, in effect, locks in one form of investments and sends out monthly checks after work. When started early with a good rate of return, these annuities can build substantial assets for retirement. Bankers Life of Des Moines, for example, recently submitted this proposal to a 45-year-old physician: "Send us $25,000 a year and we will invest the money in a fixed income annuity paying 9.75% a year. When compounded, you'll have a nest egg, at age 65, of $1,420,176. No fuss, no bother and modest costs: $25 annual fee plus a percentage-of-assets charge not to exceed $250 a year. But early withdrawals will be subject to a surrender levy starting at 7% and declining annually. After-work payments will be taxable."

The problems with an annuity come when it's tied to life insurance. With such combinations, the corporation can deduct the full payment to the insurance company but dollars used to buy life insurance become taxable, in that year, to the insured. In some cases, part of those extra taxes can be recaptured after retirement. As a general rule, it's easier, wiser and cheaper to buy life insurance outside a pension plan and to use all pension contributions for after-work income.

At retirement all or part of vested pension assets can be used to buy an annuity. This decision can be delayed until close to quitting time but the purchase must be made within 60 days after retirement date. Taxes on the payments are paid under an IRS exclusion formula:

Example: At age 60, Bachelor Bill cashes in his IRA, pays the taxes and buys an annuity for a net-after-commission cost of $10,800. At age 65, this will pay Bill $100 per month for life, which, actuarially, will be 15 years. This means a total return of $18,000 ($1,200 × 15).

To determine the exclusion percentage, Bill divides the total investment ($10,800) by the expected return ($18,000) to get 60%. Each year, $720 of the annuity (60% of $1,200) will be tax-free and the remaining $480 taxable.

Before you choose any type of annuity, consider the pros and cons. With fixed-income contracts, the return will be eroded by inflation and there will be no opportunity to take advantage of higher rates of return available from other investments where the principal remains intact.

Example: When Al retired in 1977, he used $100,000 to buy an annuity with an 8% fixed yield and another $100,000 to buy a package of intermediate term bonds with an average yield of 7.2%. Al dies in 1990. With the annuity, he received $10,400 more income over the 13 years but leaves nothing to his family. The bonds, some of which were bought at discounts, are worth $110,000 and will go to his heirs.

In many cases, the purchase of tax-exempt bonds will work out better. Here's an example cited by Executive Wealth Advisory with a one-time investment of $100,000:

With an 8% tax deferred annuity, the total accumulation will be $216,000 in 10 years; $466,000 in 20 years . . . *before taxes.*

In the same time periods, $100,000 invested in a tax-exempt bond fund that yields 6% and automatically reinvests all interest will grow to $179,000 and $321,000 respectively . . . *tax-free.*

The annuity wins only when the recipient is in a low or modest tax bracket: in 10 years, less than 17% ($216,000 minus 17% tax equals $179,000); in 20 years, under 31% ($466,000 minus 31% tax equals $321,000).

Deferred Annuities

These can be purchased directly with a lump sum or periodic payments. They are like a pension plan in that the income accumulates tax-deferred until withdrawal but the investment is *not* tax deductible. In retirement, a portion of the payout (the original dollars) is tax-free as a return of capital (see Bachelor Bill example).

The money can be invested for fixed or variable income or to acquire shares of a special mutual fund owned and managed by the insurance company solely for variable annuity customers. Most of these have an annual administration fee of $25 to $35 plus a "mortality fee" or "annual asset charge"—about 1% of the value of the annuity. This is to assure payment of a death benefit if the annuity owner dies while there is still money invested in the annuity.

You can pledge the annuity as collateral for a loan and distributions can be delayed past age 70½ as mandated for most pension plans.

Recently, there have been some problems with deferred annuities:

1. IRS ruling that excess interest is taxable to the insurance company: i.e., if the policy guarantees 4½% minimum and is currently paying 12½%, that 8% spread is taxable to the insurance company. But many firms absorb this levy because they get a credit of 87½% on the excess "dividends" paid out to the policyholder.

2. When an annuity is held for less than 10 years, withdrawals before age 59½ are subject to a 5% excise tax.

3. One major insurance company, whose policies have been widely and aggressively promoted, ran into financial

problems so that sales of new contracts ceased and there are questions as to the liquidity, if not the safety, of outstanding policies.

Advice: stash away as much as you can in personal pension plans with both deductible and voluntary contributions; consider tax-exempt securities; and if you still need to shelter income, consider deferred annuities with a large, established insurance firm.

Projecting Value of Retirement Plan

To guesstimate the value of your retirement savings, use these tables. (If you are dealing with an IRA, substitute smaller contributions.)

Table A lists the factors to use, at varying time spans and yields, to project the growth of assets. (And, later, if you're the cautious type, the impact of inflation.)

Table B shows the compounding factor to be used for annual contributions, again at different time periods and rates of return.

Table C is a work sheet. This example applies to an individual who has been in a Keogh (or Corporate) Plan for some years, has accumulated $40,000 and plans to add

$5,000 annually. The annual rate of return is 12% and he expects to work another 25 years.

The Growth Factor is 17 so the future value of his current savings will be a whopping $680,000. The $125,000 total contributions, again at 12% annual yield, have a Growth Factor of 133.33 (Table B) so the new money will total $666,650. Total fund at retirement: $1,346,650. *That's the Magic of Compounding!*

TABLE A

COMPOUNDING FACTOR

For Annual Yield or Inflation

YEARS	5%	8%	10%	12%	15%
5	1.28	1.47	1.61	1.76	2.01
10	1.63	2.16	2.59	3.11	4.05
15	2.08	3.17	4.18	5.47	8.14
20	2.65	4.66	6.73	9.65	16.37
25	3.39	6.85	10.83	17.00	32.92
30	4.32	10.06	17.45	29.96	66.21

SOURCE: David Thorndike, ed., THE THORNDIKE ENCYCLOPEDIA OF BANKING AND FINANCIAL TABLES (Boston: Warren, Gorham & Lamont, 1980).

TABLE B

COMPOUNDING FACTOR WITH ANNUAL CONTRIBUTIONS

Years to Go	6%	8%	10%	12%	15%
5	5.64	5.87	6.11	6.35	6.74
10	13.18	14.49	15.94	17.55	20.30
15	23.28	27.15	31.77	37.28	47.58
20	36.79	45.76	57.27	72.05	102.44
25	54.86	73.11	98.35	133.33	212.79
30	79.06	113.28	164.49	241.33	434.75

SOURCE: David Thorndike, ed., THE THORNDIKE ENCYCLOPEDIA OF BANKING AND FINANCIAL TABLES (Boston: Warren, Gorham & Lamont, 1980)

TABLE C

PROJECTING VALUE OF RETIREMENT PLAN

A.	Current value of fund	$40,000
B.	Years to retirement	25
C.	Annual rate of return	12%
D.	Growth Factor (Table A)	17.00
E.	Value of current savings at retirement (A X D)	$680,000
F.	Future annual contribution	$5,000
G.	Growth Factor @ 12% (Table B)	133.33
H.	Value of new additions at retirement (F X G)	$666,650
I.	Value of total fund at retirement (E + H)	$1,346,650

SOURCE: Based on ABC's of Investing Retirement Funds; C. Colburn Hardy, MEDICAL ECONOMICS, 1982

28

Stocks for Portfolios: For Investment and Speculation

It's exciting and, sometimes, profitable, to speculate with securities: to buy new or high-tech issues and watch the shares double or triple in a few months. But such success is more luck than skill. And the long-term odds are *always* against you: only a handful of fledgling firms ever grow into quality corporations.

Investments, on the other hand, can be almost sure winners if you stick to quality, buy the securities when they are undervalued and sell them when they become fully priced or, if you made a mistake, at a small, quick loss.

In the pages that follow are lists of the kinds of securities that should be the core of every pension and most personal portfolios. The target goal, in this buoyant market, should be a 20% total return with the realization that, in flat/down markets, the returns will be less so that your average annual yield will be about 16% which, after commissions, should net 14% to 15%. At that rate, you'll double your money every five years!

The stocks suggested here are in these groups:

1. Broad shopping lists of quality companies that have long, and fairly consistent, records of keys to different goals: high income and modest growth (primarily utilities); modest income and high growth (industrials, financial firms and service organizations).

2. Debt securities, more for illustration than recommendation because their values reflect the cost of money (over which you have no control) rather than the quality and money-making ability of the issuing corporation. There are few of these because all types of debt securities should be bought from your broker's inventory as their prices will be more favorable: slightly lower when buying; slightly higher when selling. And the broker will usually be ready to buy back the securities when you want to sell.

3. Speculations that are included reluctantly because of requests from long-term readers. As you will learn from experience, the research on these "future" companies is usually incomplete, often more guesswork than fact and few firms have been around long enough to prove the ability of management. You're always taking risks which, in total, usually are greater than the rewards.

4. Specific suggestions, almost all equities, for *Portfolios for Times of Your Life.* These are limited to stocks listed on the NYSE because, basically, this is where most quality stocks are traded. But with research, you can pick up winners on the AMEX or OTC.

All-Purpose Securities

The best way to describe these portfolios is as: (1) pension plan investments—holdings chosen for three or more years on the basis of fundamental quality and current value; (2) flexible holdings—in that generally all securities are suitable for all portfolios. Their choices depend on your resources, your goals and your style. If you're 31 and conservative, take a look at the stocks in the Portfolio for the 60s. If you're 66 and have extra savings, buy some of these growth stocks listed in, or suggested for, the Portfolio for the 30s. At this time, all of the suggestions are quality corporations, but conditions can change rapidly so stay alert and manage your money.

There are times (in the past few years, for example) when investors will do better, and feel safer, with high-yielding debt issues or shares of money market funds. The values of both move with the interest rate so should be considered only for a portion of savings or as temporary holdings that can be cashed in to take advantage of more rewarding opportunities. But, as explained elsewhere, discount bonds can be excellent and cash management accounts can be worthwhile because the proceeds of a sale or interest/dividends can be promptly reinvested to earn extra dollars.

Changing Market

From the time I took over the editorship of *Your Investments,* I have stressed the importance of quality. There were years when this did not produce the greatest returns but, right from the start of this bull market, quality stocks have been the leaders. This emphasis was even more pronounced in the spring of 1983 when so much money came in from mutual funds and insurance companies from IRA contributions. This demand boosted prices so that, in some cases, some stocks were no longer bargains. But fiduciary funds are always long-term holdings so that, over the years ahead, the institutions will continue to favor quality. The values of well-rated stocks may rise more slowly but, in the next 24–30 months, are likely to be much higher because the corporations will be making more money.

At this time, there are signs of a new trend: a shift of personal savings into more speculative situations. Investors who have scored unusual gains (more the result of the booming market than their own prescience) are buying new issues and high technology issues. This trend has been encouraged by hard-selling underwriters who focus more attention on their previous winners than on current offerings.

Part of this switch reflects the fact that huge corporations are just too big to be able to boost profits as sharply as in the past. As a result, their shares are becoming, relatively, less attractive. Smaller firms with revenues of $250 million to $1 billion, will, percentagewise, provide the best returns. What this means is that a billion dollar company can no longer be considered "big." In fact, only a handful of the 500 major corporations reported revenues below $1 billion! That's why more of the suggested stocks are of medium-size firms.

The remarkable rise of the market—over 400 points in one year as measured by the Dow Jones Industrials—came with amazing speed. Historically, such a gain took at least two years (1974–76) or 10 years (1962–72). Keep this in mind and temper your projections.

The market has also been characterized by sudden shifts in leadership: first, industrials, then electronics, and, lately, oil and gas companies. But throughout, one group kept plugging along steadily: utilities: a 35% rise in less than three years. Add the 10% dividend and the average annual rate of return was a hefty 22%. With prospects of still lower interest rates, this welcome trend seems likely to continue. That's why there are more utilities in the sample portfolios this year.

TABLE A
PROJECTED HIGH TOTAL RETURNS BY 1987

All itens are PLUS (+)

COMPANY	Divs.	Growth Earns.	Div. Rein.	Earned Return	Change P/E	Total Return
Baker Inter.	13.8%	16.5%	3.4%	19.9%	24.9%	44.8%
Celeron Corp.	17.6	27.1	2.4	29.5	3.6	33.1
Cooper Indus.	9.5	16.7	4.3	21.0	12.7	33.7
Daniel Indus.	19.6	16.3	1.7	18.0	16.4	34.4
Digital Equip.	0	25.8	0	25.8	5.8	31.6
Dresser Indus.	18.3	28.1	3.1	31.2	−.5	30.7
ENSERCH Corp.	11.5	14.7	8.0	22.7	16.4	39.1
1st Ci-Banc-Tex.	12.9	15.4	5.1	20.5	16.5	37.0
Flight Safety	23.5	25.0	.7	25.7	5.7	31.4
Halliburton	12.6	14.9	4.2	19.1	12.5	31.6
Helmerich/Payne	13.6	14.9	1.7	16.6	16.0	32.6
Houston Nat. Gas	12.9	15.3	4.3	19.6	14.6	34.2
Hughes Tool	13.4	14.1	3.5	17.6	12.9	30.5
Internorth,Inc.	10.5	15.4	7.0	22.4	10.6	33.0
Midcon Corp.	9.9	7.9	8.8	16.7	14.5	31.2
Nicor, Inc.	6.6	16.5	8.4	24.9	5.5	30.4
Pan. Eastern	10.5	11.5	8.6	20.1	17.4	37.5
Petrolane, Inc.	18.1	16.7	3.6	20.3	11.4	31.7
Pioneer Corp.	19.0	21.6	4.8	26.4	11.9	38.3
Rowan Cos.	31.1	16.1	1.2	17.3	19.4	36.7
Schlumberger	22.1	19.6	2.1	21.7	17.0	38.7
SmithKlineBeck.	17.7	20.8	3.2	24.0	7.0	31.0
Sonat, Inc.	15.3	12.0	5.0	17.0	17.8	34.8
Southern Union	7.0	21.1	6.5	27.6	5.1	32.7
Stan. Oil (Ind.)	8.7	13.9	6.2	20.1	10.9	31.0
Texas Gas. Trans.	11.0	11.2	7.4	18.6	12.8	31.4
Xerox Corp.	10.8	17.5	6.6	24.1	7.4	31.5

SOURCE: Wright Investors' Service

Projected High Total Returns: Table A

This shows some companies that should be highly profitable investments in the next few years. They are all major corporations, many of which play essential roles in the USA and around the world. They are managed by tough-minded professionals who must produce or be replaced. At times, their managements may be slow to move but all have ample resources in manpower, money, facilities, products, distribution or service. Most have been profitable in the past and should be more so in the future. They know how to make money so that shareholders will benefit: primarily from appreciation but also with ever-higher dividends. These are the types of stocks that are in the portfolios of major institutional investors and that should be part of the holdings of every individual who wants to build assets.

This doesn't mean that you should buy these stocks and lock them in a safe deposit box. Review them frequently, compare their returns with your investment goals and do not hesitate to sell when the company appears to be living on its reputation rather than on profits or when major investors start selling. In a broad sense, follow the leaders: buy when they buy; sell when they sell. Your broker can keep you up to date on such activities or watch the Most Active List. With wise timing of both buying and selling, you will be able to outscore the market and retire with financial security . . . or travel more after you quit work.

Stocks for High Income: Table B

This has been an ever-changing mix: in past years, REITs, bank stocks, utility stocks, convertibles and a few unpopular industries.

With ever-lower yields of Treasury bills/notes, CDs and money market funds, these securities offer a chance for both income and appreciation. As the cost of money drops, their values, based on yields, will rise. And, because most of these companies can be expected to boost their payouts, the gains should be substantial.

TABLE B
QUALITY STOCKS WITH HIGH DIVIDENDS

COMPANY	RECENT YIELD	COMPANY	RECENT YIELD
American Brands	7.8%	Peoples Energy	12.0%
ENSERCH Corp.	8.3	Public Ser. (Indiana)	11.0
Florida P & L	8.9	Southern Union	9.3
Florida Progress	9.8	Southwest P.S.	10.0
Houston Industries	11.0	Teco Energy	8.8
Internorth, Inc.	7.7	Texas Eastern	8.1
Midcon Corp.	8.5	Texas Gas Corp.	7.5
Nicor, Inc.	11.0	Texas Utilities	9.5
Northwest Bancorp.	7.5	Tucson Electric	8.4
ONEOK, Inc.	9.5	Xerox Corp.	7.5
Panhandle Eastern	8.3		

SOURCE: Wright Investors' Service

Do not take this progress for granted. Check the quarterly reports to see if profits are rising enough to warrant higher dividends. If there is one poor or flat quarter, watch out; if there are two in succession, sell. Always keep that 10%-to-15% decline in mind. Unless you plan to hold the stocks for a long time, don't argue with the market. When the stock price drops, professionals are worried and no longer want to own these shares. If you are not satisfied with the income, sell and look for other opportunities where you can get what you want.

Highly Profitable Companies: Table C

These companies make a lot of money and, since they have done so for a decade, are likely to continue to set records. They are excellent long-term investments if they maintain their high profitability. But, in some cases, they are fully priced as the result of hefty gains in the early stages of the bull market: from August 1982 to May 1983: Tandy from 24 to over 60 (and down to 34 later); American Standard from 17 to the mid 30s.

But others, especially those in the oil/gas business, are still at bargain levels. Use this list as a starting point and then make your own projections. If you cannot hope for a 50% total return in the next couple of years, look elsewhere . . . unless you are investing pension fund assets where time alone is not a major consideration.

When such quality companies start boosting profits—

and their records show that this is probable—their stocks will become popular so that their prices will rise. You may have to be patient because Wall Street is often slow to shift its preferences but when it does, action can be fast and rewarding.

The greatest gains should come from improved price/earnings ratios as more investors recognize true worth. But the bigger dividends, especially when reinvested, can be significant, too.

These are excellent stocks for those planning retirement and for gifts to children and grandchildren. They should be among the leaders in a bull market because they have the financial strength, investment acceptance and profitable growth that attract institutional money managers.

The projections are based mathematically on the past performance of the corporation. Their annual rate of earnings growth is the product of internal management; the change in the P/E ratio is external and psychological, reflecting investor attitude toward common stocks in general and the company's stock in particular. These data are valuable for comparative analytical judgments; they are not to be assumed to be predictions of the future results of the company or the value of the stocks.

For Speculators: Table D

The dream of every speculator (and many investors) is to find another Xerox: a small company (*a*) with unique products or services and competent management, (*b*) whose stock will soar in value and be split again and again until you can sell enough shares to get back your original investment and still own several hundred shares.

Only rarely does this work out and then success takes many years. For every successful, small, publicly owned company there are six failures. Table D lists some small companies that have been in business long enough and have proven, competent management. Some of these have grown very rapidly, and chances are their future growth

TABLE C
CONSISTENTLY HIGHLY PROFITABLE COMPANIES

| | 10 YEAR AVERAGE | | |
| | Growth/ | Growth/ | Return on |
COMPANY	Earnings	Dividends	Equity
American Standard	21%	31%	19%
Baker International	32	26	24
Big Three Industries	25	29	19
Church Fr. Chicken	32	30	32
Computervision	44	NC	38
Daniel Industries	25	26	20
Digital Equipment	30	0	17
Flightsafety Inter.	34	37	27
General Instrument	30	43	14
Helmerich Payne	27	28	21
Hilton Hotels	31	29	17
Hughes Tool	28	40	18
Keystone Inter.	25	38	32
Loral Corp.	36	36	28
Medtronic, Inc.	26	NC	22
National Medical Care	30	38	24
Noble Affiliate	32	39	20
Nucor Corp.	25	32	29
Philbro-Salomon	28	25	37
Pioneer Corp.	28	24	32
Rowan Cos.	39	35	29
Schlumberger, Ltd.	36	35	32
Smith International	27	29	23
Tandy Corp.	36	0	34
Texas Oil & Gas	33	80	29

NC: Not comparable

SOURCE: Wright Investors' Service

TABLE D
SMALL COMPANIES WITH RECORDS OF FAST GROWTH

| | | GROWTH | 4 YEAR |
| | S&P | RATE: | AVERAGE |
COMPANY	RATING	REVENUES	EARNINGS
CACI, Inc.	B+	66%	50%
CGA Computer Assoc.	B+	36	10
Continium Co., Inc.	B	45	130
Cullinane Database	NR	58	66
HBO & Co., Inc.	NR	55	58
Intermetrics, Inc.	NR	45	39
Monchik-Weber Corp.	NR	32	36
On-Line Software	NR	53	150
Pansophic Systems	NR	51	56
Policy Management	NR	37	91
SofTech, Inc.	NR	46	52
Software AG Systems	NR	50	28
Systematics, Inc.	NR	28	48
TERA Corporation	NR	46	49

SOURCE: High Technology Growth Stocks (Concord, Mass. 01742).

will be slower. But the risks are less and the potential rewards better than average. All of them were able to increase their earnings in the last four years—no mean feat. On the basis of past performance, their managements should continue such progress. But watch their reports carefully and get ready to take your profits when there's the first sign of trouble (usually flat or lower earnings). They are still *small* companies and do not yet have the financial strength that will enable them to keep moving ahead. And *always use only money you can afford to lose!*

Not All Winners; Table E

To re-emphasize the point that not all quality stocks are always good buys, Table E lists some companies that, probably, should not be held and, unless the situations change, should not be purchased. At this time, they still deserve a quality rating but their prices are too high when judged against future prospects. Their total returns, over the next few years, will average less than 10%. You can do better elsewhere.

Do not hesitate to sell because, almost without exception, their values are at record highs so there should be ample gains: for Gannett, from a 1982 low of 30 to a recent high of 67; for U.S. Shoe, from about 12 (adjusted for a 2–1 split) to 46.

To a degree, these higher values represent higher earnings but, as usually happens in Wall Street, they are overinflated by investor enthusiasm that boosted the multiples far above historic ranges: for Time, Inc., to a price/earning ratio of 25 compared to a 10-year range of 13–7.8; for E-Systems, to 23 vs. a decade average of around 10.

The prospects of a decline reflect the proven tendency of stocks to move back to their traditional ratios.

With all of these projections, keep in mind that they are mechanical estimates so that if and when conditions change radically, they will no longer be valid. But with all of these stocks, be cautious and remember that it is just as important not to lose money as to score profits.

TABLE E
BE CAUTIOUS; LOWER RETURNS AHEAD?

COMPANY	TOTAL RETURNS THRU 1986	RECENT PRICE	PRICE/EARNINGS RATIO	
			RECENT	1973-82
Bandag, Inc.	+7.4%	54	18	17- 9.1
Bard (C.R.)	+4.8	39	20	18- 9.7
Dayton Hudson	+3.5	68	16	10- 6.1
Diebold, Inc.	+5.1	87	19	16- 8.6
Disney Productions	+7.8	80	25	22-12
Dow, Jones & Co.	+6.2	48	33	19-11
E—Systems, Inc.	+6.9	60	23	13- 7.2
Gannett Company	+6.7	67	20	17-11
Loctite Corp.	+8.0	38	25	22-12
Mercantile Stores	+5.6	154	13	9.1-5.5
Rite Aid Corp.	+7.8	43	17	16- 7.7
Rubbermaid, Inc.	+1.6	44	24	18-10
Time, Inc.	+6.8	63	25	13- 7.8
U.S. Shoe	+7.3	37	14	7.8-4.1
VF Corp.	+6.6	70	11	8.0-4.2

SOURCE: Wright Investors' Service

Sample Portfolios

With all of these suggestions, keep these points in mind:

1. Some changes are made for illustration rather than for profit: i.e., the sale of 50 shares of Chesebrough-Pond's in the Portfolio for the 30s and the 100 shares of Warner-Lambert.

Both of these are excellent companies and their stocks have some way to go but the sales provided substantial gains and the proceeds can be reinvested for equal or better returns.

2. Even in strong markets, some stocks move up more slowly than others. This indicates lack of institutional interest due to: (*a*) shifts in popularity of industry groups: in early 1983, oil-related stocks (Exxon, Hughes Tool and Schlumberger) were in the doghouse while electronics (Digital Equipment and IBM) scored huge gains; (*b*) lower than anticipated earnings for cyclical industries battered by the slow economic recovery (Cooper Industries and Dresser Industries).

3. Over the long-term of true investments, 12 months is a short time. In normal stock markets, worthwhile gains take two to three years. If they come more quickly, take 'em and be joyous.

4. All of these securities are the *types* to consider for specific goals: for younger folks, total returns that come primarily from appreciation with modest dividends; for older folks, income of 8% or 9% in interest/dividends.

5. It is always just as important to minimize losses as to maximize gains. That's why some fine stocks were sold with a loss or small profit. Yet the majority of amateurs are reluctant to take such a realistic view. They hold on in hope . . . and usually lose more money. *If the stock does not perform as you anticipate, get out and look elsewhere. Don't argue with Wall Street.*

As stated throughout this book, be ready to sell when the price of your stock drops 15% below your cost of recent high . . . or set stop-loss orders as explained in Chapter 23.

Under these terms, several of the stocks would have been sold in the market decline in August 1982. But since the last edition of *Your Investments* was not available until January 1983, these sales are disregarded—with, in most cases, favorable comebacks in the up market that followed.

Portfolio for the 30s

This is for the young investor who has 30 years or more to build his/her assets. All of these suggestions have been, and still are, better for growth than income.

Since these sample portfolios were started in 1973, these growth-oriented suggestions have beaten the market averages but have not done as well as other age groups. In the generally down markets, the anticipated growth was not achieved within the necessary one year. But the strong surge changed this so that the overall return, from mid-1982 to mid-1983, was +28.2%.

HOLD: 100 shares of Chesebrough-Pond's which appear to be starting a strong upmove, already from 37 to 44 with a target of 60.

Nabisco Brands which rose from 35 to 42 but fell back

PORTFOLIO FOR THE 30s

SHARES/ COMPANY	COST	VALUE 1982	1983	INCOME 1982-83	TOTAL 1982-83	TARGET
HOLD						
100 Ches.-Pond's	34	37	44	$264	$964	60
100 Nabisco Brands	23	35	35	314	314	60
SELL						
50 Ches.-Pond's	34	37	44	132	482	
100 Long's Drugs	32	32	43	153	1,255	
100 Warner-Lambert	10	24	33	210	1,110	

With the proceeds of $9,800 and $1,073 income ($10,873),

BUY	COST	DIVIDENDS	TARGET
200 Daniel Indus.	11	.18	25
150 Eckerd (Jack)	30	.96	45
150 Josten's	25	.92	37
OR			
200 Flight Safety	30	.16	45
300 National Medical	14	.46	24

WHAT HAPPENED TO LAST YEAR'S SUGGESTED BUYS:

	Then	PRICES Targeted	Actual
Alco Standard	20	30	30
Barry Wright	16	35	25
Core Industries*	11	25	14
Daniel Industries	14	30	11
Josten's Inc.	17	29	25
Nat. Medical	8	24	14
Super Valu Stores	18	30	30
Waste Management**	33	55	47

* No longer meets quality standards
** Reached 62 before unfavorable publicity so should have been sold.

to 35 again. Recent heavy volume indicates an upswing soon, hopefully to that goal of 60.

SELL (with capital gains of 7 to 11 points): 50 shares of Chesebrough-Pond's (for illustration) to provide new money; all of Warner-Lambert because its price is near the 1978 peak, at which point, long-term shareholder will sell to break even and thus depress the value temporarily; Long's Drugs because 1982 earnings rose only +2% versus a 10-year average of +13%.

The purchases show alternatives: the first group more conservative; the second two, less seasoned firms.

BUY: low priced Daniel Industries, a fluid measurement firm that was hard hit by the decline in oil prices but is ready to report higher earnings and should do well in the next few years.

Expanding Eckerd (Jack) with most of its stores in the burgeoning South and a long and consistent record of higher sales and profits; steady-growth Josten's with a dominant position in the school market for rings, caps and gowns and yearbooks, with a target price about 50% above its recent 25.

OR: Flight Safety International, a junior Blue Chip that trains airplane and ship personnel and appears likely to be able to maintain its profitable growth: 29.9% Profit rate (PR) and 26.9% Earned Growth Rate (EGR) and National Medical Care, small enough to benefit from expansion and large enough to have built competent management.

Note how the *Suggested Buys* fared: Alco Standard and

Super Valu Stores reached their goals; Barry Wright, Josten's and National Medical did well; Daniel Industries was suggested too soon; Core Industries was profitable but lost its quality rating; and Waste Management was a big winner: from 33 to 62 until its stock fell as the result of unfavorable publicity concerning alleged violations of EPA dumping rules. This sharp drop, over 20 points, illustrates the volatility of Wall Street. Even though American law mandates innocence until proven guilty, the institutions panicked and unloaded with no recognition of the competence of corporate management (which, by purchases, had been lauded a few months before). If you did not sell at the target price, do so now because Wall Street detests controversy.

Portfolio for the 40s

This was a big winner: total returns of +47%: $16,502 on an original investment base of $34,650. Nuf sed.

HOLD: E. G. & G. where the strong upmove should continue because of major defense orders and growing importance in environmental and biomedical service.

Emhart which seems to have overcome its problems and, if higher earnings do come in 1984 and 1985, could reach that target of 73.

Exxon Corp., with its high 9% yield, prospects for steady

PORTFOLIO FOR THE 40s

SHARES/ COMPANY	COST	VALUE 1982	1983	INCOME 1982-83	TOTAL 1982-83	TARGET
HOLD						
400 E.G.&G.	20	18	29	$208	$4,608	52
200 Emhart	37	35	54	770	4,570	73
200 Exxon	34	29	35	600	1,800	49
SELL						
100 Ches.-Pond's	32	34	42	270	1,070	
200 Coca Cola	36	35	55	774	2,774	
250 Okla. G&E	16	17	19	680	1,680	

With the proceeds of $19,950 plus total income of $3,602 ($23,552), add $3,500 new savings:

BUY	COST	DIVIDENDS	TARGET
300 Cent. & SW	18	$1.78	27
100 CPC International	38	2.20	55
100 Hughes Tool	19	.84	33
100 Lubrizol	21	1.08	32
200 Square D	35	1.84	51
150 Xerox Corp.	46	3.00	80

WHAT HAPPENED TO LAST YEAR'S SUGGESTIONS:

	Then	PRICES Targeted	Actual
Archer-Dan. Midland*	15¼	37	22
Big Three Industries	22	50	21
Central La. Energy**	20	38	17
Cooper Industries	37	69	30
Deere & Co.	30	69	37
Digital Equipment	81	185	113
Edison Bros.	25	50	39
Malone & Hyde***	14	30	30
Medtronics, Inc.	43	72	43
Xerox Corp.	38	82	46

* Adjusted for 5% stock dividend
** No longer meets quality standards
*** Adjusted for 2-1 stock split

growth, and hopes for another stock split in another five years.

SELL: Chesebrough-Pond's (for illustration because shares are in another portfolio) Coca-Cola with a handsome profit and less likelihood of a similar gain in the near future; Oklahoma G&E because the utility no longer meets quality standards—not bad but not very good either.

With the proceeds and $3,500 new savings:

BUY: Central & Southwest, a well-managed utility in a still booming area, for excellent income of almost 10% plus strong growth.

CPC International that has almost tripled profits in the last decade and could move up 50%, from 38 to 55.

Hughes Tool, an oil industry stalwart that is at a low price/earnings ratio of 7 compared to a 17–7.3 range over the 1973–82 period.

Lubrizol, whose specialty chemicals should benefit from the economic recovery to move the stock to 32 from 21.

Square D, a leader in the electrical equipment field that is moving into electronics and should earn more with the revival of construction.

Xerox Corp., again attracting the professionals because of its low multiple of 9.5, at the low end of its 10-year range from 15 to 9.6. But watch carefully because of heavy foreign involvement which may be hurt by the strong dollar.

The results of the Suggestions are a good example of the wisdom of diversification: Digital Equipment and Malone & Hyde soared; Archer-Daniels-Midland, Deere & Co. and Edison Brothers moved up briskly but Big Three and Medtronics stayed about the same (but can be expected to do better soon); Cooper Industries was down when new orders lagged and Central Louisiana dipped slightly when it lost its quality rating.

If you still own any of these, review their prospects after the 1983 reports and then decide whether, and how soon, their stocks will come back.

Portfolio for the 50s

The total returns were a welcome 41%: $12,345 on an original base of $29,850. The bonds were up as the result of lower interest rates and the stocks moved well ahead and paid higher dividends so that the overall yield was 8.2%.

HOLD: Dart & Kraft and **Manufacturers Hanover** as both have the potential of another 50% gain.

Florida P&L bonds until around 100 when their yield will probably be less than can be expected to be available from new debt securities.

SELL: IBM for a splendid profit (again, quality pays off). This is still an outstanding corporation and the price of its stock will continue to rise but, probably, at a slower rate. This may be a hard decision but with such a huge firm, where earnings are in the billions, the chances of another 71% gain soon are slim. The proceeds can be invested to achieve such a return.

The SmithKline Beckman bond because it will mature in 1984 for a few points gain, not as much as you can make elsewhere.

The BUY list concentrates on utilities because, in their 50s, many folks, with an eye to retirement, prefer income

to growth and concentrate their savings in tax-deferred pension plans. Of course, if you have extra money, take a look at the suggestions at the bottom of the portfolio.

BUY two or three of the utilities: for high income, ENSERCH or Public Service of Indiana (about 8.5% and 11% respectively); for growth, Sonat, Inc., whose exploration potential can be rewarding.

Those in higher income brackets will do better to pick from the suggestions:

• *for the patient:* Bucyrus Erie, which dropped a few points and so is a better bargain; General Signal and Carlisle Corp . . . both of which have started what looks like a long rise.

• *for the aggressive:* Borden and SFN. Both have scored impressive gains but their able managements have indicated they plan to expand.

PORTFOLIO FOR THE 50s

SHARES/ COMPANY	COST	VALUE 1982	VALUE 1983	INCOME 1982-83	TOTAL 1982-83	TARGET
HOLD						
100 Dart & Kraft	49	53	74	$372	$2,472	100
10 Fla. P&L 8, '99	62½	62½	86	800	3,150	100
200 Man. Hanover	32	32	50	301	2,101	75
SELL						
50 IBM	75	66	117	172	2,722	
10 SmKLBeck. 8.15, '84	85	86	97	800	1,900	

with the proceeds of $9,395 (IBM: $5,850; SmithKline: $9,700) and income of $2,445 plus about $5,000 in new savings:

BUY	COST	DIVIDENDS	TARGET
200 ENSERCH	20	$320	46
200 Pub.Ser. Indiana	26	552	47
200 Sonat, Inc.	27	260	68

WHAT HAPPENED TO LAST YEAR'S SUGGESTIONS:

	PRICES Then	PRICES Targeted	PRICES Actual
Borden, Inc.	33	54	54
Bucyrus-Erie	16	35	13
Carlisle Corp.	25	59	36
General Signal	37	75	41
internorth, Inc.	28	57	28
Pioneer Corp.	21	55	23
SFN Co.	20	43	38
Sonat, Inc.	24	50	27

Portfolio for the 60s

Here, the emphasis is on income with steady growth with higher dividends and market values. Originally, I added two discount bonds but they were eliminated on the advice of a neighbor who had been a trust officer of a major bank. Said he, "From my experience with retirement planning, I believe that most people in their 60s think of bonds as their final holdings that should be left in their estate. When they are still working, they prefer conservative stocks whose income and appreciation outstrip both taxes and inflation."

HOLD: Rochester Telephone and Texas Utilities. RTC did have its first poor quarter in many years but management keeps increasing the dividend and with greater opportunities under deregulation, the company should be less a utility and more an electronic service company . . . with higher profits.

Texas Utilities, at 25, is selling at about six times earnings and, with an anticipated average annual increase of 5% in profits and payouts, a higher multiple is logical. The stock could rise 50% in the next couple of years.

SELL: Continental Group convertible preferred. The yield is excellent but the company has not yet overcome the problems of transition from forest products to insurance.

Houston Industries. The dividend is a hefty 10% but, with lower profits, the price/earnings ratio has become a high 13, double its historic level and that of many other electric power companies. For the next year or so, the same money can do better. But if you are willing to hold for that income, there should be a worthwhile comeback.

PORTFOLIO FOR THE 60s

SHARES/ COMPANY	COST	VALUE 1982	1983	INCOME 1982-83	TOTAL 1982-83	TARGET
HOLD						
200 Rochester Tel.	18½	27½	30	$408	$ 908	45
300 Texas Utilities	20	23	25	600	1,200	43
SELL						
200 Cont. Gr.						
$2 CV pf	18	16	21	400	1,400	
150 Houston Indus.	18	19	22	324	774	

with the proceeds of $8,932 (Continental: $4,200; Houston: $3,000 income of $1,732 plus $2,500 in new savings,

BUY	COST	DIVIDENDS	TARGET
100 American Brands	54	$350	73
100 1st City Texas	27	130	55
200 Southern Union	18	312	42

WHAT HAPPENED TO LAST YEAR'S SUGGESTIONS

	PRICES		
	Then	Targeted	Actual
Avon Products*	25	67	31
BankAmerica	19	40	25
Beatrice Foods	20	40	28
Dresser Industries	22	50	22
Ingersoll-Rand**	47	122	46
IBM	65	100	117
Smith International***	30	90	24
Transway Inter.	22	43	32

* No longer provides adequate income
** No longer meets quality standards
*** Target price revised to 51

BUY: American Brands with a welcome 6.5% yield, anticipated price gain of almost 20 points in the next two years and, then, the possibility of a stock split.

First City Banc Texas, a statewide holding company with prospects of earnings gains as much as 20% a year. At 24, the stock is selling at a low six times earnings despite a recent rise from about 20. Projections for the next two years: dividends, +11%; P/E: +21.3% and a target price of 55.

Southern Union, a natural gas distributor with many years of strong growth interrupted, now and then, by down periods. Still, SUG has outperformed most utilities: for the past decade, an average PR of 17% and EGR of 9%. With higher earnings, even the same multiple will more than

double the price of the stock. But such progress will reduce the dividend yield from a recent 9% to about 6%—a good trade-off.

Except for soaring IBM, the suggestions did not set any records. Avon, recommended because of its 10% yield, reduced its dividend; Dresser Industries stood still; Ingersoll Rand never did receive the anticipated orders for heavy machinery and was eliminated as a quality company; and Smith International, along with other oil firms, was buffeted so that its goal had to be revised downward.

Fortunately, the others were winners: modest gains for Beatrice Foods, BankAmerica and Transway International . . . all with good prospects of reaching their target prices.

Analyses and Projections

To give you an idea of what the experts look for, here are digests of analyses/commentaries from Wright Investors' Service. Since this international investment advisory firm concentrates only on quality corporations, attention is focused on the past and projected ability of the companies to make more money and to continue higher rates of profitability and growth: except for regulated utilities, an EGR of over 8% and PR of 15%. This means that if their progress continues, the earnings and dividends will double in another five years and these gains should be reflected in much higher stock prices.

The actual reports are far more detailed and usually accompanied by extensive tables covering pertinent data for the last 12 years with projections for the next five years. Since WIS is not selling securities and uses the data for its own decisions, there are no sales pitches as can be expected with research reports from brokers and advice-for-sale services.

Consider the stocks in the sample portfolios as starting places and be ready to switch 20% of your holdings annually. For successful investing, there are very few "permanent" holdings.

Big Three Industries (BIG). Last year (1982) the analysis noted that, despite the deep recession in the energy-related area, the company managed to post a modest gain in the first quarter as the result of broad diversification. "Over the past decade, BIG has reported consistently good results: an average annual return on equity of 19.6%, a rise in per share profits from 31¢ to $2.57 and per share dividends up from 7¢ to 60¢. With a comeback in oil stocks, BIG shares should rise sharply."

This enthusiasm was premature. The company ran into big trouble: down went the return on equity to 15.9%, the earnings to $2.08 and the dividends were unchanged. No wonder the stock dipped from a high of 38 to 15!

But the new projections are more favorable: for 1983, ROE of 16.9% and earnings of $2.43 per share; for 1984: 18.7% and $3.00 respectively. That's why there are logical prospects for the stock to move from 21 to 50.

Chesebrough-Pond's (CBM). The company is financially strong: long-term debt 18.3% of total debt and 21.6% of total capitalization. That means ample funds for expansion, which in the past has been successful: Prince, the leading manufacturer of tennis rackets, boosted sales and earnings 5% in the first year under CBM.

1983 was a rough year but early reports for 1984 indicate that the company is back to its historic double digit earnings growth. Traditional cosmetic/hospital products are moving ahead; packaged foods, led by Ragu sauce, are expanding; and the Bass footwear division has added Fun Striders and Bare Traps.

The price/earnings ratio of about 10 is at the low end of the 10-year range, 15–9.7, so the stock is currently undervalued and, with a strong market, could hit the target of 68 in the next 24–30 months.

Exxon Corporation (XON). Lower oil prices are not unequivocally bad for a major integrated oil company . . . to the extent that they translate into economic recovery so that XON's results should benefit.

Upstream operations: last year, U.S. liquids production declined −1% and natural gas sales fell −14%. Both should show improved trends soon. And in 1982, the company increased its worldwide petroleum reserves by +3% in both liquids and natural gas.

Downstream operations: the efforts to downsize refining and marketing were drastic and the new OPEC agreement eliminates Exxon's commitment to buy over one million barrels of oil per day from Saudi Arabia at $4 per barrel over market price. But LIFO profits, resulting from inventory drawdowns, will be lower.

Other operations—chemicals, coal, office systems and Reliance Electric—should benefit from lower costs and higher sales. XON profits can be expected to rise +4% in 1983 and +30% in 1984. With about the same low multiple of 6.4, the stock could hit 50 by the end of 1985.

Sonat, Inc. (SNT). This is one of the most broadly diversified energy utilities with a money-making combination of pipeline and natural gas distribution, extensive oil/gas exploration activities, and a 50% interest in a paper and wood products manufacturer with some 800,000 acres of timberland. Profitwise, SNT has been a leader: for the past decade, a PR of 14% with dividends rising from 36¢ to 1.40 per share. With a low P/E ratio of about 5, the stock is undervalued and, with ever-higher profits, should double,

from about 25 to 50 or more. Quality, value and, now, timing!

Note how even the best of projections have gone awry. Some stocks have spurted far beyond their targets; others have moved up slowly and a few just never did get going. That's why you must always review all holdings regularly, revise your estimates or take your profits or losses when things do not work out as anticipated. All of these securities will prove profitable over the years but your gains, and income, will be much greater if you play by the rules.

Spotting a Winner

Finding new quality companies is never easy but here's an example of a Junior Blue Chip worth checking further: **Church's Fried Chicken (CHU).** The company sells fried chicken, hamburgers, specialty sandwiches, and complementary food items through neighborhood take-out stores. It has 1,159 company-owned outlets in 27 states and 235 stores operated by licensees in 32 states, Canada, Mexico, Puerto Rico, Japan, Singapore and Malaysia. The units are unique in that about 40% are located in inner cities. The stock split recently . . . the third time in seven years so there are now 19 million shares—enough to be of interest to institutions.

Despite the fact that the primary customers, blue collar workers, have been hard hit by the recession, corporate sales and earnings continue to rise. With $45 million in cash and short-term investments, CHU is looking to diversify beyond fried chicken and to move into mall locations that can be expected to attract more affluent customers.

By using modular buildings which take only two weeks to assemble, the company can open new stores as rapidly as it can find new sites. Over the next five years, CHU's earnings should go up an average of +22% compound annual rate. That means the stock can double with little change in the price/earnings ratio . . . from an adjusted 20 to as high as 40+.

29

The Role of Advisers/Advisory Services

Investment advisers are worthwhile when: (1) they provide factual, intelligible, useful information; (2) you have substantial assets that require more attention than you are willing, or able, to give; (3) you can afford—or enjoy—the luxury of having someone to hold your hand . . . investmentwise. In most cases, for most sophisticated people, the benefits of investment advisers are more psychological than real. It's your money and you should always be in a position to make your own decisions.

It is essential to use advisers in related-to-investments areas: a competent lawyer to set up a retirement plan or trust; a tax expert to make certain that you are taking advantage of legitimate ways to reduce taxes; and an experienced accountant to prepare complicated tax returns. A professional money manager can be valuable when you are involved with large sums in a fiduciary capacity but for personal and pension savings, the primary role of the investment adviser should be to establish a system that will enable you to make your own decisions. Once you have a sound base, you can decide whether you want to handle your savings directly or with help, or to turn management over to someone else—for a fee.

With small sums, such as $10,000 to $15,000 in an IRA, any intelligent individual can make his/her own decisions. When assets become larger, indirect counsel—from broker's research reports, financial publications and market letters—can be helpful. And when your assets total over $100,000, it may be wise to seek professional assistance. At this point, the right kind of investment counsel can help you increase your wealth and teach you how to be your own money manager. Even hefty fees will be returned many times over, in dollars and in peace of mind.

But do not expect any financial adviser to be a genius. He or she will make mistakes. Choose carefully and do not be afraid to make changes if you feel the advice or style fails to meet your needs and goals. Too often, the most convenient counsel comes from those with selfish interests: *for investments,* from a stockbroker who relies on commissions from buying and selling securities; *for insurance,* from a broker/agent whose livelihood depends on his ability to sell policies; for *retirement and estates,* from a banker whose institution provides savings and trust services.

From my own experience, I believe that most people who are willing to spend some time in research and analysis can be successful investors on their own. All it takes is common sense and adherence to principles such as outlined in this guide.

If you do add advisers, do not let them act without your approval, or at least knowledge. It's your money. You worked hard to earn it. In most cases, you know your capacity and needs better than they do. It's well to heed competent counsel but the ultimate decision should be yours.

Investment Aid

Whether you retain a professional directly, purchase shares in a pooled portfolio or subscribe to a market letter, study all information and recommendations, check the character and reputation of the individual/sponsor and review the long-term record.

If you are interested enough in your investments to buy a book like this, you can easily learn how to achieve results far superior to those of the average amateur and of stock market averages. But even if you have such knowledge, you must also set aside time to do your own research (or study that of advisory/statistical services) and to review your holdings periodically, preferably weekly, hopefully monthly and certainly every quarter.

If, despite such preparation, you find that you are losing money by making too many mistakes or are achieving high returns primarily because of a couple of high risers, get help from a paid professional or reliable advisory service. Follow this counsel for a year to test their skill and style. Then, if you feel you've learned something, take charge again. Of course, if the results are unsatisfactory or you (or your spouse) are uncomfortable, make a change. Just as in investing, the first loss is usually the smallest.

These days, everybody and his brother/sister is getting into the act but unless you have strong reasons for not doing so, concentrate your search on firms or individuals that have been managing money for many years, have built a reputation for integrity and have long and fairly consistent records of better-then-average investment results in both bull and bear markets.

Such criteria may eliminate convenience and friendship but the primary reason for hiring investment counsel should always be SUPERIOR PERFORMANCE. Be cautious with any firm that headlines its successes and footnotes its failures (as advertised in *Barron's,* or, more likely, will be found in a direct-mail pitch). Anyone can be lucky with a few stocks for a few years, but, unless you want to speculate, look for *quality* just as you do with securities.

Broadly, these are your choices with investment advisers:

Investment companies. As explained earlier, these are professionally managed pools of funds that invest in a diversified group of securities for specific goals: growth, income, balance or a combination. In most cases, the initial investment is small, you can make additional purchases easily and you can buy and sell shares quickly.

But you turn over management to someone else and will have to pay for such service. The cost may not appear on any report but it's there all the same.

Some firms, primarily those with load funds, provide special packages that, the salesman will assert, "make professional counsel available to the small investor." You do get a certain degree of personal service but, in most cases, these are little more than standard programs in an attractive format. IDS, for example, offers four plans, each with a flat fee ranging from $250 to $5,000 a year. According to one representative, "Our goal is to keep moving you into a higher category as our system increases your wealth."

Brokerage firms. These involve a minimum outlay of $100,000 and are managed on a discretionary basis. They are best for an aggressive portfolio seeking special situations or short-term trading profits.

Typically, Shearson/American Express Asset Management Corp. accepts individual accounts of $200,000 and charges a fee of 1% of portfolio assets. You can set your own objectives and your money will be invested in the securities which, the managers feel, can best achieve your goals. The monthly reports are detailed; you won't be bothered with calls from your broker; and, in the recent bull market, the results have been excellent.

Insurance companies. This area is changing rapidly so it's difficult to be specific. Check with your insurance agent for information. Usually there are three types of investment service/advice:

Guaranteed Income Contracts (*GIC*), where a specific rate of return is guaranteed for a set period of time, typically one year. Thereafter, the yield moves with the cost of money.

Variable portfolio. This is like a mutual fund that invests in both stocks and bonds. The rate of return depends on management's skill. These are always safe but usually not as rewarding as regular mutual funds or personally managed assets.

Fixed-income fund. All savings are invested in fixed-income holdings such as bonds, mortgages, and, increasingly, liquid assets.

The major drawback of all insurance-related investments is the cost: commissions of 5% to 20% plus management fees. Since the load comes off the top, you have less money working for your goal.

Many agents concentrate their sales pitch on tax shelters with "big tax-savings" and, of course, high sales commissions.

Banks/trust companies/thrift institutions. Their "advice" departments are organized to *manage* large savings such as pension funds or estates. With few exceptions, their performance records have been poor. By training and tradition, bank officers are conservative, make decisions by cumbersome committees and pay greater attention to avoiding criticism than to enhancing the wealth of their clients.

Fortunately, with competition, there are beginning to be major changes: bank holding companies are setting up special departments (often with greater publicity than personnel) to sponsor public-invited investment seminars, provide free "personal" financial counsel to high-balance depositors and to offer more-or-less standard counseling by a bank executive who reviews your portfolio and makes recommendations with the hope that you will turn management over to the bank's "experienced" staff. Typical charges at Chase Manhattan Bank: $100 an hour with a $250 minimum.

One of the more promising developments, by medium size commercial banks and thrift institutions, is the Managed Portfolio Plan (MPP) sponsored by Wright Investors' Service. This offers investors a choice of several types of mutual funds, keyed to different objectives with deposits made at the local bank's office. The superior performance that the Wright system has achieved for many years makes these special plans valuable for both personal and fiduciary savings. Find out if such an opportunity is offered in your area.

Certified Financial Planner (**CFP**). This designation is awarded individuals who pass a series of long, detailed examinations on various aspects of investing and financial planning. Typically, the professional reviews the portfolio and prepares specific recommendations for present and future action . . . at a cost of from $60 to $150 an hour. This service can be valuable when you have ample assets and expect more in the future, but unbiased CFPs are hard to find. To make a living, most have to rely on income from the sale of insurance, tax shelters or limited partnerships. At worst, you'll get a better idea of how to plan your investments/financing; at best, you will learn how to handle your wealth more profitably.

For further information, check the yellow pages or ask the Reference Librarian for the names/addresses of national organizations.

Professional money managers. These are individuals or groups; some operate independently, but most are associated with other financially oriented organizations. Roughly, their fees are 1% of portfolio value with a minimum of $500 a year. Above $1 million, the fees are scaled down. Small savings, under $250,000, are usually handled through standard portfolios designed for various investment objectives. Larger holdings receive personal attention.

Their biggest plus: You have someone to talk to, someone who can keep you up to date on economic and financial developments, can back up recommendations with research reports, and can explain the pros and cons of various opportunities/options. And with pension funds, you have a buffer if some plan participant complains about performance.

Model portfolios. These are available from investment advisory services that publish weekly reports and letters. You don't have to follow their recommendations but when you do, you are, in effect, turning over control of the management of your money.

Checkpoints

The number one consideration in choosing any type of investment adviser is comfort: to select someone whom you respect, whose advice you are willing to follow, who operates in a professional manner (with integrity, intelligence and information) and who eases your doubts and your spouse's fears.

These criteria eliminate brokers hustling for commissions; salesmen who make quick recommendations without considering your assets, income obligations, and goals; and everyone who promises large, fast returns.

Specifically, check:

Experience. Look for individuals with at least five years of portfolio responsibility and firms whose principals have collective experience of 25 years or more.

Philosophy. You want counsel with objectives and approaches that match yours or, at least, do not make you uncomfortable. You can get a feel of what to expect by reading the promotional literature, reviewing reports and talking to one or more of the people responsible for investment decisions, not just the sales representative. When large assets are involved, dig deeper by asking for: (1) a list of the major holdings in past years: in ebullient 1975, in the 1977 bear market, in the 1981 upsurge, in the 1982 downswing and, of course, in recent months; (2) the rationale for such holdings during such periods; (3) a summary of what actions were (or were not) taken with these stocks: when they were bought, if and when they were sold, and what guidelines have been set for the future; (4) the total returns reported annually for the past 10 years with a comparison with those of T-bills. A good performance would mean a *consistent* return 1.2 times that of the yield of these government debt issues.

Target goals. If the professionals are willing to settle for less than 10% a year, forget 'em. You can do better with unmanaged bonds. If they mention 20%, be wary unless they back up such optimism with facts of past performance and logical projections. When they mention 15% a year, over a fairly long time, they are being realistic.

Willingness to sell. Successful investing relies on two factors: how much you will make and how little you lose. Check the composition of all portfolios for the past 10 years. If they are still holding glamour stocks bought at peaks and now near lows, move on! I am constantly amazed at how many so-called professionals ignore their losses. One of the major growth funds (with a good overall record) has owned a large block of Avon Products for many years. Yet, this stock sold at 140 in 1973, fell to below 20 in 1974, bounced up over 60 in 1978 and then dropped again to below 30. Trading would have been wise but there are times when even the best of stocks should be sold: when they become overvalued (1973) and certainly when they become unpopular (1974 and 1980–81). A professional should know that it does not pay to fight the market. Check the dates of purchase and sale of major holdings.

Sources of profits. Review the annual reports to discover whether the gains came from a few big winners or from a number of wise selections. Look for consistency based on clearly stated procedures and concepts. Successful investing is a long-term process.

Fees. This is most important when you are switching from one adviser to another. If the new service costs 1% more than the old one, the results must be at least 3% better to be worthwhile. And always find out about special charges.

Types of clients. Look for individuals/firms that deal with people with incomes, needs and goals similar to yours. If you're 40 and still building assets, do not select an adviser/manager specializing in trust accounts for wealthy retirees. Professionals can follow only a limited number of securities, and in this example, will concentrate on stable dividend payers, not the growth stocks/situations you want.

Integrity. If the individual or firm has had a brush with the law, the SEC or the New York Stock Exchange, look elsewhere. You cannot afford to take any chances with your savings. This applies more to smaller organizations, as large companies, with scores of offices, will always include some bad apples.

Incidentally, do not be impressed with the title of Registered Investment Adviser (RIA). All one has to do to acquire this is to send $150 to the Securities and Exchange Commission with a sworn statement that you have not violated any securities law.

Performance. This is the single most important consideration. You want someone who has a solid, if not outstanding, record. Always get the complete results of *all* recommendations, not just the "sample" portfolio. Then study the movement of *every* stock, year by year. (If this information is not shown in the annual report, get a 12-year chart book and see for yourself.) You want to know: How great were the gains? How long did they take? Were the stocks bought near their lows and sold close to their highs? or vice versa? Similarly, check the losses. Were they in line with the overall market or the results of poor choices?

If the predictions and recommendations were right 60% of the time, that's a good batting average. And always relate the results to your own experience. Why pay someone else to buy the same stocks you made money with?

Areas of responsibility. Before you sign anything, get a written schedule of when you can expect a preliminary report, the dates on which regular monthly statements will be mailed, a formal explanation of responsibilities of the adviser and the investor, and an agreement that you can withdraw at any time and will receive all documents, copies of work papers, etc. It's a horrendous task to reconstruct investment transactions.

Market Letters

These are weekly or semimonthly letters/reports that are supposed to keep you informed about the stock market and specific securities. Some are largely personal commentaries; others provide statistical data; all make specific recommendations to buy and sell. They cost from $50 to $500 a year, tax-deductible. If you're wealthy and interested in special areas such as foreign exchange, commodities and trading futures, you can subscribe to written-for-the-professional reports that cost up to $2,500 a year.

As you've probably learned from your mail, bull markets spawn a host of new letters, most of which let you in on hot new stocks—shares of small, unseasoned companies in temporarily popular industries with temporarily popular products/services. The promoters are seldom modest, and usually start their "advice" with self-congratulation (in large type with a dramatic chart), state that "once again, we were right on target" (even though this may not be quite true) and continue with fuzzy and cagily hedged forecasts on the market and more definitive recommendations on their "favorites."

Unlike the established services that present factual information with a minimum of adjectives, these newcomers tend to trumpet their profits and downplay their losses. Too often, they fail to take into account the commissions and so overstate gains and understate losses. They report a 20% gain in two months—buying at 10 and selling at 12—but neglect to note that the round trip commissions would be about $70 per 100 shares so the real gain would be $130 or 13%.

The most useless letters are those published by prophets of doom who bewail the American economy and urge that all capital be put in "conservative holdings" such as gold, silver and Swiss francs. Yet, as the records show, these have been extremely volatile, very risky and only sporadically profitable for fast-acting traders.

Some of the most widely circulated market letters are listed at the end of this guide. By and large, all market letters are better for conversation than profits. The best way to check them is by trial subscription as offered in *Barron's* and other financial publications. Or take advantage of special sample offers: 20 services for $11.95 from Select Information Exchange, 2095 Broadway, New York, N.Y. 10023 or 25 for $25 from The Hirsch Organization, 6 Deer Trail, Old Tappan, N.J. 07675.

With these letters, in addition to the checkpoints listed above, study:

Audience. If the service goes to hundreds of thousands of people, its comments will be general and useful primarily as background. If it's directed to a small segment of investors, it's probably too expensive and too limited for your needs.

Clarity. Look for advice that's easy to understand and implement. Beware of obfuscations, complex language and generalities such as "buy on weakness, sell on strength," etc. You want background data to enable you to improve your investment returns: specific buy prices, target points and logical reasons why actions should be taken.

Types of securities. If the text concentrates on swinging OTC issues, it may be helpful with speculations but, if you want investment advice, look for services/letters that analyze industries and corporations and provide you with data that you understand and can utilize.

The most you can expect from any advisory publication is that it will help you to make profitable decisions. As one of Wall Street's oldest professionals told me, "Read all market letters with skepticism. If the authors are so wise—and successful—why aren't they rich enough to retire?"

Checklist for Broker

A stockbroker is a sales representative, not an investment adviser. His job is to buy and sell securities for which he is paid a portion of commissions/profits. He has received special training, has had to pass strict examinations, must be of good character, and is subject to the regulations of stock exchanges and the Securities and Exchange Commission. If you plan to rely on research information and investment recommendations from his firm, use this checklist. (For convenience, "he" is used but an increasing number of brokers are women):

How long has he been in the securities industry with this firm?

What is the certified record of the firm's recommendations?

How does he feel about giving advice? General, to buy, to sell?

How many clients does he serve?

How diversified is the firm? Is there an economist? Technical analyst: money market expert? Commodities department? Options department? Tax shelter adviser?

How many senior analysts and how long have they been in research?

Does the firm issue reports? If so, weekly? Monthly? Periodically?

Are there fees for safekeeping of securities?

What is the commission structure? Can you get lower rates with heavy volume of trading?

Is the firm financially sound?

Will you be able to meet with the broker and some of his associates to discuss strategy and tactics?

Will the statements provide information on dividends received, portfolio value, yield estimates?

Will the firm prepare a game plan for your specific needs? If so, how detailed will it be? And how long will it take to prepare? Or will it be a prototype proposal?

If the broker or firm does provide investment management, how will this be done? Will this require minimum assets? What will be the fees?

With tax shelters, deferred annuities and other special deals, will there be a printed fee schedule?

Does the firm have any measurement-of-performance index?

What is the time lag for completing transactions? For withdrawing your securities?

Has the individual or the firm been censured by any official body?

30

Abbreviations and Averages

In keeping with Wall Street custom and financial reporting, initials are used frequently. Here are some of the most important:

Exchanges

NYSE: New York Stock Exchange. This is the major auction market for common stocks and corporate bonds. To be listed, the corporation must:

• Demonstrate earning power of $2.5 million before federal income taxes for the most recent year and $2 million pretax for each of the preceding two years.

• Have net tangible assets of $16 million.

• Have market value of publicly held shares of $16 million.

• Report a total of 1 million common shares publicly held.

• Have 2,000 holders of 100 shares or more.

AMEX: American Stock Exchange. This lists stocks of companies with fewer shareholders and smaller capital than those on the NYSE. Generally, the stocks are more speculative.

BOS: Boston Stock Exchange.

MID: Midwest Stock Exchange.

MSE: Montreal Stock Exchange.

PE: Philadelphia Stock Exchange. This lists both stocks and options.

TSE: Toronto Stock Exchange.

PSE: Pacific Stock Exchange.

OTC: Over-the-counter. This is the market for securities that are not listed on major exchanges. The trading is conducted by dealers who are members of NASD (National Association of Securities Dealers) and who may or may not be members of other exchanges. Trading is by bid and asked prices. The primary market is NASDAQ (National Association of Securities Dealers Automated Quotations) which consists of about 200 of the most actively traded issues. Some 2,500 other stocks are quoted in daily financial summaries.

CBOE: Chicago Board of Options Exchange. The major auction market for calls and puts, primarily on NYSE stocks, and recently, for special types of options such as those on Treasury bonds.

AMEX Options Exchange. The division of AMEX that trades puts and calls, almost entirely on NYSE listed stocks.

CBT: Chicago Board of Trade. A major market for futures contracts: commodities, interest-rate securities, commercial paper and so forth.

CME: Chicago Mercantile Exchange. Futures contracts for commodities, T-bills, etc., and the S&P 500 Index.

Comex (formerly New York Commodity Exchange). Futures and options of a limited number of commodities and metals (gold, silver and copper).

CTN: New York Cotton Exchange. Trading in futures in cotton and orange juice.

IMM: International Monetary Market. This is located at the Chicago Mercantile Exchange and trades in futures of foreign currency and U.S. Treasury bills.

KC: Kansas City Board of Trade. Trades in futures of commodities and Value Line Futures Index.

NYFE: New York Futures Exchange. A unit of the NYSE that trades in the NYSE Composite Futures Index.

NYM: New York Mercantile Exchange. Trading in futures of petroleum and metals.

Federal Agencies

SEC: Securities and Exchange Commission. A federal agency established to help protect investors. It is responsible for administering congressional acts regarding securities, stock exchanges, corporate reporting, investment companies, investment advisers and public utility holding companies.

FRB: Federal Reserve Board. The federal agency responsible for control of such important investment items as the discount rate, money supply, margin requirements.

FDIC: Federal Deposit Insurance Corporation. An agency which provides insurance of bank deposits.

FSLIC: Federal Savings and Loan Insurance Corporation. A similar insurance-of-deposits agency for savings and loan associations.

CFTC: Commodity Futures Trading Commission. This is a watchdog for the commodities futures trading industry.

Stock Market Averages

Dow Jones Industrial Average (DJIA): the oldest and most widely used stock market average. It shows the action of the stocks of 30 major corporations, representing about

15% of NYSE values, on a weighted basis: i.e., IBM at 110 carries more than three times the weight of Woolworth at 35.

Furthermore, cash dividends tend to reduce the average as each stock passes its ex-dividend date and, percentagewise, a stock that falls from 100 to 50 loses 50% of its value but when it moves back, the gain is 100%.

According to Lou Stone, senior analyst with Shearson-American Express, "Most of the big gains are simply recoveries in value, not actual profits realized. Out of 313 million shares of GM outstanding, only 62 million shares traded in 1982 . . . more than half were duplications so that less than 10% of the shares changed hands during the year."

In recent years, the composition of the average has been changed to reflect the growing scientific, consumer and international roles of American business; IBM replaced Chrysler and Merck was substituted for Esmark, Inc.

The DJIA is determined by dividing the closing prices by a divisor that compensates for past stock splits and stock dividends. In mid-1983, this was 1.292. This meant that a 10-point change in the average represented an actual price shift of $12.92.

Dow Jones Transportation Average (DJTA). This is made up of the stocks of 20 major transportation companies. Recent changes have substituted a trucking firm (Carolina Freight) and an airline (USAir, Inc.) for merged railroads. The recent divisor was 1.574.

Dow Jones Utilities Average (DJUA). This consists of 15 major utilities to provide geographic representation. With more firms forming holding companies to engage in oil and gas exploration, and distribution, its value is greater as a point of reference than as a guide to the market's evaluation of producers of electricity and distributors of gas. The recent divisor was 2.709.

Standard & Poor's Price Index: of 500 leading NYSE-listed corporations: 425 industrials, 20 railroads and 55 utilities. It is weighted in that it is based on the market value of all outstanding shares of these companies so reflects the action of a comparatively few large firms. *For example:* IBM accounts for 3.9% of the index; Foster Wheeler for only .06%. The recent value was 152.85.

Wilshire Equity Index. This is a value weighted index derived from the dollar value of 5,000 common stocks including all those listed on the NYSE and AMEX and the most active OTC issues. It is the broadest index and so more representative of the overall market.

NYSE Common Stock Index. A composite index covering price movements of all common stocks listed on the Big Board. It is based on the close of the market December 31, 1965, and is weighted according to the number of shares listed for each issue. Point changes are converted to dollars and cents to provide a meaningful measure of price action.

Dow Jones Bond Average. This consists of bonds of ten public utilities and ten industrial corporations.

Dow Jones Municipal Bond Yield Average. This is a changing average but, basically shows the yields of low-coupon bonds in five states and 15 major cities.

STOCKS IN DOW JONES AVERAGES

INDUSTRIALS (DJIA)

Allied Corp.
Aluminum Co.
American Brands
American Can
American Express
American Tel. & Tel.
Bethlehem Steel
Dupont, E.I.
Eastman Kodak
Exxon Corporation
General Electric
General Foods
General Motors
Goodyear Tire
Inco, Ltd.

International Business Machines
International Harvester
International Paper
Merck & Co.
Minnesota Mining & Mfg.
Owens-Illinois
Procter & Gamble
Sears, Roebuck
Standard Oil (Calif.)
Texaco, Inc.
Union Carbide
U.S. Steel
United Technologies
Westinghouse Electric
Woolworth (F.W.)

TRANSPORTATION (DJTA)

AMR Corp.
Burlington Northern
Canadian Pacific
Carolina Freight
Consolidated Freightways
CSX Corp.
Delta Airlines
Eastern Airlines
Norfolk & Southern
Northwest Airlines

Overnite Transportation
Pan American World Airways
Rio Grande Industries
Santa Fe Industries
Southern Pacific
Transway International
Trans World
UAL, Inc.
Union Pacific
US Air, Inc.

UTILITIES (DJUA)

American Electric Power
Cleveland Electric
Columbia Gas System
Commonwealth Edison
Consolidated Edison
Consolidated Natural Gas
Detroit Edison
Houston Industries

Niagara Mohawk Power
Pacific Gas & Electric
Panhandle Eastern Corp.
Peoples Energy
Philadelphia Electric
Public Service E & G
So. California Edison

Bibliography

Basic Background

Abrams, Don. *The Profitaker.* New York: Wiley, 1980.

Altman, Edward. *Financial Handbook.* New York: Wiley, 1981.

Amling, Frederick. *Investments.* Englewood Cliffs, N.J.: Prentice-Hall, 1978.

Andersen, Ian. *Making Money.* New York: Vanguard, 1978.

Anderson, Frank R. *Quality Controlled Investing.* New York: Wiley, 1978.

Appel, Gerald, and Hitscher, Fred. *Stock Market Trading Systems.* Homewood, Ill.: Dow Jones–Irwin, 1980.

———. *99 Ways to Make Money in a Depression.* New Rochelle, N.Y.: Arlington House, 1982.

Barnes, Leo and Feldman, Stephen. *Handbook of Wealth Management.* New York: McGraw-Hill, 1977

Beadle, Patricia. *Investing in the Eighties.* New York: Harcourt, Brace Jovanovich, 1981.

Blackman, Richard. *Follow The Leaders.* New York: Cornerstone Press, 1979.

Blarner, Thomas, and Shulman, Richard. *Dow Three Thousand.* New York: Simon & Schuster, 1982.

Blotnick, Srully. *Winning: The Psychology of Successful Investing.* New York: McGraw-Hill, 1978.

Blume, Marshall E., and Friedman, Jack P. *Encyclopedia of Investments.* Boston: Warren, Gorham and Lamont, 1982.

Bondy, Susan. *How To Make Money Using Other People's Money.* New York: Bobbs Merrill, 1982.

Bridwell, Rodger. *The Battle for Financial Security.* New York: Times Books, 1980.

Brownstone, David M., and Sartisky, Jacques. *Personal Financial Survival.* New York: Wiley, 1981.

Casey, Douglas R. *Crisis Investing.* New York: Harper & Row, 1981.

———. *Strategic Investing.* New York: Simon & Schuster, 1982.

Christy, A. G. *Introductions to Investments.* New York: McGraw-Hill, 1982.

Church, Albert M. *The Sophisticated Investor.* Englewood Cliffs, N.J.: Prentice-Hall, 1981.

Clasing, Henry K., and Rudd, Andrew. *Modern Portfolio Theory.* Homewood, Ill.: Dow Jones–Irwin, 1981.

Cobleigh, Ira. *Double Your Dollars.* New York: Crown, 1979.

———, and Dorfman, Bruce. *The Dowbeaters.* New York: Macmillan, 1979.

Cohen, Jerome B., et al. *Guide to Intelligent Investing.* Homewood, Ill.: Dow Jones–Irwin, 1977.

Crane, Burton. *The Sophisticated Investor.* New York: Simon & Schuster, 1964.

Crowell, Richard A. *Stock Market Strategy.* New York: McGraw-Hill, 1977.

Curley, Anthony J., and Bear, Robert M. *Investment Analysis and Management.* New York: Harper & Row, 1979.

Diller, G. *Investor's Guide to Fixed Income Securities.* New York: Van Nostrand Reinhold, 1983.

Dirks, Ray. *Heads You Win; Tails You Win.* New York: Bantam Books, 1980.

Dougall, Herbert E., and Corrigan, Francis J. *Investments.* Englewood Cliffs, N.J.: Prentice-Hall, 1978.

Dreman, David N. *Contrarian Investment Strategy.* New York: Random House, 1980.

Eder, George J. *What's Behind Inflation and How to Beat It.* Englewood Cliffs, N.J.: Prentice-Hall, 1979.

Elton, E. J., and Gruber, M. J. *Modern Portfolio Theory.* New York: Wiley, 1981.

Emory, Eric S. *When To Sell Stocks.* New York: Exposition Press, 1980.

Engle, Louis. *How To Buy Stocks.* New York; Bantam Books, 1982.

Farrell, James L. *Guide to Portfolio Management.* New York: McGraw-Hill, 1983.

Farrell, M. L., et al. *Dow Jones Investors' Handbook.* Homewood, Ill.: Dow Jones–Irwin, 1980.

Fischer, Donald E., and Jordan, Ronald J. *Security Analysis and Portfolio Management.* Englewood Cliffs, N.J.: Prentice-Hall, 1979.

Francis, Clark, and Archer, Stephen H. *Portfolio Analysis.* Englewood Cliffs, N.J.: Prentice-Hall, 1979.

Gitman, Lawrence J., and Joehnk, Michael D. *Fundamentals of Investing.* New York: Harper & Row, 1981.

Graham, Benjamin. *The Intelligent Investor.* New York: Harper & Row, 1973.

——— et al. *Security Analysis.* New York: McGraw-Hill, 1962.

Haft, Richard A. *Investing in Securities.* Englewood Cliffs, N.J.: Prentice-Hall, 1982.

Hagin, Robert. *The Dow Jones–Irwin Guide to Modern Portfolio Theory.* Homewood, Ill.: Dow Jones–Irwin, 1980.

Hayden, Vern. *Money: Use It or Lose It.* New York: Hayden House, 1980.

Helfert, Erich A. *Techniques of Financial Analysis.* Homewood, Ill.: Dow Jones–Irwin, 1980.

Herzfeld, Thomas, and Brach, Robert F. *High Return, Low Risk Investment.* New York: Putnam, 1981.

Huang, S. *Investment Analysis and Management.* Englewood Cliffs, N.J.: Winthrop, 1981.

Johnson, Timothy E. *Investment Principles.* Englewood Cliffs, N.J.: Prentice-Hall, 1978.

King, David, and Levine, Karen. *The Best Way in the World for a Woman to Make Money.* New York: Rawson, Wade, 1980.

Krefetz, Gerald. *The Smart Investor's Guide.* New York: A & W Publishers, 1982.

Lasry, George. *Valuing Common Stock.* New York: AMACOM, 1980.

Leuthold, Steven C. *The Myths of Inflation and Investing.* Chicago: Crain, 1980.

Levine, Sumner N., et al. *Investment Manager's Handbook.* Homewood, Ill.: Dow Jones–Irwin, 1980.

———. *Financial Analyst's Handbook.* Homewood, Ill.: Dow Jones–Irwin, 1980.

Levitt, Arthur, Jr. *How To Make Your Money Make Money.* Homewood, Ill.: Dow Jones–Irwin, 1981.

Loeb, Gerald M. *The Battle for Investment Survival.* New York: Simon & Schuster, 1965.

———. *The Battle for Stock Market Profits.* New York: Simon & Schuster, 1971.

Mader, Chris, and Hagin, Robert. *Dow Jones–Irwin Guide to Common Stocks.* Homewood, Ill.: Dow Jones–Irwin, 1980.

Maginn, John L., and Tuttle, Donald L. *Managing Investment Portfolios.* Boston: Warren, Gorham & Lamont, 1983.

Malkiel, Burton G. *The Inflation Beater's Investment Guide.* New York: Norton, 1980.

Meltzer, Bernard. *Bernard Meltzer Solves Your Money Problems.* New York: Simon & Schuster, 1982.

Metz, Robert. *Future Stocks.* New York: Harper & Row, 1982.

Montapert, William D. *The Omega Strategy: How You Can Retire Rich.* New York: Capra, 1982.

Nauheim, Fred. *Move Your Assets To Beat Inflation.* Englewood Cliffs, N.J.: Prentice-Hall, 1980.

Nemet, Roslyn. *Investment Tips for Today's Woman.* New York: Norton, 1981.

Noddings, Thomas C. *Advanced Investment Strategies.* Homewood, Ill.: Dow Jones–Irwin, 1978.

Porter, Sylvia. *New Money Book.* New York: Avon, 1980.

Reilly, J. *Bond Investments in the 80s.* New York: Van Nostrand Reinhold, 1983.

Righetti, Raymond R. *Stock Market Strategy.* Chicago: Nelson-Hall, 1980.

Rogers, Mary Joyce and Nancy. *Women and Money.* New York: McGraw-Hill, 1978.

Rolo, Charles J. *Gaining on the Market.* Boston: Little, Brown, 1982.

Rosenberg, Claude N. *The Common Sense Way to Stock Market Profits.* New York: New American Library, 1978.

Rosenberg, Jerome. *Managing Your Own Money.* New York: Newsweek, 1979.

Ross, Charles M. *A Guide for the Perplexed Investor.* New York: Carlton, 1981.

Ruff, Howard. *Surviving and Winning in the Inflationary 80s.* New York: Warner, 1982.

Rutberg, Sidney. *Playboy's Investment and Financial Planning Guide for Singles.* Chicago: Seaview, 1981.

Sargent, David R. *Stock Market Profits and Higher Income for You.* New York: Simon & Schuster, 1978.

Schultz, Harry. *Bear Market Investment Strategies.* Homewood, Ill.: Dow Jones–Irwin, 1981.

Shulman, Morton. *How to Invest Your Money and Profit from Inflation.* New York: Random House, 1980.

Smith, Milton. *Money Today, More Tomorrow.* Englewood Cliffs, N.J.: Winthrop, 1981.

Smith, Thurman L. *Investors Can Beat Inflation.* New York: Liberty Publishing, 1980.

Sokoloff, Kiril. *The Thinking Investor's Guide to the Stock Market.* New York: McGraw-Hill, 1978.

———. *Paine Webber Handbook of Stock and Bond Analysis.* New York: McGraw-Hill, 1979.

Stigum, Marcia. *The Money Market.* Homewood, Ill.: Dow Jones–Irwin, 1978.

———. *Money Market Calculations.* Homewood, Ill.: Dow Jones–Irwin, 1981.

Taylor, Thomas J. *Get Rich on the Obvious.* New York: Harcourt Brace Jovanovich, 1982.

Tobias, Andrew. *The Funny Money Game.* Chicago: Playboy Press, 1978.

———. *The Only Investment Guide You'll Ever Need.* New York: Bantam Books, 1979.

Touhey, John C. *Stock Market Forecasting.* New York: AMACOM, 1980.

Tracy, John A. *How to Read a Financial Report.* New York: Wiley, 1979.

Train, John. *The Money Masters.* New York: Harper & Row, 1980.

Tucille, Jerome. *Everything the Beginner Needs to Know to Invest Shrewdly.* New Rochelle, N.Y.: Arlington House, 1978.

———. *The Optimist's Guide to Making Money in the 1980s.* New Rochelle, N.Y.: Arlington House, 1979.

———. *Mind Over Money.* New York: Morrow, 1980.

———. *Dynamic Investing.* New York: New American Library, 1981.

Van Caspel, Venita. *The New Money Dynamics.* Englewood Cliffs, N.J.: Reston, 1982.

Whitman, Martin, and Shubik, Martin. *The Aggressive Conservative Investor.* New York: Random House, 1979.

Widicus, Wilbur W., and Stitzel, Thomas E. *Personal Investing.* Homewood, Ill.: Dow Jones–Irwin, 1982.

Williams, Arthur. *Managing Your Investments.* Homewood, Ill. Dow Jones–Irwin, 1980.

Williams, Gordon. *Financial Survival in the Age of New Money.* New York: Simon & Schuster, 1981.

Zarb, Frank G., and Fabozzi, Frank J. *Handbook of Financial Markets.* Homewood, Ill.: Dow Jones–Irwin, 1981.

Technical Analysis

Edwards, Robert D., and Magee, John. *Technical Analysis of Stock Trends.* John Magee, Inc. 103 State Street, Boston, MA 02109.

Frost, A.J., and Prechter, Robert. *Elliott Wave Principle.* New York: New Classics, 1980.

George, Wilfred R. *The Profit Box System of Forecasting Stock Prices*. Homewood, Ill.: Dow Jones–Irwin, 1978.

Granville, Joseph E. *New Strategy of Daily Stock Market Timing for Maximum Profits*. Englewood Cliffs, N.J.: Prentice-Hall, 1976.

Holt, Thomas J. *Total Investing*. New Rochelle, N.Y.: Arlington House, 1978.

Jiler, William. *How Charts Can Help You in the Stock Market*. New York: Trendline (Standard & Poor's), 1976.

Pring, Martin J. *Technical Analysis Explained*. New York: McGraw-Hill, 1980.

Special Securities/Speculations

Ansbacher, Max G. *The New Options Market*. New York: Walker, 1978.

Beckhardt, Israel. *The Small Investor's Guide to Gold*. New York: Manor Books, 1979.

Beckner, Steven K. *The Hard Money Book*. New York: Dutton, 1980.

Bernstein, Jacob. *The Investor's Quotient: Psychology of Successful Investing*. New York: Wiley, 1980.

Brown, Thomas E. *A Layman's Guide to Oil/Gas Investments*. Houston: Gulf Publishing, 1981.

Browne, Harry. *You Can Profit from the Monetary Crisis*. New York: Macmillan, 1979.

————. *Inflation-Proofing Your Investments*. New York: Morrow, 1980.

Cavetti, Peter. *How To Invest in Gold*. New York: New Century, 1980.

Clasing, Henry F. *The Dow Jones–Irwin Guide to Put and Call Options*. Homewood, Ill.: Dow Jones–Irwin, 1980.

Dames, Ralph. *The Winning Option*. Chicago: Nelson-Hall, 1980.

Darst, David M. *The Complete Bond Book*. New York: McGraw-Hill, 1980.

Donoghue, William E. *Complete Money Market Guide*. New York: Harper & Row, 1980.

Duhy, Rodin V. *Alternative Investment Guide to Opportunities in Collectibles*. New York: Times Books, 1980.

Fischer, Robert. *Stocks or Options?* New York: Wiley, 1979.

Freedman, Michael. *The Diamond Book*. Homewood, Ill.: Dow Jones–Irwin, 1981.

Gastineau, Gary L. *The Stock Options Manual*. New York: McGraw-Hill, 1979.

Geczi, Mike. *Futures: The Anti-Inflation Investment*. New York: Avon, 1980.

Grushcow, Jack, and Smith, Courtney. *Profits Through Seasonal Trading*. New York: Ronald Press, 1980.

Hardy, C. Colburn. *ABCs of Investing Your Retirement Funds*. Oradell, N.J.: Medical Economics, 1982.

Herzfeld, Thomas J. *The Herzfeld Hedge*. New York: McGraw-Hill, 1979.

Holt, Robert L. *The Complete Book of Bonds*. New York: Harcourt Brace Jovanovich, 1981.

Homer, Sidney. *The Great American Bond Market*. Homewood, Ill.: Dow Jones–Irwin, 1978.

Kinsman, Robert. *Guide to Tax Havens*. Homewood, Ill.: Dow Jones–Irwin, 1979.

Lamb, Robert, and Rappaport, Stephen P. *Municipal Bonds*. New York: McGraw-Hill, 1980.

Lin, Tso. *Complete Investor's Guide to Listed Options*. Englewood Cliffs, N.J.: Prentice-Hall, 1981.

Loosigian, Allan N. *Interest Rate Futures*. Homewood, Ill.: Dow Jones–Irwin, 1981.

McLendon, Gordon. *Get Really Rich in the Coming Super-Metals Boom*. New York: Simon & Schuster, 1981.

McMillan, Lawrence G. *Options as a Strategic Investment*. Englewood Cliffs, N.J.: Prentice-Hall, 1980.

McQuown, Judith. *Tax Shelters That Work*. New York: McGraw-Hill, 1979.

Powers, Mark J., and Vogel, David J. *Inside the Financial Futures Market*. New York: Wiley, 1981.

Rodolakis, Anthony, and Tetrick, Nicholas. *Buying Opportunities: Wall Street on a Shoestring*. New York: McGraw-Hill, 1979.

Rosen, Lawrence R. *When and How to Profit from Buying and Selling Gold*. Homewood, Ill.: Dow Jones–Irwin, 1981.

————. *The Dow Jones–Irwin Guide to Interest*. Homewood, Ill.: Dow Jones–Irwin, 1981.

Schwarz, Edward W. *How to Use Interest Rate Futures Contracts*. Homewood, Ill.: Dow Jones–Irwin, 1980.

Simon, Arthur C. *How to Invest in Diamonds, Metals and Collectibles*. New York: Future Press, 1980.

Smith, Charles W. *The Mind of the Market*. Totowa, N.J.: Rowman and Littlefield, 1981.

Welch, William B. *Strategies for Put and Call Options Trading*. Englewood Cliffs, N.J.: Winthrop, 1981.

Wilson, James A. *Investing in Call Options*. New York: Praeger, 1982.

Commodities

Angell, George. *Winning in the Commodities Market*. Garden City, N.Y.: Doubleday, 1979.

Barnes, Robert. *Profitable New Commodity Trading Methods*. New York: Van Nostrand Reinhold, 1983.

Bernstein, Jacob. *Handbook of Commodity Cycles*. New York: Stein & Day, 1982.

Gould, Bruce. *Guide to Commodities Trading*. Homewood, Ill.: Dow Jones–Irwin, 1981.

Huff, Charles, and Marinacci, Barbara. *Commodities Speculation for Beginners*. New York: Macmillan, 1980.

Kaufman, P.J. *Commodity Trading Systems and Methods*. New York: Wiley, 1980.

Prestbo, John A., et. al. *The Dow Jones–Irwin Commodities Handbook*. Homewood, Ill.: Dow Jones–Irwin, 1977.

Seeley, Arthur W. *How You Can Profit from Strategtic Metals in the 1980s*. New York: Real Equity, 1983.

Zieg, Kermit C., and Nix, William E. *The Commodities Options Market*. Homewood, Ill.: Dow Jones–Irwin, 1978.

Information on Investment Companies

Investment Company Institute, 1775 K Street, N.W., Washington, D.C. 20006.

Lipper Analytical Distributors, 74 Trinity Place, New York, NY 10006.

Mutual Funds Almanac, 6 Deer Trail, Old Tappan, NJ 07675.

No-Load Mutual Fund Association, 11 Penn Plaza, New York, NY 10001.

United Business Services, 210 Newbury Street, Boston, MA 02116.

Vickers Associates, 226 New York Avenue, Huntington, NY 11746.

Wiesenberger Services, 870 Seventh Avenue, New York, NY 10019.

Chart Services

Chartcraft, Inc., One West Avenue, Larchmont, NY 10538.

Commodity Research Bureau, 1 Liberty Plaza, New York, NY 10006.

Daily Graphics, William O'Neil & Co., Box 24933, Los Angeles, CA 90024.

M. C. Horsey & Co., 120 South Boulevard, Salisbury, MD 21801.

R. W. Mansfield Co., 26 Journal Square, Jersey City, NJ 07306.

Securities Research Company, 208 Newbury Street, Boston, MA 02116.

Trendline, Inc., 25 Broadway, New York, NY 10004.

Wall Street Graphics, Inc. P.O. Box 562, Wall Street Station, New York, NY 10268.

Real Estate

Bruss, Robert. *The Smart Investor's Guide to Real Estate.* New York: Crown Publishers, 1982.

Brueggeman, William B., and Stone, Leo D. *Real Estate Finance.* Homewood, Ill.: Dow Jones–Irwin, 1981.

Case, Fred E. *Investing in Real Estate.* Englewood Cliffs, N.J.: Prentice-Hall, 1978.

Hall, Craig. *Real Estate Investing.* New York: Holt, Rinehart and Winston, 1982.

Harney, Kenneth R. *Beating Inflation with Real Estate.* New York: Random House, 1979.

Mader, Chris. *The Dow Jones–Irwin Guide to Real Estate Investing.* Homewood, Ill.: Dow Jones–Irwin, 1978.

Miller, Daniel A. *How to Invest in Real Estate Syndicates.* Homewood, Ill.: Dow Jones–Irwin, 1978.

Seldin, Maury, et al. *The Real Estate Handbook.* Homewood, Ill.: Dow Jones–Irwin, 1980.

Walters, David W. *The Intelligent Investor's Guide to Real Estate.* New York: Wiley, 1981.

Sources of Information

Barron's, 22 Cortlandt Street, New York, NY 10007.

Better Investing, Box 220, Royal Oak, MI 48068.

Chronicle, 120 Broadway, New York, NY 10005.

Commodities, 1000 Century Plaza, Columbia, MD 21033.

Donoghue's MONEYLETTER, Box 416, Holliston, MA 01746.

Executive Wealth Advisory, 589 Fifth Avenue, New York, NY 10017.

Finance, 8 West 40th Street, New York, NY 10018.

Financial Weekly, P.O. Box 26565, Richmond, VA 23261.

Financial World, 1250 Broadway, New York, NY 10021.

Forbes, 60 Fifth Avenue, New York, NY 10011.

Fortune, Time-Life Building, New York, NY 10020.

Institutional Investor, 488 Madison Avenue, New York, NY 10022.

Investment Dealers' Digest, 150 Broadway, New York, NY 10038.

ML Market Letter, P.O. Box 60, Church Street Station, New York, NY 10008.

MONEY, 1271 Avenue of the Americas, New York, NY 10020.

The Money Manager, 77 Water Street, New York, NY 10007.

Money Reporter, 509 Madison Avenue, New York, NY 10022.

Sophisticated Investor, 2095 Broadway, New York, NY 10023. (A catalogue-type magazine listing hundreds of advisory letters, reports, etc.)

Tax Hotline, 500 Fifth Avenue, New York, NY 10110.

Value Line, 711 Third Avenue, New York, NY 10017.

The Wall Street Journal, 22 Cortlandt Street, New York, NY 10007.

Wall Street Transcript, 120 Wall Street, New York, NY 10005.

Investment Trading Information

American Stock Exchange, 86 Trinity Place, New York, NY 10006.

Canadian Business Service, Suite 700, 133 Richmond Street, West, Toronto, M5H 3M8 Canada.

Chicago Board Options Exchange, La Salle at Jackson, Chicago, IL 60604.

Chicago Board of Trade, LaSalle at Jackson, Chicago, IL 60604.

COMEX (Commodity Exchange, Inc.), 4 World Trade Center, New York, NY 10048.

International Monetary Market, 444 West Jackson Boulevard, Chicago, IL 60606.

Kansas City Board of Trade, 4800 Main Street, Kansas City, MO 64112.

Moody's Investors Service, 99 Church Street, New York, NY 10005.

NASDAQ (National Association of Securities Dealers), Inc., 1735 K Street N.W., Washington, D.C. 20006.

New York Mercantile Exchange, 4 World Trade Center, New York, NY 10048.

New York Stock Exchange (NYSE), 11 Wall Street, New York, NY 10005.

Securities and Exchange Commission, 500 North Capitol N.W., Washington, D.C. 20549.

Standard & Poor's, 25 Broadway, New York, NY 10004.

Index

Index of Securities